THE FOLKLORE
OF CONSENSUS

*Theatricality in the
Italian Cinema,
1930–1943*

MARCIA
LANDY

STATE UNIVERSITY OF NEW YORK PRESS

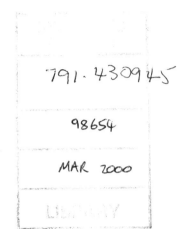

791. 43094-5

Published by
State University of New York Press, Albany

© 1998 State University of New York

All rights reserved

Printed in the United States of America

No part of this book may be used or reproduced
in any manner whatsoever without written permission.
No part of this book may be stored in a retrieval system
or transmitted in any form or by any means including electronic,
electrostatic, magnetic tape, mechanical, photocopying, recording,
or otherwise without the prior permission in writing of the publisher.

For information, address State University of New York Press,
State University Plaza, Albany, N.Y., 12246

Production by Marilyn P. Semerad
Marketing by Patrick Durocher

Library of Congress Cataloging-in-Publication Data

Landy, Marcia, 1931–
    The folklore of consensus : theatricality in the Italian cinema,
1930–1943 / Marcia Landy.
        p.   cm. — (The SUNY series, cultural studies in cinema/video)
    Includes bibliographical references and index.
    ISBN 0-7914-3803-1 (hc : alk. paper). — ISBN 0-7914-3804-X (pb :
alk. paper)
        1. Motion pictures—Italy—History. 2. Motion pictures—Political
aspects—Italy. 3. Motion pictures—Social aspects—Italy.
I. Title. II. Series.
PN1993.5.I88L37 1998
791.43'0945'09043—dc21   97-44015
                                                                      CIP

10 9 8 7 6 5 4 3 2 1

CONTENTS

LIST OF ILLUSTRATIONS

Cover: from *Cavalleria*. Courtesy of New York Museum of Modern Art, Film Stills Archive.

PREFACE

In *Fascism and Film* (1986), I examined the character and contributions of Italian sound cinema during the twenty years of the Fascist regime. The book was indebted to critical studies that had already appeared in the 1970s and early 1980s in Italy,[1] studies that were instrumental in exhuming the "skeletons in the closet,"[2] those films produced during the Ventennio (the twenty-odd years of Fascism). Through an examination of these neglected and maligned films, *Fascism in Film* explored the relation between film and Italian culture of the Ventennio and found a place for these films in the history of Italian cinema. Since that time, a number of critical studies have appeared that explore the nature of cultural production of the era particularly focusing on the position of women, relations between Italian cinema and Hollywood, the forms and impact of advertising, the role the cinema played in creating a culture of modernity, and extensive discussion of popular genres, particularly comedy and melodramas.[3] In the present book, I focus on what I call "theatricality," a politics of style that is less about spectacle in a monumental sense and more about the everyday aspects of performance. The commercial feature films of the era are preoccupied with theatricality in terms of role playing, performance, and spectacle. This dimension of the films has been often neglected, minimized or still reduced to questions of ideology, propaganda, and "escapism." In rethinking the Gramscian terrain of common sense as folklore, I seek to unsettle monolithic assumptions about national and social identity, affirmation, and adherence. However, I am not arguing for the presence of "resistance" and "subversion," so much as trying to shift the discussion of media to another register, involving the role of antirealism as a profound symptom of modernity: the theatricality of the films not only reveals the unstable elements of identity and common sense but even more a crisis of representation concerning the nature and effects of cultural production. Particularly in the spirit of recent studies of literary, theatrical, and cinematic melodrama, I seek to identify how discourses of national identity, gender, and sexuality are staged for a reconsideration of the complex workings of consensus, at least to the illusion of a shared social and cultural enterprise, the "folklore" of consensus.

My concern, in returning to the character of films produced during the twenty-year era of fascism is to extend the discussion of cinematic representation beyond conventional considerations of melodrama as a genre and to view it as conduit for a more differentiated and nuanced sense of affect, and as a locus for reexamining the possible ways of understanding the reception of cinematic texts. I seek to chart and identify the complex character of affect as a major instrument in the dissemination of a modern folklore, a folklore that is characteristic of popular forms of representation. I define affectivity as a form of labor expended in the consumption of cinematic images, in the enterprise of voluntarily offering up our lives "as free contributions to capitalist power." The history of cinematic reception is too often inflected by a monolithic economism that focuses on the profit nexus of the media and, correspondingly, sees the media from the vantage point of top-down ideological control. What gets easily overlooked (except perhaps in psychoanalytic studies) is the labor invested on the part of the consumer, a labor that is intrinsic to all forms of commodity production including cinema. Often dissociated from obvious forms of work identified with and measured in terms of time expended in the factory, the office, and other workplaces, the labor time invested in the consumption of cultural narratives, images, and sounds is a necessary labor in the maintenance of social life under capitalism. For much too long, analysis of the popular media has been identified with "escapism," neglecting or misreading the quality of affective investment on the part of viewers.

If, in world film histories, the tendency persists to regard the cinematic production of the Ventennio as "white telephone" (e.g. frothy comedies of upper-class life) and to classify the films as "escapist" and hence as evading political concerns, the reason must lie largely in an ongoing misrecognition of the texts produced during the fascist era and perhaps of fascism itself with its anti-realist bent and theatricality. The lingering nostalgia for the narrative of neorealism as a significant rupture in Italian cinema is also responsible for the dismissal of the previous cinema of genres. This continuing disregard for the Italian films of the 1930s and 1940s by many international scholars is akin to the earlier disregard for Hollywood cinema, its dismissal as vacuous and as pernicious in its vacuity. In the spirit of interrogating the relation between film and politics, I want to rethink the meaning of "escapism." I do not regard the notion of "escapism" as being apolitical in the sense of being voided of political signification. If the term is useful, it is advantageous for situating popular cinema's involvement in the production and dissemination of modern folklore and in the relation of folklore to a form of politics that functions as indirect discourse. As in fetishism, where boundaries between subject and object are blurred and the inanimate object comes to assume an animated character, in cinema the spectator's affect is cathected onto the object, the film, that magically comes to take on a life of its own. However, the assumption that the process of fusion with cultural representations is total needs to be examined in the light of the meaning, character, and practices of common sense and folklore which can account for the simultaneous involvement and detachment that constitutes the theatricality essential to popular and mass cinema.

In seeking to elaborate on folklore and draw parallels between it and popular cinema, I am heavily indebted to the writings of Antonio Gramsci. In particular, I find his comments on folklore as common sense in his *Prison Notebooks* indispensable to a consideration of cinema and its relation to consensus. I extend Gramsci's conception of the relation of folklore to common sense and the role of popular culture in the creation of consensus. He does not discuss folklore as primitive, prerational, and picturesque, identified solely with rural and nonindustrial societies, but as a major (and modern) means for the dissemination of knowledge instrumental in the construction of hegemony. While offering the appearance of unity, organicity, and affective power, the strengths of folklore lie in its fragmented and heterogeneous character. For folklore to be effective, it has to depend on commonly shared but ever-changing representations of the world and of social life. Gramsci's writings on popular culture are largely devoted to literature, the theater, and opera, but they are equally applicable to cinema. Though his allusions to cinema are brief, the general tenor of his concern with folklore is consistent with his concerns to analyze the political nature and importance of cultural expression. Recognizing that his observations on popular culture and its relationship to common sense as folklore belong to a specific historico-socio-discursive formation, I seek to align them more closely to contemporary thought,

especially to the work of such thinkers as Gilles Deleuze in his explorations of the cinematic image as heterogenous, theatrical, sensory, as
related to differing conceptions of temporality, and especially (and most
Gramscian) as contributing to modes of thinking differently about
thought.

My enterprise is interrogative, not prescriptive. By examining theatricality and its ties to melodrama, by probing its affective value, by
regarding its expenditure of affect as tied to gender and sexuality, I seek to
identify the dual registers of "escapism," the portraits as constraining and
entertaining, as familiar and estranging, as engaging and disorienting.
When the question of sexuality is apparent in film melodrama, the
romance paradigms, the portraits of family conflicts, the images of masculinity and femininity are not predicated on the notion of cinema as a
reflection of reality, on cultural images as an instantiation of the real. The
uses of melodrama in films offer more powerful images than fidelity to
"actual social practices." Melodrama is, in my terms, the entrance to the
problematic character of consensus, its fluidity, its tension between stasis
and innovation, conformity and rebellion, and its reliance on an affective
bonding of films and their audiences.

My intention in the reexamination of Italian cinema is not to name,
classify, judge, or reiterate truisms about Fascism—its totalitarianism, its
worship of the power of the leader, its fascinating public spectacles. These
have been abundantly commented upon by others. I am interested in
moving away from the clichés that have circulated concerning Italian Fascism. While I am unwilling to abandon the term "fascism" in relation to
the cinema, I am eager to regard it anew, seeing it in its relation to a
remapping of modernity and, further, to a relation between Americanism
and modernity. Following Gramsci, my object is to interrogate the affective dimensions of the creation of a new type of individual engendered by
industrialism, to underscore those dimensions of Americanism that are
unleashed by cinema—the Hollywood cinema, and its relation to the
emergent cinema of the Fascist years. In assessing the character of cultural
representations of the era, I seek to map various qualities that comprise
the cinema as popular culture, to identify the affects that are inherent to
the "melodramatic imagination," and hence, in the words of Gilles
Deleuze, to "go beyond the states of things, to trace lines of flight, just
enough to open up in space a dimension of another order favorable to
these compositions of affects."[4] These "lines of flight" entail an examination of cinema that does not focus exclusively on the conventional dimen-

sions of narrativity and on the valorization of "realism," but reveal different, multilayered, and complex relations to the cinematic image, to what has been termed "escapism," and, hence more broadly, of the nature of representation.

The directions that I propose to follow, therefore, involve the various and manifold strategies for the generation of affect found in the uses of cinematic comedy, melodrama, and history as the carriers of cultural folklore in the Italian popular cinema of the Fascist years. The melodramas of the period offer a way of understanding consent not as affirmation but as an expression of complex and heterogeneous responses to the role that cinema plays in culture. In their narrative structures, iconography, and visual style, the melodramas offer a fascinating glimpse into the heterogenous character of the common sense of popular representation.[5] The conjunctions that have been forged between Italian cinema of the sound years and Hollywood cinema are not eccentric to a consideration of the pervasiveness and centrality of melodramatic affect but indicative of a mode of representation that characterized Hollywood and European cinemas of the 1930s and early 1940s, a mode of representation that contributed to the folklore of consensus, whether from the right, center, or left of the political spectrum. Distinctions between the nature of consensus under Italian Fascism and that of "democratic" societies such as the United States and Great Britain have become increasingly tenuous, forcing a reexamination of the notion of consensus, of the role of cultural production, and also of the nature and character of fascism, especially of its exclusive connection to the Italian nation. In the past, the exceptional nature accorded to Italian Fascism served to mute an analysis of similarities between the culture of Italian Fascism and of other Western nations. The evidence of important differences in the political structure and practices of Italian Fascism should not obscure points of convergence. My discussion of the films produced under Fascism should help to shed light on certain common problems arising from the increasingly central role played by media in social and cultural life, even more, to locate the persistence of ways of thinking that emerged at that time, that have not disappeared but have intensified.

Most central to my argument is that economic and cultural value are complicitous, and that the task of understanding the production of cultural commodities is one of identifying their multifarious connections to the production of other commodities, the speed at which the circulation of commodities operates, and the ways in which connections between culture and economics are effaced but not inaccessible. My method is textual, but textual in the sense that I regard the text not as a closed and finite entity but as a social text. I do not regard the film text as disjoined from the larger social fabric, as its mere "reflection," but as a prime source of knowledge, a commodity that presupposes and instantiates certain modes of consumption and reception. However, I do not regard this social text as a monolithic and seamless narrative or, for that matter, as a "reliable" narrative, but as a conduit for discourses of nation and of masculinity that circulate broadly, directly, and indirectly and that rely heavily on the cultural capital of femininity.

In the chapters that follow, I discuss the films of this era not narrowly to locate "fascism in film," but to locate connections (and discontinuities) between "fascism and film." I continue, as I did in *Fascism and Film*, to focus on the intricacies of the film texts as my archive. Hence the chapters rely heavily on a description of the films as a means for locating the various and reflexive uses of theatricality, their strategies and their connections to folklore and other art forms. I focus mainly on the sound cinema of the 1930s and early 1940s, grateful that such works as Giuliana Bruno's *Streetwalking on a Ruined Map* have undertaken to examine and rethink the character of the silent cinema, tying it to questions of nationalism and regionalism, feminism, and popular culture. My interest continues to lie predominantly in the texts of the 1930s and early 1940s, but my hope is that the work in this book connects backward to the cultural problems posed by the silent cinema as well as to those posed by the films and film theory identified with neorealism.

Chapter 1, "Introduction: Film, Folklore, and Affect," is an overview of the historical context for the films, of the critical work that has been done on Fascism and on the Italian cinema, and of the critical methodology I employ in charting the character of the "melodramatic imagination" and its relation to folklore, theatricality, and escapism. The films selected to discuss in each chapter range from the earliest sound films to the films produced at the end of World War Two as a means for tracking repetition but also for identifying differences among them. My argument is predicated on the assumption that, there is more diversity among the films than is usually acknowledged, a diversity attributable to the differing critical outlooks on the deployment of various genres, the predilections of particular filmmakers, the conditions of censorship, changing conditions of production, and, most importantly, the political vicissitudes of the regime. Particularly, in relation to theatricality, I assume that there is an ongoing concern with its nature and effects *throughout* the sound era, but I also assume that a greater self-consciousness emerges about performance in the films in the late 1930s and in the 1940s that contributes possibly to a different understanding of the nature and impact of neorealism and its relations to the cinema of genres that preceded it. Each chapter begins with highlighting a particular film that is exemplary in its deployment of the various aspects of theatricality that I seek to highlight. Thereafter, the films follow a chronological progression, focusing on different dimensions of theatricality identified by the introduction to the chapter and by the overall strategies identified through the analysis of the initial text.

Chapter 2, "Comedy, Melodrama, and Theatricality," reexamines the debates that have surrounded the meaning of "white telephone" films, their style and their reception. In particular through a discussion of such films as *Figaro a la sua gran giornata, Rubacuori, La segretaria privata, Il Signor Max, Gli uomini che mascalzoni, Una moglie in pericolo, Darò un milione, Batticuore, Mille lire al mese,* and *Quartieri alti,* the chapter undertakes a reconsideration of the notion of escapism, challenging the contention that these films are apolitical by exploring the oblique and masked character of their politics of style. In exploring the nomination of escapism for many of the films, especially the comedies, I have recourse to contemporary reevaluations of Hollywood cinema, transplanting certain modes of reading mass cinema from that medium to the Italian comedies of the 1930s and 1940s. Unlike the costume dramas, melodramas, and historical films, the comedies are not concerned with exceptional and unique figures and with the transcendence of suffering and renunciation. These films seem more concerned, in their narratives, their choice of characters, their images, and their uses of sound, with creating a sense of the immediacy of survival and accommodation. However, this difference from the melodramas may be more apparent than real. The films are concerned with role playing, disguises, and dissimulation not as a problematic largely to be interrogated and challenged, but more with their necessity as strategies for survival, if not success. Many of the comedies explore secrecy, deception, and impersonation as a precondition for acceptance of a settled and respectable, if not modest, form of existence. The films' self-reflexivity calls attention to the film as artifact and, hence, to the artificial character of the cinematic world. Their self-reflexivity and intertextuality does not necessarily serve as a means of resistance. Through their theatricalization, the films involve audiences, often cynically and even self-consciously, in a bifurcated rather than a completely naturalized and unified sense of the cinematic world, contaminating the relationship between "reality" and representation.

Chapter 3, "The Uses of Folklore: History and Theatricality," explores links between melodrama and folklore, interrogating strategies for identification: the role of hyperbole and excess in the treatment of narrative, the use of stars, and the cultural sources that constitute the films' milieu. My primary objective in this chapter is to track the affective character of a handful of melodramas in terms of the ways that these films produce history through such films as *Scipione l'Africano, Condottieri, La corona di ferro, Un'avventura di Salvator Rosa, Ettore Fieramosca, Lorenzino de' Medici, 1860, Piccolo mondo antico, Passaporto rosso, Il Dottor Antonio, Cavalleria, Squadrone bianco,* and *L'assedio dell' Alcazar.* Rather than viewing the films as expressing a unified portrait of Fascist ideology as public spectacle, I examine how images of the past are wedded to the melodramatic imagination, resulting in the creation of an even more "fascinating fascism" than the public spectacles of the regime. The historical film is not monolithic, and my discussion explores the forms available for representing the past: in epic forms, biopics, films of adventure, war films, romances. An examination of the films reveals that even where they appear to be polemic and doctrinaire, they, like the comedies, are engaged in theatricality, posturing, and stylistic excess, thus undermining any sense of their immersion in any sense of the "real." They are further validation of the cinema's power to produce the world as artifact and to flaunt the powers of artifice, impersonation, and masquerade, as a means of confounding connections to the "real."

Chapter 4, "From Conversion to Calligraphism," examines two prominent expressions of melodrama that I identify as "conversion" and as "calligraphism," a term that I borrow from the criticism of the era. The affective emphasis addresses representations of masculine protagonists in the texts. The films under examination are *Il fu Mattia Pascal, Terra madre, Acciaio, Rotaie, Vecchia guardia, Squadrone bianco, Napoli d'altri tempi, Napoli che non muore, Quartieri alti, La morte civile, Un colpo di pistola,* and *Gelosia.* The focus of the discussion is the phenomenon of conversion (or its failure) as a dominant strategy of melodramas that feature dramas of masculinity. The melodramas of the era, in many ways bearing a certain relation to British and Hollywood melodramas of the 1950s that have been the focus of attention in recent film criticism, are preoccupied with images of transcendent or failed struggles on the part of the male protagonists, focusing on their struggles to achieve attitudes and behavior appropriate to familial, class, romantic, or militant political and warlike expectations. The scenarios are not seamless. The narratives dramatize alternatives confronted by the characters in their quest for personal transcendence, resulting finally in the mystification and elimination of the road that leads to personal freedom and pleasure, a way often identified with anarchy and libertinism.

The "calligraphic" films, while entertaining similar conflicts (between heterosexual and homosocial bonding, duty and pleasure, paternal or maternal identification), invert and complicate the scenario of conversion, opening up into a menacing and dangerous world that threatens to engulf the characters. If the films are not a direct reflection of a crisis-laden social and political situation inherent to Fascism, they validate the role of melodrama as popular form and as a response in its own terms to social crises. More than the comedies of the era that seem to be more attuned to Hollywood style and values, these films, especially those identified with the formalism of "calligraphism" identified with such directors as Ferdinando Maria Poggioli, Mario Soldati, and Amleto Palermi, are cast in the tradition of Italian literary and dramatic modes and especially with a tendency toward the operatic. I distinguish these films from the ones discussed in chapter 3 largely on the basis that they focus on the interiorization of conflict, on a self-conscious fascination with power and subjection, and particularly on the vicissitudes of identity ending in dissolution. Through their preoccupation with disguises and impersonation, they disclose the absence of shared values despite their conventional narrative structures that seek to uphold them.

Chapter 5, "The Affective Value of Femininity and Maternity," concludes the book, exploring the problematic of femininity as central to any discussion of theatricality. I discuss femininity as imbricated in the growing preoccupation with performance, challenging to notions of escapism, and especially familiar conflicts concerning realism, illusionism, and representation. I discuss films that feature female protagonists: *Il carnevale di Venezia, Sissignora, Sorelle Materassi, Come le foglie, T'amerò sempre, La peccatrice, Zazà, Ballerine, La donna della montagna,* and *Malombra.* However, in my linking of femininity and theatricality I am concerned with femininity as fiction and, more broadly, with representation as tied to the illusion of woman. The representations of feminine sexuality in the films mask the epistemological and physical violence inherent in familial and, by extension, all forms of social and political relationships, but in their style the texts cannot totally efface traces of sexual conflict. While in theme the narratives remain attached to familiar images of feminine sexuality as spectacle, I read the stylistic excesses as suggesting an uneasy relationship to familiar conflicts between the home and the world, the public and private spheres, and personal desire and perceived social imperatives. Theatricality appears particularly to be associated with femininity, with maternity, and especially with an emphasis on masquerade and impersonation. The films that feature feminine figures offer a repertoire of maternal figures and maternal surrogates who, in their excessiveness, appear to be caricatures of service and self-abnegation. While the maternal figure, as a paragon of self-abnegation or as errant and destructive, is ubiquitous, her portrait is not seamless and unproblematic. Even when the mother is not directly invoked, the scenario of femininity guides the narrative, the images, and relations among characters, drawing on a traditional iconography embellished and brought up to date to conform to modern aspirations. The image of woman is identified with the maintenance of the family, which is, in turn, identified with melodramatic images of loss and compensation for sacrifice. The theatrical as operatic is the mainstay of such fictions, identified with performance and not with authenticity. A sole focus on Fascist institutions does not adequately reveal the character of Fascist representations of femininity. In the popular commercial films, their theatricality calls attention to the blurring of boundaries between theatricality and life endemic to the cinema of the era, a blurring that validates the existence of a crisis in representation that affected all aspects of the cultural and political life of the era.

While theories of "fascinating fascism" call attention to the ritualistic and spectacular manifestations of Fascism—its public spectacles and political rhetoric—they underplay the immediate, everyday, and dynamic dimensions of representation characteristic of many of the films produced. The films' texts are clever about politics, but I designate their politics as a politics of style. Self-conscious about their need to be entertaining, the films stress spectatorship, artifice, doubling, disguises, and impersonation. The films' theatricality merges with images of quotidian life to offer clues that, for better or worse, invoke the fantasies, needs, and aspirations of their audiences in ways that complicate and force a modification of notions and judgments of escapism. Through theatricality, escapism reveals itself as entailing identification and participation as well as a cynical awareness of the posturing necessary to "keep the show going." The notion of performance is not restricted to the fictional constructs on the screen but inflects conceptions of everyday life. Rather than dismissing the films of the era as trivial escapist texts, the texts should be regarded as providing new insights into the complex character of difference that modifies prevailing notions of coercion or consensus.

Obviously, I am not alone in this enterprise of rethinking Italian films of the Ventennio. I share the field with others, most notably the work of Gian Piero Brunetta and Lino Miccichè, who have done more than any other Italian critics to make these films critically accessible. In the United States the critical works of Philip Cannistraro, James Hay, Elaine Mancini, and Angela Dalle Vacche have paved the way for the growing works in English on Italian cinema of the 1930s and 1940s as have those of Geoffrey Nowell-Smith in Britain and Pierre Sorlin in France. I am indebted particularly to the work of Peter Bondanella, whose exemplary *Italian Cinema* situates the cinema of the Fascist years within the broader trajectory of Italian cinema. I am also indebted to him for his ongoing support of my work, typical of his generosity toward scholars and his commitment to scholarship. I wish also to express my appreciation to James Hay whose meticulous critical reading of the manuscript forced me to rethink many aspects of my methodology. I only hope that his prodigious efforts are evident in the final product. As always, I am grateful to Amy Villarejo for her interest in and critical reading of my work. Lucy Fischer, director of the Film Studies Program, Mary Louise Briscoe, dean of the College of Arts and Sciences, and Alberta Sbragia, director of the West European Studies Program, at the University of Pittsburgh have been intellectually and materially supportive of my work over the years, enabling me to do indispensable archival work. Stanley Shostak has been an ongoing source of critical insights, a stringent reader of my work, and a tolerant observer to my attempts to meet his standards, and I am grateful for his intellectual companionship and friendship.

CHAPTER ONE

Film, Folklore, and Affect

Antonio Gramsci's conception of folklore pays particular attention to popular cultural production and reception, though he is not silent on the relations between high and popular culture. In reconceptualizing the notion of folklore and tying it to common sense (as earlier propounded by Giambattista Vico),[1] Gramsci reminds his reader of the many sources from which popular culture draws its sustenance, sources that are largely eclectic and heterogeneous. He stresses the role and importance of traditional religious, medical, psychological, and legal discourses that are at the heart of "common sense as folklore." His interest in folklore is not divorced from considerations of the labor entailed in the creation of social value. He is concerned to investigate the sources and character of particular conceptions of the world, their role in enhancing or inhibiting the creation of a popular culture, and how these are constructed and function as powerful incentives in creating the illusion of social cohesiveness and continuity, in inhibiting social transformation, and in working against those subaltern groups for whom change is imperative. His work is deeply inflected by a sense of history.

I trace his observations on common sense as folklore and their relation to his conception of popular culture to his notes on Italian history and particularly to his discussion of the Risorgimento as a "passive revolution" and to the formation of Italy as a nation in the nineteenth century. Gramsci identifies the Risorgimento, the struggle to unify the separate states and regions that comprised what later became identified as the

Italian nation, as a crucial moment for Italian politics and culture, a moment when the possibility of a revolution from below became a reformation or "passive revolution" from above in the reconsolidation of social classes through the alliance of the aristocracy, particularly the southern landowners with the northern bourgeoisie. Gramsci's writings, his fragmentary notes in the *Prison Notebooks* in particular, offer a view of popular culture that must be situated in relation to his conception of the subaltern, in relation to the peasants and working classes and in the context of the imperative not merely to describe but to produce conditions for social transformation in their behalf and through their efforts.

Critical of many prevailing Marxist views of the time that first one must change the economic means of production, he insisted on the need to integrate economic, political, and cultural concepts as a means for understanding and overcoming obstacles in the way of social change. Consistently, he challenges the notion of "economism" identifying it finally with "corporatism" (and with Fascism) as a strategy for reducing social phenomena to purely monetary considerations and, hence, to the operations of the state in conjunction with capital. Since his primary concern was to create a popular movement, that is, to create a revolution from below on the part of peasants and workers, he is constantly attentive to the ways in which knowledge and hence radical action are obstructed through all the various institutions of the nation-state, involving religion, the law, family, language, literature, theater, and the media. While Gramsci states that the "'industrial' city is always more progressive than the countryside which depends organically upon it . . . [but] not all Italy's cities are 'industrial,' and even fewer are typically industrial."[2] However, the opposition between the regions served to maintain the power of northern interests and the divisions between south and north, agrarian and urban life.

A persistent symptom and concomitant of these divisions entails the conflict between rural and the urban forces exemplified in contending notions of the dominance of one region over the other. In Italy the division between north and south was expressed in the rhetoric of *stracittà* (urbanism or cosmopolitanism) and *strapaese* (ruralism or regionalism). The proponents of *stracittà* identified the popular with technological modernization, while the advocates of *strapaese* were suspicious of modernity and sought instead to valorize a vision of Italy tied to provincial life and uncontaminated by modernity. Both views are indicative of profound cultural rifts relating to tradition and modernity and further to conceptions of popular culture.

Gramsci's call for the creation of a national-popular culture and politics is thus tied to the imperative of creating affiliations between these opposing subaltern groups as a strategy for analyzing and overcoming "the present primitive sentiment of [their] being a despised race."[3] Toward that end, a rethinking of popular culture could serve as a means for identifying assumed and actual differences of interests deeply embedded in every aspect of Italian life that legitimated this "primitive" sentiment. He identified the cosmopolitanism of many Italian intellectuals and artists (both north and south) as an indication of their turning away from the people, as finding respite in a nostalgic contemplation of the past and in identification with social and class positions that were inimical or indifferent to subaltern groups in Italy. However, Gramsci is not offering a prescription for popular culture. His method is critical and interrogative. He does not indulge in creating ready-made definitions of popular culture but rather in examining a rationale and methodology for identifying its character and the ways in which it has been appropriated by different constituencies for different ends. In referring to the people, he writes "'The people!' But what is the people? Who knows them? Who has ever defined them? . . . The 'people' though, has provided the title for many important newspapers, precisely those that today ask 'What is this people?' in the very newspapers that are named after the people."[4]

Gramsci was not calling for a patriotic and nationalistic polemics or for "paternalistic" and "picturesque" portraits of the "people" and of popular culture.[5] These he identified with Fascism. He was arguing for the creation of critical thought, for the creation of forms of knowledge that could combat the tendency of many intellectuals and artists to espouse ideas and forms that operate in opposition to any expression of existing struggle and change. Hardly programmatic in his call for the national-popular, Gramsci is testing the possibility, the necessity, of the role of culture, specifically a popular culture, to function in such a way so as to serve the needs and interests of subaltern groups (a problem that has by no means disappeared from our critical concerns with popular culture). His comments on the popular are not confined to his critique of the Risorgimento but serve more powerfully as a means of understanding the nature of Fascism as a further extension of and instantiation of a "passive revolution," an intensification of its myth of national unity. Important aspects of Fascism have to be seen as drawing sustenance from the fiction of national unity in the name of the people, of nationalism, and increasingly of imperialism and war.

He identifies the significance of and adherence to formulations of *strapaese* (ruralism) and *stracittà* (urbanism) in Italian culture, the distinctions and tensions between ruralism and urbanism, tradition and modernity, and conceptions of modernity that were prominent in conceptions of the United States and Hollywood films of the era. Gramsci was aware of the role that Americanism had begun to play in the twenties and thirties.[6] Ambivalent relations to modernity—not unique to Italy—expressed in Italian cultural works of the era were identified with the dangers and challenges of urban life expressed in both the romanticization of rural life as well as in the presentation of the sinful pleasures derived through the portrayals of the sights and sounds of the city. These relations to geography were paralleled by ambivalent relations to nation and empire, also not unique to Italy but rampant in international culture, as was the heavy reliance on historical epics to bolster this folklore.[7]

In his notes on literature and drama, Gramsci underscores the persistence of melodramatic forms of literature and drama that were endemic to Italian culture, often identified with the operatic and with forms of legal and funerary oratory. He writes that "popular theaters, with what are called arena performance (and today perhaps sound films, but also the subtitles of old silent films, all done in an operatic style), are of the utmost importance in the creation of this taste and its corresponding language."[8] Melodrama is a form of theatricality, an ensemble of effects that generates intensity of emotion. While ostensibly appearing as synthetic, uniform, and unified, its strategies can be described as commonsensical in the Gramscian conception of *senso comune* as "disjointed and episodic . . . strangely composite: it contains Stone Age elements and principles of a more advanced science, prejudices from all past phases of history."[9]

The affective dimensions of common sense exceed narrativity and temporality, signaling its protean and polysemic nature. In its disunified and pastiche-like qualities, common sense is not univalently oppositional, though in its fragmented nature it does expose tensions and ambiguities that are at the heart of consensus.[10] These conflicts are endemic to the cinema of the Fascist years, where traditional images and values are not abandoned but transposed into a new register. Common sense as the "philosophy of the masses" valorizes the past, especially the folkloric, and is, as such, dependent on traditional, formulaic, and experiential knowledge such as truisms, clichés, and proverbial wisdom. But commonsense investments in the past are not innocent. The attachment to the past functions, in the Nietzschean sense in the excessiveness of affect, [11] as an overinvestment in representations of the past, bespeaking the presence of conflict and the attempt to suppress it. In particular, monumental, antiquarian, and critical forms of history rely on the sense of history as a vast panorama where the events are staged in terms of great actors and grandiose events. This excessive treatment is also the hallmark of melodrama, where its theatricality reveals the incommensurability between desire and its attainment.

The melodramatic conflicts presented in the films are clothed in operatic and histrionic scenarios, involving sexual antagonisms tied to conflicts between social classes as well as tensions between rural and urban existence. For example, Gramsci wrote that "the new industrialism wants monogamy: it wants man as worker not to squander his nervous energies in the disorderly and stimulating pursuit of occasional sexual satisfaction."[12] The female serves as a procreator, nurturer, disciplinarian of the husband, self-disciplinarian, and guarantor of the integrity of the family unit.[13] Many of the films stage sexual relations, whether set in the domestic or public spheres, emphasizing a puritanical ethos of restraint in greater or lesser degrees. The family appears as the source of continuity, nurturance, social stability, and, as seen particularly in the films of Mario Camerini, a haven from conflicts. However, the family portraits are not quite so innocent. Representations of gender and sexuality in the films, to a greater or lesser extent, in direct or in oblique fashion, dramatize the epistemological and physical violence inherent in familial and, by extension, all forms of social and political relationships, but in their style the texts cannot totally efface the traces of conflict. While in their narratives the films remain attached to familiar images of gender, sexuality, and work, the stylistic excesses arising from the conflicts presented can suggest an uneasy relationship to familiar conflicts between the home and the world, the public and private spheres, and personal desire and perceived social imperatives. The element of theatricality, involving impersonation, disguises, and doubling inherent to melodrama enables a tracking of the vagaries of affect, its displacement, disavowal, and even, in certain instances, its disappearance.

How does affective value circulate through melodrama, and, beyond formal analysis, how can one determine the impact of these films? There is no definitive method for determining the conditions for and the nature of the reception for the films. The method of assessing "popularity" on the basis of box-office receipts can give information about a film's accessibility and perhaps account for movie-going habits and predilections for certain kinds of films, but beyond this, it cannot provide a nuanced sense of reception. Anecdotal material by critics and movie-goers can offer one means to assess consumption. As is characteristic of discourse generally, the texts are implicated in evasive, fragmentary, and contradictory strategies that are inherent to the struggle to achieve acceptance. Thus, the films do not provide a transparent or univalent sense of the culture and social life. One cannot dissociate the modes of reception from production, since production is dependent on consumption. Producers and consumers are complicit in the creation of cultural commodities, sharing in their value-creation. In the creation of value, the problem that confronts the critic, therefore, is to understand the social character of these hieroglyphs, and this understanding involves challenging the purely economic character of the commodity to comprehend the affect that is entailed in producing not merely monetary but social value as a means of producing the folklore of consensus.

Hence, such considerations as sexuality and gender are not mere appearances but fundamental components in production, circulation, consumption, and in determinations of value. While the profit motive is constant, the production process itself is hydra-headed, utilizing multivalent and constantly changing strategies to ensure circulation and consumption. And the concept of woman is central to the production of social meaning as affective labor through forms of representation and representativeness that provide the semblance of a subject who ostensibly participates willingly, and of necessity, in the dissemination and maintenance of social and cultural forms. In relation, therefore, to the ways in which femininity circulates in dynamic fashion as the crucial component in the generation of cultural value, its valuation appears to operate primarily at the level of gender differentiation, but this differentiation has tentacles that reach into considerations of domestic and public spheres, into the division of labor that touches questions of sexuality and reproduction, and, at the most abstract level, considerations of social order or chaos.

In assessing the role of sexuality and its ties to gendered forms of representation, attempts to identify an originary or homologous source (e.g., biological conceptions of gender) for the role that sexuality plays in the construction of social value usually end up in the morass of essentialism and reductionism, mystifying the power assigned to sexuality and obfuscating how affective value circulates and signifies in multiple fashion so as to seize and harmonize different and even dissident constituencies. However, value "does not wear an explanatory label. Far from it, value changes all labour products into social hieroglyphs."[14] The multivalent and heterogeneous ways cultural texts work simultaneously to reveal and conceal textual and, hence, sexual value cannot therefore be determined in terms of what Gilles Deleuze describes in the terminology of arborescence. An arborescent mode of reading would rely on fundamental assumptions of unity and totalization, arising from a defined and binary origin, whereas a rhizomatic conception "establishes connections between semiotic chains, organizations of power, and circumstances relative to the arts, sciences, and social struggles. A semiotic chain is like a tuber agglomerating very diverse acts, not only linguistic, but also perceptive, mimetic, gestural, and cognitive."[15] Instead of unity, there is multiplicity. Instead of simple determinations, there are overdeterminations, and instead of seamless signifying continuities, there are asignifying ruptures. Thus, both the production and the consumption of a text, while presupposing a homogenous community, reveal attempts at both unification and the fractures and fissures that belie such unity. In reading the films to identify their representations of gender and sexuality, I seek to locate the relations between their production and reception as instantiating this dual movement toward unity and resolution while at the same time eluding any fixity.

In his discussion of the pre– and post–World War Two cinema, Deleuze in *Cinema 1*, departing from narrative analysis, has explored the character of the "movement-image," and, following Henri Bergson, explores the illusion of unity and organicity that seems to characterize earlier cinema. In ways that do not seem to undermine Gramsci's tantalizing notes on folklore as common sense, Deleuze states that "movement relates the objects of a closed system to open duration, and duration to the objects of the system which it forces to open up. Movement relates the objects between which it is established to the changing whole which it expresses and vice versa. Through movement the whole is divided up into objects, and objects are re-united in the whole, and indeed between the two the 'whole' changes."[16] His analysis of the various forms of montage—pathetic, dialectical, sublime (mathematical and dynamic)—elaborates on the ways in which movement through the sensory-motor image functions through forms of perception, affection, and action (in contrast to the time-image associated with post–World War Two cinema) and on the changing relations between the part and the whole, the image in relation to other images. His writings on cinema are an intervention in the dominant tendencies to valorize narrative and to interpret texts in terms of fixed meanings.

Deleuze's preoccupation with affect is particularly developed through what he terms the "affection-image" in relation to the uses of the close-up and the face in particular. He describes the affection-image as follows,

> The affect is the entity, that is Power or Quality. It is something expressed: the affect does not exist independently of something which expresses it, although it is completely distinct from it. What expresses it is a face, or a facial equivalent (a faceified object) or . . . even a proposition. . . . The affection-image, for its part, is abstracted from the spatio-temporal coordinates which would relate it to a state of things, and abstracts the face from the person to which it belongs in the state of things.[17]

Deleuze shifts attention from narrative onto the image itself in an attempt to see the image as part of a process of de-individuation.

> Ordinarily, three roles of the face are recognisable: it is individuating (it distinguishes or characterises each person); it is socialising (it manifests a social role); it is relational or communicating (it ensures not only communication between two people, but also, in a single person, the internal agreement between his character and his role). Now the face, which effectively presents these aspects in the cinema as elsewhere, loses all three in the case of close-up. . . . These functions of the face presuppose the reality of a state of things where people act and perceive. The affection-image makes them dissolve and disappear.[18]

In this context, the image ceases to be a product of its historical and ideological context and instead lures the spectator into a realm beyond meaning bestowed by forms of historicizing and ideology.

The two affective poles of faciality involve reflection and intensity, wonder and desire, and "quality and power." The poles are not strictly disjoined from each other but depend on particular filmmakers, different moments in the films, and the oscillation between different affective states. Both suggest an affective relation to the image, but rather than assigning a fixed meaning to the affect, Deleuze invites reflection on affects that have not been considered in relation to the perception of the image in close-up. These affects are not the conventional, schematic, and preformed notions of sentiments as opposed to thoughts that are presumed to constitute "experience." Instead, his configurations of affect are based on a Nietzschean and Spinozan view of affection in relation to the body and to power. In describing Deleuze's conception of affection and its relation to Spinoza, Michael Hardt states that, "To understand the nature of power, we must first discover the internal structure of the body, we must decompose the unity of the body according to its lines of articulation, its differences of nature. Deleuze reminds us that the investigation of this structure must be conducted not in terms of the power to act (spontaneity) but rather in terms of the power to be affected."[19] Deleuze's emphasis on affect is not a formal study or history of cinema but applies more broadly to the character of modern thought, which the cinema embodies in its forms of expressive affect, its aporias, and its possibilities for thinking differently.

Distinguishing between "passive affections" that relate "only to our power to feel or suffer," and active affections that relate "to our power to act," the preoccupation in *Cinema 1* with the affection-image is precisely Deleuze's attempt to "discover the internal structure of the body" rather than assuming "the primacy of the passive affections."[20] The importance and distinctiveness of Deleuze's studies of the character of the affection-image, his preoccupation with the relation between affection and action, is in the interest of attacking the traditional disjunction between rationality and irrationality, body and mind, and unity and multiplicity. This enterprise of distinction involves an interrogation of static conceptions of meaning that are most often associated with melodrama and its obsession with victimage. Deleuze's work forces a reexamination of conventional melodramatic scenarios that hierarchialize the relations between victim and oppressor. His rethinking of affectivity invites a reconsideration of negative notions of power. In his writings, there is a consistent emphasis on the need to configure power in the context of affection, in active not passive terms. In relation to an examination of the cinema produced during the Fascist years, Deleuze's examination of affect is productive in so far as it generates a series of questions around representations of power, desire, multiplicity, and difference.

The complex nature and role of affect is inextricable from the commodity form and the commodity form inextricable from representation—of money and of commodities. In the famous passage in *Capital* on commodity fetishism, Marx tells us that:

A commodity appears at first sight an extremely obvious, trivial thing. But its analysis brings out that it is a very strange thing, abounding in metaphysical subtleties and theological niceties. As far as it is a use-value, there is nothing mysterious about it. . . . Whence, then, arises the enigmatic character of the product of labour, as soon as it assumes the form of a commodity? Clearly it arises from this form itself. . . . The mysterious character of the commodity-form consists therefore simply in the fact that the commodity reflects the social characteristics of men's labour as objective characteristics of the products of labour themselves, as the socio-natural properties of these things. Hence it also reflects the social relation of the producers to the sum total of labour as a social relation between objects, a relation which exists apart from and outside the producers. Through this substitution, the products of labour become commodities, sensuous things which are at the same time suprasensible or social. . . . It is nothing but the definite social relation between men themselves which assumes here, for them, the fantastic form of a relation between things. In order, therefore, to find an analogy we must take flight into the misty realm of religion. There the products of the human brain appear as autonomous figures endowed with a life of their own, which enter into relations both with each other and with the human race.[21]

Marx's comments on fetishism, the "mysterious character of the commodity form," are central to an understanding of how film as economic and affective commodity—its modes of production and circulation—serves in a dual character as commodity, as both use-value and exchange-value, as concrete and as abstract, and of how the relations between use and exchange are masked through representation, making it appear that commodities have a life of their own independent of the mind and giving rise to forms of economic reductionism through quantification and discrete classification. Thus, cultural objects such as cinema can be considered as independent of other forms of labor. In rethinking Marx on the question of value formation, Gayatri Chakravorty Spivak asks, "What narratives of value-formation emerge when consciousness itself is subsumed under the 'materialist' predication of the subject?"[22] Stressing the "irreducibly complicitous" relation between the cultural and the economic, she suggests that "the best that one can envisage is the persistent undoing of the opposition, taking into account the fact that, first, the complicity between cultural and economic relations is acted out in every decision we make; and, secondly, that economic reductionism is, indeed, a real danger."[23]

Hence, an analysis of film as commodity must, first of all, undo the binary distinction between mental and physical production, then it must conjoin production to reception in seeing it as a circular, endlessly mobile process that unites the labor of reception to that of production, necessarily folding back on itself so as to ensure the reciprocity of the process. The question of subject predication is not a given but inextricably tied to the cultural production of knowledge as a commodity form. And cultural production is inseparable from the reciprocal nature of production and reception, How does representation enter into the exchange? To answer this question, as Spivak indicates, considerations beyond the exclusive economic predication of the subject must be brought to bear. The social relations of production involve questions of value produced through representations of the family, gender, sexuality, and of the nation. Their affective value, while not quantifiable, is intrinsic to the "metaphysical subtleties and theological niceties" that are inherent to the commodity form. What forms of analysis permit an investigation into value formation that enhances and maintains, even alters, the terms of exchange? What enables the seemingly endless production of cultural commodities and their consumption? How can affectivity be brought to bear on an understanding of the value and power of representation?

To answer these questions, we return to Gramsci's notion of folklore as common sense. Distinct from polemic and interpretation, folklore is germane to what Deleuze identifies as affectivity and what Raymond Williams termed "structures of feeling," a composite and affective relation to "the world and life." Gramsci does not invoke folklore in the strict anthropological sense of the concept, though he does not preclude its ethnographic potential. For him, folklore is

a "conception of the world and life" implicit to a large extent in determinate (in time and space) strata of society and in opposition (also for the most part implicit, mechanical and objective) to "official" conceptions of the world (or, in a broader sense, the conceptions of the cultured parts of historically determinate societies) that have succeeded one another in the historical process. (Hence the strict relationship between folklore and "common sense" which is philosophical folklore.)[24]

Gramsci's use of the term "mechanical" also suggests a sensorimotor relation to images of social life distinct from notions of false ideology as false consciousness, one based on habit that is distinct too from any conception of a fully articulated consciousness that is "elaborated and systematic."

Elaboration of the form of folklore charted by Gramsci enables an identification of the major tropes that animate the cinema of the era through a careful disarticulation of their sources in the broader culture. One of the difficulties in examining folklore involves the exclusive privileging of the role of narrative and the assumption that these narratives are static, identified with ruralism and with unchanging tradition. The familiar narratives are characterized by repetition and difference, and the treatment of sameness and difference offers clues to the texts' adherence to and departures from any presumed norm. The images in which these narratives are couched are far more revealing of tensions surrounding cultural continuity and change than the narratives taken in isolation. The striated nature of folklore, its discontinuities, are tell-tale signs of conflict and attempted foreclosure. One of the basic characteristics of folklore is its investment in the semblance of sentiment: folklore does not function consciously or rationally, but affectively. Its heterogeneous character, according to Gramsci, is "much more unstable and fluctuating than language and dialects."[25] Despite its ostensible appearance of uniformity, its affective elements are unstable and indicative of the greater importance of affect than as mere deliberate and univalent belief. In Gramsci's description of the sedimented nature of folklore, he acknowledges a necessary yoking of high and popular culture and of past and present. Folklore, relying as it does on tradition, contains the residue of earlier cultures united to contemporary situations.

The glue that binds the disparate elements of folklore is "experience," experience based on and valued as proverbial wisdom, popular song, intuition, memory, and habit. Gramsci's "folklore" bears similarities to Gianni Vattimo's notion of "myth." Akin to myth, folklore is "narrative and fantastic, playing on the emotions with little or no pretense to objectivity."[26] "Myth" functions in affective fashion and seems to identify participation in and passive assent to social structures.[27] Folklore and myth do not assume *a priori* a set of unified assumptions about the world. On the contrary, they call attention to the multifaceted dimensions of received culture as seen in its emphasis on archaism, cultural relativism, and limited rationality. In relation to modernity, the prevalence of mythical and folkloric knowledge signals the "dissolution of metaphysical philosophies of history."[28] However, this dissolution does not signal the end of myth, but demythologization itself comes to be seen as a myth: "A secularized culture is not one that has simply left the religious elements of its tradition behind, but one that continues to live them as traces."[29] While common sense as folklore might appear as the foundation of hegemony and consent, a reading of the art, literature, and cinema of the Fascist era dramatizes profound schisms and, even more, antagonisms, in relation to conceptions of the movement and meaning of history. In the period that Gramsci wrote, he recognized through his discussion of folklore similar signs of dissolution of unified forms of thinking: in certain liberal notions of progress, in the ultimate rationality of the state through the triumph of Americanism, in the philosophy of action as against rationality expressed through the writings of Giovanni Gentile, and in the ascendancy of mass media. However, Gramsci's conception of folklore is relevant to modern thinking insofar as he is concerned to understand the cultural/political forces that inhere in the philosophical thinking of each person and of social groups.

For Gramsci, if there is a possibility for social transformation it resides in the conviction that intellectual work can produce significant changes, given the understanding that when he refers to intellectuals he is not describing what he terms professional or traditional intellectuals who are aligned with the state. His definition of an intellectual is predicated upon the notion that there is no such thing as a nonintellectual. Rather he writes that

> There is no human activity from which every form of intellectual participation can be excluded; *homo faber* cannot be separated from *homo sapiens*. Each man, finally, outside his professional activity carries on some form of intellectual activity, that is, he is a "philosopher," an artist, a man of taste, he participates in a particular conception of the world, has a conscious line of moral conduct, and therefore contributes to sustain a conception of the world or to modify it, that is, to bring into being new modes of thought.[30]

Thus, he rejects the notion of the ignorance and mindlessness of the people, though he does not reject the possibility that political change may come too late or not at all.

His conception of popular culture is further tied to his comments on common sense and folklore. He does not regard popular culture as retrograde and nonintellectual but as the repository of thoughts and beliefs that are fragmentary and in need of critical elaboration. Common sense, in his terms, is not to be radically differentiated from systems of philosophy; nor is high culture to be considered radically different from popular culture. As an historically determinate "conception of the world and life," common sense is related to folklore but is not, Gramsci writes,

> elaborated and systematic because, by definition, the people (the sum total of the instrumental and subaltern classes of every form of society that has so far existed) cannot possess conceptions which are elaborated, systematic and politically organized and centralized in their albeit contradictory development. It is, rather, many-sided—not only because it includes different and juxtaposed elements, but also because it is stratified from the more crude to the less crude—if, indeed, one should speak of a confused agglomerate of fragments of all conceptions of the world and life that have succeeded one another in history. In fact, it is only in folklore that one finds surviving evidence, adulterated and mutilated, of the majority of these conceptions.[31]

Gramsci in referring to folklore is not identifying it as "primitive," as pastoral, ethnographic, or as "quaint." He is not interested in nostalgia, in a return to an impossible source. Folklore is not restricted to rural and past societies and their ethnographers; it inheres in urban societies and it survives well into the present. Gramsci is not suggesting that it is false. He is also not suggesting that in itself common sense as folklore is "true" and liberating. Instead, he is seeking a mode for understanding how popular thought is composed, circulated, and legitimized and its contributions to group and individual perceptions of requisite behaviors for survival, fantasmatic and imaginary as they might be. The importance of studying folklore as common sense is not traditionally academic and passively descriptive. His objective is, as always, addressed to questions of subalternity, to understand the ways in which the subaltern knows the world but may not be in a position to know how to change it. Inherent in common sense and its expression of folklore is a rudimentary sense of the world, of how social, political, and cultural forces are aligned, the obstructions to action, and ways for warding off and circumventing likely retaliation for thinking and acting differently. Common sense as folklore, as a dominant characteristic of the popular, is thus a mode of self-censorship, conformity, and a strategy for survival.

Similarly Vattimo's comments on contemporary myth, with some caution, can be applied to the struggles that characterized Italy during the Fascist years albeit with an awareness of significant changes in culture and politics that have transpired since that time: "Modern European culture is . . . linked to its own religious past not only by a relation of overcoming and emancipation, but also, and inseparably, by a relation to conservation-distortion-evacuation: progress is in a sense nostalgic by nature, as the classicism and romanticism of recent centuries has taught us. But the significance of this nostalgia only becomes apparent once the experience of demythologization is taken to its extreme."[32] One of the characteristics of myth is its ability to abrogate time and specificity. Though often identified as myth, the notion of folklore is more nuanced, less identified with the suprahistorical, bearing less of a problematic relationship to history and ideology. In its formulaic nature, its pastiche qualities, its stubborn adherence to experience and affect, folklore seems to de-individuate, appearing to obliterate time and space, comprised as it is of proverbial wisdom, aphorisms, nostrums, truisms, clichés. However, these familiar strategies are not voided of history. As folklore circulates through the culture, it is dynamic, complicit with change, assuming different shapes to meet historical exigencies. Gramsci too eschews a strictly ethnographic conception of folklore, avoiding folklore's identification with primitivism, exoticism, cultural backwardness, and nostalgia for a return to an uncomplicated mode of existence. Folklore as projected in his writings is a dynamic rather than static way of accounting for behavior and activity, amenable to accommodations to the new, particularly to modern exigencies. In this sense, folklore can provide insights into the character of mass cinema—its narratives, motifs, styles, and melodramatic strategies.

Melodrama, like opera, relies on folkloric narratives of searing injustices to be righted, the demonic uses of power, the imperative to revenge, unrequited love, and loyalty betrayed. These scenarios are composite, relying on earlier history for explanation and legitimation but deeply invested in the present. This is not a static world of automatism, paralysis, or archaism. In fact, melodrama's reliance on the fluidity and changeability of common sense ensures a dialogue between past and present. Most importantly common sense as folklore in Gramscian terms is the philosophy of subaltern groups, and this philosophy serves certain immediate social and psychic needs. While it may not provide a critical view of the world that is rational and "coherent," it is not blind and mindless. Folklore as common sense is wily in its strategies of suturing perceived needs and desires to contemporary exigencies as evident in its cautious weighing of the new, its distrust of change, its mistrust of power and authority but, at the same time, its willingness to make modest concessions to the present. Suspicious of intellectualism, reformism, and language, common sense as folklore is melodramatic not necessarily in the formal and generic sense, but in its reliance on proverbial wisdom, truism, and cliché, in short, in its attempts to reduce complexity. Its composite quality bespeaks a certain encyclopedism in its drawing on historical figures and events, its reliance on juridical discourses, its preoccupation with the body and with disease and health, and its secularism that bears a religious taint. The affective component of folklore is melodramatic, preoccupied with sentimentality, romance, litigiousness, obsessional quests, jealousy, and aggression. The role of affect, rather than serving as the servant of meaning and action, and arising from their failure, must be regarded in opposite terms. Affect reverses the usual primacy of meaning. Affect is in search of a signifier to which it can attach itself. Overriding the limits of signification, the excessive character of melodrama spills over into and is capable of negating sexual and familial conflicts, contaminating narratives ostensibly devoted to the circulation of truisms, "underlying meanings," and "messages." Through its theatricality and operatic character, melodrama, working in tandem with folklore, draws attention onto the unsettling presence of affect that exceeds the unity of consensus.

In "Americanism and Fordism," Gramsci described how Americanism had made its inroads in Italian and, more generally, in European culture, and he was aware of the cultural institutions that were emerging, including cinema, and their potential for providing an appearance of change. He wrote:

> In the case of Americanism, understood not only as a form of café life but as an ideology of the kind represented by Rotary Clubs, we are not dealing with a new type of civilisation. This is shown by the fact that nothing has been changed in the character of and the relationships between fundamental groups. What we are dealing with is an organic extension and an intensification of European civilisation, which has simply acquired a new coating in the American climate.[33]

This "new coating," he identified in the arenas of industrialism, economics, wages, and Fordism, expressed particularly in relation to "supercountry" and "supercity," the "sexual question," and feminism and "masculinism." His comments are couched, as are so many of the notes in the prison writings, in schematic fashion as issues to which he might return at some later point. Needless to say, his observations in the notes on "Americanism" and "Fordism" are cogent, requiring elaboration in the context of more recent research that has augmented and documented the complicated role of America in the interwar era as well as in the post–World War Two era. Specifically in relation to the role of cinema, Gramsci commented that its currency and appeal, its cultural substance, derive from its nonverbal, neologistic character, involving

> gestures, tone of voice and so on, a musical element that communicates the leitmotiv of the predominant feeling, the principal passion, and the orchestral element: gesture in the broad sense, which scans and articulates the wave of feeling and passion. These observations are indispensable for establishing a cultural politics and they are fundamental for a cultural politics of the popular masses. They explain the current international "success" of the cinema and, earlier, of the opera and music in general.[34]

In an assessment of the eclectic nature of popular and mass culture, the concept of folklore helps to identify the absorptive character, the assumed experiential and protean quality, and, above all, the investment in affective experience that characterizes the multivalent and quotidian involvement in social life. In relation to the construction of value, the concept of folklore provides an alternative on the one hand to monolithic psychoanalytic hypotheses about oedipality, castration, and desire, and, on the other, to equally monolithic economistic explanations. The importance of folklore in connection with popular memory and history has been dramatized by Italian filmmakers of the 1970s and 1980s, most notably Federico Fellini, Pier Paolo Pasolini, and Paolo and Vittorio Taviani, who, in their differing styles, have returned to the 1930s and explored the role of cinematic language in the context of cinema as a form of modern folklore. And the Italian cinema of the Fascist years offers an opportunity to assess the role of modern folklore as a means for rethinking the complex nature of consensus.

REVALUATIONS OF FASCISM:
CINEMA AND CONSENSUS

In the process of revaluation of fascism, Italian and German studies on gender and sexuality have corrected the predominant attention paid to public manifestations of "fascinating fascism" that tended to occlude the immediate, everyday, and eclectic dimensions of representation that ensure its reception. These studies reveal that an understanding of popular culture under fascism must be tied to a synoptic examination of cultural and political life. The cinema of the era cannot be considered in isolation from international cultural developments especially involving relations between modernism and modernity in the formation of mass culture. In recent studies of national cinema, the emphasis has shifted away from the concern with defining the unique character of national identity and toward situating considerations of nation more properly within an international context and under the rubric of national conceptions that are shifting and ambiguous. One of the most prolific and fruitful directions of critical investigation involves antagonisms between tradition and modernity; specifically the role of modernization and connections to America and Americanism have become central to revaluating the history of Italian cinema. Such examinations have complicated relations between cinema and politics and particularly the character of fascism.

Since the late 1970s and early 1980s, critical work on Italian cinema of the Fascist era has increased dramatically, not only building on these earlier studies but opening up new directions for rethinking the character and impact of the cultural production of the era and, equally importantly, for conceptions of Fascism. Cultural studies of the late 1980s and 1990s have complicated the dominant preoccupation with the nature and role of ideology, prompting the need to interrogate and think anew models of coercion and consensus through offering multivalent examinations of relations between cinematic production and consumption under Fascism. In the examination of Italian Fascism, such critics as Philip Cannistraro and Victoria de Grazia have stressed the practices of the regime through its public spectacles, the restrictive laws that governed woman's reproductive life, the repression of alternative sexualities, the erosion of civil life, the increasing intervention of the state into all areas of social life, the preparation and execution of an imperialist war, and the racist practices that are the inevitable accompaniment of nationalistic and imperialistic aspirations while overlooking the shared heritage in the West of such practices.[35] Focusing on differences to the exclusion of similarities, critics can make the case for significant differences between Italy and Germany, on the one hand, and the United States and Great Britain on the other.

By focusing on the unique, coercive, and repressive character of Italian Fascism, the possibility of understanding the interdependent character of emergent global politics and the ways that the masses were implicated is occluded. The object is not to obscure or minimize the barbarism of Fascism but to assess its forms differently, to interrogate the complex and contradictory ways in which social relations came to be represented and particularly its relation to conceptions of consensus. In his examination of "everyday life" and the different modes of coercion and consent under Nazism, Detlev J. K. Peukert has commented that "A study of everyday life under National Socialism, then, provides basic insights into the ambivalence of political activity, and shows how pervasively elements of inadvertent conformity or conscious approval entered into calculations about opposition and compromise."[36] Because of its seeming escapist character, the commercial cinema can serve as tutelary instance of "the ambivalence of political activity." The popular cinema was a site of conflicts over consensus, revealing conformity as well as opposition and compromise. Mobile rather than static, tenuous rather than univalent, and fragmentary rather than unified, it is a challenging enigma of the complexity and materiality of cultural representation. Even more dramatically, the cinema can tell us something about the illusory nature of representation through its self-conscious articulation of its strategies through theatricality and hence, through making its designs evident to its audiences.

In discussing the character of the Italian cinema of the 1930s, Pierre Sorlin asks, "Was cinema a mere instrument which allowed political leaders to entertain people and establish an illusory consensus?"[37] According to him, looking at the cinema in this fashion "does not tell us much about Italy."[38] His conclusion is that one must ask other, different, more pragmatic questions about film and politics, involving production, exhibition, and, above all, reception. In examining commercial films and newsreels, Sorlin points to numerous inconsistencies, stressing that "Flagrant propaganda does not exist in the Italian films of the 1930s, but historians often stress the importance of oblique publicity."[39] While at moments overstating his case, Sorlin is correct to challenge a reductive conception of consensus and of a close fit between film and politics; he raises disturbing questions about strategies for understanding the character of Italian cinema of the 1930s and early 1940s. The naming of the cinema of these years as "fascistic" serves to define the cinema in advance of any examination of the meaning of the term and its efficacy for characterizing cultural life during the Fascist era. However, in jettisoning consensus, a concept that he treats reductively, he inhibits the possibility of recognizing the complex relation between the viewers and the films that he invokes. In James Hay's terms,

> The notion of cultural production and a processual approach to cinema raises questions about the permanence of social consensus. To understand the fabrication of social consensus, it is again necessary to examine the rhetorical practices, the techniques and models, through which viewers visualize possibilities of continuity and change. Cultural production does not occur in a unilinear fashion; discursive practices do not (as traditional "mass culture" theorists suggest) replicate traditional beliefs or attitudes in a mechanical fashion. Formal change and diversity are part of cultural production, even in a state-controlled or so-called totalitarian society.[40]

Hay's position, while taking into account the role of consensus as necessary precondition to profitability, tracks the nature of change and diversity rather than adhering to a rigid set of ideological prescriptions. Consonant with Sorlin's call for a study of reception, Hay's enterprise presupposes a strong correlation between text and audience for an understanding of the workings of popular culture that is not isomorphic with a uniform sense of ideology. Thus Hay addresses the economics of the industry, but extends the notion of production to include the crucial role played by cultural knowledge as a reciprocal and dynamic process that circulates between producers and consumers. This knowledge is embedded in the texts themselves as social texts. Rather than performing a quantitative analysis of audience composition by class, gender, or region—an impossible task—such an analysis probes the multivalent character of cultural production: its inseparability from industrial production, the union of subjective and objective considerations in the determination of value, and hence the interdependency of economics, politics, and culture. Cultural production takes on the character of a "fantastic form of a relation between things," and the project becomes one of discerning the ways in which this fantastic relation can be understood to come into existence and establish a hold through representation.

Thus, Sorlin's question concerning the instrumental and consensual role of cinema under Fascism has a direct bearing on any consideration of the complicitous nature of economic, cultural, and political forms as they impact on the audience/consumer.[41] Inherent to his critique of consent is a proper resistance to a conception of consensus as reductive and monolithic, thereby revealing nothing about the workings of popular culture. Moreover, he is correct in his assumption that the notion of consensus, if a workable concept, is applicable more broadly to the popular cinema than uniquely to the Italian cinema of the Fascist years. However, the question of the "instrumentality" of cinema is at the basis of the return to a Gramscian analysis and of the attempts to elaborate on his observations concerning the forms of culture and the nature of consent. The character of consensus as defined by Gramsci, refined by Raymond Williams, and further explored by Stuart Hall and others of the Birmingham school is not a simple matter of control over representation as determined by political leaders and assimilated by the populace.[42] Consensus is part of a complex process that draws on existing and developing forms of cultural knowledge.

These writers share a concern to understand the nature of production and reception, the ways they are tied to existing and emergent forms of cultural knowledge as they are in the process of assuming new forms. They are attentive to the ways these forms are disseminated, especially through mass culture, as they are heterogeneous rather than unified. Nowhere from their writings can one conclude that consensus is seamless and monolithic, nor that it is unique to a fascist state. On the contrary, their elaboration of the nature of consensus takes into account its constitutive, not absolute and essential character and, most particularly, its simultaneous involvement in and distance from formal politics. In Gramsci's writing on common sense, he describes and underlines repeatedly its fragmentary and protean character. Given his emphasis on the importance of understanding the uses and abuses of popular culture, his scattered comments on culture, common sense, and folklore are a way of focusing on the all-important dimension of the creation and reception of cultural positions.

In the case of the Fascist years, recent scholarship has underscored the importance of the tension between modernity and tradition, myth and the appearance of rationality, modernism and folklore, the bolstering of nationalism in the face of imperialism and global threat. Thus, a reading of the cultural productions of the Fascist years, much like Renzo De

Felice's refusal to name D'Annunzio as fascist or antifascist, must inevitably come to terms with the conflicting elements that are imbricated in the folklore of consensus.[43] Contemporary examinations of folklore and its ties to Italian cinema as well as to world cinema more generally have had to address the role of America specifically as constructed through the lens of Hollywood. In exploring the cultural impact of Italian cinematic production in the 1930s and 1940s, its ties to theater, music, spectacle, and popular literature, it has become important to abandon conceptions of national cultural purity and focus instead on the eclectic nature of film production.

If the work on postcolonial literatures and cinemas has stressed the "hybridity" of cultural forms, the critical examination of European cinema has also been characterized by a recognition of its assimilative character, its dependency on America and on the American cinema as the locus of modernity. The antipathy to genre cinema characterized in the immediate aftermath of World War Two has been steadily eroded, replaced by the recognition (as took place earlier in relation to studies of Hollywood) that a refusal to address the nature of Italian popular film constitutes a major obstacle in understanding the Italian cinema, its relations to Hollywood and to other European cinemas. Even more, this refusal is also responsible for misrecognizing how the cinema under Fascism created a folklore, built on the past but responsive to new trends, trends that were to bear fruit in the succeeding years including those that are identified with the "neorealist aesthetic." Merely acknowledging the productive growth of filmmaking in Italy in the 1930s will not address this misrecognition. Nor will drawing affinities to other cinemas correct the situation. The continuing assumption is that the films are escapist vehicles conveying "the exhilarating sensation of being able to emigrate temporarily to the world of their own dreams, and of returning to their own lives and private spaces enriched and enlivened."[44]

While such a formulation foregrounds the centrality of popular cinema in the cultural transformations that were taking place during the Fascist era, it does not offer a great deal by way of understanding how this modern folklore may have functioned by way of reaching audiences. The reinvestigation of the films of the era requires a deeper understanding of the nature of "escapism." Were they perceived as trivial and diversionary, entertaining but mindless? Is an analysis of the relationship between Italian cinema and that of Hungary and France of the same era as well to the Hollywood cinema sufficient to account for the nature and effects of popular cinema? Or has a conception of popular cinema as a "dream factory" merely been resuscitated with new dimensions? If the films were instrumental in generating new desires, in producing new images of the world to which audiences responded with pleasure, how is it that they generated this value? And what does this tell us about the mobile, ever-changing, and slippery nature of consensus? In the numerous domestic comedies embodying the fantasies of department store clerks, engineers, actresses, erring and disgruntled husbands and wives, dreams of acquiring a "million lire a month" are not removed from the general tendencies of the popular commercial cinema to entertain genre codes and conventions that are derivative, repetitive, reassuring in their familiarity, while at the same time amenable to permutations.

The challenge is to produce critical strategies to identify and understand the persistence of characters and motifs not as mere escapism but, as in the case of Hollywood cinema, through identifying the ways they create a bond with audiences, a bond that relies on the union of realism and fantasy. In addressing a group of films, the British Gainsborough films, similarly identified as "escapist," Sue Harper describes the films' styles as requiring "a high degree of audience creativity . . . a site for the development of a carefully costed 'expressionism.' . . . [I]t was precisely in this expressionism that the audience's fears or desires could be pleasurably rehearsed."[45] Similarly, many of the Italian melodramas of the 1930s and early 1940s seek strategies that are conducive to new relations between production and consumption, generating "fears or desires" within the parameters of a recognizable world. Sue Harper's work on the Gainsborough films, particularly the costume dramas of the 1940s, is a model for exploring the question of pleasure afforded by their highly choreographed and stylized decor. In ways applicable to the Italian melodramas of the late 1930s and 1940s, these British films, geared to a feminine audience, according to Harper, "address a female sexuality denied expression through a conventional signifying system."[46] In relation to reception, she concludes, "British costume melodrama (as opposed to historical film) manifests a positive interpretation of the past, and grants a freedom to the audience to maneuver its own way through narrative codes."[47] Harper seeks to attach a positive, rather than negative, value to the so-called "escapist" tendencies of these melodramas and excludes other expressionist forms of representation in her account. I would extend her comments more broadly to the commercial cinema of the 1930s and 1940s, including the various forms of the historical film. The "freedom to maneuver through narrative codes" and the reliance of these codes on the cognitive and affective character of melodrama can be extended to other genres, including comedy. However, in addressing the question of the "positive" dimensions of the uses of the past, it is also necessary to examine the codes in such a way as to allow for their simultaneous openings and closures, for the complicated ways that their uses of folklore function as a limited site for a recognition of difference and also as a means of inhibiting its potential.

Recent work on Italian popular cinema and its relations to other national forms of film production, involving the desire on the part of the industry for profit through increased and modernized forms of production and circulation (even to the detriment of political correctness), and the challenging role of Americanism, has paved the way for rethinking the nature of consent. Instead of abandoning any attempt to account for consensus, it is more productive to provide an elaborate and complex notion of the slippery and contradictory character and reception of popular texts and, more generally, of the complex nature of the commodity form. The fact that consent is not unique to the Italian cinema of the Ventennio does not invalidate the consensus character of the films. Rather an examination of consensus challenges the critic to examine the ever-changing forms that characterize what is subsumed under the term, "mass culture." The rethinking of consensus may make Italian Fascism less unique but consent is still important for understanding the relation between Fascism and mass culture. The relations among common sense, folklore, and consent are central to any consideration of the adherence and consent with the caveat that they are neither univalent or totally uncritical.

In the context of consent, Victoria de Grazia has documented the importance of the *Dopolavoro*, the state's afterwork organization. The state's management of leisure life was yet another means for confronting changes that were part of creation of new forms of entertainment encouraged by the regime—even if at the expense of traditional conceptions of the centrality of the family, so central to Fascist ideology.[48] Her extensive examination of the positioning of women under Fascism, also reveals the contradictory effects of social and political life during these years of fascism. She finds that women's "lives were a disconcerting experience of new opportunities and new repressions: they felt the enticement of things modern; they also sensed the drag of tradition."[49] The "woman question" was a major instance of challenges to familialism and its relation to changing and conflicting notions of femininity that crossed national boundaries and complicated the question of coercion and consent in the culture and politics of the era. Work on representations of femininity in the literature and art of the Italian cinema has been long overdue, though representations of masculinity have been highlighted. Representations of femininity and masculinity, expressed especially through the star system, are part of the folklore essential to mass cultural production for the appearance of social stability, offering insights into the sources of its construction and its presumed power over its consumers. An examination of the folklore of consensus involving questions of nation, gender, and modernity, thus complicates any assessment of Italian film production of the era, inviting a closer accounting of similarities and differences between production under Fascism and so-called democratic societies.

As feminist critics have pointed out in their examinations of representation and sexuality, woman's sexuality in particular is central to an understanding of the nature of consensus under fascism. Situating the question of feminine sexuality within the larger context of cultural conflicts inherent to the time, de Grazia writes:

> Because Italian fascism's positions on women were not merely of its own invention, nor were they, in the last analysis, that distant from the attitudes, policies, and trends prevailing in non-authoritarian states, they need to be studied in a wider time frame and in comparative context. Mussolini's sexual politics crystallized deep-seated resentments against broader changes in the condition of women in Western societies.[50]

Sensitive to the role played by mass culture, in commenting particularly on the cinema, she states that "Mass culture, especially that consumed by women, has usually been treated as escapist, the assumption being that it diverts from social engagement and deadens critical thinking."[51] Resisting such a judgment, de Grazia acknowledges the role played by mass culture through radio, cinema, and journalism as "an empowering force for young working-class and lower middle-class women."[52] But she asks why such issues as dating, more daring notions of sexual expression, new forms of beauty care, and the examination of courtship did not "result in more sexually emancipated behavior" and "freer life styles?"[53]

De Grazia's question raises the problem of how to interpret the role of media. On the one hand, media are the source of new, more "modern" images of femininity, as de Grazia indicates. However, modernity can never be considered apart from economic, cultural, and hence political considerations. The role of modernity in the 1930s and 1940s was highly ambivalent. While images of modernity exploited consumerism and while consumerism was inextricably linked to notions of gender and sexuality, these images were still closely fused to traditional conceptions of the family as a stabilizing force. In the vein of folklore, the new images were superimposed on the old. The affect generated by the cinema can be situated in a disorienting space between past and present. Cinema is not the window on prevailing conceptions of reality so much as it is an index to the composition of affects that evade the binary schism between fiction and the real. The spectator is suspended between the real and the illusory, the familiar and the new in the strategies adopted by the Italian cinema as it represented "the tensions, fears, and desires of Italy's rapidly changing social and cultural environment."[54]

What is important about Gramsci's observations on cultural politics is the value he consistently accords to affect, stressing not the content per se, but focusing on expressive forms of articulation: particularly gesture, feeling, and passion, attributes most closely associated with melodrama, opera, and with Hollywood cinema in particular, its genre system, its stars, and its tie-ins to the wide range of cultural commodities—fashion, vehicles of locomotion, furniture, and advertising. In this vein, James Hay, in his discussion of the "myth of the Grand Hotel" and the relationship between "*stracittà* and the department store," has sought, in this vein, to identify changes wrought in Italian cinema involving modernity, while Karen Pinkus has examined Italian advertising of the era, focusing particularly on its exploitation of "bodily regimes." She comments that "Fascism brilliantly exploited the inextricable reciprocal exchange that pertains in any state formation between the body politic and the formation of the individual body."[55] She explores in great detail the iconography of advertising that inflects notions of the "black body," the bodies of women and men, and their relation to the machinic, to production and consumption, especially in relation to fashion and maquillage. The impetus of the Pinkus text—to open up more avenues to understand representations of the body—extends the Gramscian concern to identify connections between politics, economics, and "the sexual question."

The "tensions, desires, and fears" expressed in the images and narratives of commercial cinema appear most blatant and obvious in melodrama with its excessive, hyperbolic style, removed from prevailing conceptions of realism. The critical interest in melodrama was resurrected in conjunction with a critique of realism. This critique challenged cinema's presumed approximation of conditions as they exist, its naturalization of socially constructed values, calling attention rather to cinema's status as artifact. By historicizing melodrama, by pointing to its readability within the lens of excess, and by relating this excess to its preoccupation with pleasure and danger, critics have been able to articulate its presumed silences in relation to questions of the family, sexuality, and gender. The work of critics on the melodramatic imagination has had a discernible and important effect on film studies. Melodramas are no longer regarded as a despised, trivial, and meaningless mode of expression or as simply a genre among many genres. Film melodrama has become a means of access to thorny questions of production and reception. It has offered critics a language to identify the ways in which conflicting presentations of the everyday—particularly of family, gender, national identity, and sexuality—are embodied in the commercial cinema. Through an examination of narrativity, the functioning of stars, the uses of music, fashion, and *mise-en-scène*, the study of melodrama, often in concert with psychoanalytic concepts, has forged methods for reevaluating the processes of identification between filmic text and spectatorship particularly through addressing the affective components of melodramatic style.

These studies have challenged the traditional valorization of realism as a transparent form for arriving at textual meaning and reception. They have forced a rethinking of the bifurcation between realism and highly coded forms of expression, pointing to ways of reading melodrama's hyperbolic expression, its reliance on affectively charged images and sound, its penchant for pleasure in its narratives and in its address to the audience through spectacle, and its reliance on cultural folklore as a more reliable indication of textual strategies and effects. In Christine Gledhill's terms,

> melodrama is a dramatic narrative in which musical accompaniment marks the emotional effects. This is still perhaps the most useful definition, because it allows melodramatic elements to be seen as constituents of a system of punctuation, giving expressive colour and chromatic contrast to the story line, by orchestrating the emotional ups and downs of the intrigue. The advantage of this approach is that it formulates the problems of melodrama as problems of style and articulation.[56]

The relevance of Gledhill's observations for a study of the films produced under fascism is its emphasis on style, not authenticity, thus opening the way to interrogating the opportunistic, theatrical, and contradictory aspects of articulation.

The problems of articulation are not univalent and transparent but are polyvalent, ambiguous, and strife-laden. Peter Brooks's study of melodrama makes abundantly apparent the ways in which melodrama operates in a nonverbal register. The language of melodrama, rather than affirming the pro-filmic status quo, opens a window to different readings of the face, the body, and landscape. Melodramatic language may not set out to subvert or undermine conventional values, but in its fascination with power, eroticism, and violence, melodrama inevitably unleashes a host of cultural antagonisms. Brooks stresses the centrality of what he calls, the "the text of muteness," the preoccupation with the inarticulate that signifies the inadequacy of constructed and apparently fixed social meanings which emerges when one analyzes gesture and music as contestatory.[57] The relation between the melodramatic and operatic text is located in the uses of music and gesture not merely as diegetic support but as a telling sign of the insufficiency of verbal language, and hence of institutional values.

In his "Tales of Sound and Fury," Thomas Elsaesser describes melodrama in term of its identification with the victim, its tendency toward rapid and extreme oscillations in response to tensions, underlining their inadequacy in confronting the world they seek to escape but cannot. Irony and pathos are the responses to the characters' inadequacies, their inability to alter their world. Irony and pathos are also a conduit to the audience and to their responses to the dilemma they witness. Elsaesser writes:

> Irony privileges the spectator vis-à-vis the protagonists, for he registers the difference from a superior position. Pathos results from non-communication or silence made eloquent—people talking at cross-purposes, . . . a mother watching her daughter's wedding from afar . . . or a woman returning unnoticed to her family, watching them through the window . . . where highly emotional situations are underplayed to present an ironic discontinuity of feeling or a qualitative difference in intensity.[58]

Thus, irony and pathos are the means to audiences' investment in melodrama and facilitate their involvement with the characters and events. Incest, violence, betrayal, exploitation, misrepresentation, misrecogni-

tion, jealousy, obsession, and thwarted power are the motors of melodrama, and the style in which they are presented is seductive, touching
chords of response on the part of the spectator.

The notion of excess has played a key role in the critical delineation
of the workings of melodrama and, nowadays, in more general relation to
cinematic texts. The presence of excess becomes the locus of difference,
the link between the social and the filmic text (but not as a reflection of
the real but as the real). The critical reading of the melodramatic text has
also served to level the ground between popular and modernist texts
through imposing a writerly relation to the text generated through textual
excess. Following the lead of Roland Barthes, Kristin Thompson states
that, "The minute that a viewer begins to notice style for its own sake or
watch works that do not provide such thorough motivation, excess comes
forward and must affect narrative meaning. . . . [E]xcess implies a gap or
lag in motivation."[59] Thus, in melodrama, the texts invite consideration
of style for their own sake. More importantly, this recognition would suggest that (1) most texts, especially those identified with Hollywood classical cinema, communicate a greater or lesser degree of excess (e.g., Griffith or von Sternberg), (2) that excess need not be in conflict with
identification but plays a role in both distancing yet involving the spectator in another register even if only to return her affectively to a more
involved relation to the narrative, and finally (3) the presence of excess
signifies the impossibility of the melodramatic text to present a seamless
and untroubled relation to its scenarios of pain and disaster. The important aspect of the concept of textual excess is how it undermines narrativity, directing the spectator to other aspects of the text, the star, relations
between director and star, discrete images, especially the close-up, the specific uses of sound, and the singularity of gestures. Far beyond the role of
the concept of excess as a defamiliarizing strategy is its usefulness for recognizing the theatricality of feature films, their metacinematic character,
the ways in which the films perforce share with their audiences a knowledge of their commodity status, a slippery relation to conformity and
opposition, and a simultaneous sense of involvement and detachment.

The excessiveness of the star persona plays a key role in unsettling a
narrative's impetus toward transparency, clarity, and unity. Gledhill
describes how

> If realism presumes the adequacy of given linguistic and cultural
> codes for understanding and representing reality, and modernism

embraces the infinite regress of meaning in the self-reflexive play of the signifier, melodrama's rootedness in the real world, its ideological mission to motivate ordinary lives, leads into an opposing stance. Faced with the decentred self, the evasiveness of language, melodrama answers with excessive personalisation, excessive expression.[60]

This personalization clashes with the tendency toward either naturalizing the signs or also partaking of the self-reflexivity of modernism though attaching this reflexivity not to a critical insight but to a particular fascination with the image and its affectivity. The star serves several complex, even conflicting, functions: as a way of interrupting the diegesis, of blurring the lines between the real and the imaginary, of seeking to humanize identity formations, and, simultaneously, to unsettle identity but not intentionally or necessarily as a means of subversion or resistance.

The Italian cinema of the silent years at its height was characterized by a love of spectacle, a preoccupation, though not exclusively, with historical and mythical themes, not at all dissimilar from other national cinemas, and especially with its star system, the system of *divismo*. Such divas as Francesca Bertini, Lyda Borelli, and Eleonora Duse, were intimately identified with Gabriele D'Annunzio, closely tied to melodrama and to the operatic and affective powers of the cinematic medium. According to Brunetta, the diva

> is not solely a body, a look, tied to characteristic and stylized gestures, it is also, at this time, the most incarnate emblematization of a world over which she exercises absolute dominion. The woman-diva, thanks to her fascination, her sexual power, dominates and can destroy a world over which she possesses economic and political power.[61]

Brunetta connects the dominion of the diva with "a series of variable factors internal and external to the cinematic apparatus."[62] Her appearance coincides with massive immigration to the United States and to Latin America as well with Italian imperialist expansion in Libya. Her reign coincides with the development of the new language of the cinema and with the successful circulation of these films abroad. This new language resides in the specularization of the body and, in particular, the feminine body. Her image is particularly associated with the materialization of a sense of power inherent to the cinematic image that carries great affective appeal. The diva is identified with prevailing conceptions of beauty that are not merely attributed to slimness and glamour. Associated with D'Annunzian melodramatic excess in her radiation of eroticism, exoticism, and hyperbolic affect, she largely, though not exclusively, inhabits a world of decadence, romanticism, and oneirism.

However, by the end of World War One, the Italian historical spectacles and melodramas that had been so successful internationally were no longer profitable. The system of *divismo*, so expensive now, and so theatrical, had become a deficit. The eclipse of the diva and the types of films with which she is identified, particularly historical, mythical, and melodramatic films, must be attributed to a combination of economic, social, aesthetic, and cultural factors. In relation to the cinema, in particular, Brunetta and others have underscored the perilous condition of the Italian film industry. On the economic front, *divismo* was a costly operation. The staggering salaries of the diva could not be maintained in the face of small audiences for films in Italy. Those films that shook the world, *Cabiria, The Last Days of Pompei, Maciste*, and others, with their spectacular settings, their exaltation of the sights and sounds of classical Rome, their fiery divas, and their large casts had ceased to attract audiences in the interwar years. Other factors pertaining more largely to the organization (or rather disarray) of the Italian film industry also played a role. Too many companies were competing with each other. There were too many unrealized scripts with accompanying financial losses. The lack of innovation in the face of foreign competition was starkly evident along with a stagnant and backward mode of production that was technically inferior. And, of course, Hollywood (and to a lesser extent Germany) had successfully initiated its colonization of world cinema, the "long march" of Hollywood in Italy described by Brunetta.

The "long march" was "in fact, a single-short-lived episode, the version organized by the American cinema was a long-term affair, carried out by degrees, at times appearing to be carried along in the wake of the regime, at others moving in parallel with it, always however at the same, ever-increasing rhythm that the regime dictated."[63] Brunetta reminds us that the Hollywood "march on Rome" was in no way threatening to the ideology of Fascism, and certainly Fascism had no concern about Hollywood's deleterious effects on the indigenous Italian cinema. Moreover, the Church, despite its mistrust of "film as a major danger to moral order" was sympathetic to Hollywood cinema, seeing in it a form of representation that "would not only provide entertainment, but would also illuminate the public and lead it along the narrow path of virtue."[64] Hollywood was, in Brunetta's words, "reality with a radiance of its own, an almost pentacostal light with the spiritual potential to bring to life, desires, dreams, and hopes, and to help the average man or woman, the homeowner and the *petit bourgeois*, to imagine his or her own future. The stars, the heroes and heroines, and even the run-of-the mill John Does of American cinema, gradually became perceived as disturbing projections of that which the average Italian, indifferent or alienated from Mussolini's imperial adventures, really wished to become."[65] Even after the law of 1938 that curtailed the importation of foreign films, the "inheritance of the images stored away by millions of cinema-goers continued to circulate in the collective imagination, undergoing various metamorphoses in the process."[66] Brunetta's comments reveal a complex state of affairs concerning any assessment of the relations of Italian commercial cinema and fascism as well as more broadly of the nature of cinematic production and reception.

In particular, Brunetta's observations shed light on important changes that had transpired in the interwar era in Italy as well as changes that were to continue throughout the twenty-year history of cultural production in Italy. The struggles of the Italian film industry cannot be exclusively tied to the ideology of fascism but must also be tied to the general state of the culture and economy of the time. It is clear, therefore, that the development of Italian cinema and any understanding of the history of that cinema must cope with the role that Hollywood and Europe played in its transformation for both good and ill. The role of mass culture, its evolution during the 1930s and 1940s, must also be addressed, in particular, its creation of popular images that resonate for contemporary audiences. These popular images address the desires and fantasies of the viewer rather than representing the official political line couched in images of historical monumentalism often associated with a handful of films of the era. Centrally, the "collective imagination" so successfully embodied by Hollywood cinema was of an affectively contagious nature, capturing the common sense of upward mobility, consumer gratification, new, more modern, models of femininity and masculinity, and contemporary conflicts more generally. Of course, these images were couched within prevailing constraints and contradictions of contemporary Italian social life.

The "long march" of the Americanization of Italian cinema had its effects on the character and quality of the modes and styles of cinematic

production. While the advent of Fascism did not immediately effect production in dramatic fashion, it did begin to set in place measures to
address the economic crisis of the film industry. Neither new narratives
nor forthcoming financial support were evident to bolster the ailing
industry. The most notable attempts at rejuvenating production involved
the creation of ENAC (Ente Nazionale per la Cinematografia) that was to
create ties with foreign film companies in 1926, but this effort failed in
1930. More successful, though still fragile, were the efforts of Stefano Pittaluga, who not only bought up many theaters, but attempted to find a
balance between foreign imports and indigenous production. The Società
Anonima Pittaluga was a joint state and private entity designed to regularize production, but it, too, faltered after Pittaluga's death in 1931. The
transition to sound in 1930 brought with it both further financial and
technical problems, but it also introduced and mandated innovation. The
early 1930s witnessed the entry of new directors, technicians, and actors
into the cinema as well as experimentation with tradition and new forms
of narratives. The directors associated with this movement were Raffaello
Matarazzo, Guido Brignone, Mario Serandrei, Alessandro Blasetti, and
Mario Camerini. New faces became more apparent in such actors and
actresses as Amedeo Nazzari, Vittorio De Sica, Sergio Tofano, Isa
Miranda, Elsa Merlini, Assia Noris, and Maria Denis, among others. The
theater helped supply new talent. Apparent too were gradual changes in
physiognomy, bodily contour, costume, makeup, and acting. The role of
music, both popular and operatic, as in other national cinemas, became
an important factor.

The sound cinema from 1929 to 1943, actually to the advent of
neorealism, is a drama of crisis and of strategies to meet that crisis successfully. One can chart changes in personnel, types of narrative, technical expertise, and modes of organization of production. The coming of
sound posed problems for the Italian cinema much as it did for other
European cinemas. According to Elaine Mancini, "The existence of
sound caused a host of thought and discussions; those who never before
had been interested in cinema now became engrossed by it; those who
had mastered silent film techniques questioned the artistic motives of this
new element that drew cinema closer to the theater; those who did want
to work with sound nonetheless questioned its validity in marketing
terms. In short, the coming of sound gave, sometimes directly, occasion-
ally indirectly, the strongest incentive the Italian cinema had known in
years."[67] Citing the successful *Figaro e la sua gran giornata* (1931) as a

milestone in the Italian sound cinema, Mancini comments that "Italy had successfully found her own style of sound film that related to her own cultural tradition."[68] Directed by Mario Camerini, the film eclectically draws on opera, theatricality, comic misrecognition, and pastoralism and reflexively plays with questions relating to cultural reception, revealing a familiar preoccupation most evident through the genre of the musical and its self-reflexive preoccupation with entertainment.

By the mid-1930s, the film production and reception of sound films increased. By 1942, the Italian film industry ranked fifth in the world, having risen from "260 million seats in 1936 to 470 million in 1942."[69] Sorlin asks why the number of spectators increased at a time of economic hardship. In response, he points to the recruitment of new viewers, both suburban and rural. The creation of the Venice Film Festival in 1932 was also an incentive as was the creation of training and educational facilities at the newly created Centro Sperimentale di Cinematografia and the building of new studios at Cinecittà. Thanks to the increased technical quality of the films, to the diversification of the types of narratives offered, the adoption with modification of Hollywood and European models of narration and acting, and the creation of new stars, Italian cinema was on the road to renewal, a renewal that is only now evident as a result of research on this long-neglected moment in Italian cinema. Thus, the question of consensus must be reconfigured in the context of priorities relating to the modernization of the industry as part of a more general drive toward enhancing Italy's position in relation to capitalist reformation.

The first priority (then even as now) of the Italian commercial cinema, more than that of ideological conformity, was the development, enhancement, and expansion of cinematic production. As Sorlin comments, "intellectuals were content with manifesting their allegiance, never deepening their knowledge of a constantly changing programme."[70] Sorlin's comments are instructive for calling attention to the opportunistic aspects of life under Fascism. The cinema of the Fascist era was instructive for the disjunctions that are evident between official culture and economic opportunism. To insist on the contamination between cultural politics and economic opportunism is hardly to eradicate the existence of Fascism, to minimize its excesses, but to arrive at a different understanding of the relations between civil society and the state under Fascism. Official history often elides or overgeneralizes the effect of political events on a populace, thus making judgments about the character of an age that often tends to subsume contradictory elements. According to Detlev J. K. Peukert, studies of Fascism have been "based either on the theory of fascism or on the theory of totalitarianism." The effects of such approaches, were that they "both dealt with the political system of authority, the wielders of power and the mechanisms of suppression, and they largely ignored the experience of those affected by the system, namely the mass of the population."[71] Thus, Peukert, while not eradicating the exceptionality of Nazism, suggests that a focus on the experience of the mass and on the character of everyday life, " provides a critical anti-fascist historiography with opportunities."[72] These "opportunities" are not in opposition to eradicating the nature and effects of formal power, but provide different insights into the culture of the time, complicating the nature of consensus. The formal, institutional aspects of the politics of the era need to be measured against the contradictions, evasions, and indifference that also characterize its cultural and political life.

Mussolini's rise to power in Italy was symptomatic of a crisis of liberalism and capitalism that also characterized Germany. Since the Risorgimento, the policy of transformism had been the cornerstone of Italian politics, identified with the convergence of interests between the "educated and propertied middle class and the liberal aristocracy."[73] As Philip Morgan maintains, "In blurring political differences, *trasformismo* at best represented a kind of liberal parliamentary consensus for the defense of liberal institutions and the political hegemony of the liberal political class against those forces, Catholic, democratic, and socialist, which threatened the disintegration of the state. At worst, *trasformismo* perpetuated government by corrupt parliamentary oligarchies."[74] The Italy of the 1870s and 1880s was not a mass democratic society, but a society of patronage and bureaucracy. The 1900s, a time of political and revolutionary agitation, strikes, and antimilitarism, also heralded Italy's involvement in Libya. Italy entered into World War One, first on the side of Austria, Hungary and Germany, then in 1915 on the side of France and Britain, and the involvement in the war did not consolidate the nation, but instead was productive of social and political conflict and division.

The interwar period was characterized by class conflicts, opposition to the liberal state, inflation, strikes, land occupations in the south, struggles for higher wages, and reduced working hours, reaction against the traditional leadership of the country, and increasing and aggressive nationalism, leading to the occupation of Fiume under the aegis of D'Annunzio and the Arditi. The failure of the factory takeovers, the

adoption of a Bolshevik-style revolution that was ill-adapted to the resolution of Italy's unique problems of economic growth and national inte-
gration, and the rise of the syndicalists with their emphasis on produc-
tivism only intensified the political disarray and assisted the rise of
Fascism in the 1920s. The initially congruent links between socialists,
futurists, and incipient fascists signaled the failure of traditional transformism and paved the way for Fascism. Fascism initially drew on these
several constituencies.

The character and contributions of Gabriele D'Annunzio have
become increasingly central to conflicts about the character and evolution
of Fascism. In *Nationalism and Culture: Gabriele D'Annunzio and Italy
after the Risorgimento,* Jared Becker has insisted that "Italy's fascist history . . . continues to resist a settled interpretation."[75] In contrast to Renzo
De Felice's *D'Annunzio politico 1918–1938,* Becker does not want to
exonerate D'Annunzio from a major role in the creation of fascism: "In
many ways, D'Annunzio is the pivotal character . . . for it is he above all
others who orchestrates the shift from a nineteenth-century culture of
nation-building to a culture of radical nationalism and imperialist aggression."[76] The significance of this difference between Becker's assignment of
a key political position to the poet and De Felice's is central to an understanding of deep divisions in recent assessment of Fascism. According to
De Felice, "one cannot reduce the problem of D'Annunzio to whether he
was or was not a fascist. . . . He was never a fascist, not even formally, even
when, with the war in Africa, it was obligatory to sustain and exalt the
works of Mussolini."[77] De Felice does not suggest that the poet was apolitical. What he seeks to examine are the historical and economic grounds
of D'Annunzio's cultural and political relations to Fascism (and by implication) the efficacy of assigning such a commanding position to one individual and naming him as "fascist." Once again, the propensity to name
inhibits an understanding of the character and evolution of Fascism, particularly its multivalent character and eclecticism.

Becker names D'Annunzio "Italy's most original architect of Fascist
ideology."[78] While he illuminates the style and character of the poet's
works (themes relating to racism, nationalism, colonialism, homoeroticism, massification, antidemocracy, and imperialism), his sole reliance on
the writings of the author disregards, for the most part, how these concerns are endemic to Europe of the 1920s and 1930s and are not exclusive to Fascist Italy. In one sense, Becker's work resurrects, with some difference relating to his concerns with sexuality, a familiar linear and

melodramatic form of historical and ideological analysis that relies exclusively on formal textual analysis. The usefulness of the work resides in its
careful attention to the work of D'Annunzio. Its problematic nature
resides in its foreclosing on the complex relations between a political
movement, other forms of cultural creation and, even more, audience
reception.

From another direction, involving the failure of Marxists to read
Fascism carefully, David Forgacs writes that the "fundamental category
which led the left into error was the instrumental view of the relation
between social classes on the one hand and political systems and ideologies on the other."[79] A conception of Fascism "explained by an illusory
identification with . . . bourgeois ideology" does not take into account the
complex and heterogeneous nature of social life, the nature of consensus,
and the direct and indirect ways in which economics, politics, and representation function to account for the various and contradictory forms of
adherence.[80] Following Gramsci's discussions of consensus and common
sense, Forgacs asserts that "Ideology is not something unreal and ethereal
that floats about in people's heads but is something set in motion and
constantly relayed through the school, the newspaper and periodical
press, the radio, mass meetings, hand-painted slogans on walls."[81] The
period was obsessed with media and with the transmission of slogans,
manifestoes, and the dissemination of images of collective aspirations.
However, the assessment of the character of "real needs and desires" has
to be further qualified by what Gramsci identified as "the folklore of common sense," which does express perceived needs but in terms that are con-
taminated and qualified by an excess derived from an uneasy conjunction
of traditional lore and its relation to the material exigencies of the present.
In this context, while the media play a crucial role in the ways in which
this folklore is expressed and received, it is necessary to abandon notions
of consensus that imply univalent acceptance and adherence on the part
of the populace in behalf of more striated, mobile, and dispersed analysis
of "real needs and desires."

While there is some agreement about the ways the regime sought to
create consensus through institutional structures, there is less unanimity
about the regime's success in achieving its aims. In consolidating its
power, the regime created a number of organizations after the March on
Rome as a means of fascistizing society, in both urban centers in the north
of Italy as well as in the south and Sicily. In relation to economic policies,
the regime expressed "A general commitment to private property and any

policy likely to favour economic efficiency and maximise production was translated into specific proposals for the privatisation of public utilities, cut-backs in and tight control over government spending, and tax and fiscal reform to stimulate private enterprise. This was a rolling back of the state, in other words, in the interests of taxpayers and entrepreneurs."[82] Significantly these policies seemed to be at odds with the statist predilection associated with Italian Fascism, and would continue to create tensions between entrepreneurs and the Fascist leaders.

The church was eventually brought into the fascist orbit, subordinating or eliminating to a great degree opposition from Catholic political parties. Most striking, of course, were the ways that the regime sought to organize the social and work life of Italians. The Balilla (Opera Nazionale Balilla) was aimed at young people from eight to seventeen years of age in an effort to indoctrinate them in the values of Fascism. The OND, the Dopolavoro (Opera Nazionale Dopolavoro), was designed to organize people's leisure time. The OND was responsible for welfare disbursements as well as recreation, and by 1938, its membership had grown to 3.8 million. Women were also organized through the OND and through the ONMI (Opera Nazionale per la Maternità ed Infanzia) that sought to establish "desirable" qualities that emblematized fascist womanhood: "maternity became tantamount to the physical act of making babies." Women were not only excluded from political life, but their "rights in the workplace, their contributions to culture, and their service as volunteers were called into question by the official message that their permanent duty was to bear the nation's children."[83] Edicts were also promulgated to ban "illegitimate sexuality," and prostitution resulted in the imprisonment, regulation, and surveillance of those involved in its practice. Restrictions were also instituted against those who practiced abortion, making abortion illegal and countering attempts to control reproduction by rewards to those women who produced big families. Mass spectacles were designed to promulgate maternity and reproduction in the interests of the state. A "Mother's Day" was instituted to be held on December 24th when prolific women were rewarded for their fecundity, another public spectacle designed to highlight mothers' services to the state.

These attempts were not unanimously adhered to and were productive of contradictions: "Propaganda insisted on the sexual puritanism, economic frugality, and austere leisure habits associated with early industrialism. Meanwhile burgeoning consumer industries often of foreign, especially American, provenance, publicized ready-made clothing, synthetic fibers, cosmetics, household items, and processed foods, as well as the commodified sexuality typical of a modern consumer economy."[84] The anastomosis of traditional and reiterated views of the sanctity and privacy of the family was in tension with modern life, its consumerist and its outward look, thus foregrounding and putting strain on yet another area of Fascist eclecticism and potential conflict. An examination of women's position under Fascism thus offers a corrective to the notion of the complete totalization of Italian life. Not only was subversion through forms of birth control and through family management practiced, but the regime in fact created the terms of conflict. Every aspect of woman's everyday life—her growing up, role in the family, child rearing, uses of leisure time, work, forms of organizing, role in the war effort and later role in the resistance to fascism—presents a checkered story of involvement not a seamless and unified picture. Since the cinema draws liberally on prevailing and timely cultural images, even when it purports to restrict itself to the past, circulating and conflicting representations of femininity insinuate themselves into the commercial narratives to the extent that they open a window onto the problematic construction of the national imaginary.

In the commitment to and reaffirmation of the mission of the Italian nation, the cinema of the era offered its historical spectacles, empire films, war films, and melodramas that glamorized both imperialism and colonialism. These films too cannot be read merely as reflections of propaganda but were further indices of the tenuousness of consensus. Their often blatantly theatrical styles tended also to expose the grandiosity and artifice of imperialist adventure. The imperialist aspirations of the regime were not universally endorsed. They were also a source of its weakness in relation to the garnering of consensus and were to account ultimately for its failure. While not unique to Fascism, the emphasis on nationalism and imperialism was developed as another aspect of the regime's designs on the hearts and minds of the populace. Morgan comments that "from its inception, Fascism was imperialist . . . the movement consistently had as its declared aim a general commitment to realising the grandeur of Italy, specifically through the founding of an empire."[85] Under Mussolini, Italy sought to expand into the Balkans, Greece, the Danube, and plans were set in motion as early as 1927 for expansion into Libya and realized in 1935. The Rome-Berlin accords, the Italian involvement in the Spanish Civil War between 1936 and 1939, the establishment of Nazi-style racism, and the entry into the global war along with Hitler are the fruits of the expansionist policy and are also identified with the "crisis of consent" that characterized the latter years of the regime.[86]

These imperialistic and warlike policies and the actions to which they gave rise had the effect of creating a series of critical problems in domestic affairs exemplified by inflation, shortages in foodstuffs and other consumer items, and the Allied bombings of Italy in 1942 resulting in the disruption of production, homelessness, and mass evacuations to rural areas. These dislocations strained urban and rural populations, engendering a further loss of confidence in Mussolini's leadership. In relation to the woman's situation, the war, in particular, produced new contradictions. At the same time that the war created new opportunities for women in leadership positions, militarism also accentuated the "polarization of gender relations, frustrating the efforts of women to identify with the fascist hierarchy and national collectivity."[87] Concomitantly, the new man so prized, advertised, and lauded by Fascism, was also undermined, so that the former "homoerotic pride of comrades-in-arms gives way to the pathos of men abandoned," resulting in rebellion, desertion, and resistance.[88]

An examination of actual behaviors derived from accounts of the time reveals that there was a range of responses to fascist practices ranging from expediency and adaptation, to a withdrawal on the part of many to private life, and "other more abrasive forms" characterized by refusals to "take the Fascist Party card, to make the Fascist salute, or to wear the black shirt where public occasion demanded it."[89] These views of apparent nonconformity are not the same as resistance or opposition in a large sense, but, they are revealing of the nonunitary nature of consensus. Moreover, they offer a clue to the specific expressions of discontent, ranging from Fascist attempts to control the body to matters of style, and to the disparity between the everyday and the ritualistic. The emphasis on daily life further offers a corrective to the long-reigning notion of "fascinating fascism" that does not take into account the mixed, immediate, and contradictory dimensions of power that help to account for the ultimate failure of Fascist consensus. Moreover, in relation to the cinema of "escapism," white telephone or otherwise, one might see the cinema as expressing indifference or even low-grade annoyance in response to the regime's totalizing ambitions and the church's attempts at control through censorship.

Only recently have critics suggested that there may be closer ties between LUCE (L'Unione Cinematografica Educativa, the Light Institute), the official organization for the creation and dissemination of propaganda and the commercial film industry, than have previously been acknowledged, challenging the notion that propaganda and feature production were radically different. Both are characterized by unwittingly exposing the difficulties of the regime as well as by nonpropagandistic and opportunistic elements.[90] For example, Sorlin has asserted that

> When looking at the newsreels, one cannot but be amazed by the presence of new, unprecedented features: more and more priests, young people, or Fascist bosses or captains fill the background. Moreover the framework has changed, the countryside tends to be replaced by towns. . . . Newsreels unwittingly document the difficulties of the fascist agrarian policy. . . . Documentaries and newsreels tell us a contrasting, ill-constructed story. *Il Duce* is always present but, around him, the scenery and the extras vary greatly . . . most of the time movies exhibit the opportunism and uncertainties of the regime.[91]

Correspondingly, the images and the sounds of the feature films present an oblique and contradictory relation to the practices of Fascism. There, too, Sorlin finds the films are unable to deliver a "precise, coherent message."[92] In fact, "no precise, coherent message" is possible given that consent functions in imprecise, incoherent fashion. The ideology, like the bureaucratic apparatus of the regime, allowed for many lacunae, for spaces if not of freedom, then at least of indifference and opportunism. The commercial films make contact with a world familiar to audiences drawn from Italian history, myth, folklore, and everyday life. This is an eclectic culture constituted through the images received through the radio, public spectacle, popular music, opera, the visual arts, theater, sports, advertising, and Hollywood cinema. These images are ambivalent, adopted as they are from past narratives and fused to a modern means of transmission.

Without conflating cultural and political differences among various national cinemas, one can say that the Italian cinema of this period (in its general configurations) shares the tribulations and eclecticism of other national cinemas of the era. If (in certain marked ways) the cinema encodes conflicts that are endemic to Fascist culture, that fact does not rule out its affiliation to other mass cultural developments on the international scene. The notion of "fascinating fascism"[93] takes on new resonance when linked to the notion of theatricality and its ties to a politics of style that introduces the theater of everyday life, or, more succinctly, links life to performance and makes of everyday life a spectacle. The "fascinating" character of fascism emerges in another, less monumental, form, one that takes on the features of modern folklore, its complex relations to gender, the family, urban and agrarian life, and to modes of survival. Regarded from this vantage point, the problematic character of Italian Fascism (and its lingering effects) has more to do with the politics of style and its relation to the theater of everyday life that I seek to identify in this book. An examination of the memorial reconstruction of the Fascist era in the films of Federico Fellini, Pier Paolo Pasolini, Lina Wertmüller, Sergio Leone, Bernardo Bertolucci, Luchino Visconti, the Taviani brothers, and many other Italian filmmakers from the postwar era underscores the importance of rethinking connections between the everyday, Fascism, and theatricality.

An overview of the vicissitudes of the regime are revealing of the folklore of consensus, inviting a reconsideration of its meaning and effects, making inroads into standard notions of totalitarianism and univalent subjection to Fascism, and enabling a reconsideration of cultural politics. The tension between tradition and modernization, the uneven development between northern and southern Italy, between *strapaese* and *stracittà* were central themes in the Fascists' attempts to develop a political and economic program and to ensure hegemony. While there is abundant evidence for the role of mass culture in the 1920s through the early 1940s as an instrument for consensus, the problem remains of characterizing the subtle ways in which mass culture was instrumental in furthering the Fascist agenda. For example, the articulated objectives of the regime as conveyed through radio, journalism, and mass spectacles, are a mixture of familiar, new, and makeshift signs: in their recourse to conceptions of familialism wedded to images of femininity and masculinity, in their flirtations with modernity and their reliance on traditional concepts of social life, in their reliance on discourses of the nation infused with imperial aspirations, and in their reliance on war as a major strategy for national enhancement and for consolidating domestic programs. The cinema cannot be considered outside of these other cultural and political practices and their effects. In exempting cinema for the most part from other aspects of Fascist cultural life, an opportunity is lost for gaining a synoptic, albeit heterogeneous, sense of the various and competing factors that constitute the everyday dimensions of social life. In acknowledging and demonstrating consent as a major feature of mass societies, in ascribing to it a protean, fragmentary, and heterogeneous nature, it is possible to identify the cinema of the period as a crucial index to the character and effects of representation in the popular culture of the 1930s and early 1940s as they shed light on new and more subtle aspects of the culture of modernity too superficially labelled as totalitarian and Fascistic.

CHAPTER TWO

Comedy, Melodrama, and Theatricality

One of the most difficult and challenging tasks in cultural criticism is to undo the consequences of rigid naming, classification, and aesthetic judgment that inhibit the possibility of further investigation into the genealogy, character, and reception of the textual object under examination. In the case of the Italian cinema of the Fascist era, the appellations that seem to have occupied an unshakable position in the history of this cinema are the designation of the comedies as "escapist" and "white telephone." These designations have served to identify the films as homogenous, frivolous, and as indicative of the Fascist regime's monolithic hold on the cinema. The term "white telephone" has been circulated as a way of subsuming the entire Italian production from the coming of sound to 1943. Roberto Villa has stated that he did not remember the appellation, "white telephone," being applied "until well after the war was over, after 1948, 1949, or 1950."[1] But, according to one critic writing on the history of cinema, "Early Italian sound films traveled between the two poles of pro-Mussolini propaganda and escapist comedies, historical spectacles, and musical romances, so-called 'White Telephone' pictures (because of the inevitable white telephone in the fancily decorated apartments that served as sets for these films)."[2] This narrative proceeds to regard Italian neorealism as the movement that saved Italian film from its decadence and its subservience to ideology. While a growing number of critical texts in English and Italian have sought to examine and reevaluate the cinema under Fascism, and while notions of "escapism" and "propaganda" have long since ceased to function in histories of Hollywood cinema, these assessments still have currency in general histories of film that describe the Italian cinema prior to "neorealism."

The critical work on Italian comedies of the era suffers still from an ongoing problem of establishing their character and nature, both those films identified with Hollywood styles and those with contemporary European, especially Hungarian comedies. Given the highly stylized and formulaic character of the Italian film comedies in the 1930s and early 1940s, their reliance on indirect discourse, their tendency to mask "serious" conflicts, their highly theatrical nature, it is tempting and easy to dismiss them as trivial and "escapist." The comedy of the time cannot be characterized by a single paradigm, namely white telephone comedies. Instead of one dominant form, the cinema of the era reveals a variety of comedic forms set in contemporary or historical situations—romantic comedy, upper-class comedies of endangered marriages, musicals, schoolgirl comedies, and folk comedies of group life, among others. The common denominator of all of these films is their striving to create a sense of commonality or community among the genders and social classes portrayed. In some instances, the films strive to cross class lines to dramatize a commonly shared involvement in adversity; in others, the films distinguish the lives of the upper class and the working classes, identifying safety in separation. The common sense of folklore is apparent in the films' narratives, the images of gendered and sexual conflict, the dramatization of conflicts between work and leisure, the treatment of romantic love, generational and familial relations, entertainment, upward mobility, and the vicissitudes inherent to rural or urban life. As a form that addresses fantasies, the imagined needs and desires of the protagonists, comedy appears to be the site par excellence of ideological manipulation, its presumed escapism serving as instantiation of the genre's false and misleading ludic nature, but, unlike work on melodrama, the work on comedy seems to elude an analysis of its structure and effects. Andrew Horton comments that "No totalizing theory has proved successful. The vastness of the territory which includes the nature of laughter, humor, the comic, satire, parody, farce, burlesque, the grotesque, the lyrical, romantic metacomedy, and wit, precludes facile generalizations."[3]

Major stumbling blocks in the consideration of the nature and effects of comedy reside in the difficulty of deciphering the antirealist narratives of comedy, their enjoyable character, their popular appeal, and their ostensible social conservatism. The problems posed by comedy are compounded by the persistence of the term "escapism," which is more often applied to this genre than to others. Does escapism signify the complete negation of life in the everyday? Is it a mode of diverting audiences from pressing conditions of life? Is it a form of the channeling of consent through entertainment, propaganda by indirection? Is it characterized by a conspiracy to implant and legitimize dreams of money, upward mobility, and power in the minds of its audiences?

In connection with Hollywood cinema, answers to these questions have been sought in recent years.[4] Assessments of Hollywood comedy have been closely tied to the development of a critical understanding of popular culture where critics have sought through the theories of ideology, deconstruction, and psychoanalysis to account for its effects and for its popular appeal. In addition, the popular cinema is acutely sensitive to the market, to the material demands of circulation and consumption. By virtue of its relation to economic and social exchange and value, the film industry must perforce be able to gauge its public, its desires as well as its resistances. The public is thus an active force in creating conditions of exchange and value. Gian Piero Brunetta's account of the disastrous years following the "golden age" of Italian cinema reveals the effects of not gauging changes in public taste, in particular the Italian film industry's attempts to meet the challenges posed by Hollywood as well as by other European cinemas and the contradictory ways in which the cinema participated in the struggle to meet the challenges of modernity and the social changes it sets in motion.

In their various forms (romantic, comedian, slapstick, parody, and satiric comedy), comedy constructs a world that is predicated on prescribed but constantly changing images and patterns that are neither absolute nor univalent. Consonant with Gramsci's description of common sense as built on past modes of knowledge fused to contemporary forms of belief, fragmentary and unstable, designed to provide the semblance of truth, the comedies are indicative of how popular culture is constantly engaged in "a continual process of recombination and appropriation."[5] More than other genres, comedies thrive on common sense as folklore, drawing on folk rituals, festivals and carnivals, local customs, and modes of combating threats to collective survival and to the well-being of a community. In Hay's terms, "popular movies appeal by simultaneously demonstrating the inadequacies and adequacies of established models [of social interaction and discourse] . . . by eliciting from viewers an ambivalence about the movies' massages."[6] Comedy, in particular, thrives on eclecticism, on reducing philosophical complexity to questions of behavior and action, and on the fantasy of resolving antagonisms. Its strategies are multilayered, combining traditional lore with modern exigencies, anastomosing past wisdom onto present conflicts, revealing its protean nature that exceeds rigid ideological prescription in the interests of reception and hence profitability. Hence, a rigidly economistic and totalizing explanation for the popularity of the genre restricts an understanding of the nature of popular production which entails constantly shifting affective positions to entertain as wide an audience as possible. Thus, the character of consent has to be understood in dynamic terms: its instability becoming the impetus for working toward a mode of consensus that can incorporate different groups through the *appearance* of commonality, a commonality that is based on a recognition of differences to be managed. That the comedies produced under Fascism (the "culture of consent" par excellence) have been trivialized and considered unworthy of such analysis reveals the existence of *a priori* assessments and judgments about the nature of Fascism and its relation to popular culture. This kind of blindness does a disservice not only to the history of film, but even more to an understanding of the dynamic and slippery nature of consent.

The term, "escapist" has also been applied to the films as a means for describing the character of the comedies as well as their reception, suggesting that popular genres function to situate the spectator in an illusory realm divorced from quotidian exigencies. The comedies produced in the 1930s are highly conventionalized, produced within the terms and conditions of genre production. However, one of the dangers of reading genre texts is the tendency to emphasize the reiterative structures without due attention to the differential elements in the uses of image, sound, and editing. The overvalorization of the familiar narratives, their reliance on repetition, elides how the strategies of popular culture entail a constant and opportunistic plundering of the cultural lexicon. A strict genre approach also occludes the parasitic character of genres that, as part of their opportunism, feeds on other genres. While a highly codified form, genre is above all else reflexive, situating itself within a specific mode of production, but, even as it seems hermetically closed, it has recourse to other cultural and institutional forms as a means of establishing its terms of address. The eclectic nature of comedy is a source of its success, enabling it to provide an aura of plenitude and the pleasure of recognition. It is not unusual for the films to allude to literary works, theater, popular song, painting, journalism, other films, and institutional practices involving law, commerce, religion, education. The films often blend melodrama and comedy, Whether set in the past or in a contemporary context, the comedies "mirror, contain, and ultimately transform . . . melodramatic themes and motifs."[7]

Recent work on the so-called white telephone films and comedies has been attentive to the ways in which the films are sensitive to modernity not merely as a thematic but as inhering in the types of actors and actresses selected for the roles, the costumes, the *mise-en-scène*, the architecture, images of street life, the foregrounding of trains and cars, forms of technology (including television), the portrayal of places of work (factories, department stores, and shops) and of leisure (hotels, inns, places of gambling, and sports events). These images are most often couched in the familiar and potentially melodramatic context that involves conflicts concerning the dangers of misalliance, the vagaries of marital infidelity, the threat of familial dissolution, the salvation of a potential (often feminine) miscreant, the planned entrapment of and obstacles in the way of finding a suitable mate, gender competition on the job and its temporarily destabilizing effects. Many of these motifs are common to the films of Mario Camerini, but they also permeate the films of other, sometimes less prominent, directors. What has been overlooked until recently is the fact that the films are not structured exclusively according to Italian national characters but are heavily reliant on Hollywood forms and on the works of European directors (e.g., René Clair and Jean Renoir).

Unlike the costume dramas, melodramas, and historical films, the comedies are not concerned with exceptional and unique figures nor with the transcendence of suffering and renunciation. They are more concerned with their narratives, choice of characters, images, and uses of sound to create a sense of the immediacy, familiarity, and manageability of social conflict. However, the difference from monumental forms may be more apparent than real. The romantic dilemmas the comedies present are no less removed from questions of power and sexuality, but the terms in which they are couched reveal that they are less affectively invested, preferring to dissipate affect through the focus on their goal-oriented behavior, and, even more, through their concerted, seemingly almost self-conscious effort, to work against inflated conceptions of theatricality and posturing, making them appear intrinsic to survival. If the films are not direct attacks on pompous rhetoric, in their portraits of the world of family, work, and leisure, they minimize rather than heighten the melodramatic conflicts that initiate their scenarios.

The texts do not stand in binary opposition to melodrama but are engaged in absorbing, mitigating, and neutralizing melodramatic conflict.

Their relation to melodramatic affect is one of management and control. Based on melodramatic scenarios involving courtship, marriage, adultery, betrayal, and disloyalty, they mask affect through reflexivity, disguises, and obvious social masks. Their preoccupation is with success and failure rather than with psychic or spiritual conversion or its impossibility. The films are concerned with role playing, disguises, and dissimulation as a problematic, and with their necessity as strategies for survival and even more for success. Many of the comedies explore theft and deception as a precondition for acceptance of a more settled and respectable, if not modest, form of existence. However, their mode of reconciliation is ambiguous, a form of craftiness that appears to cancel out the more malevolent and melodramatic dimensions of manipulation and control but remains nonetheless deceptive. The films' self-reflexivity, while calling attention to the film as artifact and the artificial character of the world created, does not necessarily serve as a means of resistance. The films manage through theatricalization, through impersonation and disguise, to involve audiences, often cynically, in a bifurcated rather than completely naturalized and unified sense of the filmic world and hence of the culture, enabling a broad range of responses to the conflicts posed. In the confrontation of the changing and often threatening terms of modern existence, the films stress the importance of ingenuity through dissimulation. One of the major conflicts seems to be the tension between naturalness and artifice, and often it is artifice that is valorized as a necessary means for negotiating between conformity and desire.

In this chapter, I discuss a range of Italian film comedies from the era in an attempt to probe the ways the films complicate the nature of consensus. I focus on the complex portraits of courtship, familialism, and the forms of sexual conflict that animate the films, paying attention to the ways in which they at the same time seek to contain disorder while exposing gendered antagonisms particularly through their preoccupation with impersonation, dissimulation, and life as fiction, theater, and film. I examine the symbiotic relationship between melodrama and comedy, regarding the oscillation between the two as necessary for the proper channeling of affect in the narratives. I stress the importance in comedy of performance, of "putting on a show" as a means of managing social reality. The self-reflexive uses of fiction drawn from drama, opera, and novelizing are quintessential strategies for juxtaposing questions of authenticity with the demand for conformity. In the portrayal of the texture of modern life, the comedies rely on doubling and impersonation to underscore disjunctions between the impetus toward transgressing social norms and the demands for accommodation. Thus, at the heart of the comedies is a recognition of the impossibility of escape and of reconciling personal desire with institutional realities.

FOLKLORE, OPERA, AND "PUTTING ON A SHOW"

The cinematic form most identified with escapism and with antirealism is the film musical, where song and dance are considered as evasions from the hardships of life—failure, violence, unrequited interpersonal relations, and abuses of power. The prime characteristic of musicals is their emphasis on a show within a film that serves to present art as life, and to celebrate performance over naturalism. Their antirealism is mainly identified in their preoccupation with theatricality, artifice, romance, and resolution of conflict. Their eclecticism is evident in a reliance on earlier literary, theatrical, and cinematic sources, but recasting them to meet the exigencies of the contemporary moment.[8] One of the first Italian sound films was *Figaro e la sua gran giornata* (1931), a musical directed by Mario Camerini, that links life and art. Melodrama is present even in the comic scenarios, in their motifs as described above, and in their theatrical styles. As the title indicates, the film, directed by Mario Camerini, is indebted to *The Barber of Seville* and to a play by Arnaldo Fraccaroli, *Ostrega che sbrego!* The narrative is structured around the attempts of a waning baritone, Basoto, played by Gianfranco Giachetti, to insert himself into a performance of *The Barber of Seville* to be performed by a visiting opera troupe. His boasting of his once-great career is unmatched by his actual performance: while a braggart about his talent, Basoto cannot sing on key. On the other hand, Nina (Leda Gloria), the source of the melodramatic scenario, a victim of parental control, is abundantly talented, and Basoto and Rantolini, the manager, seek to enlist her as their Rosina, against the efforts of her father and later of her lover Chiodini (Maurizio D'Ancora). Her life is also complicated by the refusal of her parents to entertain marriage between her and Chiodini. The dual lines of the narrative—between romance and theatrical performance—meet in the trials and tribulations of Nina and her relationship to Chiodini, suggesting that "the symbolic wedding celebrates the ongoing relationship between film and spectator as much as it celebrates the union of the couple,"[9] and, further the union of art and life.

FIGURE 1. The beleaguered young lovers in *Figaro e la sua gran giornata*. Courtesy of New York Museum of Modern Art, Film Stills Archive.

FIGURE 2. Plotting the opera performance, *Figaro e la sua gran giornata*. Courtesy of New York Museum of Modern Art, Film Stills Archive.

Figaro blurs the distinction between life and theater by consistently calling attention to the role of spectatorship, involving several audiences in the film—the townspeople, the opera troupe, the parental figures, and Basoto and Chiodini as eavesdroppers to Nina's singing. As in the Hollywood musical, the film, "seeks to bridge the gap [between audience and performance] by putting up 'community' as an ideal concept."[10] The focus on "live entertainment" in the case of *Figaro* and of musicals more generally serves "to speak more directly to the spectator. . . . [M]aybe that's why so many musicals are about putting on a show rather than about making films."[11] The plight of beleaguered and helpless feminine figures beset by irate parents and jealous spouses, a traditional source of melodramatic conflict, is overcome through artistic performance not only for the characters but for the internal and external audiences.

Figaro is not an unusual Camerini film and hence offers a possible key to the popularity of Camerinian comedy during the Fascist era. This film does not seem to participate in official Fascist discourse. The emphasis on familialism, central not only to his work but to other films of the era, can be read as a counterpart in the Fascist exaltation of the family, aligning the film with Fascist propaganda that, it is claimed, sought to beguile the masses through cinematic spectacle. However, the film invites a more contradictory reading that eludes rigid ideological analysis. In the context of entertainment, the misunderstandings, misrecognitions, deceptions, and prohibitions associated with "real life" appear momentarily suspended, relegated to an oneiric, fantasmatic world. However, this suspension does not necessarily mislead the audience, rendering it unable to distinguish between art and "reality." While the text offers a momentary respite from constraints, it never lets the audience forget that what it is watching is artifice, mere "entertainment." Nor does the text conceal conflict. The film offers an image of community in the contemplation of shared conflict and even of shared knowledge about the impossibility of reconciliation except through entertainment. Escapism in this film can be construed as the transformation of life into theater where all problems can be resolved. However, the "coincidence" of the parallel between the opera and the film, the consequence of "putting on a show," has a more substantial and contradictory valence. While the film eschews a realist form of representation in favor of illusion, its reflexivity in calling attention to the parallels between art and life, ironically suggests a lack of consonance between social reality and representation. Theatricality (in this case, melodrama), the acknowledgment of the necessity of performance, becomes a strategy for exposing and contending with, not denying, conflict. In the disruption of the final staging of the opera, sabotaged by Nina's father, the film seems to undermine the familiar strategy of ending with a union of successful stage performance and romance. The parallels between art and life have worked in a reverse direction, so that the conflicts besetting the characters have taken on the characteristics of the opera; the lives of the protagonists and the townspeople are, in fact, more theatrical than the performance.

LIFE AS FILM

One of the staple devices of 1930s' comedies involves an actress aspiring to a career in the cinema. The conventional scenario portrays her attainment of success in work and in romance after a series of vicissitudes. This scenario is also preoccupied with dramatizing homologies between artistic and social performance. Mario Soldati's *Dora Nelson* (1939), a comedy that resembles Hollywood comedies of the era, employs the conventions of the poor young woman who, after a series of obstacles and misrecognitions, is assimilated into the world of the upper class. This Cinderella narrative is commonplace enough, but what is interesting about the film is its reliance on impersonation and doubling, a strategic device in comedy for challenging the primacy of "real" life over fiction. The film, a remake of a French text, hinges on dual identity, the similarity in appearance but difference in attitude between an upper-class woman and her lower-class counterpart. From the opening moments of the film, through the device of a film within a film, the spectator is thrown into confusion about appearances. A group of gypsy performers are singing and dancing as a bemedalled officer greets the arrival of a princess. Suddenly, the "Princess," played by Assia Noris (in the dual role), has a tantrum and it then becomes apparent that this is a film within a film and that the woman is an actress. At home, she, a widow of an ex-Russian prince, berates her second husband, Giovanni, a wealthy industrialist (Carlo Ninchi), for being a bourgeois; her aspirations are tied to the aristocracy.

In the narrative's gesturing toward self-reflexivity and its relations to theatricality, the director of the film within a film is confronted by the fact that he needs to replace his star in order to finish the production. Fortunately, a look-alike (also played by Noris), who happens to be a clerk in a hat shop, is found to fill the role in the film. The doubling characteristic of many of the comedies and melodramas underscores the preoccupation with sameness in difference that the films portray. Pierina is brought to the studio, outfitted, and made up for the part, but she is not eager to make a name for herself in the cinema. Not only are the two female characters doubled but the plots of the film and the film within a film mirror each other. There the similarities end. Dora is the consummate diva, enemy of middle-class life, given to tantrums, and hostile to the burdens of maternity and family. She has a daughter who is engaged to a respectable young man (Massimo Girotti), but her lack of maternal concern and her willful behavior threatens their marriage. As one might expect, the confusion between the identities of Dora and Pierina escalates. Giovanni, who has come to the set to find his wife, instead finds Pierina. He marvels at the visual similarity between the two women. Desperate, he asks Pierina to play the role of wife and mother for a few days during the engagement festivities for his daughter so that the occasion will provide an illusion of a united and harmonious family.

Giovanni brings Pierina to the house and she outdoes herself in performing the role of Dora, entertaining the guests, seducing them with her charm. The only person she cannot charm is the daughter, who is antagonistic toward her "mother." Pierina, experiencing the daughter's hostility, has a tantrum herself and angrily tells Giovanni that she wants to leave, but another woman, thinking that the couple is having a marital squabble, tells them to kiss and reconcile. They kiss, and the kiss seals their love, bonding them in the conspiracy of dissimulation. The festivities for the daughter are successful, and Giovanni tells Pierina that he is happy for the first time in his adult life. The dual plot involves Dora in nefarious dealings with the self-styled aristocrats, their hangers-on, and shady financial machinations that make the headlines, thus distinguishing unproductive from productive performance. Her intrigues are intercut with scenes of family life, culminating in the marriage of the daughter, and their departure for their honeymoon, ending the necessity of Pierina's acting the part of Dora. Marriage and role playing are fused. Realizing the hopelessness of her love, Pierina humbly informs the husband that nothing can come of their relationship since he is married. Moreover, she tells him that she is an insignificant person, while Dora is important. Before she can leave, Dora returns. Seeing her, Pierina hides but before she can warn Giovanni. He thinks that Dora is Pierina and tells her how bad and capricious Dora is, but the melodrama is truncated when the chauffeur runs in, bearing a newspaper that announces, "The strange case of the dead revived . . . the first husband of Dora Nelson, believed dead in a train crash has been restored to life after eight years, and the marriage to the noted industrialist Giovanni Ferrari has been dissolved." The film ends with Giovanni and Pierina on the road in an open convertible. They stop to observe the making of another film, starring Dora and her prince. They look at the actors, laugh, and drive off.

The film can be easily written off as yet another "escapist" film that legitimizes middle-class life, stressing the proper virtues of monogamy, feminine charm and service, and romantic love, all adding up to the consummate mythology of familialism. Pierina is "deserving" of her good fortune, since she has all the attributes of the romantic heroine: she is not scheming, does not care for Giovanni's money, but loves him despite the apparent vanity of their relationship. By contrast, the bad other is Dora, who is adulterous, impatient, temperamental, indifferent to her child, and aggressive toward her husband.

While in its narrative of doubling and through the iconography, the film seems openly to evoke the notion of cinema as a "dream factory," encouraging the assumption that the Italian cinema of the era was escapist, there is another dimension to the film, a dimension endemic to the functioning of popular cinema and to its reception. The other side of this film, as with so many comedies of the era, involves the film's reflexivity concerning cinema. The emphasis on role playing, on the slippery line between acting and "reality," serves a dual and complex function. Not a disavowal of the narrative of upward mobility and the selection of the fittest to receive the rewards of money and privilege, it does upset simplistic notions of the film as a mere carrier of an air-tight ideology identified as escapism that assumes the diversionary powers of spectacles of the rich and famous. By setting up the film within the film against the film itself, *Dora Nelson* shares with its audiences the knowledge of the fictional status of cinema and its narratives. In this manner, the film winks at the audience, confirming the audience's commonsense knowledge about narratives of romance and upward mobility—that they are "make-believe." The film's visualization of the movie set, its images of the fast life through Dora, its images of opulence through the scenes where Pierina impersonates Dora, and the blurring of the lines of vision through the device of doubling suggest that the romance narrative and its familiar conventions are a pretext to explore and exploit spectatorship. The comedy thus lies less in the repetition of the Cinderella folklore and more in the shared joke between the audience and the film, the knowledge that film viewing entails theatricality and, even more, the complex notion that impersonation *is* life. Thus, the reflexivity is not in the service of "radicalism" or even of subversion, but it offers tell-tale markers to indicate that in order to gain an audience popular models have to be smarter than the critics, providing space to attend to the potential of audiences' knowledge of illusion and play.

The reflexivity does not invalidate impersonation so much as it seeks to make distinctions between different forms of theatricality and the ends to which they are put. While the preoccupation with exploring boundaries between reality and illusion, art and life, persists, the film seems to want to make distinctions between forms of spectacle. Pierina's acting in the interests of rescuing the family and ultimately is "excused" and finally exposed as a benevolent and necessary act canceling out bad performance, similar to homeopathic magic where like drives out like. The film's preoccupation with performance suggests audiences' increasing ability and competence to recognize cinematic conventions in the interests of differentiating forms of spectacle. The comedy's preoccupation with performance also suggests that cinema's relation to modernity involves an increasing theatricalization of social life, including the public spectacles of Fascism. Above all, the film's reflexivity suggests a necessary decomposition of notions of the "real." While not valorizing "authenticity" and realism in the conventional sense, the film reveals that it is not merely imposing a fictional construct on an innocent and unsuspecting audiences; in more complicated fashion, the film exposes that it is engaged with the audience in acknowledging the social value (and profit) of fictionalizing.

THE EVERYDAY AND DOMESTIC
DIPLOMACY OF FICTION

Theatricality relies on the clever management of knowledge, hence the predominance of masks, disguises, and impersonation. Based on common sense as folklore, popular narratives focus on the necessity of withholding information. Certain characters within a text serve to expose secrets to the external audience, placing the audience in a position superior to many of the characters, thus serving to confound distinctions between artifice and "reality." *Una moglie in pericolo* (A Wife in Danger, 1939), directed by Max Neufeld, is an exemplary text to explore the forms of escapism of the so-called white telephone films as it highlights not only the ubiquity of deception but its necessity for social harmony. In its predilection for upper-class subjects and an upper-class environment, the film appears to have no direct connection with Fascist politics, or any politics for that matter. The comedy is set in the mythical world of sexual intrigue that seems to be removed from the everyday. Yet the scenario is deeply rooted in folklore. This folklore has its basis, albeit indirectly and not in polemic fashion, in familialism and in the sexual division of labor that cuts across class and even national and regional divisions. In assessing the film's theatrical character and its reflexivity, unexceptional attributes for the films of the era, the critical viewer cannot miss the familiar scenarios with their strategies that have their roots, by way of folklore, in the everyday world of sexual politics.

Max Neufeld has been described as a master, as the inventor of white telephone films and as a "little miracle of efficiency."[12] He was a "hands-on" director who paid careful attention to the ambiance of the film, to the photography, and especially to the clarity of the lighting.[13] Laura Solari, who acted the part of the maid in *Una moglie*, confirms Neufeld's attention to the slightest detail, though his choice of her costume, she felt, was "absurd in Italy."[14] This film is an example of the hybrid union of Hungary and Hollywood with Italian comedy, focusing on the world of the middle class and on threats to domestic harmony. In its brittle dialogue based on double entendres and in its self-reflexivity, it produces an antisentimental and pragmatic treatment of the requisite sexual intrigue after first presenting a potentially destabilizing and threatening domestic scenario reminiscent of such comic operas as *The Marriage of Figaro* and *Die Fledermaus*.

The narrative is located is Budapest in a modern setting. A photograph of a woman, his wife, Mary (Marie Glory) sits on Pietro's (Antonio Centa) desk. He goes to switch off a phonograph player as she approaches him to divert him, and he tells Mary to let him work. Having lured her husband to bed, she again interrupts him with her curiosity about a book he is reading, "A Woman in Trouble," about a wife who gets into trouble though not of her own making. She responds that a "good wife never gets into trouble." This prologue sets the terms for the marital intrigue to come: habituated relations between husband and wife, the expectation of infidelity, and the element of superstition exemplified in Mary's receipt of tickets that bear the number thirteen. The motif of infidelity and womanizing is further developed through the introduction of Giorgio, a Don

Juan figure and a diplomatic colleague of Pietro's. Mary's father also spends his time and money on women. By contrast, Pietro is committed to his work as a diplomat, having little time to pursue such pleasures.

At home, a forlorn Mary wants to go to a masked ball but Pietro is unavailable. She tries to convince her father to accompany her, but he tells her he's going to bed. Aware of his subterfuge, Lina complains to Mary in the language of common sense that "All men are cheats." Setting the motif of impersonation in motion, the disguised mistress and servant both go to the ball where Mary sees her father. There she also makes Giorgio's acquaintance and he becomes enamored of her, though because of the disguise he cannot ascertain her identity. He goes to the telephone to call Pietro to tell him that he has met the ideal woman and that he is determined to pursue her. He follows her home. Mary orders him to leave. Compliant, he jumps down from the balcony, but he complains of pain as a consequence of the fall, and insists that he must come in and sit down. Once again in the house, Giorgio phones to tell Pietro that he is at the house of the woman of his dreams, and Pietro calls him an "incorrigible Don Juan." A policeman arrives, inquiring if everything is all right, since a man was seen jumping from the window. In another permutation of the motif of subterfuge, the maid deflects his curiosity, and he leaves.

The following day, Mary receives an anniversary present from Pietro as the aunt prates about the previous evening's ball. Later, Giorgio arrives at a reception to celebrate Pietro and Mary's anniversary, where the couple is being toasted. He brags to Pietro about his escape and the fact that the woman he was chasing never removed her mask, so that he is still uncertain about her identity. Oblivious to the fact that Giorgio offers a threat to his own honor, in melodramatic terms, Pietro tells him that if he were the cuckolded husband he would kill Giorgio. Mary is then "introduced" to Giorgio, and he tries to ferret out if she was the woman with whom he danced at the ball. Informing him that she never went to the ball, Giorgio asks her if there are other women in the house, and she responds "an older aunt and the maid." Through Lina's machinations, the aunt appears wearing the dress that Mary wore the previous evening sprayed by Lina with Mary's perfume. Giorgio is completely routed. As Mary and Pietro dance, they discuss the ending of the novel, "A Wife in Danger." Pietro decides that, although in the novel the husband and wife separate, it is better not to confess. She, however, decides to "confess"—the confession being her love for him.

The family constellation involves an absent mother, an inept aunt who stands in as a mother-surrogate, a womanizing father, Mary, a childlike wife whose dominant occupation is to maintain the fiction of an ideal marriage, and a son-in-law, Pietro, who is redeemed from being a cuckold. With his wife Mary's complicity, Pietro emerges as hard-working, sincere, and responsible. Giorgio, Pietro's colleague and the irrepressible Don Juan of the film, who threatens the family by his amorous designs on Pietro's wife, is chastened for his exploits by being threatened with exposure and, hence, with social ostracism. The maid-servant, Lina, now mistaken for Mary by Giorgio in his attempt to uncover the identity of the woman with whom he danced, remains silent and assists her mistress in the conspiracy to maintain Mary's integrity, nor does she implicate others. Not only does Lina tidy the house but she orders the family's sexual affairs. The film makes no pretense of elevating her status, or of rewarding her in any way for her efforts. Mary and Pietro's marriage is saved from potential disaster, thanks to Lina and Mary, the guardians of family secrets.

The domestic politics of the film center on the drama of "diplomacy" and "intrigue" as a central fiction in the negotiation of domestic life. The emphasis on concealment is reinforced by the vocation of the masculine characters. Ironically, Pietro and Giorgio are diplomats, though the real diplomats turn out to be the women who keep the men pacified and monogamous. The women are the ones who channel the narrative from melodrama into comedy. The common sense of the comedy, its pragmatic and theatrical nature, is apparent in the film's access to and management of cultural knowledge, specifically the knowledge of marriage as a masculine encumbrance and of the female as the guarantor of domestic order, legitimacy, and social continuity. The comic elements revolve around the danger of the husband's potential cuckoldry, hence the insult to his honor. The contrast between Pietro and Giorgio is between an apparently domesticated male and Don Juanism, thus averting the danger of elevating promiscuity.

The world in which the characters move alternates between work and parties, receptions, and balls. The film focuses on consumer objects—clothing, handkerchiefs, perfume, expensive fans—as the signposts of wealth and leisure. They are also the source of tricks the characters play on each other, signifying the fetishized character of this world, the interchangeability between women and things. And they also are the conduits through which misunderstanding and misperception circulate. The emphasis on disguises and on diplomacy elevates the notion of impersonation that provides the necessary ingredients of comic misperception, serving to underscore and minimize the potential consequences of the sexual games that are being played. But the impersonation has a more serious side insofar as it highlights artifice, providing a defense against the possibility of confrontation with and legitimation of socially transgressive behavior.

Thus, the film can, on the one hand, invoke the possibility of promiscuity, while at the same time reining it in. Nothing is ever consummated, but there is a great deal of posturing and double entendres about sexual games. The three women in the film, while differentiated according to social class and age, are, in fact, the same. They are united in their role as women who are instrumental in keeping the show going, in cleaning up the family mess, and, more profoundly, in being identified with fiction and its dissimulations. Finally, the ending of the film serves as the ultimate disclaimer about theatricality, reinforcing not only the sense that nothing untoward has happened but that the essence of the "fiction" is concealment. By extension, concealment also implies a bond between the audience and the text to maintain the fiction. The connections to social life are masked but not inaccessible.

The importance of impersonation and of concealment dramatizes the opportunism and cynicism that underpin consent in its dual character that simultaneously acknowledges recognition and concealment like the husband and wife's commonsense decision not to confess what actually transpired. The film's duality, its simultaneous stabilizing and destabilizing strategies, give the lie to the sense of the monolithic and claustrophobic character of escapism. What the film reveals is that change and crisis rather than stability are embedded in the text, illuminating the fragile and contradictory nature of the world presented and of the tenuous nature of performance. Despite its ostensible frivolity, the film is saved from triviality in its reflexivity, its acknowledgment of the necessity of fictionalizing, specifically of maintaining the fiction of domestic harmony. In this context, the theatricality involves a certain "realism" in the acknowledgment of performance and its connection to the maintenance of social appearances.

FORMULAS FOR SUCCESS

The fascination with the world of the wealthy and with the struggle of "ordinary people" to achieve success is considered a hallmark of the 1930s popular comedies, earning them the appellation of escapism. In seeking to understand the "escapism" of the Italian popular cinema of the era, Gian Piero Brunetta writes: "The cinema hall in which the rites of film watching were celebrated with ever-increasing regularity and frequency under Fascism, became a specialised area for the cultivation of emotions and hopes of an entire people, which was aware of the transposition on the screen (in a kind of mirroring or doubling effect) of its own private or subconscious impulses."[15] This "cultivation of emotions and hopes" was based on the power of the cinematic image to create an opportunity for audiences "to emigrate temporarily to the world of their own dreams, and of returning to their own lives and private spaces temporarily enlivened."[16] The character of this emigration, the nature of the dream world, and the return to "private spaces" is not simplistic. In the case of the Italian comedies that are dependent on American and Hungarian models, the pleasures they offer through the promise of upwardly mobile expectations are mixed, holding out a promise of success, while at the same time relegating aspiration to the virtual world of entertainment. It is this dimension of entertainment deemed as escapism that is hardest to grasp, since it seems to depend on notions of the audience as uninformed, passive spectators, totally consumed by the narratives, beguiled by the spectacle, and, especially, of the fictional world as divorced from something known as reality. Common sense as folklore is more complex, suggesting that the audience members are not mere dupes but recognize the validity and necessity of subterfuge in maintaining social appearances. More importantly, the notion of escapism relies not only on a binary opposition between fiction and truth, but also between fantasy (escape) and life.

The presence of Americanism and its ties to performance is evident in Guido Brignone's *Rubacuori* (1931), another early sound film. The film also features a Don Juan character in the world of upper-class machinations. Opening with the arrival of a prizefighter from a successful tour of America, the scenes highlight the adulation of the crowds gathered to greet him, with the exception of a pickpocket who takes advantage of the situation. The fascination with personality and success is reiterated in an office scene where the women employees, suspending their work, are gathered around a radio listening to the description of the fighter's arrival. The boss, Giovanni (Armando Falconi), enters, sending the women scurrying back to their work. He, however, goes to his office and picks up a letter, sniffs, and then opens it. The letter is from an entertainer who informs him that she is expecting him at the night club. Thus, the film introduces a fascination with celebrities as well as a contrast between the vagaries of upper-class men and their workers. The film also develops a contrast between the world of entertainment, its association with transgression and criminality, and the constraining world of domesticity.

The domestic axis of the narrative unravels as Giovanni returns home to dress and to inform his wife and mother-in-law that he has a business commitment for the evening. When he is greeted at the night club, it becomes evident that he is a regular customer and moreover that he is a gull. His innamorata is busy with an accomplice planning a jewel robbery that will involve him, since they will plant the stolen goods on him. Also at the club is the prizefighter and his companion, Ilke, the contemplated victim of the robbery. The action takes place against the background of popular songs and dances, including an Argentinian tango, thus reinforcing the film's concern with entertainment. When the entertainer takes Giovanni to the dance floor, the lights go out. When they go on again, Ilke discovers that her ruby heart necklace has been stolen. The police arrive but do not discover the location of the jewelry. When Giovanni arrives home in the early hours of the morning, he discovers the jewelry in his pocket. Going to bed, he spends an uneasy night as he mutters in his sleep, "I am innocent," provoking his wife to ask him what the problem is. He merely responds that he was dreaming. The potentially melodramatic complications involving guilt and domestic betrayal are mitigated through Giovanni's compulsive, involuntary, and bumbling behavior and his innocence of theft.

On the following day, he tracks down Ilke and goes to her apartment to return the jewelry. The maid greets him while Ilke is occupied with bathing, powdering herself, and dressing. While he waits, Giovanni uneasily scrutinizes the portrait of the prizefighter. His guilt is further enhanced when he sees a pair of man's slippers and movement from behind a curtain. However, the culprit turns out to be Ilke's dog. When she arrives, he gives her the necklace, whereupon she asks if he is a policeman, and he responds, "No, an involuntary thief." As he leaves, he embraces her and, the necklace clings to his jacket. Giovanni scurries off, chased by Joe, the prizefighter, who has arrived and is jealous in finding a man in Ilke's suite. In his chauffeur-driven car, content that he has relieved himself of the jewelry, the necklace drops to the floor to be discovered by his wife and a friend after he has gone. The friend advises her to assume that the jewelry is a gift from Giovanni and she puts it on. At work, Giovanni is confronted by the entertainer, who threatens to blackmail him if he does not turn over the necklace. At that moment, the wife arrives, delighted with her "gift," and the entertainer leaves with a menacing look. Now the ruby heart links the married couple, the entertainer, and the prizefighter.

The film climaxes at the prizefight, which like the opening of the film links audience and spectacle. The prizefighter sees Giovanni and his wife wearing the ruby heart. The couple is also observed by the crooks, and the domestic drama competes with the scene in the prizefighting ring. Giovanni tries to signal reassuringly to the fighter, but Joe, disconcerted, is knocked out. Eventually Giovanni stealthily removes the necklace from his wife's neck. Now his wife screams theft. The police arrive and the truth of the robbery emerges. Giovanni returns home with an angry wife, who refuses to speak to him despite her mother's efforts to mediate. The scene fades, again to a pair of slippers that through animation dance from one side of the bed to the other and on the sound track Giovanni's voice can be heard asking, "Are you asleep," and her voice responding, "No." The following day, Giovanni on his way to work stands on the street as he observes a pair of legs pass him by. He hesitates, then follows, and the drama begins again.

The film reiterates formulas of romantic comedy, updating and enlivening them through the emphasis on a modern setting, clothing, automobiles, street scenes, and popular entertainment. The focus on entertainment stresses the element of artifice and performance in opposition to authenticity, this time in the context of the dangerous and fascinating world of the night club. From the beginning of the film, the motif of theft is highlighted. Stolen objects circulate in protean fashion between the daylight world of respectability and the sexually transgressive night-time world. Theft thus serves not merely to identify the misappropriation of material property but is transposed onto the register of sexual politics. The thief turns out to be the husband who must conceal his "crime" of violating his conjugal commitments. The Don Juan figure as exemplified by Armando Falconi is older, stout, and inept, a caricature of Don Juanism. His treatment of his women workers may be authoritative, but his relations with the other women in his life, both his wife and the entertainer, are not. His behavior is characterized by compulsion from which he must be rescued. The women in the narrative are portrayed as either victims of his womanizing, as victimizers, or as rescuers. The terrain of conflict thus centers on the battle of the sexes.

The comedy is derived from the typification of the characters, from their inability to control their behavior, and from the ways in which attempts to cover up clandestine behavior backfire. Chaos threatens constantly to erupt. The metaphor of boxing fuses connections between domestic and public relations. It is at first identified with adulation and success, and later it is identified with sexual antagonism in the sparring between Giovanni and the women in his life, but particularly with his wife. Thus, *Rubacuori* orchestrates its sexual politics through exposing the fragility of conjugal life, challenging provincial notions of marital responsibility and monogamy, linking the threats to the family to the sinful pleasures of urban life and to the blandishments of new forms of diversion, namely sports and night life. The Lothario figure, the bored and wandering husband, has its counterpart in the long-suffering wife who is forced to subvert and to punish his vagaries. The attention to theft and to the role of the police dramatize that law must intervene to reestablish and regularize affronts to social order but not until their unruly and disruptive characters have been exposed. The presence of entertainment again serves in self-reflexive fashion to mitigate melodramatic suffering caused by promiscuity and to provide a form of enjoyment based on images of leisure and subversion that are made safe through the humorous treatment of transgression and through its ultimate management. But the film is not silent about its strategies: both concealment and revelation are the medium of entertainment, the *sine qua non* of common sense that provides a sign that the texts are not hermetically sealed but that they are involved in the complex management of social relations.

AMERICANISM AND FORDISM

In his notes on "Americanism and Fordism," Gramsci wrote that "The elements of a 'new culture' and a 'new way of life' which are being spread around under the American label, are still just tentative feelers. They are not due to a new 'order' deriving from a new basis, because that has not yet been formed, but are due to the superficial apish initiative of elements which are beginning to feel themselves socially displaced by the operation (still destructive and dissolutive) of the new basis in the course of formation."[17] The films of the era bear the signs of this "displacement," this "new basis in the course of formation." The "superficial" character is evident in the attempts to unify the "old and the new," the traditional and the modern. Gramsci's comments are applicable to many of the comedies of the era, especially Camerini's, in the ways that the films ambivalently straddle tradition and modernity, the world of the family and the world of commerce, the world of work and that of pleasure, and the world of comedy and that of melodrama. Particularly apt in relation to the films' emphasis on theatricality is the notion that the flirtations with Americanism are not indicative of a "new culture" and "new way of life," but rather are indications of the "tentative feelers" that are being expressed in relation to Americanism. The union of comedy and melodrama in these films underscores the fascination as well as perceived dangers identified with Americanism.

Due cuori felici (Two Happy Hearts, 1931), directed by Baldassare Negroni, is a comedy that in content and style bears the imprint of Americanism. The film revolves around Mr. Brown (Vittorio De Sica), an automobile manufacturer, who is first seen on a train arriving in Rome. He comes to the Italian offices of his father's firm where regimented workers are awaiting his arrival. Never having seen him before, the only way they have of recognizing him is through a picture of a bearded man that hangs in the office, identified by the name, "Brown." The workers are primed to say upon his arrival, "How do you do, Mr. Brown?" Anna (Rina Franchetti) is a secretary for the firm and is left in charge when the engineer, Mr. Fabbri (Umberto Melnati), is called home immediately.

When Brown arrives, none of the workers recognizes him, and Anna assumes that he is a customer looking to buy a car. Fabbri returns home to find that the emergency was his dog who has indigestion. At Fabbri's home, the phone rings and the caller is Brown. Having indoctrinated the workers to the phrase, Fabbri mechanically intones, "How do you do, Mr. Brown," and invites him to dinner. Anna comes to the house for dictation in the midst of bedlam and is enlisted by the family into preparing for their guest. The conflict over the care and feeding of a dog continues as Clara, the wife, insists that her dog, Bibbi, must eat with them and Fabbri says "no Bibbi at table." Outraged, she decides to leave, for good. The doorbell rings, and the maid repeats as prompted, "How do you do, Mr. Brown?" Fabbri tells Brown that he looks different from the picture hanging in the office, and Brown informs him that the picture is of his grandfather, the founder of the firm. Brown reveals that his family was born in Italy, in the Tyrol, and Fabbri says, "Where they make cuckoo clocks."

Anna finally appears at Fabbri's house and is assumed by Brown to be the engineer's wife. Cued by Fabbri, she plays the game of impersonating his wife, changing into one of Clara's dresses as the men converse over aperitifs. Brown confesses to Fabbri that he does not have "everything," for he lacks a wife. In the bedroom, Anna puts on the wife's elegant clothes and perfume, brushing her hair and dancing before a mirror.

When she enters the room with the two men, Brown gives her a gift of jewelry that Fabbri pockets, and the trio enter the dining room. Meanwhile, Clara, Fabbri's wife, is at the theater with Bibbi, but people around her begin to complain of the dog. When she returns home, she discovers that her dress is gone. She hears music coming from downstairs where Anna has charmed Brown, who expresses the wish to have a wife like her. The maid signals to Fabbri to inform him of the wife's return. Clara confronts her husband and tells him she's going to reveal the truth to Brown, but relents and instead impersonates Fabbri's secretary. When Brown suggests that they all go out and celebrate, she says she can't go dancing without her "fiancé," but after a fake telephone call in which she pretends to ask her fiancé for permission, she agrees to go along.

The increasingly familiar image in the films of the era of the night club with its art deco setting and floor show, and where Brown orders champagne, becomes the setting for the foursome as the comedy of confused identities intensifies. A man from the office approaches the table but Fabbri wards him off to avoid revealing the charade being enacted. When Brown asks Clara to dance, Anna becomes morose and decides to leave. Fabbri begs her to stay, saying he'll raise her salary, and they return to the table, to discover that Brown and Clara have left. Outside, Clara delays for time, because she cannot tell Brown where she lives. The two instead go to a bar that contrasts with the supermodern night club environment. Instead of champagne, Brown orders wine, and an audience gathers around to listen to Brown and Clara as they sing, thus enhancing the element of spectatorship necessary to theatricality. Clara finally gets rid of him with the excuse that her "fiancé" gets violent when he is jealous. Brown gets into a taxi and asks the driver how he likes the car, one manufactured by Brown, and the man says it is "not very good." At his home, Fabbri is concerned about the whereabouts of his wife, and calls Brown, who informs him that he intends to take Fabbri's "secretary" back to America. However, Fabbri offers his "wife" instead and Brown assumes that the reason for this offer is that Fabbri is having an affair with the secretary. When Clara arrives home, the couple quarrels but then reconciles. When Brown, who has said that he abhors lies, learns about the mix-up, he finally proposes to Anna and says that he will take her with him to America. The film ends as it began with the refrain, "How do you do, Mr. Brown?" as the couple exits, calling attention through repetition to artifice and theatricality.

The comedy centers on impersonation, role reversal, marital discord, and potential adultery. The reversal between the secretary and the wife generates jokes and misunderstandings that involve sexual transgression. Deception is central to the narrative, working on several levels. The substitution by the secretary for the wife is justified in the name of protecting Fabbri's job, but more fundamentally it is the hinge that enables the renewal of the faltering marital relationship and the development of a romance between Anna and Brown, since Anna is thus given the opportunity to display her ability at acting the part of an upper-class woman. The class difference between Brown and Anna is subordinated to the sexual conflict between the upper-class couple. Social and class conflict are neutralized in the romantic union of the secretary and the American capitalist. The transgressive elements reside in the implications of woman swapping, but they are legitimized by the fact that Brown is an outsider, an American now, though of Italian origin. Eccentricity, a feature central to characters in comedy, permits the possibility of a union between an industrialist with a secretary.

According to Steve Neale and Frank Krutnik, "the play between 'eccentricity' and convention in the field of love and marriage . . . moves towards the reassertion of the latter."[18] In the disarming of transgression, the affective character of comedy unlike melodrama involves another duality in the "*play* between identification and distanciation."[19] Comedy oscillates, too, between forms of work and leisure. In a caricature of Fordism, work is associated with regimentation, repetition, and subservience, but through the benign and romantic figure of the industrialist, work is a prelude to pleasure and social mobility. The film contrasts the anxiety-ridden figure of manager Fabbri against Brown, who is associated with play, mobility, and sexuality. The double-edged nature of this contrast reveals, on the one hand, the limiting and repressive aspects of work but, on the other hand, the promise of leisure as diversion and potential escape. In the context of Fascist attempts to reshape the lives of workers through new forms of workers' organizations and through forms of leisure such as the organization of Dopolavoro, the film becomes itself a form of "after work."

The "Americanism" of the film not only involves the character of Mr. Brown. The film's tentative feelers toward America and its identification with modern life include the world of commodities: automobiles, fashion, popular forms of entertainment, and domestic ease through the aid of complicitous servants. The melodramatic potential of marital conflict involving Fabbri and his wife is diverted through the focus on Anna's impersonation and its effects on Brown, whose Americanity can excuse his complicity. One of the ways in which comedy creates distanciation and dilutes melodramatic affect is through depersonalizing, even mechanizing, characters, often identifying them with animality. The role of Bibbi, the dog, thus appears more than a gag, and becomes a protean image that serves to emblematize the relationship of Clara to her husband. She lavishes her attention on Bibbi, according him a status superior to Fabbri. Due to her attachment to Bibbi, Fabbri is called away from work to minister to the dog's indigestion as if the dog were a child. This act enables Brown to arrive at the firm undetected by the workers and especially Anna. The dog also becomes the strategy for eliminating Clara long enough for Anna to make her impression on Brown. Other accidents insure the "innocence" of impersonation: Anna's accident of wetting her dress, Brown's assumption that she is Fabbri's wife, Clara's being told to leave the theater because of her dog. While the film does not feature an entertainer as in *Rubacuori* or make allusions to novels, plays, and other films, its insistence on impersonation as a prerequisite for harmonious sexual relations and social order provides another commentary on the necessity of entertainment, calling attention to disguise, protean identities, and the importance of dressing to proper performance.

Brown becomes a mouthpiece for the film's ostensible position on fictionalizing. While he asserts that he cannot abide a lie in his acceptance of Anna as his mate, he participates in the "lie," the fiction of his acceptance of Anna. Without the impersonation, their union would have been impossible. In a vein similar to advertising, the film is not silent about its "duplicities," since it is engaged in selling itself to an audience. The key product seems to be entertainment and the key word that echoes throughout such texts as this one, *La segretaria privata, Mille lire al mese*, and Mario Camerini's films, but in another form, is happiness. The dancing, singing (off stage and on stage) is identified with being "felice." But what of their audiences? Are they beguiled by the "happy ending?" Is the reference to "happiness" to be construed as another successful resolution to the Cinderella fable? Or, given the film's portrait of regimentation through work and marriage, does the litany to "happiness" assume a more ironic significance, tied as it is to the acknowledgment of the necessity of dissimulation?

TYPISTS AND "HAPPINESS"

La segretaria privata (1931), directed by Goffredo Alessandrini, was identified with its feminine protagonist's theme song, "Come sono felice," the Italian equivalent of the Roosevelt era's "Happy Days Are Here Again."

The film focuses on the aspirations of petty bourgeois figures struggling to attain an economic and social foothold in the middle class, though only few are chosen. A remake of *Privatseketärin*, the film bears some of the marks of the German original in the use of music and in its characterization. The film fuses Hollywood, Hungarian, and German popular comedies of the 1930s with their emphasis on female workers: shop girls, secretaries, typists, and department store clerks. That this form of comedy was viable, durable, had a profitable life, and crossed national boundaries is evident in the popularity of Camerini's comedies that focus on working-class characters and in British films such as Victor Saville's *Sunshine Susie* (1931) also based on *Privatseketärin* and Lubitsch's later Hollywood comedy, *The Shop around the Corner* (1940), where the world of typists and clerks is temporarily transformed into melodrama and finally redeemed as comedy. These texts rely on the devices of impersonation, misrecognition, and chance to sustain the tension between fantasy and everyday reality. That not all of the characters are redeemed plays as important a role as the delivery of the protagonist from her humdrum existence.

Segretaria begins with an image of a suitcase, before it even travels to the female protagonist, Elsa (Elsa Merlini). The train arrives at the station and men swarm to help Elsa with her suitcase, but a nattily dressed man with spats calls a taxi for her, expecting a "reward" for his assistance, but she rides off—alone. The suitcase functions in hermeneutic and proleptic fashion to identify Elsa as the film's "baggage," raising the question of who will carry her away and under what circumstances. The feminine "baggage" is the fiction on which the film rests, the baggage of folklore and especially of the Cinderella narrative. At the "Pensione Primavera," Elsa joins other working-class women who are also waiting for opportunity to strike it rich. The women complain of the food, their regimented life, and poor salaries, while the owner, like a headmistress, reminds them that the payment for their room and board is overdue. Elsa is optimistic, hoping to earn her "mille lire al mese," and the following day she strikes out to seek employment. At an office of the bank, she sees women applicants turned away by the porter, Otello (Sergio Tofano), and she too is sent off. However, she manages to capture his attention by talking to him about music, especially opera, further enhancing the film's reflexive allusions to theatricality and particularly to its operatic dimensions. He asks her what music she prefers, and she responds, "Verdi." When she informs him that she likes *Otello*, she wins him over, and he informs her that he is the director of a chorus. He invites her to a concert but she tells him pathetically that if she does not get a job she must return to the country. When he learns her name, Elsa, he identifies her with Elsa in Wagner's *Lohengrin*. Given these signs of shared interests in opera, Otello is now determined to help her get a position. He takes her to the head of personnel (Cesare Zopetti) and she is hired provisionally, not for her talent but because he sees her as a potential object of seduction. After the interview, Elsa dances on the street, singing, "Come sono felice" (How happy I am), repeating the song on her balcony to the world outside the pension.

She reports for work on the following day. The office is a model of regimentation, desks equidistant from each other and lined up in symmetrical rows. The head of personnel inspects the typists like a general reviewing his troops, a not uncommon Fordist image in many of the comedies that feature workers. Elsa finds a seductive note from him among her papers. At first, she is ebullient about her work, then through a series of dissolves, her look of joy alters to one of fatigue. The head of personnel becomes annoyed with her evasion, and begins to find complaints with her work, forcing her to work longer hours. At one of these sessions, she is discovered by Berri (Nino Besozzi), president of the bank, as he leaves his office. Unaware of his identity, she complains of her situation, and he sits down and helps her to finish her work, discovering in the process that the mistakes attributed to her are really those of the head of personnel, mistakes that she has tried to correct. He invites her to dinner, but the two end up at Otello's concert at a restaurant-club. There Otello conducts a group of singers in a variety of songs, and when he sees Berri in the audience, Berri signals to him to remain silent about his identity. Elsa is vivacious. She dances with Berri and the two drink champagne. When Otello joins them, she talks about the bank director as probably fat and pompous. The festive evening ends with Otello singing again as the camera pans the happy audience. In the taxi, Elsa tells Berri how happy she is, and the scene cuts to Otello on the street, drunk and staggering, but singing about how happy he is.

Happiness turns to melodramatic conflict when Berri tries to seduce Elsa by inviting her to his house and she is driven to defend her embattled virginity. To his annoyance, she insists that she be driven home. At the pension, while other women are seen kissing their escorts good night, Elsa merely shakes Berri's hand and enters the pension where she again breaks into song. In his taxi, Berri smiles. The final shot of this episode is

FIGURE 3. Performing for the world, *La segretaria privata*. Still from New York Museum of Art compilation film, *Antologia del cinema italiano* (1929–1945).

of the women's shadows at their windows as light after light is extinguished. At work, the following day, a perplexed Otello asks Berri how to behave toward him and is told to return to their formal relations. In the main office, the typists are working as the head of personnel surveys them. Elsa is berated for being late, but seeing Berri behind him she discovers his identity. She tries to talk to him but he appears indifferent. Otello impersonates Berri on the telephone and sends his secretary on an errand to Florence so as to enable Elsa to get into his office. The plan backfires when Berri tells her to leave and fires Otello. Afterward, Berri calls his secretary and tells her to remain longer in Florence. He calls Otello and rehires him, then calls Elsa, now packing to leave, and tells her to come to his house for dictation. Joyful, she sings and her pension mates help to dress for the occasion. She exits the pension looking very chic as the other women gaze at her admiringly.

Berri's home is modern, an advertisement for the latest in modernist geometric furniture and interior design. When Elsa arrives, greeted by the major domo, Berri offers her refreshments, and then acts seductively toward her. She slaps his face, and exits as he says, "She loves me." When she does not appear at work, Berri calls in the head of personnel and tells him to order Elsa back to the office or be fired. The man goes to the pension to beg her to return to work, but she refuses. Finally, Berri arrives, confesses his love for her, and proposes marriage. At the keyhole, Otello peers in at the couple as the other women vie also to get a view of the romantic scene. The film ends with Otello conducting the women spectators in song.

Made during the early years of the transition to sound, similar to Hollywood comedies of the era, *La segretaria* indulges "in a favorite Depression fantasy: the poor working girl, trapped in her dingy life, suddenly gets the chance to spend the rest of her days with a rich and handsome prince."[20] The film is characterized by its upbeat character, the liveliness of the songs, and the sense of collective optimism even among the other not-so-fortunate women at the pension. Elsa, like her American counterparts, is a resourceful and independent person. However, she is nonetheless exceptional in contrast to the other women in her shrewdness about her sexual morality, the key to her success. Her upright sexual morality, her common sense of saving her virginity until marriage, is central to her gaining the attention of the bank president. Thus, the dangers of women's independence are stressed as are the importance and inevitability of marriage. From the outset of the film, the dangers besetting the single woman are underscored, but so is Elsa's wit and shrewdness in avoiding entrapment. Her merit, therefore, is not her talent as a secretary so much as her traditional, if not puritanical, sexual behavior, and her happy and optimistic demeanor. The Cinderella motif is augmented by the heavy and unmasked emphasis on sexual restraint.

The film is not silent about the oppressiveness of work, its regimentation, the subjection of the workers to tyrannical intermediaries (never the owners) of the establishment. The bank president has a finer sense of fairness and justice and becomes the savior of his employees, though he may put them to certain trials to test their merit. His impersonation is important in developing the motif of Elsa's trial and initiation. Cinderella cannot immediately have access to her prince. Only after a series of tests does the shoe fit, and the role of Otello is the agent in Elsa's salvation. His role as a conductor of a glee club extends beyond his literal role, introducing the film's reflexive elements. He is the director of the action, finding Elsa the job, keeping silent about Berri's identity, and impersonating him at one point. His identification with musical entertainment serves as a surrogate for the film's director, making impersonation and the upside-down world of carnival the *sine qua non* of success. He introduces the element of spectacle that underpins the entire film in his directing of the singing but also in calling attention to the element of looking that introduces and closes the film. Elsa is the object of surveillance: the head of personnel looks her over, she and Berri enjoy the spectacle of Otello's performance, and the young women at the pension observe her with admiration and envy.

The final episode at the keyhole with Otello and the young women is a visual motto for the film in its highlighting of the pleasure of looking, particularly at images of success. The theme song, "Come sono felice," bears relation to Hollywood forms of Depression entertainment. The film also valorizes the pleasures associated with the commodities made possible by capitalism in its focus on elegance of clothing, automobiles, visions of modern and sumptuous decor, and in its treatment of the banker as the dispenser of equity and happiness. In the process, the film also sells film itself as entertainment in the image of its star as the conduit for happiness and optimism. Thus, this film seems to validate the assumption that films like this one are pure escapist fare designed for "little shop girls" who "go to the movies" to gratify their fantasies.[21] Such a reading maintains the assumption that audiences, particularly female members of the audience, are totally swept away by the dreams of love and wealth and that romance comedies are unashamedly given over to ideology. *La segretaria* not only portrays the drudgery, humiliation, and cramped lives of the working women at the pension, a fate from which Elsa escapes, but stresses, in the face of economic and social constraints, the necessity of ingenuity and wit for personal survival. The emphasis on Elsa's "purity," the threat from the opening shots of the film to her feminine vulnerability, is melodramatic: the romance between Elsa and Berri invokes the threat of violated femininity neutralized through the marriage proposal and especially through the acknowledgment that Elsa has been put through a test. The melodramatic affect is dampened through the musical numbers, through the emphasis on spectatorship, and through the playing with impersonation, shifting the emphasis from narrative exigency to the formal dimensions of entertainment.

La segretaria also bears the marks of its German origins, in its allusions to Wagner, in the image of the German newspaper that Berri reads before meeting Elsa, and in the image of collective song and toasting at the restaurant. The film opens a window on another face of Italian Fascism with its images of benevolent industrialism, pacified and happy workers, and the valorization of merit and productivity, but in the film's treatment of women and work, their subordinate and expendable status is not suppressed in the film's recourse to images of regimentation, foregrounding of difficulties in finding work, and in the reiterated portrayal of the drudgery of the work. This unattractive version of work operates on several levels: it makes contact with the audience in the knowledge of unemployment, underemployment, and oppressive employment despite prevailing propaganda that exalted work; it also suggests that if women are chaste, fortunate, and resourceful, they can, through marriage, be redeemed from work; it also functions metacinematically to identify entertainment as a compensation for drudgery. The film invites a reconsideration of the notion of escapism, which, in order to posit escape, has first to make contact with images of discontent and conflict that are by no means trivial. The potentially melodramatic scenario requires the presence of antagonism that, only later, through entertainment and a comic scenario of misrecognition and then restitution, is affectively neutralized.

SCREWBALL COMEDY, ITALIAN STYLE

The motif of "mille lire al mese" seems to extend beyond the title of Max Neufeld's film of that title (1939) to capture the sense of the 1930s as purveyed in popular film, through the comedies identified with Holly-wood and Budapest and especially through the "screwball comedies" that highlighted the "dual tensions of sexual and ideological conflict between its romantic leads."[22] Neufeld's film, too, bears many similarities to the comic films of the Depression, focusing on entertainment as subject and object, on struggling couples seeking to attain a modicum of financial and social respectability, and dramatizing how, after many vicissitudes and misunderstandings, merit is acknowledged and rewarded even if only in modest terms and uniting the disgruntled couple. Unlike *Segretaria, Mille lire* relies heavily on the emancipation of the masculine figure through the agency of the woman who is the instigator and the "director" of comic confusion, the familiar figure responsible for confounding the boundaries between illusion and reality. The allusions to entertainment are embed-ded throughout, containing references to its creation and reception. The opening moments of *Mille lire* involve a singer performing the title song on the radio, her audience a young woman, Magda (Alida Valli), who is entranced. However, Magda's fiancé is not enthusiastic about the music and its sentiments since, though he is a trained television engineer, he is at present unemployed and the couple cannot marry. Like Elsa in *La seg-retaria privata,* Magda is effervescent and indomitable, even aggressive as befits the female protagonists of screwball comedies. Accusing Gabriele of not having sufficient ambition, she herself goes to Budapest to find him work. Her plans in Budapest involve Theo, a pharmacist, and his assistant Lili. Theo's contact is the night porter at the television station, and Magda sets out to gain access to the director. On her way to the station in a taxi, she has an altercation with a man who tries to seduce her but she rebuffs him.

Once at the station, she again sees the offensive man from the taxi and ignores him. Exiting from an elevator, passing the performance of a dance number, she goes to the director's office only to learn that he is her nemesis from the taxi ride. However, he calms her, tells her to sit, and lis-tens to her as she rehearses Gabriele's situation. He informs her that he has no need of an engineer at the present time, but takes Gabriele's name and address. Fortunately for Gabriele, the engineer at the station, nervous at anticipating the birth of his fifth child, manages to confound thor-oughly a demonstration for a visiting dignitary, superimposing scenes of dancers on images of a ship's christening. The director contacts Magda, telling her to contact Gabriele. The couple's troubles are hardly over: Gabriele manages to get into a fight on the train to Budapest, being mistaken for the rival to the station manager's mistress. As a consequence, Magda enlists Theo to impersonate Gabriele to the manager, while Gabriele performs the actual labor behind the scenes. Among his ideas for the station, Gabriele develops the idea of closed circuit television whereby whatever happens anywhere in the station can be made visible. In fact, in his disguise as Theo, he demonstrates to the director how such a system can work, revealing men in an office playing cards when in fact they should be gainfully employed. Thus, he is on his way to becoming a suc-cess—except for the fact that he cannot appear as himself. Theo must continue to impersonate him, speaking in an language he has invented to conceal his lack of knowledge about the television medium. Confusion escalates as Theo manages to push all the wrong buttons as lights begin to buzz and papers to fly about the room. Theo escapes, and Gabriele manages to carry off a demonstration for the director without being seen.

The climax of the comedy takes place in a restaurant where Theo, seeking to placate Lili, who is feeling neglected, is assaulted by the direc-tor, who, still under the impression that Theo is Gabriele, accuses him of two-timing on Magda. The setting for this sequence is as the scenogra-pher for the film asserted, "Modern, most modern," and "decorative."[23] Theo runs from table to table, playing himself and also Gabriele, quickly substituting one identity for another. Theo becomes jealous when, during one of his frequent absences, Lili dances with a man at the next table. Gabriele also becomes jealous when he sees Magda with the director, and, finally, when the director tells Theo he must choose between Magda and Lili, Theo "quits" as engineer. The confusion is unraveled when Gabriele informs the station director of his true identity, and all is forgiven. He now has his "mille lire al mese." He can marry Magda, and the film ends as it begins with the singing of the theme song. Magda as the real man-ager has carried off her plan to assist Gabriele so that she can marry him. Her beauty and "good intentions" serve to enhance her image of covert power. Articulate and combative, she is the source of the confusion; she is also the source of order restored. The character of Gabriele is more vul-nerable, mechanical, and puppetlike, his role is invested in the anxieties of masculinity that verge on the melodramatic, arising from the fear of never finding employment, of being unable to earn a proper income and, hence, of not being able to marry and be respectable. The film's preoccu-pation with success and failure, competence and incompetence, has the potential to become melodrama, but the comedy of impersonation set in motion by Magda minimizes the intensity of affect associated with economic failure and masculine dependency. Identity conflict is played out in the hectic scenes of impersonation by Theo and Gabriele that are set aright by the station director. The temporarily topsy-turvy world is restored to "normal," but only after the prospect of disorder can be entertained and made to appear entertaining.

As the film addresses sexual and gendered relations, they are cast within the traditional terms of female service in behalf of a male figure. Magda's aggressive actions are, after all, channelled in the interests of marriage. However, in a vein different from the Hollywood heroines of screwball comedies, the question of equality and reciprocity between Magda and Gabriele is not the major issue at stake. Unlike many Hollywood screwball comedies, the dialogue and the action/counteraction between the male and female protagonist are not balanced and reciprocal. Magda is the fast-talking, shrewd, even unscrupulous director of the comedy, the source and the reconciler of the comic misrule, while Gabriele is largely acted upon. However, Magda's role seems to lead to several different readings of her role. First of all, Magda recreates a desired image from the era—a maternal image of power in the service of family and continuity; secondly, she offers a modern image, almost a tomboyish one, of femininity, acting rather than reacting; finally, as the source of the topsy-turvy events in the film that produce the comedy, she is identified with the entertainment, the television within the film and the film itself.

The role of television has interesting implications for the way comedy aligned to entertainment functions in the film. While hardly a mass medium in 1939, television identifies the futurist orientation of the film in relation to notions of work, leisure, modernity, and entertainment. The film's playing with television as a medium for the surveillance of workers also adds a strange and unsettling dimension to the comic text, introducing the coercive dimensions of the medium that involve the obsessively controlling aspects of Magda's pursuit of the job for Theo. Like the ambiguous image of femininity conveyed through Magda, television is the source of confusion, an instrument of surveillance as well as of entertainment. In this film, the images of entertainment orchestrate several positions: the necessity of impersonation for success; the potential of media for control; the increasingly greater role of media as a feature of modern life; and the importance of performing a role of competence and expertise in this technological world. Above all, the film confirms that the comedies are not invested in reiterating traditional pastoral and religious values, nor are they escapist in the sense of their taking flight from the exigencies of daily life, but are, in their preoccupation with modernity and cosmopolitanism, willing to contemplate modestly new forms of social life within the parameters of conventional familial and gendered relations.

COMEDY, FOLKLORE, AND THE LAW

While impersonation may be a central feature of comedy realized in a play or film within a film, there are other paradigms derived from folklore. One of the oldest and most familiar scenarios involves the law and the potential miscarriage of justice. The courtroom drama is rich in possibilities for theatrical display. Like melodrama, comedy has thrived on portraits of the law and particularly the rights of inheritance. In the case of both melodrama and comedy, the law, administered in the name of the father or a paternal surrogate, is a fragile barrier against a world that threatens to be devoid of justice. Dramatic scenarios involving judges, lawyers, and courtrooms include murder, incest, bigamy, succession, and property rights. In the case of melodrama, the intensity of affect concerns acts that have been perpetrated to the detriment of the protagonists— lives that are lost and property that has been misappropriated—whereas in comedy these actions are threatening but ultimately contained. The comic narratives hinge on the threat that a miscarriage of justice will take place.

The comic world introduces the necessary danger of misrule and disorder, but, in the last instance, the danger is averted and order is restored. In the case of the Italian cinema under Fascism, a number of comic films involve miscarriages of justice. The lawyer Marchi in *Il birichino di papà* assists the sisters in asserting their claims. In *L'eredità dello zio buonanima* (1934), directed by Amleto Palermi, one of the classic scenarios of comedy is enacted—the contention over the will of a dead relative. The film begins with a procession on the street by the "Congregation of the Pious," but then quickly cuts to an image of a legal document, announcing the reading of a will of the late Cavaliere Favazza. A hand turns the document over and the camera glides to the image of a sleeping man. The music is loud and lively and a series of dissolves reveal Don Antonio Favazza's (Angelo Musco) fantasies. His corpulent cousin, Maria Antonia Favazza Sgamba (Rosina Anselmi), a competitor for the estate, taunts him, laughing at his situation, thus presenting a challenge to his paternity and masculinity. Still another fantasy reveals his three daughters begging for alms on the street. Suddenly, the threat of melodrama gives way to an image of the uncle in the clouds as the family learns that they are now rich.

When Antonio awakens, he is convinced that he will be a wealthy man, and he orders his wife and daughters to prepare themselves for their good fortune. He buys himself expensive mourning garb, a painting of his deceased uncle, and also black dresses for the women in the family. The film relies on strict parallelism and stylization as in a folk tale. Antonio has a submissive wife and three daughters; Maria Antonia has a submissive husband and three sons. The offspring of both families seek to evade the surveillance and discipline of the dominant parental figure, who, chastened at the end of the film, will unite the warring families. The sons are musicians, and they serenade the young women with their romantic music. The conflict in the film climaxes with the reading of the will. The scene begins with altercations over the proper seating of the relatives, but the legal drama is not without its appreciative audience. The people on the street await the news. The theatricality of the occasion, the sparring of the combatants, the unctuous oratory, is especially associated with Antonio, who, in his self-confidence, swaggers, speechifies, frequently interrupting the lawyer in his reading, a reminder that the language of folklore, as Gramsci indicates, is built on oratory, especially arising from legal language. At one point, Antonio stops the lawyer's reading, prematurely announcing that he is the heir. He rushes out to the street, announcing free drinks for all as the spectators applaud him. When he returns to the room, he is reminded that the reading is not yet finished, and he learns that Maria Antonia's sons and the Congregation of the Pious are the beneficiaries, not he. She laughs as Antonio's daughters weep.

Distraught, Antonio returns home, rips off his mourning garb, has the painting of his uncle removed as he curses him. Maria Antonia's sons arrive and pay their respects to him, and a scene follows as they court the young women in the countryside, prefiguring the film's resolution. However, the problem of the wound to Antonio's honor has yet to be addressed. The president of the congregation comes to him with another will written by the uncle, sealed at four corners and at the center (an image which had appeared under the film's titles). Antonio discovers that his daughters have each inherited money and that he is to go to the bank to collect the cash. He arrives at the bank only to discover that it is closed and that all payments have been suspended. He becomes hysterical as people gather around him. Returning home, bandaged, he finds his house in disarray, his goods collected for his creditors, himself an object of scrutiny by his neighbors. Maria Antonia's sons are persistent, courting Antonio's daughters, and Maria Antonia arrives in a state of high dudgeon, seeking to avert any union of the families. The cousins reconcile, and then the news arrives that the bank will honor its commitments to Antonio. Once again he returns with an empty suitcase to collect the money, this time successfully. The film climaxes with shots of Antonio throwing money into the air, reminiscent of his fantasies at the beginning of the film, accompanied by the united couples singing.

The film is a melange of forms—musical, melodrama, comedy, folk tale, and American genre codes. The foundational dimensions of the nation form appear intact, involving the connection between the family, juridical institutions, and their relation to money. According to Etienne Balibar, the modern nation form involves "the dissolution of relations of 'extended' kinship and the penetration of family relations by the intervention of the nation-state, which runs from legislation in respect of inheritance to the organization of birth control."[24] In the film, the melodramatic elements involve the motif of the threat to the family's integrity by way of the contested inheritance, and inheritance is tied to the social position of the paternal figure, which is in turn connected to the integrity of the family. Paternal power and its status in the community is at stake. It is this power that can insure the proper marriages of the daughters under the aegis of the father. The inheritance money is the lever, the measure of the father's ability to maneuver in the community and to garner respect. The film's reliance on folklore is evident in the appeals to tradition and the past, in the stylization of the characters, in the conflict between the male and female figures of power, in the symbolic use of the number three as it applies to the tripartite structure of the narrative, the balance of three daughters and three sons, and the well-worn scenario of conflicts over inheritance.

The romantic scenario with three daughters for three sons is balanced against the antagonisms produced between conflicting claims to power between the maternal and paternal figures. Both Antonio and Maria Antonia inherit money, but the comedy focuses on the necessity of satisfying Antonio's paternal claim. The presence of these conflicts over power expose the inevitable conflicts that attend the passage of wealth and power from one generation to the next, threatening to expose the fragility of the social order. The film music, associated specifically with the courtship of Antonio's daughters by Maria Antonia's sons, is aligned to the romanticization of heterosexual coupling that works against the crass economism and conflict of the older generation. Like the romantic pairing, the music militates against the threat of melodrama. The film shares with the audience the commonsense knowledge that the rejuvenated family is the instrument for mitigating the inevitability and the harshness of conflicts that are inextricably tied to the law, private property, and the state. While this comedy does not rely on reflexive allusions to other media or the conventions of impersonation characteristic of many of the other comedies discussed in this chapter, in its emphasis on misrecognition, fantasy, and stylization, the film reveals that a more subtle form of theatricality is essential to the maintenance of community. This form of impersonation is not restricted to one individual but is the common property of the community in the ultimate roles that they are assigned to play within the social order and upon which the film and other social institutions rest.

FAMILY AS THEATER

Increasingly the comedies of the era seem to be critical of performance, if not rejecting theatricality totally. Mario Soldati's *Quartieri alti* ((Exclusive Quarters, 1943–44), appearing two years after his melodramatic *Piccolo mondo antico* (1941), explores impersonation. The film combines melodrama and comedy to dramatize threats to the family, threats engendered by obsession with material benefits through the older generations' expectations of being supported by the younger in a style that is commensurate with their fantasies of aristocratic leisure. In *Quartieri alti* the protagonist, Giorgio, played by Massimo Serato, is a young gigolo who reforms to become a respectable member of bourgeois society. The film portrays his family as totally corrupt. *Quartieri alti's* melodrama focuses on the domestic sphere and on Giorgio's growing conflict with the materialist values of his family. Initially, Giorgio lives off the income of the rich, avoiding any productive work and seeking only to gratify personal desire. The element of impersonation is central to the film, and it serves as yet another symptom of the preoccupation in the comedies with the motif of theatricality as opposed to authenticity. Giorgio and his family pretend to wealth and status in their attempts to rise in the world, even hiring actors to enhance their performances. However, this film is geared to unmasking disguises and exposing the duplicity, greed, and pretensions of the protagonist's family. Visually, the film focuses on enclosed quarters, cramped rooms, and framed perspectives. The characters are involved in spying on each other. A recurrent image, the revolving doors of the hotel, is a visual coda for the film's movement, signifying loss of direction, and circularity.

Quartieri alti presents a negative image of the aristocracy, portraying them as manipulative, self-aggrandizing, decadent, and even violent. The film does nothing to make them appear attractive or to encourage voyeurism through the women's fashions, the *mise-en-scène,* or the glamour of wealth and status. Opposed to the vision of aristocratic decadence are the bourgeois values of monogamy, security, and work. The narrative develops through oppositions: real parents and paid actor-parents, thematic oppositions between play-acting and social realities. These polarities remain intact despite the protagonist's conversion. The narrative probes the economic underbelly of the family, focusing on the exploitation and violence that are part of domestic relations through the deleterious effects of misrepresentation engendered through impersonation.

Within this context, Giorgio's conversion to respectability identified with authenticity, as opposed to play-acting, can be read as a gesture of capitulation to the familial and bourgeois common sense of Fascism. His physical wounding, by a representative of the unscrupulous upper class, is a symbolic wound that tames and disciplines him into bourgeois responsibility. However, the staging of his confession of complicity is significantly different from that of films that present impersonation and secrecy as necessary to family unity. Nor is the film's reconciliation festive. It lacks the playfulness of Camerini's films with their communities of like-minded people, common histories, and interests, but it shares with Camerini a critical reflexivity about performance, its ubiquity but its destructive effects on individuals and the community. Giorgio's renunciation of play-acting, his movement toward respectability, constitutes a frail and insufficient gesture when measured against the images portrayed in the film of the decadence of the larger society. His retreat to a modest position of work and respectability constitutes a submission to conformity and nostalgia as well as a critique of the status quo. In this respect, the film invites speculation on its relation to and role in the growing disaffection with the regime, if not with Fascism, in its waning years. In contrast to such films as *Dora Nelson, Una moglie in pericolo*, and *Rubacuori*—where impersonation is raised to a principle of necessity, an oblique commentary on the theatricality of media and on simulation, a solidifying bond with the audience—Soldati's film operates closer to a melodramatic register, in its negative treatment of dissimulation, indicative of the long-standing conflict between realism and antirealism in Italian cinema that was to become so prominent in the last years of the regime and in the postwar era. Nonetheless, in its negative treatment of impersonation, the film validates the prevalence of the motif of theatricality.

DOMESTIC COMEDY AND "ORDINARY" PEOPLE

If the films of Mario Camerini were among the most popular of the era, this may have much to do with the consummate ways in which they addressed domestic situations, the drive toward materialism, upward mobility, consumerism, and social pretensions while avoiding the extremes of legitimation of the status quo, on the one hand, and of high theatricality and moral pomposity on the other. Of the many comedies produced in the 1930s and early 1940s, his are the most exemplary of a form of domestic comedy with its roots in both Hollywood and Europe, especially France. His use of such stars as Assia Noris and Vittorio De Sica also lent a different aura to the texts, bordering on a form of acting and iconography that most resembled Hollywood comedy in its use of stars that projected a sense of ordinariness. Unlike such films as *Mille lire al mese, La segretaria privata,* and *Dora Nelson,* which follow Hollywood formulas for success in terms of upward mobility and the rewards of performance and virtuosity, Camerini's films most dramatize what Gian Piero Brunetta has described as exemplifying the motto from *The Wizard of Oz,* "There's no place like home." In describing Hollywood comedy of the thirties, Ted Sennett comments that while it "revolved around the sardonic, even mean-spirited behaviour of eccentrics, one large portion was reserved for the kinder, gentler folk. These were the people who resembled or at least approximated the members of the audience: ordinary people, whose tranquil, often small town, lives were disrupted by one crisis or another."[25] Existing alongside many of the German- and Hungarian-based comedies, the comedies of Camerini followed a different trajectory. Their "characters and settings were altogether different from those of the 'white telephone' comedy . . . ordinary people, far removed from the heroes proposed by the Fascist regime."[26]

In the 1932 comedy *Gli uomini che mascalzoni* (Men, What Scoundrels), the "ordinary hero" is a working-class protagonist, Bruno, played by Vittorio De Sica, and its treatment of mistaken identity and disguises, takes a direction other than many upper-class comedies: it becomes a reflexive strategy for exploring the nature of spectatorship, for differentiating audiences, and for ironically playing with conceptions of life against, not as, art. Through impersonation, working-class characters get into trouble, producing a chaotic and topsy-turvy world as they take on identities that are removed from their familiar world. The film does not condemn theatricality so much as it satirizes those forms that are aligned to self-deluding forms of behavior. The film begins in Milan with a taxi driver, Tadino (Cesare Zoppetti) who comes off the night shift, returns home, and awakens his daughter, Mariuccia (Lia Franca), for work. Their patterned and orderly behavior, a prelude to the incipient disorder to follow, is conveyed through her dressing, eating, and saying farewell to her father. This peaceful, routine moment is disrupted on the street as she is pursued by Bruno on a bicycle, following her tram. He knocks over a garbage can, is sprayed by water, but she merely laughs at his escapades. Joining her fellow workers from the shop where she is employed, she and they all have a laugh at his expense, teasing him about his bicycle. He tells Mariuccia that if she wants him to have a car, he will get one. After a scene of her in the shop, the scene shifts to Bruno at work in an auto shop. Bruno takes his employer's car, drives to her place of work and invites her to ride with him and take a trip to the country. They go to an inn in a peaceful pastoral setting where customers are singing and dancing. They dance and he sings to her a song that became popular from the film, "Parlami d'amore Mariù."[27] This pleasurable moment is disrupted by Bruno's chance encounter with the wife of his employer, whom he must drive to town. Manufacturing an excuse, he leaves Mariuccia with the promise to return quickly. However, his plans are foiled when he gets into a fight with the a driver of a cart after a collision. After waiting for Bruno until closing time, Mariuccia has insufficient funds to pay the bill. However, the innkeeper and his wife are sympathetic, allowing her to spend the night with them and promising to return her home in the morning after their consensus that "men are scoundrels," a familiar motif of the comedies. She arrives home before her father arrives from work and is given a blistering by her father.

Bruno comes to the shop to make amends and ends up buying an expensive bottle of perfume as Mariuccia wreaks her revenge. Having been fired from his position, Bruno scans the want ads and finally takes another job as a chauffeur. The focus on cars and driving is an opportu-

FIGURE 4. Bruno (Vittorio De Sica) at the Samples Fair, *Gli uomini che mascalzoni*. Courtesy of New York Museum of Modern Art, Film Stills Archive.

nity for the film to create vignettes of city scenes. Their inevitably con-
flicted romance takes another turn when his new boss becomes interested in Mariuccia. Having to drive the pair while seeking to disguise his
presence, Bruno, after viewing the man through the rearview mirror kissing a reluctant Mariuccia's hand, stops the car in mid-traffic and tells his
boss, "Drive yourself." The passage of time is signaled by a sign that says,
"January," and Bruno enters Mariuccia's shop and is told that she is no
longer an employee. Learning from her friends that she now works at a
commercial fair for an industrialist, he goes to see her and the two have
a rapprochement. She offers to get him work as a guide through the
firm's factory. Assisted by a megaphone, he points out the different elements involved in production as shots of machinery accompany his narration. When he returns to the fair to see Mariuccia, he learns that she
has gone out with the industrialist. Peeved, he invites the woman from
the candy stand to go out with him. Later, at a restaurant where he has
followed Mariuccia, and after a series of shots of each of them at separate
tables, both looking miserable, they finally reconcile with the aid of her
father. He first drives Mariuccia home, where he locks her in, then calls
Bruno a taxi, then along with a customer drives Bruno, explaining that
Bruno is his future son-in-law as they drive off. The film ends with the
an image of an empty street as at the beginning, thus reinforcing the
motif of repetition with difference that is essential to the comic world
where everything changes, yet remains the same within the theater of
everyday life.

The film is replete with images of cars that are at the basis of the sexual and class tensions. Bruno's occupation as a chauffeur and Mariuccia's
father's as taxi driver are the agents of the conflict as well as of its resolution Collisions and traffic jams underscore the sense of movement and the
precariousness of the urban landscape. The narrative relies on the conventional comic codes of pursuit, misunderstanding, separation, and
finally union. The fast pace of the film relies on type casting, quick
repartée, disguise, misrecognition, and confusion of identities. The location shooting also enhances the film's ambiance, like the automobile,
identifying the world of Rome and Milan with modern life and linking
the misunderstandings of the characters to its inherent complexity and
vicissitudes. Especially the scene at the Samples Fair demonstrates, as
James Hay describes, "Camerini's ability to transform a radically com-
mercialized and technological environment into a dramatic stage and to
infuse it with an almost mystical aura and a symbolic value."[28]

The elements of impersonation begun by Bruno's "borrowing" his employer's car set in motion the narrative confusion concerning social class. Cast in the mold of other Camerini characters, Bruno is not averse to representing himself as having access to commodities that he deems necessary to his courtship. His initial presence at the inn where he withholds information from Mariuccia about the real owner of the car leads both to his firing as well as to obstacles in his wooing of her, obstacles that involve them in relations with the upper class that produce further misunderstanding and separation. In a number of ways the film is reflexive about its status as a film, emphasizing the importance of looking—Bruno's observing Mariuccia on the tram and on the street, the spectators at the inn who observe Mariuccia and Bruno as they dance, the onlookers to Bruno's conflict with the cart driver, the workers at the department store who observe his machinations to reconcile with Mariuccia, the role of spectators as Bruno guides people through the factory. Looking is intimately associated with the character of urban life and urban life with the tendency toward misperception that animates the narrative, inciting characters such as Bruno to place emphasis on the connection between commodities and desire and, further, of the pitfalls of mistaking the illusory for the "real" character of social class relations. In Camerini, this confusion is mainly conveyed through a fetishizing of objects that produces misperceptions.

Camerini's formulas for comedy are based on mistaken identity, a quest for upward mobility that gets derailed, and the redeeming character of romance between equals. In films later than *Gli uomini*, his frequent use of Vittorio De Sica and Assia Noris served to establish an iconography for his working-class protagonists. In fact, Noris herself acknowledged to Savio that she had become an icon for "una ragazza di tutti," "la donna ideale," "la fidanzata di tutti."[29] In contrast to Isa Miranda, whose roles were identified with suffering, and Luisa Ferida, who was identified with wildness, Noris projected a gentle vulnerability and also shrewdness. De Sica's ability to personify commoner and self-styled aristocrat was central to the effectiveness of the films' dual scenarios of allowing an entry into both the world of the upper class and that of the working class, while leaning toward a more sympathetic portrait of the working-class milieu and its values. In the case of both stars, their ability to personify "ordinary people," while at the same time conveying exceptionality, is a central feature of stardom and its popular appeal,[30] and served De Sica well throughout his career as an actor.

HOME IS WHERE THE HEART IS

A more trenchant exploration of the nature and consequences of impersonation in relation to social class, Camerini's *Il Signor Max* (Mr. Max, 1937) features De Sica in the title role as a Roman newspaper vendor, Gianni, and as a would-be upper-class gentlemen, Mr. Max. His impersonation as Max is not the consequence of his consciously undertaking to enter into the upper-class world so much as the result of a misrecognition that triggers his fascination with the rich. He undertakes a cruise as a consequence of the largesse of a well-to-do friend and as his aunt and uncle bid him farewell he queries them as to whether he looks like an English gentleman, whereupon they deflate his pretensions by telling him that he looks more like an English news vendor. The name, Max, derives, significantly, from the name on the camera that Gianni carries that belongs to his well-to-do acquaintance. On his way to board the ship, he encounters two women who are also going aboard, and he sees them again at the ship's dance. In particular, he is attracted to Lady Paola (Rubi Dalma). Gianni recognizes the disparity in their backgrounds immediately when she asks him if he plays bridge, and he answers too quickly, "No," betraying his lower-class origins. Seeing the shocked expression on her face, he adds, "tonight," and thus begins his attempt to acquire the accoutrements and habits of the upper class. Using his limited funds, he overspends on shaves, haircuts and, above all, on a bouquet of orchids for Lady Paola and is forced to return home early. Further differences between Gianni and Lady Paola and her friends are underlined in the nomadic character of the upper classes as they move from New York, to Shanghai, Greece, and so on, whereas the only world Gianni knows is Rome and Naples.

While his family is following Gianni's itinerary with a map, he returns home, broke. Displeased with Gianni's pretensions, his uncle ironically and angrily offers him money to continue his impersonation, which he accepts. The family home is modest with a picture of Mussolini in evidence on the wall. Gianni is determined to play the role of Max and a montage sequence traces his crash education into upper-class life, his learning bridge, tennis, golf, and foreign phrases. At the newsstand, he sees Lauretta (Assia Noris), the governess for Lady Paola's sister, Pucci. She is astounded by the similarity between Gianni and Signor Max, but he disguises himself by his Roman accent and his bodily deportment. Realizing that he can once again find Lady Paola through Lauretta, he follows her car, but in his recklessness to keep up with her, he crashes into a taxi.

Concerned, she gets out of her car and assists him along with a policemen into a pharmacy to be treated. Determined to get her address in spite of her coyness and refusal to provide the information, Gianni tells the policeman that he will need her as a witness, and thus he once again is back in business as Max. He goes to the Grand Hotel, the ultimate in art deco setting, where the guests are clothed in the most expensive-looking and modern of garb. He arrives dressed elegantly in evening clothes, ascending the stairs, nonchalantly smoking a cigarette. He sees a companion of Paola's who tells him that he and Paola are engaged, but when she arrives on the scene she discredits this news, saying that was only a joke. She appears to be taken with Max, though she teases him when he tells her that the reason for his leaving the cruise prematurely was jealousy, rebuking him for being "bourgeois."

At work again at the newsstand, his business partner assists him with acquiring a riding habit, since Gianni has agreed to go horseback riding with his new friends, playing at being an international playboy with the necessary costume befitting a member of the leisure class. Once again Lauretta appears, though Gianni appears quite indifferent to her. However, his uncle comes to the newsstand, has a brief conversation with her about her work and the amount of money she earns, deciding that he likes her. He invites her to a concert sponsored by the Dopolavoro (an after-work, leisure organization established by the regime), and she accepts readily. By contrast to the images of upper-class life, the film now focuses on the concert, where Gianni is a member of the chorus. The scene emphasizes Lauretta's and the uncle's alignment, their scrutiny of Gianni, and the event as an expression of community values. The uncle manipulates Gianni to dance with her, while he is eager to leave and meet Paola. Lauretta tells him how much she admires him compared to people she works for who are idle and irresponsible, echoing Gianni's uncle's praise of his nephew as hard-working and serious. She asks him to come to the station to say farewell.

At the station, Gianni's play-acting is put to the test as he quickly switches between his two personas, one for Lauretta, the other for his new friends. He ascends the train dressed as Max but when he sees Lauretta he enlists his partner, who is selling papers, to aid him by putting on his coat and hat and standing at the window, facing inward. He then runs out to say "good-bye" to Lauretta, then runs to the other side of the train to board. The final phase of his flirtation with upper-class life occurs as he sits at table listening to Lady Paola and her friends gossiping about divorces and remarriages. When he takes part in a bridge game, he bids totally wrong, angering Paola, and exits from the game. He bumps into Lauretta, who is in tears, having been subject to Pucci's tantrums and verbal abuse. He follows her and as Signor Max tries to comfort her, she talks of her life, her loneliness, her affection for Gianni, and, carried away, he tries to kiss her. However, she thinks that Max is trying to seduce her and she slaps him, despite his insisting that he is Gianni. Called on the carpet by Lady Paola after Pucci makes a scene, Lauretta quits. Overhearing that she is returning to Rome, Gianni also changes trains, and he and Lauretta meet again at the newsstand where he has preceded her. His partner urges Gianni to take her for a carriage ride, and the two declare their love for each other, though Gianni teases her (or gets revenge for the slap?) by asking her if she has ever kissed a man. At first, she claims she is a good woman, but then confesses that she kissed someone who looked like Gianni. However, Gianni does not confess his impersonation, and when he arrives home with Lauretta he is counseled by his uncle not to tell about this escapade. Lauretta is received into the house and the door closes on the family, like a curtain falling, leaving the audience outside. Once again, secrecy prevails in the interests of family harmony.

In following the conventions of romantic comedy, the heterosexual couple is matched after a number of complications involving the desire for upper-class luxury as portrayed in magazines (such as the *Time* and *Esquire* carried by Lady Paola and her friend at their first encounter with Gianni) and through the implied images of wealth derived through cinema, which the film counteracts by the homely scenes of singing and dancing at the Dopolavoro event and by its ambivalent relation to the images of the Grand Hotel, its guests, and their entertainment. Through the Gianni/Max duality, the film sets up the contrast between different lifestyles relating to work and to leisure—one sedentary, the other nomadic; one productive, the other parasitic; one associated with family and community, the other with exclusiveness and cruelty. The motif of impersonation comes more clearly into focus here as part of a dialectic between authenticity and theatricality. Not only does it enable the film to penetrate two opposing worlds and to set up a modest case for petit bourgeois familial life, but it implies a critique of spectacle and of images to relate to underlying concerns with realism that will become more clamorous.

The film's duality is also related to the relationship between melodrama and comedy. The potentiality for melodrama involves the image of modern upper-class rootlessness, its mobility, its wastefulness, its commitment to appearances, and its imitation of Americanity. The film, however, includes these images that are in Brunetta's terms part of the "Long March of Hollywood on Rome," but one that Camerini's film acknowledges but seeks to undermine. There are other gendered and sexual elements that are conveyed through the characters. As De Sica plays Max in contrast to Gianni, he ascribes a putative effeminacy along with snobbishness to upper-class men. Gianni is clearly more "virile." In the case of Assia Noris, who is pitted against Rubi Dalma's Paola, she is characterized by her vulnerability, her avowed isolation and expressed need to be adopted by a family which is what the uncle does and what ultimately Gianni reinforces.

The film's ironic treatment of "home is where the heart is" is central to the pathos at the heart of the film, which is never really mitigated. The film is not so much a celebration of familialism as it is a satire on and critique of the threatening social forces that inhere in modernity. Unlike Blasetti's *Terra madre*, the film does not completely indict modern life. It presents it in such a way as to acknowledge the character of modernity that seems to belong as yet to the upper classes, identified with alienation and associated especially with leisure. The external audience is invited to see this world of movement and commodities. What the audience does not glimpse, however, by way of a contrast, is any celebration of working-class life. The door is abruptly closed on the audience at the end of the film as if to share knowledge about the fictional status of the "happy ending." Aside from the musical concert, the world of "common folk" and the affective compensations of family life are not visible. As the film develops relations between Gianni and his family, his uncle's relationship to Lauretta, and finally Gianni's relationship to her, there seems to be the implication that "home" is not a physical but a spiritual (and, hence, unvisualizable) space, involving the pathos of redemption from loneliness and survival in a threatening world. Ironically, this knowledge becomes possible only after the character has, through impersonation, entered into that other world. "Home" thus appears to be a stage, involving roles and rules that are set in opposition to the theater of the upper classes. It is not that this arena is more real and natural than the other; what the film seems to suggest, as if a metacommentary on its own operations, is that there are many theaters, identified with different social classes, and that the comedy derives from their interaction and the confusion that results from one group's impersonating the other, particularly in the case of the working class. The issue does not seem to be authenticity but rather decorum to suit the situation and context.

ESCAPISM AND CARNIVAL

The carnivalesque as an image of an inverted world, a world turned upside down, is fundamental to comedy and satire, and many of the comedies of the era are set within the context of the carnivalesque. Familiar behavior is suspended; roles are interchanged and reversed. Instead of impersonation, there is masquerade. Instead of collectivity and community, there is romantic coupling and escapism as the protagonists flee this world at the end of the film. The comedy is predicated on a familiar hypothetical question designed to overturn existing social roles: "What would happen if you met a millionaire who was willing to bankroll you?" This hypothesis sets in motion a carnivalesque atmosphere that facilitates a momentary upsetting of expectations, allowing different and critical perceptions to emerge. *Darò un milione* (I'd Give a Million, 1935) is hardly as legitimation of the status quo. The film, which won a prize at the Venice Film Festival, also stars De Sica and Noris. The collaboration between De Sica and Zavattini precedes *The Bicycle Thief* by a decade, since Zavattini was one of the writers for this film.

Blim, a hobo (Luigi Almirante) reminiscent of Boudu in the Renoir film *Boudu Saved from Drowning* (1932), is trying to drown himself by tying a weight around his leg. (Chaplin's tramp is also evoked.) The film cuts to a ship and a series of shots involving a tuxedoed man, Gold (De Sica), water, a closer shot of the man, his movement on the ship's deck as he observes the hobo seeking to end his existence. Finally, he jumps into the water to rescue Blim. The men struggle and Gold restrains Blim. The scene cuts to an elegant room where people are gathered by the radio listening to news of Gold's disappearance as outdoors the hobo and the millionaire sit by a fire. Gold hangs his own clothes to dry as Blim observes him, especially ogling the wet money that is hanging out to dry. As they sit by the fire, Gold tells the beggar that he "would give a million" if he could find a person who was interested in him for reasons other than his money. When Blim awakens in the morning, his clothes are gone, and so is Gold, but the millionaire's clothes remain and so does the money. The scene dissolves to a carnival and again to a clothes line, a familiar image in this film and also in *Il cappello a tre punte*. In Camerini's films, objects are highlighted, especially clothing, serving to identify the attachment to or detachment from commodities.

At a circus, we once again meet Gold with a dog by his side, again another allusion to *Boudu*. As he awakens he sees a shadow of a woman on the sheet. He looks again then sees a heavyset woman, not the same as the shadow figure. Finally the woman from the shadow appears: it is Anna (Assia Noris). A crisis occurs that brings the couple together: the dog, "Bob," a mathematical whiz, takes off down the road following a cyclist and Anna and God chase after him. Blim meanwhile has gone to the newspapers with his story, informing them about the millionaire's offer. A lengthy sequence introduces the editor's interview of the beggar, the plans for capitalizing on the story involving pictures, headlines, and culminating in an image of the layout with headline, "I'd give a million to whoever makes a disinterested and generous gesture toward me." The sequence follows the circulation of the paper, people reading it and then passing on the information to others, thus emphasizing the notion of the modern media as information (or rather as misinformation). Beggars are shown now helping each other in the hope that one of them is the millionaire. Suddenly, they are no longer undesirables and a sign from a store window that read "Beggars forbidden to enter" is removed. Thus, this prologue to the film has stressed role reversal between rich and poor, impersonation, the blurring of class identities, the notion of the circus as the site for such reversals, and the role of media in enhancing the confusion between impersonation and social identities. The characters are typed in terms of occupation and gender and the film involves a journey through a gallery of social types—mendicants, entrepreneurs, hustlers, self-styled millionaires, romantic lovers.

At the point that the couple is about to recapture Bob, he is grabbed by dogcatchers. Heroically Gold grabs the dog, freeing the other dogs as well, but then is arrested. Anna, however, escapes with Bob. Given the ambiguity of who is a beggar and who a millionaire, Gold is released. Beggars are seen being overwhelmed by people wanting to do good deeds. At the circus, a banquet (as in Blasetti's *La tavola dei poveri*) is prepared for the beggars. The camera travels up and down the table capturing the beggars in various postures. The beggars are being scanned in the hope of finding the millionaire. The feast of the beggars serves a number of functions in the film: it satirizes the role of charity; it offers an image of the poor but without idealizing their image or, conversely, making it appear

FIGURE 5. Blim, Gold, and Anna, *Darò un milione.* Courtesy of New York Museum of Modern Art, Film Stills Archive.

grotesque; it also reinforces the notion of saturnalia, the idea of the suspension of the normal and everyday. The feast is connected to a notion of public spectacle that seems characteristic of the 1930s newsreels as well as calling attention to the role of the media, newspapers and radio, in publicizing and disseminating misinformation.

Blim, who has been trying to escape from the clutches of the newspaper editor, finally is chased away. The editor's wife had been in bed with a beggar, but Blim is mistakenly perceived to be the culprit. At the circus, the stage is set for the lottery to be held as planned by the manager. The scene is crowded with equestrians, acrobats, floats, beggars, as a billboard with a million lire note painted on it is lowered. The spectacle in this scene involves dance, as a musical number is performed miming the beggars and millionaires. There is a lottery, and the number called is "32," ironically Gold's number. The element of chance or coincidence is again highlighted. When the beggars discover that Gold has the winning number, they douse him with water. Anna takes him to her room to help him dry his clothes. Outside, the world has gone mad. Gold's "abdication" has turned the world upside down, destabilizing relations, producing greed masked as altruism. While Anna irons his clothes, she finds a diamond ring. He approaches her and kisses her, offers her the ring, which she refuses. Suspicious, she interrogates him, wondering why he doesn't work. The manager enters and expels Gold from the circus, thinking that he has compromised Anna. Gold returns to see Anna again, but with the same shadow technique as at the opening of the film, he sees the two talking and assumes that they are plotting to get his money.

Gold has decided to return to his boat, explaining to Blim his disillusionment with people: once again men are cheats, scoundrels, and impersonators. But life is beginning to normalize as the greedy people begin to return to their habitual bad treatment of beggars. Gold tells Anna that since he is not the millionaire there is no reason to pursue him. In his rage at her, he breaks some dishes, and she goes to pay the woman for the damages. As he prepares to get into a boat to row to the ship, she tells him good-bye. She turns to leave, then turns back, wishes him luck and presses some money into his hand to help him. This gesture melts his anger. He kisses her, and says that he has finally found a truly generous friend. He takes her to his ship where they are greeted by his captain, and where Gold puts his ring on her finger. The scene cuts to the beggars and Blim having their own party. Blim takes the money that Gold had left him and spends it on rides for the beggars, and the film ends on this saturnalian note.

98

FIGURE 6. Carnival and Woman as Spectacle, Assia Noris in *Darò un milione*. Courtesy of New York Museum of Modern Art, Film Stills Archive.

Like all satire, the film relies on role playing, role reversal, irony, and burlesque. The "circus" becomes the synecdoche for the society where all these different groups converge. Gold, like his English name, is the force that sets these agencies into motion and that also disrupts their normal functioning. What the film does not do, any more than any other Camerini film, is resort to a utopian vision, offering instead a cynical view of competition, the quest for wealth and power, and even the operations of institutionalized altruism. Furthermore, the narrative suggests that the vision of a transformed society is illusory. The exceptions to this view reside in the notion of pleasure as exemplified by the beggars who with Blim enjoy the amusement rides at the end, perhaps too ambiguous a comment on cultural predilections for bread and circuses to divert the masses. The notion of escape pervades the film, beginning with Blim's suicide attempt, Gold's disappearance from his yacht, the dog's attempt to escape from the circus, and Blim's escape from the newspaper editor among others. In fact, at the end of the film, Gold and Anna escape from the "circus."

The romance element with Anna and Gold serves to balance against the portrait of greed and opportunism. In terms of the conventions of romance comedy, Anna becomes the saving remnant, the one truly worthy person. Here the poor woman and the rich man are united in contrast to *Il Signor Max*, their bonding based on their shared indifference to wealth and quest for authenticity. With Gold's wager, the film becomes one vast competition much as in myths of Diogenes to find the one deserving person. Anna is put on trial and of all the needy in the film, she is deemed the most worthy and rewarded. As each group in the film finds its own counterpart, Anna finds hers with Gold. The sexual conflict in the film not only serves to mate the compatible couple, but suggests that there is some connection between the competition for wealth and sexual desire. In fact, the element of clothing seems to be the dominant carrier of the film's preoccupation with fetishism as tied to the confusion between money and needs, objects and people.

Clothing serves to highlight the various disguises, impersonations, and role reversals. At the outset Gold exchanges clothes with Blim. Later clothing comes to be associated with Anna, who is a maker of costumes. Her slip becomes an object of contemplation by Gold as she irons his clothes. He strokes it as if it were Anna even though Anna is in the same room. In ironing his clothes, she comes across the diamond ring that becomes the pivotal object in their relationship, first separating them and then later uniting them. The other images that are central to the film's preoccupation with the attempt to unite materialism and spirituality are of shadows. Gold first encounters Anna as a shadow. Later, he misperceives her motives as he looks at her as a shadow figure with the manager.

Most particularly, this film, like Camerini's others, appears to be uneasy about spectacle and spectatorship. A platonic preoccupation with the illusory nature of appearance, a suspicion of looking, governs the text. In its treatment of femininity, the film seems to equate woman with spectacle, and, as we have seen, spectacle with hypocrisy and deception. Gold and Anna, united at the end, could be conceived of as the progenitors of the family, but since the film satirizes everything, it is difficult to isolate the romantic from the satiric elements. One is tempted to read their union in the same fashion as the ending of *Il Signor Max:* as a predictable convention of comedy, as a necessary coupling but hardly as a celebration of the family and the future to come or as an escape to anywhere. Escape functions less as a celebration of romantic love and more as a reproach to the status quo as the film dissects and exposes the illusory character of theatricality. Like *Una moglie,* the film is reflexive, acknowledging the power of performance, but unlike the Neufeld film, it is suspicious of theatricality and of vision, using masquerade to undermine the powerful sway of role playing identified with the role of cinema and with the power of the image. The film seems to suggest that representations are closely linked to self-interest and self-interest to monetary values. The romantic comedy (and especially the role of woman) thus becomes the entry into the ambiguous world of representation.

REGARDING FRIENDLY FASCISM

Escapism is often identified with playful immorality, a flouting of heterosexual coupling, of marital and familial responsibilities, as well as a disregard of polemic and formal politics. The reflexivity of the comedies, their allusion to other films, and their incorporation of conventions characteristic of genre films, can be construed as a disregard for reality and even a reassertion of conventional values. One of the virtues of escapism is how it evades formal strictures and censorship through its ostensible claims to frivolity. Yet an examination of so-called "escapist" films, reveals that the stance of indifference masks a knowledge of and investment in social realities. In the case of *Batticuore* (Heart Beat, 1939), also directed by

Camerini, the film's archness and theatricality mask a more serious notion inherent in relation to political economy that "property is theft." The "escapism" involves the formal apparatus of the film that challenges more fundamental issues concerning property relations, the hypocrisy of the upper classes, and the ambiguous nature of the law as it defines crime.

Batticuore offers another satiric excursus into the world of the upper class and pretenders to this world. It adopts a range of melodramatic and comic devices to explore rather complicated relations between property, theft, and the law. The film is set in Paris, providing abundant and typical touristic shots of the city. In voyeuristic fashion, the camera moves to a window, remaining outside as a professor (Luigi Almirante) lectures. Another window is half-shaded, impeding vision, and soon the professor pulls the shade on the other window, leaving the spectator on the outside. So far, the scene seems innocuous, suggesting nothing disreputable. The professor is testing his pupils, while a stuffed mannequin is evident as the focal point of the testing and interrogation. On the street, Arlette (Assia Noris) and a young man talk about the professor's assignments and his expectations. She takes a letter from her purse to mail and as the couple walks, they talk about gaining employment. The narrative takes an unexpected turn as the man approaches a fat man with a cigar and tries to pick his pocket. The affair backfires and the victim calls for help. People gather, and Arlette and her companion escape. Returning to the school, Arlette hides behind a door and peers through the window opening, observing the professor and his students, recapitulating the opening scenes that involve a dichotomy between inside and outside, relating to film's thematic of surveillance.

She enters the room and joins the others as Professor Comte lines up his pupils. Like a drill, he conducts them through various movements, asking them to look to the right and left, having them raise their hands, palms out. Then Arlette is singled out as she goes through certain paces. The group then practices pick-pocketing on the mannequin. Some are too fast, others are "not bad." For their final exercise, they pretend they are riding on the bus, plying their trade. Their practice is cut short by the entry of the professor's wife, who reminds them of a celebration in the evening as their send-off into the world of crime. At the party, the professor further observes Arlette to make sure she looks sufficiently professional. He has her practice an alibi should she get caught, namely that she is basically an honest and virtuous person, that she has never had any run-in with the law before and therefore begs leniency. Satisfied, he prophesies a promising career for her.

After another attempt to find legitimate work and failing, she finds herself on an elevator with a well-to-do looking man wearing a jeweled stickpin. A series of cuts between her in close-up to a close-up of the stick pin leads to a shot of him minus the pin. On the street, she opens her hand containing the pin. Seeking to evade her victim, she goes to a movie theater that has an ad for a Rogers-Astaire film and sits only to find the man in a seat next to her. She then rehearses her innocent victim routine with him while the film on the screen replays the same scenario. The man, Count Maciaky (Giuseppe Porelli), orders her to come with him to the Stivonian Embassy, where she is merely told to impersonate a Stivonian baroness at a ball. She enters a grand hall in clothes provided by Maciaky, who introduces her as a baroness. Maciaky tells her to dance with Jerry, Lord Salisbury (John Lodge), an English nobleman, and steal his pocket watch. After doing the job, the company gathers to watch a television broadcast from Stivonia that, as in *Mille lire al mese*, gets scrambled. During the broadcast, Arlette removes a woman's picture from the watch. She then returns the watch to Jerry's pocket, thinking that he was unaware of her machinations.

The narrative shifts to the professor and his students as he is informed of Arlette's success at the embassy. All are duly excited at the future prospects. After the ball, Jerry insists on escorting Arlette home. She tells him she would rather walk alone but, insistent, he follows her. She stops at a hotel where she pretends to take a room. However, she exits to find him waiting. He invites her to restaurant, the "Lapin Rouge," and tries to get information from her about the "secrecy he sees in her eyes." They have their picture taken and again Jerry comments on her eyes, telling her she does not look like a sinner, while she looks remorseful. When they exit, he kisses her as they are observed by the professor in the bushes, disguised behind a beard. Jerry tries to catch him, but all he finds is a discarded beard. She returns to the hotel, takes a room, and the following day, Jerry calls her. She tells him she cannot see him, since she does not have her baggage from Stivonia. At his residence, Jerry tells his butler (the victim of Arlette's companion earlier) that he is in love with Arlette but that he plans to teach her a lesson. He then goes to see her and has a wardrobe brought to her. She accuses him of trying to seduce her, but after he reassures her, she agrees to spend the day with him. She has also received a threatening note from Maciaky to return the borrowed clothes or be exposed, but the note is accompanied by a bracelet. Then the Professor arrives and offers to help her. He takes the bracelet and in return gives her money to pay her bill. Hoping to escape from Jerry, she leaves but sees him on her way out and tries to dissuade him from any future relations, saying that he knows nothing of her past, but he is undeterred. In the lobby, too, is her former companion in crime, jealous of Jerry's attentions.

Jerry discovers that his watch is missing and thinks that Arlette is the culprit. However, incompetent as always, the young man is caught by the hotel security. Jerry insists that the man must be tried and punished. The scene shifts to police headquarters where Arlette tries to confess to her crimes. The young man refuses to acknowledge her. When called to testify, the count asserts that nothing of his had been stolen, and shows that he is in possession of the stick pin that Arlette said she stole from him. In private, he tells the commissioner that the stealing of the watch was a secret matter of state, involving political motives. There were secret plans in the watch. After prying the watch open, it is revealed that the only thing in it is the photo of Jerry and Arlette taken earlier, and he leaves to find his countess. Jerry and Arlette are reconciled as she begins to recount a narrative of her life, fading to a scene of their wedding. The film ends with the wedding festivities and with the professor and his students, enjoying the opportunity to fleece the rich guests; however, since they agree it is a special day, they decide to return the stolen items.

The element of thievery is potentially the material of melodrama, involving transgressions of the law, but the melodrama is subverted through comedy. Melodramatic expectations associated with crime are short-circuited at the film's outset. The usually negative associations of criminals is undermined through the comparison of the school for thieves with a respectable pedagogical enterprise, thus blurring differences between conventional and marginal institutions. The incompetent nature of the crooks also mitigates the usual association of thievery with malevolence. They are, after all, only trying to earn a living. Also, the comparison of the homeliness of the thieves community with the professor, his wife, and their charges militates strongly against negative identification with the thieves. Most of all, Arlette, as their "star" pupil, is attractive and desirable as the romance plot demonstrates. Furthermore, when placed against the image of the foreign diplomats and their knavery, the boundary between the thieves and respectable folk blurs. The thieves' society seems more interesting and variegated than that of the upper classes, reminiscent of Camerini's continuing predilection for "ordinary" folk against the predations and hypocrisy of the rich. Jerry's illicit relations with the countess undermines any clear moral binarism between criminality and respectability.

Not only are respectable structures called into question, but the satire dramatizes the common sense wisdom that crime and impersonation do pay. They are the entry into the upper reaches of society. In being presented as a form of work, as a "profession," it stands in contrast to the leisure and machinations of the upper class. Also, it is established early that Arlette has tried to find respectable employment only to fail and is therefore thrown back to the profession of theft. Furthermore, crime appears to be useful to the upper classes as the hiring of Arlette seems to indicate. Camerini's seemingly "light" comedy (underestimated as such) touches at the heart of basic social structures as they are implicated in Italy's contemporary society. The film's ostensible escapism resides in its playful amorality, its use of parody, and its maintaining romance conventions to set aright conventional morality at the end, masking the more serious notion inherent in critiques of political economy that "property is theft." The "escapism" thus involves the formal apparatus of the film that challenges more fundamental issues concerning property relations, the hypocrisy of the upper classes, and the ambiguous nature of the law as it defines crime.

The film reproduces conventional voyeurism, allowing a window opening onto the world of wealth and luxury, but the mechanisms of spectatorship are such that this view into the life of the other half exposes its moral imperfections. From the opening shots, the issue of looking is highlighted. The inside-outside images play with the audience, withholding and then revealing what goes on inside this society. The audience is playfully indicted as a voyeur and then invited to participate. The element of surveillance involves bystanders to the acts of pickpocketing. Arlette is observed by her first victim. Maciaky surveys Arlette as she steals the watch. Jerry observes her. The professor spies on Jerry and Arlette. That Arlette is "caught" by Maciaky while watching a film is not an empty reflexive device but another indication of an urban world where looking has primacy, and especially, as in *Gli uomini che mascalzoni* and *Il Signor Max*, where looking enhances the desire to be something else and to possess that which one sees.

The recognition of cinema as the consummate purveyor of these images appears central to Camerini's films, offering a meditation on representation as unstable currency, circulating through many and untrustworthy venues. Thus, impersonation, that is, performance, is also more than a self-reflexive device. As in so many melodramas of the era, impersonation begins to resonate with supplementary meanings involved in cultural politics. It raises the question of authenticity, of the meaning of truth. In *Batticuore*, the film undermines confession as truth telling exemplified by the fact that the film ends with the withholding of the count's motives to his "crime." Also, Arlette's attempts at confession are thwarted by Jerry and the police. In foregrounding looking and linking it to crime, the film not only undermines any simplistic notion of escapism but it offers an insight into the cinema of the era that exceeds intentionality and becomes part of the dense texture of a world devoted to spectacle. Spectacle exceeds the sense of Sontag's "fascinating fascism," complicating the usually externalized descriptions of fascism as public show, pointing rather to the contradictory ways in which media consumption functions and circulates. The film complicates any simplistic notion of consent, paving the way to further investigations of ways in which common sense operates as a rudimentary consciousness of the necessary deceptions and compromises embedded in cinematic culture through its portraits and images of social life.

Along with the other films discussed in this chapter, Camerini's comedies are not naive about the power of the cinematic image. In their various explorations of theatricality—whether they acknowledge the necessity for social survival in the blurring the boundaries between art and life, the value of withholding information, and the necessity of impersonation (even of theft) rather than authenticity—they provide insights into the complex character of the affective value of cinema, which thrives on generating a sense of the image as real and desirable while also conveying a sense of its fictional status. For better or worse, the relation of the films to their audiences and the audiences' relations to the films is more reciprocal and knowledgeable than is usually assumed. In their stylization and in their self-conscious attention to the powers of theatricality, they demonstrate that they cannot be relegated to a limbo of escapism where the audience is assigned a position of passive consumption of dream images. The texts work rather to enlist the audiences in the work of constituting a world that is both familiar and estranging.

Ernesto G. Laura says that "in order to understand the evolution of Italian film comedy, mention must be made of a journalistic phenomenon peculiar to Italy between the two wars: the enormous popularity of comic weeklies."[31] The weeklies, "made up of cartoons (often moderately sexy), jokes, and short stories" were "a tolerated corner where some irony and a little social criticism could be indulged in."[32] Many film comedies of the era also provide a "corner" for irony and even social criticism. A close examination of these comedies alerts the critic concerned with the politics of culture, especially popular culture, to reexamine the binarism of much film reception that asserts, on the one hand, that cinema is an opiate and conducive to beguiling audiences away from "reality," and on the other, that it is a transparent window to the "real" world. The film comedies produced under Fascism force a rethinking of such monolithic views of representation, particularly as they are exemplified in the negative appellations assigned to the genre as "white telephone" and, more recently, as "escapist."

If the term "escapism" is to be maintained, it has to incorporate a more striated sense of the character of the cinematic medium (if not all forms of representation) which blurs and complicates boundaries between fiction and "reality." Escapism must not be seen as a process whereby sense is evacuated but rather one in which "reality" is more elusive, heterogeneous, and produced, not given. By calling attention to performance, the comedies find a meeting ground with the spectator, even if it is often only one of cynicism, that subsumes political platitudes and truisms about the uniformity of consensus by underscoring the ubiquity and inevitability of the artifice of performance as endemic to art and to social life.

What is evident above all in the comedies is the ongoing and obsessive preoccupation with performance, utilizing the strategies of comedy—impersonation, misrecognition, and doubling—for enlisting audience participation, allowing it to play a role in the construction of fictional worlds, but, at the same time, also underscoring the notion of the role of play as imbricated in the everyday and commonsense conflicts in which this theatricality is couched. Not wholly masked, this cynicism serves to bring producer and audience together in a shared enterprise that sheds light on the power of the popular Italian cinema of the era and of its role as a social text, its increasing competence in finding points of affinity with its audiences, who are not bereft of the knowledge of fictionalizing. Even such films as *Quartieri alti*, which appear to cast a critical eye on impersonation, validate the ubiquity of theatricality, the necessity and the limits of "putting on a show," cannibalizing on a confusion between the private and public spheres, a characteristic that seems to be shared by the sound films of the era from the 1930s into the early 1940s (and resurgent in many of the comedies of the 1950s). What differs from film comedy to film comedy is the degree of irony, cynicism, and affect attached to the theatricality.

CHAPTER THREE

❀

The Uses of Folklore:
History and Theatricality

Along with the negative critical assessment of the era's "white telephone" comedies, the historical spectacle has come in for its share of misrecognition and disrepute. While the so-called white telephone films have been termed fascistic because they evade pressing political problems, the historical spectacles and costume dramas have been considered fascistic because they are deemed expressions of Mussolini's belief in "the persuasive power of cinema to shape a people."[1] A close examination of the Italian cinema of the period reveals that it had a much more opportunistic, contradictory, and, in certain instances, problematic relation to uses of the past. Like other national cinemas of the era, the cinema under Fascism ransacked earlier historical moments, to create a pastiche of elements drawn from popular folklore, literature, theater, opera, and current events. According to Walter Adamson and others, there was no coherent political viewpoint at any time from the inception of fascism in 1922 through 1932, "when the first attempt to state a fascist 'doctrine' was made. On the contrary, fascism made a fetish out of being an 'anti-ideology,' just as it was an 'anti-party.' . . . [I]f we nonetheless take it as a political doctrine in the strict sense, we are apt to miss many of the mythic and performative elements (rituals, styles) that most clearly link it to the culture out of which it grew."[2] The cinema's uses of "factual" history are a major source of the mythic and performative elements endemic to Italian culture during the Fascist era. However, as one seeks to disarticulate the relation between present exigency and elements derived from the past, one is confronted by the difficulty of defining cinematic uses of the past against factual notions of history. One is also confronted by the problem of how to read and understand the nature and effects of performance, the rituals and styles alluded to by Adamson.

Cinematic history is, as Robert Rosenstone reminds us,

> a vision game that involves such an enormous perceptual and conceptual change from the academic sense of the past that to find its equal we would have to skip past the significant alterations in historical practices of the last three hundred years and return to that period over two thousand years ago when, in the Western world, the written word began to replace the oral tradition. . . . [F]ilm must be taken on its own terms as a portrait of the past that has less to do with fact than with intensity and insight, perception and feeling, with showing how events affect individual lives, past and present.[3]

In the case of the Italian cinema under Fascism, which produced a goodly amount of historical films, it is tempting and comfortable to ascribe its uses of history monolithically as serving Fascist culture and society. Taking film "on its own terms" implies a less programmatic sense of its uses of the past. As with the era's "white telephone" comedies, the historical film has been a victim of facile judgment. While the so-called white telephone films have been termed fascistic because they do not directly address contemporary events and the political exigencies of life under Fascism in critical fashion, these texts are nonetheless historical. Their uses of history are, in Robert A. Rosenstone's terms, dependent "less on data than upon what we might call vision, upon how we look and think about and remember and make meaningful what remains of people and events."[4] (6) The sense of history communicated through the cinema is fictive and eclectic: it is also affective, inflected by the structures of melodrama concerning the efficacy of action, questions of justice, and considerations of power.[5] To acknowledge its fictiveness and its affectivity is to invoke a sense of history as construct, further, to extend the ways in which it functions in more heterogeneous ways than is often acknowledged in the quest for an objective measure of the "truth" of the events enacted.

The cinema of the fascist years reveals not one but a range of models—monumental, antiquarian, and critical—for the uses of the past. The cinematic forms take the forms of the historical film proper, the costume drama, the adventure film, and the biopic. These forms are further altered depending on the filmmaker's predilections, the genre employed, the particular historical moment selected, and the point in time that the films are produced (whether early or late in the lifetime of the Fascist regime). In some instances, the films appear to be celebrating a glorious national past, portraying the past as a locus of spectacle, a site of visual pleasure. In other instances, the earlier world is a source of nostalgia, in others a place of fantasy, and in others, a judgment on the present. The common denominator resides in the ways affect is mobilized in the uses of narrative, image, and sound, focusing on the energetic and zealous efforts of exceptional individuals to direct events of the nation in the name of the people, the struggle to attain power, and the violence generated from these struggles. The drama of the imperiled nation, the clash between insider and outsider, loyal leader and traitor, and legitimacy and illegitimacy is central. In many ways, these films are not so different from the British Empire films or the Hollywood western. The signs of nationalist rhetoric, with its reliance on melodramatic conventions drawn from nineteenth-century literature and opera, are evident.

In writing on questions of Italian national-popular culture and its relation to the operatic, Gramsci writes,

> Verdi's music, or rather the libretti and plots of the plays set to music by Verdi are responsible for a whole range of artificial poses in the life of the people, for ways of thinking, for a "style." "Artificial" is perhaps not the right word because among popular classes this artificiality assumes naive and moving forms . . . a means of escaping what they consider low, mean, and contemptible in their lives and education.[6]

The relationship between opera and the cinema of the era can be seen in the productions of such films as *Giuseppe Verdi, Tosca, Carmen, La serva padrona,* and *Zazà.* However, the literal uses of opera are overshadowed by the operatic character of many of the melodramas of the late 1930s and early 1940s directed by Mario Soldati, Renato Castellani, Ferdinando Maria Poggioli, and Amleto Palermi, who derived many of their scenarios from nineteenth-century literary works. Giuseppe Adami, who wrote the libretto for Puccini's *Turandot,* was also responsible for the scenario of such films as *Ballerine.* Camerini had recourse to the literary text on which the opera *Il cappello a tre punte* was based, and Palermi's *Cavalleria rusticana,* while operatic in its style, was based on the literary text not on the libretto.

Connections between the novelistic, the operatic, and the melodramatic are traced and described by Gian-Paolo Biasin, who writes that if "we may follow a line that begins with Cuoco and Foscolo and passed through Manzoni and D'Azeglio," we can identify "the aesthetics of astonishment, moral manicheism, and the rhetoric of excess . . . brought to extreme consequences (logical if not artistic) as functions of the *école du coeur,* of civic education, and of the democratization of morality and its signs."[7] The style of these writers is marked by a straining toward sublimity, religiosity, and sensuality. In their writings, history and memory play a significant role in the fascination with folklore, with the ambiance of a past world and often with a pastoral world. As in romanticism, the landscape and especially the ruins of the past are objects of reflection and semiotic markers for the psychic state of the characters. According to Caroline Springer, the ruins function as part of an effort to interiorize the landscape, revealing its as an elegiac, nostalgic locus of aspirations and fears.[8]

The operatic character of the cinematic text with its fascination for spectacle drawn from the past can be identified in its uses of music and choreography, especially the choreography of groups, and its emphasis on heroic themes and a heroic treatment. Movement is juxtaposed to stasis, horizontality to verticality, and symmetrical arrangements against threatening randomness. In particular, the rhetorical quality of the monologues and dialogues function in a fashion akin to operatic arias. The use of music as song and as accompaniment functions as a major expressive mode. The music serves not merely to create a sense of the ambiance but carries the emotional valences of interactions between the characters. In the sense that Peter Brooks describes the "mute gesture" as the attempt to express the ineffable and inexpressible, music is the carrier of the characters' attempts to convey what words cannot encompass.[9] The emphasis on ritual is also prominent, conveyed most often through scenes in a church or its equivalent even if the film does not seek to convey Christian attitudes. Dance is also central, evident in the spectacle of balls, military formations, and festivals and serving as a means of choreographing group relations. Often, the protagonists and antagonists are set apart from the common people and their gestures are stylized and posturing.

The operatic style most emulated is Verdean with its emphasis on the motif of sacrificial leadership. The accent is on heroic service and self-abnegation. The melodrama functions in manichean terms, differentiating hero and villain. The landscape serves not merely as background but as analogue for and extension of the dramatic conflicts and oppositions, in particular. The forest, grotto, and caves, are the typical loci for the dramas of conversion, conveying the magical quality of the filmic world. Magic, like religion, provides an index to the supernatural character of the conflicts, the index to their spiritual character, identified with the overarching sense of the power of the protagonist's will and power. Linked to nationalistic themes, these operatic works situate the protagonist beyond individual and personal interests and identify his actions with the fate of the people in whose name the actions are undertaken. The trappings of national power, in the use of the effects of painting, tableaux, and statuary, are identified with the national culture and especially with its patriotic symbols. Moreover, the allusion to other arts suggests a form of continuity with what has proceeded in time and what is to be resurrected, as well as reflexively drawing attention to the artifice of the *mise-en-scène*.

Melodrama, as in opera, is closely tied to romantic, grandiloquent, patriotic, and nationalistic motifs and to a highly theatrical mode of performance. The cult of sentiment is inextricable, especially in the second half of the nineteenth century, from a more individualistic and subjectivist mode of representation. In the literary and dramatic texts upon which so many films depend, three authors are exemplary: Verga, Manzoni, and D'Annunzio. These sentiments can take the form of monumentality as in the works of D'Annunzio or move in a more domesticated vein as in Manzoni, whose focus is on the "common people" as opposed to the great and exceptional. *I promessi sposi* conforms to melodramatic expectations, particularly in the struggles of the two simple protagonists, Renzo and Lucia, to marry and lead pious lives in the face of threatening and malevolent forces—from unscrupulous to foreign oppressors—that would separate them. The intimidating nature of natural disasters and disease also poses a danger to their well-being and serves to define a world that is precarious. Gramsci asserts, however, that "the 'humble' people, are often presented as popular 'caricatures,' with good-natured irony, but irony nonetheless."[10]

According to Gramsci, Manzoni's Catholic "paternalism" produces "an attitude dictated by an external feeling of abstract duty decreed by Catholic morality but corrected and enlivened by a pervasive irony."[11] The irony to which Gramsci alludes is an inevitable concomitant of melodrama's reliance on a Manichean view of the world in which good and evil contend for dominance and in which the action is seen in terms of clear ethical dichotomies. This irony is not merely the consequence of the author's superior knowledge to or condescension toward the characters. Irony is inherent to melodramatism, where affect exceeds the Manichean conflict between good and evil, creating a sense of unease with the common sense of judgment, and with the constraints of litigious and moralist views of behavior. The presence of irony does not ensure that good sense emerges from this encounter with the possibility of an alternative, but it validates the connection that Gramsci makes between common sense and good sense, namely that common sense contains the seeds of critical thinking. The audience is buffeted between moral reductionism and the excessive character of affect produced by the excesses of theatricality, the emphasis on performance. This binarism also results in a schematic treatment that stresses typicality rather than individuality, a strategy that can be identified with caricature. In discussing the evolution of melodrama from the eighteenth century to the present, Thomas Elsaesser comments that the *"dramatis personae . . .* figure less as autonomous individuals than to transmit action and link the various locales within a total constellation."[12]

The novels and short stories of Giovanni Verga offer another instance of the porousness of the melodramatic imagination and its links to the operatic and to the past, particularly to Italian folklore. His works were to provide a fecund source for filmmakers of the Fascist era and beyond as exemplified by Palermi's *Cavalleria rusticana* and Visconti's *La terra trema.* Verga's use of regionalism is tied to the operatic quality of the treatment of the characters' conflicts. His fiction relies on his creations of Sicilian life, the consonance between the landscape and the characters, and his affinity for folklore drawn from the customs, habits, and history of the region. Millicent Marcus describes how "Verga's peasant Sicily offers the laboratory conditions most conducive to clinical observation of man's fate."[13] His naturalism is not, however, devoid of affectivity. In the stark milieu he portrays, the characters are driven by impulse and are bound stubbornly to an unyielding natural and social environment where there is no mitigation to their misery. What has been described as the tragic element in his work is, in effect, melodrama, providing the sense of fatality against which the characters struggle. In Verga's work, filmmakers found the repetition, parataxis, formulaic patterns, the use of proverbial wisdom, and the limitations and deceptions of verbal language so central to the melodramatic and operatic character of folklore.

The other major figure, altogether different in style and discourse from Verga, who exerted a major influence on cinematic uses of the past both in his literary and cinematic texts was Gabriele D'Annunzio. The preoccupation in his works with incest, fratricide, death, dionysian desire, and sensuality are conveyed in terms of hyperbole, rituals derived from antiquity, and a spectacle that valorizes image and sound as signs of the need to transcend the banality of verbal language.[14] Influenced by Nietzsche, he attacks the weak, the "loathsome morality of abjection" and seeks to resurrect " a decayed ideal of power and glory."[15] In his portrait of a world of supermales, his portraits of homoeroticism, there is fascination with sacrifice and death. His attraction to the past is fused with national and imperial designs, a monumental vision of glory through a destruction of the banality of the everyday. His works are not dissonant from earlier nineteenth-century romanticism, though expressed in the language of the modern avant-garde with its antibourgeois sentiments, its exaltation of modernity and the machinic, and its ambivalent relation to the past. The rhetorical and oratorical cast of his writings, the reliance on myth, the affective excess of the images situate his film work, his dramas, and his poetry in a melodramatic and operatic context.

The penchant for generic classification has obscured the overarching role of melodrama inherited from the nineteenth century but is in tension with the demands of modernity. Too often, melodrama has been confined to a single generic category rather than being seen as a dominant discursive and aesthetic mode of expression, contaminating even the movement toward realism as well as spectacular forms of production. In his study of the relations between theatrical, novelistic, and cinematic melodrama, A. Nicholas Vardac writes that "The most popular single expression of the combined romantic and realistic theatrical modes of the nineteenth century is to be found in melodrama."[16] And in the cinema this union can be seen in Italian spectacles such as *The Last Days of Pompei* and especially *Cabiria*, a film that D'Annunzio not only supervised but also wrote. The "screen spectacle," writes Vardac, "presented forces in conflict whose significance, by virtue of a clever editorial pattern, surpassed that of mere human beings."[17] This type of spectacle did not exhaust the tendency toward excessive forms of expression but was also evident in the films set in modern contexts that featured the diva, films that highlight romantic scenarios, more European than exclusively Italian, based on social and class differences, "fantastic adventures in which we see girls seduced, unmarried mothers abandoned, orphans restored to their parents, innocent men found guilty, spectacular acts of revenge, factories in flames, and crimes receiving their long-delayed punishment."[18] These motifs did not disappear but assumed new styles in the treatments of history in the sound cinema of the 1930s and early 1940s.

The biographical film in particular, the biopic, has played an integral role in the popular cinema in the rhetoric of nation-building and its plundering of the past. From the silent cinema to the present, the biopic has foregrounded the "life story" of the exceptional individual. In contrast to the historical film proper where the protagonists are part of the larger canvas of significant moments in the life of the nation, the biopic uses the portrait of an exceptional individual's life to isolate "a single life from the flow of history."[19] This "personalisation of history" involves the employment of conventions not unique to the cinema but derived from short stories, folk tales, novels (especially the nineteenth-century novel), and oral tradition. The techniques for narration can be first-person narration, narration by a figure involved in the protagonist's life, authorial and omniscient narration, either direct or masked through the portrayal of events. The uses of flashback are commonplace in literature and in cinema, and in the cinema the role of montage is created from diverse aspects of cultural lore and representation including paintings, opera, architecture, and national symbols. Melodrama is essential to the portrait of the protagonist's trials in his or her journey to fame and glory. The trials involve the numerous obstacles to be overcome in the attempts to vanquish the malevolent and deadly forces that threaten the society and his or her personal well-being. At stake is the protagonist's ability and endurance to accomplish the tasks that destiny or fate has preordained or that he or she has determined as just and right. These obstacles may be traced from the early years of life or telescoped onto the present, involving familial antagonism, antagonisms between opposing factions, competitors for the rewards of wealth, status, or recognition.

The values of the protagonist may be conceived as deviant and destructive initially from the perspective of the majority, though a few loyal comrades or loved ones may side with him or her. Parental figures and romantic attachments are instrumental in the uniting family with the nation. The problem of winning over the people is thus essential but tenuous. The protagonist may undergo a conversion from indifference to commitment, from self-preoccupation to altruism, though in many instances the issue of conversion resides in the community and its learning to accept, trust, and affirm the protagonist's moral position and actions. The character of the protagonist need not necessarily involve great physical strength, though in the adventure form of the biopic it is often the case that physical power is a requisite. Intelligence and wit are equally important if not overriding attributes. Romantic love is generally fused with the larger social goal and good, confirming the protagonist's largesse of soul, affirming the importance of heterosexual desire, underscoring its endangerment, and providing the necessary emotive dimension to the character. The dominant reservoir of melodrama is binarism, its quest for a clear demarcation between virtue and villainy, justice and injustice, loyalty and betrayal. Secrets, disguises, and dual identities are essential to the process of differentiating between these oppositions, providing the melodramatic affect that arises from the desire for unity, identity, and certainty that is constantly threatened.

In this chapter, I examine the different ways in which folklore animates historical representations: through monumentalism, the uses of biography, and the recourse to legend, fantasy, and adventure. Many of the films are reliant on the mythology of romantic nationalism, where desire is transposed from an individual, individuating, and heterosexual register onto the romance with the nation. Aestheticization is central to many of the texts through a foregrounding of the artist as protagonist and savior. Aestheticism also functions through the identification of characters with monuments, architecture, and works of art. History appears as theater not only through the emphasis on architecture, landscape, costumes, and artifacts but through the presence of melodramatic conflicts involving threats to national and individual survival, transgressions of the law, violence, and the fear of death. The melodrama undermines a monolithic reading of the films as escapist, polemic, and as simplistic affirmations of Fascist ideology and its assertion of a moral order. The affective treatment of events, the texts' addiction to spectacle, artifice, and affective excess points rather to conflictual and irresolvable elements within the narrative. Contrary to notions of escapism or to notions of resistance, I suggest that the texts' theatricalization of events serves a dual function: linking the text to contemporary politics as spectacle, and also, as with the comedies, sharing a cynical knowledge with their audiences of the strategies of political power. In short, the films are not predicated on a notion of escapism as pure flight, as ignorance or as mere accomodation to the status quo, but on a more complex sense of being uncomfortably implicated in power.

MONUMENTAL HISTORY

Monumentalism has its roots in nineteenth-century historicism, and Nietzsche in his *Untimely Meditations* has much to say about the theatricality, melodrama, and excessiveness of this type of historicizing. For him, monumental history is the

> masquerade costume in which . . . [the historians'] hatred of the great and powerful of their own age is disguised as satiated admiration for the great and powerful of past ages, and muffled in which they invert the real meaning of that mode of regarding history into its opposite. Whether they are aware of it or not, they act as though their motto were: let the dead bury the living.[20]

The key term from Nietzsche for an understanding of this type of historical creation is "masquerade." The portrait of the "great and powerful of past ages" has been a staple of the commercial cinema, exemplified particularly by the films that are set in classical times. This type of history, closely identified with the teens through the 1930s in Hollywood and in Europe, seeks parallels between different periods, identifying great moments in the past with the present, and also working to universalize the events. The major Italian sound spectacle of the 1930s was indebted to a classical subject involving the events of the Second Punic War, 297 B.C. Created in a vein reminiscent of the earlier historical epics, but modified to meet the demands of the sound cinema and the tenor of popular film of the 1930s, *Scipione l'Africano*, directed by Carmine Gallone, offers a cinematic spectacle to vie with the "epics" of D. W. Griffith and C. B. De Mille. The film deploys every aspect of melodramatic representation to provide a monumental and spectacular treatment of the past. In encyclopedic fashion, the film conjoins familial relations, homosocial bonding, unrequited and doomed passion, relations between the Roman populace and the military forces, and an imaginative recreation of the decisive battle between the two nations. The film draws on the conventions associated with the historical film: paintings, murals, costuming, architectural models, large casts, ritualistic ceremonies, and elaborate choreography of crowd scenes. Relying on orchestrated uses of long and medium shots and the frequent use of close-ups, the film conjoins perception to action and action to affect, thus providing the necessary connections between the subsets of the film and the whole film: "each of these movement-images is a point of view of the whole film, a way of grasping this whole, which becomes affective in the close-up, active in the medium shot, perceptive in the long-shot—each of these shots ceasing to be spatial in order to become itself a 'reading' of the whole film."[21]

The narrative focuses on differences between Romans and Carthaginians conveyed through the images in the Roman Senate, the Carthaginian camp, and in the battle scenes. But the action relies predominantly on the two protagonists—Scipio and Hannibal—who contend for power. The melodrama centers on the feminine figures, particularly Sofonisba (Francesca Braggiotti) and Velia (Isa Miranda). As is predictable in films focusing on past events, a title situates the time in which the filmic events will take place, alluding to the century-old rivalry between the two nations. The initial images are of a smoking field, then of the exterior of the Roman Senate with crowds gathered awaiting the arrival of Scipio (Annibale Ninchi). The spectacle of the masses is intercut with the arrival of Scipio. The editing stresses the singularity of Scipio through intercutting his image with that of the Roman people, connecting yet also separating him from others. The element of spectatorship is introduced through point-of-view shots, first in long-shot, then in close-up, providing a perspective on the scene through the individuals and groups in the massive gathering. Similarly in the scenes that follow in the Senate, shots alternate between the gathered senators and the individual speakers as a debate ensues over the feasibility of Scipio's undertaking a campaign against Hannibal in Carthage. Similarly, spectatorship is highlighted through the intercutting of the groups within the Senate and those without, serving to underscore the unanimity of sentiment between insiders and outsiders. The episode culminates with the appearance of the victorious Scipio, who is tracked by the camera as he emerges from the building and walks through the parted masses. The choreography of his movement in relation to the thousands of people is accompanied by singing and loud orchestral music.

In contrast to the public spectacle that opens the film, the scene shifts to the home of Scipio and to his wife as she gathers her jewelry to contribute it to the Roman cause. A contrast is set up between the madonna-like image of the woman with her baby and the image of Scipio in his uniform of a Roman warrior with his boy child also in uniform, a miniature version of the father. The images of domestic harmony are shattered in the following scene as a Roman woman, Velia, is taken captive by the Carthaginians with her child, thus introducing the melodra-

FIGURE 7. A domestic tableau in *Scipione l'Africano*. Courtesy of New York Museum of Modern Art, Film Stills Archive.

matic element of the defenselessness of women in the face of war, particularly as is revealed the danger of their sexual exploitation at the hands of the enemy. Hannibal, seeing her, desires her as his concubine, but she refuses to succumb to him and is ultimately saved by Scipio and Velia's husband, Arunte, who also had been a prisoner of Hannibal. The film is built on escalating parallels and contrasts. Velia is contrasted to the seductive and tigress-like Sofonisba, Hannibal to Scipio, the Carthaginian senators and masses to the Roman senators and masses, and the alternating views of each of the armies. The contrasting montage visually stresses the thematic of order and disorder, discipline and rebellion, duty and desire.

The affective, visually excessive, and, hence, highly theatrical character of the narrative resides particularly in the figure of Sofonisba as a Cleopatra and Dido-like figure, a throwback to the femme fatale of the Italian silent cinema (e.g., *Cabiria*, 1914) whose power is so great that she can cause men like Massinissa (Fosco Giachetti) to forsake their principles. Her sensuality is conveyed through costuming, make up, languid and affected gesture, exotic *mise-en-scène*, and an identification with fire. She is also filmed frequently in close-up, especially for the scenes of her suicide. In a nocturnal sequence, an image of the restless queen on her bed is superimposed with an image of her being dragged through the flames. An image of Carthage burning foreshadows not only her end but the end of her reign. After the defeat of Carthage, she commits suicide in a highly operatic scene. Beginning and ending with a wipe, the camera focuses on a cup of poison, with a hand and its tapered nails wrapped around the chalice. Then the camera captures her face in close-up as she expresses her desire as queen to die for Carthage. She drinks, and intense music accompanies her gestures. The death scene is significant for the ways in which femininity is identified with fragmentation and dissolution. Once again, spectatorship is stressed as an old man comes in, witnesses her dying, covers his face, and exits.

The film appears to recapitulate motifs aligned to contemporary events: in the exaltation of the wise and powerful leader, the emphasis on preparation for war (in Africa), and the highlighting of the importance of agricultural production as well as the production of armaments to support the war effort. This meeting of past and present is consistent with the conventions of the historical film and is, in the case of *Scipione*, a sign of its eclecticism and its ambivalent relation of past to present that characterizes the cinema of the era's uses of the past. Aside from the affective power of the images of violence, suffering, and death conjured through the scenes of battle, the rhetorical uses of women and children are not merely further devices for enlisting sympathy in the face of the blood-thirsty and arbitrary Carthaginians but are closely tied to the preoccupation with style and performance. The film, while tied to the cinema of the silent era, adds new, self-reflexive, elements in its visual acknowledgment of the importance of style, design, posture, and observation. History becomes a stage. The role of composition and choreography, the emphasis on *mise-en-scène* points to the uses of the people as objects, machines, and geometric patterns. The spectator is bombarded with affects and actions, invited self-reflexively to entertain the spectacle. Gesture and physical movement become a form of seduction, an invitation to enjoy historical pleasures, aided by the music that overwhelms the dialogue, geared toward enhancing sentiment and evoking admiration for the vastness and virtuosity of the cinematic canvas.

Hay suggests that "the feature that distinguishes Scipione from many of his counterparts in silent movies and that aligns him with a more petit-bourgeois ideology is his dual role as family man and as a statesman/warrior."[22] Scipio's return to the land and to his family naturalizes the preceding violence. And, yet, reading the film from the vantage point of the film's excess that surrounds the figure of woman, especially in relation to Sofonisba and her association with the all-consuming fire, these final domestic images invite speculation on the reception of such a film. Can this final image of order and domesticity be reconciled with the operatic (and familiar) spectacle of Sofonisba's disruptive femininity, also identified with nature? What is not so straightforward are the conditions of the film's reception, posing the nagging question of whether its uses of genre, its spectacular uses of image and sound, revealed or occluded its nationalistic ideology or even whether this aspect of the film was a primary feature of its reception. While well received by critics, winning the coveted Venice Cup, and while a reading of the film in terms of its patriotic and nationalist images might confirm its consonance with Fascist ideology and its celebration of the regime, the film invites a more multivalent assessment. As is characteristic of popular cinema, the film's uses of the past are heterogeneous, even fragmented rather than totalizing. The style—its spectacle associated with its stars, its choreography of crowd scenes, its preoccupation with spectatorship, theatricality, and intertextuality—suggest a looser and more eclectic relation to audiences. The style speaks to the use of history as a realm of fantasy in ways described by Sue Harper that "grants a freedom to the audience to maneuver its own way through narrative codes."[23]

MELODRAMA AND LEGEND

Legend and folklore have served as major supports for historical narration in cinema: as a way of confronting interdiction through indirection, as moral parable, as a means of bypassing censorship, and as an exercise in a cinematic style that can convey affect. The cinematic image invokes admiration, wonder, despair, and terror specifically in its uses of the face, the body, and magical objects, "tear[ing] the image away from spatio-temporal coordinates."[24] Of the films that treat medieval subjects (twenty-two in all) and particularly legend, *La corona di ferro* (1941) is exemplary for its linguistic, figurative, and fantastic "experimentation in style."[25] The film's uses of verbal and visual language have been commented upon, while its folklorist and particularly its operatic treatment of the past has received less attention. Set in the thirteenth century, the film draws on motifs from fairy tale and legend: the good and bad father-kings, the sleeping beauty awakened by her prince, the Arthurian legend of the sword in the stone, the noble young man who lives among the animals and is initiated through trials into civilized society, terrifying giants of superhuman strength, the threat of incest through misrecognition, contending suitors for the hand of a princess, and the salvation of an ailing kingdom. The lavish spectacle relies on ornate costuming, a lavish *mise-en-scène* for the court and for the outdoor shots. While seeking to create the aura of an earlier age, the film does not primarily convey a sense of an actual time and place, so much as the requisite sense of "once upon a time."

After a title that announces the time and place of the events, the narrative plunges into a scene of war and violence with the wounding and then death of King Licinio and the usurpation of his crown by his brother Sedemondo (Gino Cervi). Sedemondo is confronted by a messenger from the Pope, bearing the iron crown, asking permission to pass through the land. According to legend, the crown remains wherever injustice and corruption prevail. Seeking to rid himself of the crown, Sedemondo takes it to the gorge of Natursa and it sinks into the earth. He orders a slave to remain and kill others who seek to enter. Sedemondo is further challenged by the prophecy of an old wise woman (Rina Morelli) in the forest who predicts that Sedemondo's wife will bear him a girl child, while Licinio's wife will give birth to a boy child. She also prophesies that, when grown, the two will fall in love with tragic consequences, and that the young man will ultimately wrest the kingdom from him. Sedemondo returns home and receives the news that his wife has given birth to a son, since the babies have been switched to protect the boy, Arminio. Believing that the prophesy was erroneous, Sedemondo declares that the girl child be raised as his own, a sister to the male child. Soon signs of strife between Arminio and Sedemondo become apparent as the child rebels against Sedemondo's cruelty, and the boy, on Sedemondo's orders, is taken to the gorge by a slave to be killed. Twenty years pass. Elsa (Elisa Cegani) lives imprisoned in the castle, and Arminio (Massimo Girotti) has grown up in the wild, a companion to lions. A tournament that has been announced by Sedemondo to find a worthy prince for Elsa becomes the event that will lure Arminio back to the kingdom of Kindaor through the magical agency of a stag who beckons him to follow.

A cross between Tarzan and Robin Hood, Arminio makes his way out of the forest, saving a group of abused slaves along the way. Here he comes across a woman dressed in man's clothes who frees the stag that has been directing Arminio. More adventures befall him as he allies himself with Tundra (Luisa Ferida), whose identity and gender initially are a mystery. Only when the two protagonists get into combat with each other does he discover that Tundra is a woman and also that she is a leader of the people enslaved by Sedemondo. She urges him to assume the role of champion of her oppressed people at the tournament. At Kindaor, Elsa, like the proverbial princess of folklore, imprisoned in a tower, is shown languishing in her quarters. The proverbial ceremonial scene follows in which the king greets the various suitors and receives their gifts. Arminio enters the city as Elsa is lavishly clothed for her first appearance in public. However, she complicates the scenario by exchanging clothes with a waiting woman and exits the palace, whereupon she meets Arminio, though she keeps her identity secret.

The tournament is choreographed in spectacular fashion, with processions, banners, drummers, and patterned formations, stressing ritual encounters, recalling the style of Blasetti's earlier *Palio* (1932). The leading contender for Elsa's hand is Arriberto, a Tartar prince, who overcomes the other suitors. Sedemondo, not without affection for his daughter and responsive to her antipathy to the suitors, offers land and riches in exhange for Elsa's hand. The Tartar, threatens violence if he does not get his due, but Tundra arrives in the nick of time to aid Arminio in defeating the villain. Arminio is then greeted as the champion, and announces that, rather than assuming his rights as victor, he respects her right to choose. Tundra, unhappy over the possibility of a union between Elsa and

FIGURE 8. Elisa Cegani as the legendary princess in *La corona di ferro*. Courtesy of New York Museum of Modern Art, Film Stills Archive.

Arminio, refuses to be friendly with Elsa despite Elsa's friendly gestures toward her. Later Elsa and Arminio meet in a palace grove, while an angry Tundra eavesdrops. At a bacchanalian feast, Sedemondo reveals that he does not intend to keep his promise of sharing the kingdom with Tundra, while Elsa struggles with her jealousy of Tundra. She attempts to turn Arminio against Tundra, but again fate intervenes as Erminio discovers a scar similar to his own that had been inflicted on them by Sedemondo as children. Now the threat of incest emerges, since the lovers believe that they are brother and sister. Distraught, Elsa rushes to the gorge at Natersa and is fatally wounded by Sedemondo's slave. Before she dies, she learns that she is not Arminio's sister. A battle between Sedemondo's men and the enslaved followers of Licinio threatens but the gorge divides them. The iron crown appears, and peace is restored.

In the conventions and motifs of the adventure film that specializes in heroic feats, the emphasis is on the salvation of the family, the restoration of the benevolent paternal figure, and the importance of establishing legitimacy and continuity. In the contrasts between the claustrophobia of the kingdom with its ornate but imprisoning gates and the vastness and openness of the natural setting, the film visualizes the conflict between oppression and resistance, between paralysis and action. The imagery foregrounds the tension between unity and disorder, stasis and movement, and the individual and the masses. Folklore, melodrama, and spectacle meet in the ways the narrative relies on the visualization of binaries: Sedemondo and Licinio, Erminio and Sedemondo, Tundra and Elsa. Scenes of war, combat, and aggression punctuate the film, culminating in the death of Elsa, the innocent victim of Sedemondo's illegitimate usurpation of the throne. In this threatening world, the woman becomes the martyr and the instrument of reconciliation.

The prophetic role of the old woman in contrast to the willfull actions of Sedemondo shifts the focus from suspense to irony. From the outset, there is no question but that her predictions will be realized. The irony lies in the highlighting of the motif of vision. The audience knows from the outset of the film what Sedemondo refuses to see: that the woman's predictions will be realized. The use of spectacle highlights the destructive consequences of the refusal to see. The film underscores the problematic of representation: in the contrasts between the spectacle of royal opulence and the rugged and wild natural setting, in the frequent recourse to the imagery of veiling and exposure, in Arminio's misperception of Tundra as a man, and, above all, in Sedemondo's efforts to conceal and obliterate any evidence of his illegitimate actions. Thus, while the spectacle serves to enhance the filmmaker's ingenuity in creating a make-believe world, it is also presents a dual relationship to the act of seeing. Through the spectacle, it underlines the motif of vision in relation to knowledge and power, but it also ties that motif, if only indirectly, to the power of the cinematic image to conceal but also to expose.

La corona won the Mussolini Cup at Venice in 1941 for the best Italian film,[26] but the film was not without its critics. Goebbels excoriated the film for having a pacifist perspective. Given the outbreak of war, the steadily declining fortunes of the regime, the role of Sedemondo as having usurped rightful authority and as enslaving the people could be seen as subverting Fascist ideology and so it has been read. The adventure format, however, tends to operate on a most conventional level as an "escapist" entertainment film, and can thus be read innocuously. In Brian Taves terms, "History is reduced to mutually opposing personalities, away from complex, ambiguous socioeconomic forces and political systems, substituting such dramatically appealing motivations as a tyrannical despot's desire for riches and power."[27] Thus, audiences can appreciate the film's theatricality and spectacle, while the "historical" and "political" dimensions can be read or ignored, assimilated or rejected. This is not to suggest that the politics of the films is irrelevant but rather to complicate the ways in which contemporary politics must be seen in less programmatic and more affective and dispersed terms. This costume drama with its folkloric characteristics—its stylization, binary structure, formulaic treatment, and emphasis on magic—more than Blasetti's historical films (e.g., 1860) bears comparison with Hollywood formulas for mythologizing history. The nature of the reception of such a film thus becomes more problematic than the designation of innocuous escapism at one extreme or simple moral platitude on the other. Its adoption of a genre mode with its penchant for fantasy does not preclude its being read, if only by some, as a critique of the present through the uses of the past.

AESTHETICS AND FOLKLORE

Although Louis Trenker's Condottieri (1937), a German-Italian production, is constructed along the monumental lines of such films as Scipione l'Africano, it evokes a different atmosphere and ideological context. Trenker was fascinated with myths of the American West as well as with the sublime landscape of the Alps. A Tyrolean with Italian citizenship, Trenker was imbued with nationalist aspirations. His films, akin to the mountain films that starred Leni Riefenstahl, placed great emphasis on "pioneering odysseys (of the 'mountain' variety), in which *rites de passage* were used to symbolise the hero's strength of purpose."[28] The style of his films is inspired by a form of "agrarian mysticism" and "the combination of epic grandeur with highly sentimental 'domestic' scenes." [29] His fascination with rebels, his penchant for portraying sacrificial leadership, his vision of a world of necessary revolutionary struggle, and his reliance on mythology are equally evident in his *Der Kaiser von Kalifornien* (1936) based on the lore surrounding Thomas Sutter and his quest for gold. *Condottieri*, based on the Renaissance figure, Giovanni de' Medici, dramatizes his struggles with his "bande nere" to attain political power. *Condottieri's* uses of history and mythology are noteworthy because of the ways in which the film uses landscape, statuary, and conjoins German and Italian national mythology. The film was shot both at Cines in Rome and at Tobis studios in Berlin, but the cast was predominantly Italian. Trenker himself stars in this film as he did in his film on the American West.

The film celebrates the leader, the adherence of the masses to his authority, and national destiny, but Trenker's film also inscribes racism, a rare element in the Italian films of the period. The presentation of character and situation is monumental, not dynamic. Historical events are portrayed as on a large painting or tapestry. The viewer's position can be likened to that of an observer at a church service, and the film depends heavily on a merging of Christian and Germanic myth to present its allegorizing of the historical events. The film opens with monumental images of military men, flags, and a background of clouds. A title announces that the film was made with the assistance of the Armed Forces, "This film is a re-creation of the times of the Italian adventurers who, in the spirited context of the Renaissance, for the first time led the civil militia of the people that rose against the mercenaries with the common purpose of unifying the Italian people." A statue of a horseman appears set against a sky of clouds. In the midst of the raging battle, two children are brought to a chapel, one of whom is Giovanni de' Medici and the other a young girl, Maria, who will later be his wife. In this battle Giovanni's father is killed. The boy is taken into exile but a title announces that "he will return from exile when he had made a name for himself." He is now shown as the man on horseback, looking like the statue in the earlier sequence.

The music is Wagnerian, contributing to an aura of spirituality and transcendence. In the background, mountains and clouds are visible, serving here and throughout the film to reinforce the mystical qualities associated with the characters and their actions. Giovanni rides to the fortress on the hill where Malatesta (Loris Gizzi) has control, makes his way to the camp, and joins the men. After a "trial" in which he establishes his credentials, the young man is invited to join Malatesta's band. The men plan to go to Florence to rid the state of its French element. In a series of victories Giovanni consolidates his reputation. He also meets again with Maria (Carla Sveva), and he tells her he will return to claim her. Giovanni and his men march to Florence, singing patriotic songs. The film stresses his affinity with the common people, though the aristocracy is suspicious of him. The Florentine nobles call him mad and accuse him of being a visionary. Defiant, Giovanni gathers his men and asks them to swear an oath of fidelity, to serve their leader and the cause of unity to the last drop of their blood. But Giovanni is tried by the council in Florence and declared a traitor. He is placed on the rack, but saved by his men who spirit him away. As he escapes, a proclamation is read declaring his excommunication. His second exile is spent in the mountains, where he again sees Maria and proposes marriage to her against a background of sky and mountains. Maria is blonde and light-skinned, an ideal image of German, not Italian, culture of the period. Like the natural context with which she is associated, she is presented as the opposite of Tullia della Grazie (Laura Nucci), the dark-haired courtesan at Malatesta's court, who is enamored of Giovanni but whom he rejects. According to Hay, Giovanni's "eventual preference for the more pure ideal of women occurs, as he realizes where his political allegiances lie. Italy must be identified in his and his follower's minds with an ideal, something to be protected; and, in order to realize this ideal, he must reject the image of Italy as courtesan—one who, while alluring as a result of her outward trappings, has been defiled by foreigners."[30]

Maria and Giovanni return secretly to France, where they now confront Malatesta, whom he fights and overcomes. After his victory another scene of processions, flags, statues, and gathering masses is shown as the crowds shout, "To Rome," thus suggesting a parallel with the Fascist march to Rome. In Rome, the Pope blesses Giovanni and, following this scene of reconciliation, Giovanni and Maria are married in a service that seems more military than religious in spite of its taking place in the church. Giovanni and Maria return to the country and to a pastoral setting of flowers, rippling wheat fields, and domestic serenity. The dramatic cloud-filled sky is always evident in the background. The pastoral idyll is broken, however, by renewed political conflict announced by the now-familiar image of the statue of the man on horseback and images of marching men with banners and weapons. Giovanni leaves Maria with the vow to return again when the battle is over, joining the enthusiastic throngs on their way to fight. On the battlefield, Giovanni is fatally wounded. The enemy is routed and the dead Giovanni is carried into his tent and laid out with his sword at his side. The music is elegiac. The final image of the film is of Giovanni's sculpted figure on his tomb in the cathedral. The organ music and the image of the tomb reinforces the film's religious aura.

In his study of the Nazi cinema, Julian Petley identifies the components of *Condottieri's* ideology, stressing particularly the film's presentation of Giovanni as "the 'born' charismatic leader . . . a 'man of the people'" who is also "represented as a quasi-mystical, superhuman figure." [31] The mystical dimension is represented in the "recurrent apotheosized 'ascension' scenes in the mountains." According to Petley, Giovanni, "metamorphoses from an ordinary child into an heroic figure in imagery reminiscent of *Die Nibelungen.*" A religious element is also apparent in parallels between Giovanni and Christ: in his trials, temptations, and sacrifice. Giovanni is also portrayed as a peacemaker in contrast to the nobles of Florence and the adventurers who seek to undermine him. The inclusion of the scenes of reconciliation with the Pope suggest a specific reference to Mussolini's role in creating the Lateran Concordat in 1929. Although Petley correctly identifies the film's insistence on the mystical power of the leader and the strange fusion of populism and authoritarianism, he underestimates the importance of the way the film looks, and the possible ways it can work on the spectator. The Wagnerian elements to which he refers and which others have noted are indeed apparent in the music,[32] the uses of myth, and the emphasis on heroic combat, but an important ingredient of Wagnerian dramaturgy is missing. The film does not contain the dynamic movement so central to Wagnerian art. The scenes of combat seem to arrest action rather than advance it, and the presentation of character is as immobile as the statuary to which it is likened.

The film's aestheticism exposes itself in the final scene where the figure of Giovanni on horseback is transformed from a moving image into a still statue. This blatant effect at aestheticization reflects back on earlier images of Giovanni in the film, where he also appears as more mythological than human, icon rather than man, godlike rather than human. The film both seeks to celebrate his superhuman qualities and at the same time reveals the insubstantiality and fictional character of the figure, lending him the aura of a work of art. The human figure has been metamorphosed and fixed in stone. The freezing of the figure and actions can be read back into the narrative as an ultimate image of control that immobilizes everything around it. It can also be read as a sign of the film's exposure of the fictional and aestheticizing strategies that are endemic to monumental history.

Moreover, the emphasis on nature in the film, the countryside, the identification of Maria with animals and fertility, which seem intended to create an aura of innocence and to overcome any opposition between nature and culture, is also undermined by the images of statuary that are based on the transformation of living things into dead objects. The blatant ruralism to which the film appeals is also undercut in this fashion. Petley has noted that Fascism made "an especial bid for the attention of the rural classes, particularly the rural proletariat to which fascism presented a demagogic face . . . making false promises of 'colonisation' and land distribution. But there was more to it: fascism thoroughly exploited both the particular forms assumed by petty bourgeois rebel ideology in the countryside, and the ideological theme of the solidarity and community of the soil. . . . Like the emphasis on ties of blood and ties of the soil, on personal loyalty . . . this aspect linked up with the survival of feudal ideology in 'rural fascism.'"[33]

These contradictions are apparent in the film's imagery but also in its designs on the spectator, drawing on rituals conducive to an attitude of awe and worship. The film's allegorical project of linking Giovanni and Mussolini is developed beyond the relations between church and state to include a history of Italian Fascism: the identification of Giovanni's men with the Black Shirts, the emphasis on the rituals of oath-taking, the battles for power, and the march on Rome. The film, which fuses the history of Fascism and Nazism, is an encomium to the German leader as well as the Italian. Giovanni's struggles can also be read in relation to Hitler's rise to power: his conflicts with authorities, his reliance on the bands of Brown Shirts, his arrest, and his wooing of rural elements. Thus, the motif of nationalism is transformed and underscored like everything else in the film. Unlike the other historical films that celebrate nationalism, *Condottieri* seems most drawn to the public spectacle of Fascism and its glorification of violence and death. Signficantly, the romantic elements in many of the other historical films serve to create a form of spectacle that appears to eroticize heroic action, but this film throughout desexualizes the relationship between the man and woman, and especially the role of the protagonist, through their transubstantiation in religion and art. The film's aestheticization of history reveals, like many of the Italian historical films of the 1930s, a "capacity to displace current ideological conflict to a mythical setting, and, in turn, to reduce History to a diegetic world where the present suddenly becomes charged with value."[34] The images and symbols in the films reach deep into cultural mythology, tapping the elementary roots of kinship, the sanctity of the family and of the land, and sacrificial rituals that regenerate the culture and insure its continuity.[35]

In discussing Nazism and war, Walter Benjamin wrote that the language of war appears mystical, contributing to generally augmenting or impoverishing social life. In either case, the imagery and symbolism of war are crucial to sustaining the folklore of war.[36] Mystical images and symbols mask the commonplace reality that war is sustained in fact by the captains of finance and professional soldiers. In a strongly polemic passage, Benjamin attempts to describe this mysticism that "crawls forth on its thousand unsightly conceptual feet. The war that this light exposes is as little the 'eternal' one which Germans now worship as it is the 'final' war that the pacifists carry on about. In reality that war is only this: The one, fearful, last chance to correct the incapacity of peoples to order their relationships to one another in accord with the relationships they possess to nature through their technology."[37] Benjamin's discussion of the mystico-religious symbolism of war reiterates his famous dictum that fascism aestheticizes politics, whereby history loses its specificity and becomes myth. In *Condottieri*, the verbal and visual language is inflated and Manichean, and the events, characters, and conflicts portrayed assume an aura of determinism. The analogies presented between past and present serve to create the sense that repetition is inevitable, necessary, even desirable.[38] But while the film appears as hermetically sealed, in its Wagnerian excess, its stylization, and its theatricality, it further validates Nietzsche's notion of monumental history as masquerade.[39]

ROMANTIC NATIONALISM

More subdued and literary in its treatment of history, the 1938 *Ettore Fieramosca* directed by Blasetti is set in the sixteenth century and relies on

a specific novelistic text by Massimo D'Azeglio. Though set in the Renaissance past, the novel had contemporary designs on its readers. Gian-Paolo
Biasin claims that this popular historical novel "sparked the flame of
Romantic nationalism that then blazed in Verdi's operas."[40] The novel
operates in the vein of melodrama with its familiar "moral
manicheanism"—friend and foe, foreigner and Italian, hero and traitor—
and is replete with its share of intrigues and antagonisms as well as
romance. D'Azeglio's work was inspired by the historical novels of Sir
Walter Scott. In adopting this novel as a model for his film, Blasetti drew
on a rich vein of cultural production, one that was generative of action
and spectacle, and one that relied on the language of patriotism and
nation. Having a long tradition in British and European culture of the
nineteenth century, the conjunction of romance and nationalism is not
unique to the historical film. That the historical novel became wedded to
the cinema is a familiar sign of the reliance of popular cinema on the
other arts, including painting and theater. One of the major characteristics of the historical novel is its reliance on biography, on the exceptional
individual around whom the action revolves and who is the repository of
the political hopes of the people.

Like *Condottieri* and *Scipione*, *Fieramosca* is a biographical film, a
biopic that focuses on the actions of the protagonist as political savior. In
examining the uses of history in Italian cinema of the Fascist years, Gianfranco Mino Gori claims that the biopic tends to be most often aligned
to Fascist ideology.[41] Gori links these films under the rubric of texts that
emphasize the charisma of the leader. However, Gori's classification once
again reveals the limitations of genre analysis as well as of the reductionism in assuming a transparent and monolithic relationship between a film
text and its social milieu. The films have to be more carefully examined
to identify difference in ostensible sameness, if only to understand the
dynamic nature of the film's uses of the historical image, the bases of its
appeal, and its viability as cultural commodity.

In *Fieramosca*, the dominant motif involves occupation of Italian
soil by foreigners. The action centers on the need to expel these usurpers.
The melodrama entails the motif of national honor and its besmirching
by both the foreigners (the French) as well as by treacherous Italians, and
the importance of an heroic savior who through physical power, mental
agility, and devotion to the nation sets matters aright. The endangered
country is linked to the fate of the endangered Giovanna di Monreale
(Elisa Cegani), who weds the exploitative Graiano d'Asti (Mario Ferrari)

rather than Fieramosca (Gino Cervi), who is completely devoted to her. Visually, the film sets up contrasts between town and country, the country associated with Italians, the city with French and Spanish foreigners. After a series of intrigues and combats, choreographed by the film in a fashion reminiscent of the painting of D'Azeglio, Fieramosca and his followers are victorious. He is also finally united with Giovanna, all obstacles to their love having been removed.

As played by Cervi, Fieramosca is the romantic adventurer, youthful, single-minded, and true to the code of the adventurer. His actions are portayed as involving the conventional codes of honor, including chivalry, patriotism, and faith. According to Brian Taves, "In the populist view of the genre, the inherent traits of the adventurer—following the standards of the code—provide the moral compass. Goals are achieved through a hero who embodies the beliefs of the code, personal and political events becoming intertwined and inseparable."[42] Giovanna is portrayed as chaste and nunlike, akin to the lady of courtly love, and Fieramosca, in the position of the courtly wooer, is doomed for a while to worship her from afar. There is a parallel between the obstacles in his way to achieving her hand and the obstacles in the way to freeing the country. She is the motivation and the reward for his heroism.

The film's uses of history are thus shaped, as was the novel, in imaginative and folkloric fashion without regard for fidelity to factual events but with fidelity to its melodramatic concerns with power.[43] If the film can be compared, as Gori has done, to *Condottieri* and *Scipione*, the comparison resides in the films' invocation of melodramatic excess surrounding the constant obstruction of the protagonist's objectives, the tribulations of Giovanna, and the obstacles in the way to their desire for unity. Equally important are the ways in which the film draws on the combined artifice of other forms of artistic expression, involving music, paintings, and statuary. The emphasis on the youthfulness of the protagonists, the typology of the characters that marks them as good or bad, the sense of a landscape that belongs to a past is portrayed with almost religious zeal, problematizing the strict consonance between the film and Fascist ideology. The film calls attention to the complex character of folklore, not to its easy accessibility.

The romance element in its fusion of Fieramosca's love for Giovanna to the love of nation situates the text more broadly in the tradition of nationalist representation where the woman is derealized, abstracted as a symbol for national unity. In his discussion of the nation form as an imag-

FIGURE 9. Gino Cervi in *Ettore Fieramosca*. Courtesy of New York Museum of Modern Art, Film Stills Archive.

inary community, Etienne Balibar writes that "*every social community reproduced by the functioning of institutions is imaginary,* that is to say, it is based on the projection of individual existence into the weft of a collective narrative, on the recognition of a common name and on traditions lived as the trace of an immemorial past (even when they have been fabricated and inculcated in the recent past)."[44] In Fieramosca, the conflicts around the motif of national unity are concentrated in the figure of the Lady. Giovanna is an illusion, a retrospective hallucination, for the nation. Like the film, she is the fiction that enables unity, the spectral form that is recoded to enable the collective narrative.

THE BIOPIC, MACHIAVELLI, AND REALPOLITIK

The cinema's uses of the past cannot be reduced to simple formulas; as can be seen in the various forms described above, the films are amenable to assuming different political and aesthetic directions. Moreover, like many of the comedies, the historical film is theatrical and in its theatricality often reflexive about its role as spectacle, entertainment, and even as polemic. Guido Brignone's *Lorenzino de' Medici* (1935) is set in the Renaissance, in the early part of the sixteenth century, and the period is portrayed as a time of political intrigue, luxury, wanton and excessive cruelty. Like *Condottieri*, the narrative relies on material drawn from official history, literature, and especially philosophy and art. Beginning in the studio of Benvenuto Cellini, who serves the reigning prince by creating art works for him, *the mise-en-scène* creates an aura of the splendor of Renaissance art and architecture. By contrast to the visually opulent milieu portrayed, the viewer is introduced to scenes of intrigue, of men spying and the anticipation of violence. The romantic element is introduced through the character of Bianca Strozzi (Germana Paolieri), who is seen to emerge from a cathedral accompanied by another woman. The camera tracks her from the perspective of a man observing her movements. That man is Lorenzino (Alessandro Moissi). When the two meet, we learn that her father, Paolo Strozzi, is in danger from Duke Alessandro (Camillo Piloto), since Strozzi is identified with a political faction opposed to the duke. Leaving Bianca, Lorenzino goes to the palace library where he reads until interrupted by the duke. Lorenzino is introduced as an intellectual, identified with books and particularly with philosophy in contrast to the duke, who is devoted to a life of sensual pursuits and power. As Lorenzino assists the duke in dressing, the scene shifts to a man who is being tortured in order to extract information from him about Strozzi's activities. The man finally reveals Strozzi's plans, which will give the duke license to eradicate the conspirators. While appearing to be an ally of the unscrupulous duke, Lorenzino is, in effect, developing a counterplot to save Strozzi.

The duke's cruelty is not restricted to his political opponents. His sensuality involves his attempts to overpower young women to feed his voracious sexual appetite. Nella (Maria Denis), another potential victim, is tied up before her mother's eyes and carried off by the duke's men on his orders. A lavish feast with abundant food and entertainment, hosted by Alessandro, follows, attended by ornately dressed courtiers. The feast is interrupted by Nella, dragged in for Alessandro's delectation. When her lover who is among the company sees her, he becomes enraged at the duke and others seek vainly to restrain him. However, Lorenzino intervenes to save the man's life, and the young man escapes. Lorenzino meets Bianca, who is distraught over her father's situation, and he advises her not to ask questions but to be patient for the momen. Following his encounter with her, he meets with the conspirators among whom is Strozzi, and counsels them that open rebellion would be impossible at the present time; no insurrection would be successful.

As if to reinforce and intensify the power and unscrupulousness of Alessandro, a subsequent scene portrays a bound man accused of conspiracy and brought before the executioner. The man is promised that if he reveals the names of his fellow conspirators he will be set free. He confesses only to be executed. Strozzi's arrest quickly follows, effected with the aid of Francesco Giucciardini, who does not trust Lorenzino. Strozzi is brought before the duke. Proud and defiant, he refuses to be intimidated by the duke. Bianca begins to lose confidence in Lorenzino's ability to save her father. Undaunted by others' suspicions of his behavior, Lorenzino continues to curry favor with the duke, biding his time. But further clues to his character are offered in a following scene. Alone, as in an earlier scene reading a book, the camera focuses on Machiavelli's *The Prince*, glides from the book to Lorenzino, and then back to the book. The passage he is reading is a familiar one, involving the idea that it is in the interests of the people to bring on cruelty all at once. The image of the text dissolves to his dagger being laid on the book, thus prefiguring his determination to act against the duke. He, in turn, reassures her that he is on her side and that he has a plan in mind that will succeed.

Lorenzino now sets his plan against the duke in action. He offers Bianca as bait to the dissolute duke for his pleasure that evening during a festival. Outside the palace, groups of people are seen singing and marching with torches. Inside the palace, Lorenzino, having gained Bianca's consent to his plan to use her as a decoy, whets the duke's appetite for the sexual encounter. The duke, eager to consummate his desire for Bianca, agrees to the condition that Lorenzino sets before him: he must sign a release for her father. Lorenzino dictates as Alessandro writes, and then he leads the duke to the prepared bed, excusing himself on the pretext that he must get Bianca. The sound of the crowd's revelry muffles the dying sounds emitted by the duke. Lorenzino then goes to Bianca to inform her that the deed is accomplished. The scene dissolves to a celebration. Flags bearing the *fleur de lys* wave as a man comes out on the balcony and notifies the people of the duke's death. The final scenes take place in Venice, where shots of St. Mark's, and then of a gondola with Bianca and Lorenzino, dissolve to images of the water and then of the sky.

The film is, in the spirit of the quotation drawn from Machiavelli, a parable of realpolitik with its reliance on common sense. A dissolute, self-preoccupied, and sensual tyrant unconcerned for his people, reigning by intimidation and violence, the duke is eliminated not by an idealist but by a man of practical politics. He is contrasted to Strozzi and the other conspirators who desire open confrontation and rebellion. Lorenzino's strength resides therefore in his ability to plan effective strategies and tactics. An incarnation of Machiavelli's prince, he is not a martyr but an opportunist. He wants to marry Bianca, to rid the duchy of Alessandro, but not to sacrifice himself or to fail in the enterprise. If he requires trickery to accomplish his ends, he is amenable to performing a role, to masquerading as an ally of a tyrant. Thus, the motif of dissimulation, so endemic to the films of the era, reappears and is accorded prominence.

The film, in fact, subdues the melodramatic conflicts usually attendant on the struggle between adversaries, shifting the focus on victimization from protagonist to the people who have been threatened by Alessandro. The portrait of the people as a community is not foregrounded. The presence of the masses is restricted to scenes of revelry or spectatorship, suggesting their indifference to the important events that are taking place in the palace. In its rendition of Machiavellianism, the film restricts the notion of people and politics to the select community of intellectuals and artists. *Lorenzino* maintains the familiar focus of the biopic on exceptionality and on masculine leadership, the necessity of a strong man to resolve conflict, but replaces the usual emphasis on physical force with that of intellect. Its concerns with history thus reside in the ways it draws on the spectacle of Renaissance Florence and on Machiavelli reincarnated in the figure of Lorenzino. In the face of intrigue and adventurism as well as in the face of potential civil war, the film suggests that the strong man is the savior. However, if there are links to contemporary history, the connections seem ambiguous. In the presentation of the two types of leadership—Alessandro's and Lorenzino's—the parallels are not clear. Given the confrontation between two "strong men," which is the portrait of the dictator? Is it the unscrupulous duke, greedy, sensual, cruel, and intellectually limited? Or is it Lorenzino, who is able, in a situation of siege, to overcome dictatorial power? The film could be said to entertain two different audiences. In any case, following the conventions of the biopic *cum* adventure film, and given its melodramatic bent, the film masks any clear propagandist agenda that would strictly align it to a celebration of the status quo, but it highlights the spectacle of contested power in ways that aligns it with contemporary politics—and even more with contemporary politics as entertainment.

THE ARTIST AS *DOPPELGÄNGER*

Blasetti's *Un' avventura di Salvator Rosa* (1940) is another version of his frequent recourse to history and myth and of its relation to the figure of the artist as an exemplary figure, the creator of the world of simulacra, through whom "the very idea of a model or a privileged position is challenged and overturned."[45] Using the figure of the Renaissance painter, the film combines history and fiction, art and politics, biopic and adventure film, and style and theatricality. The public arena is a stage and the protagonist is a star (and usually played by a star). The titles that introduce the film describe Rosa as artist, poet, painter, and "friend of the people," alluding as well to the liberties taken with the biography that "inspired" this "fable." From the opening moments of the film, the oppression of the community is highlighted simultaneously with the promise of its ultimate salvation, and notions of community are tied to art and to the role of the artist as a tranformative agent. Initially, the abject figure of Masaniello, a fishmonger, is the object of attack. He has been condemned to death by the viceroy of Naples, condemned to be taken to a dungeon where he and others will be executed according to Rosa's suggestion in his other, socially conforming identity. Their hope of reprieve resides in a note left by "The Ant," the figure of Rosa (Gino Cervi) in his benevolent and heroic disguise, and he saves them. Rosa, while antagonistic to the Duchess of Torniano (Rina Morelli) and to Count Lamberto D'Arco, nephew to the viceroy (Osvaldo Valenti), engages, like Lorenzino, in subterfuge and impersonation in order to defeat these enemies of the people.

The count seeks to wed the duchess, but she has vowed not to marry anyone until the Ant has been apprehended. She is determined to refuse the peasants water from her gardens, despite the fact that the peasants in the duchy are suffering from a drought and require the water for their land. In his role as Rosa, the painter comes to the duchy under the pretext of a holiday, and the duchess invites him to stay at her villa. The villa is presented in images that are highly stylized, linear and diagonal, emphasizing doors, windows, and enclosures. A dinner is interrupted by rocks crashing through the window. The rock thrower is a peasant woman, Lucrezia (Luisa Ferida), who is militant in behalf of her oppressed people. Lucrezia's dark, wild, and fiery image is set in opposition to that of the blonde, petite, shrill, and capricious duchess. Brought in and ordered to be whipped, Lucrezia is saved by Rosa, who has her brought to his room where he informs her that he is a friend of the Ant's. She confides in him that she and four of her cohorts intend to divert water from the duchess's garden. He confuses her as to his loyalties when he orders her to be taken to a cell.

In his guise as the friend of the aristocrats, Rosa suggests to the count that the peasants be used for target practice for the count's archers the next day. After scenes of the impending execution with different point of view shots of the archers, the duchess, Lamberto, and the peasants, the Ant appears and in a swashbuckling scene routs the soldiers. Later, Rosa is discovered at his painting and claims that he scuffled with the Ant in an unsuccessful attempt to capture him. The Ant sends a message to the duchess not to marry Lamberto. Rosa interprets this message to Lamberto as a trick to make the arbitrary woman do just the opposite, and Lamberto, pleased, rewards him with a ribbon. The duchess disappears, kidnapped. Lamberto, now suspicious that Rosa is the Ant, learns that she is with Lucrezia at Lucrezia's farmhouse. He intensifies his malevolent designs, planning to kill the duchess, blame the deed on Rosa, and take over her lands. His plot is, of course, thwarted by Rosa, who deceives the duchess into thinking that he will trap the peasants and discredit Lucrezia. Sorely pressed to maintain his disguise as the Ant, he is forced

FIGURE 10. Courtly ritual and intrigue in *Un'avventura di Salvator Rosa*. Courtesy of New York Museum of Modern Art, Film Stills Archive.

to send Lucrezia to prison again. His identity as the Ant is now tenuous as he is mistrusted not only by Lamberto, but by the duchess and Lucrezia as well. His plan to entrap Lucrezia's captain with a harmless instrument backfires. The knife is lethal, killing the captain, not only undermining the Ant's credibility with the aristocracy but also with the peasants. To regain the duchess's confidence he spends the night with her, resulting in her decision not to marry the count but also to share her water with the people. Rosa defeats Lamberto in a fight. In a ceremony, the duchess formally announces her decision to share the water and her resolve to marry Rosa. The final episode takes place in the rustic surroundings of Lucrezia's home as a carriage arrives with the Ant. She is swept up into the carriage, learning as he removes his mask to reveal himself as Rosa, that he is the painter whom she asserts she now loves, not his disguise. The two ride off. The melodrama thus has a "happy ending." The land is saved. The wicked interlopers are driven off. The peasants are dealt with justly, thus able to work their land. The duchess has been forced to behave humanely. Justice and love triumph.

As in so many Blasetti films (e.g., *Terra madre*, 1931), the preoccupation with the land, with ruralism, and with the need for a strong leader to reclaim and reinvigorate the land is central. Through the folklore of the wasteland with its emphasis on drought and regeneration of the land, the artist (like the filmmaker?) becomes the savior. The dual identity is a common convention of the adventure film. It enhances the cleverness and versatility of the protagonist. It serves to emphasize the importance of theatricality as a means for confronting situations that cannot be resolved in direct fashion. It also foregrounds the melodramatic preoccupation with the fear of the loss of meaning and identity and the necessary struggle to reinstate trust. The motif of trust is reiterated in the film's frenetic editing, its use of nervous, short sequences, moving camera, and frequent point of view shots from differing perspectives. The montage produces constant juxtapositions between the duchess and Lucrezia, Rosa and Lamberto, peasants and nobility.

The film employs the idea of painting in several ways, calling attention to artifice and impersonation. The protagonist is a painter, the walls of the villa are covered in paintings; Rosa's painting is highlighted; and the look of the film, both of the landscape and of the villa and environs, is painterly. The emphasis on painting, like the film itself, thus reflexively calls attention to the fictional, artifactual, and constructed nature of the fable, stressing in yet another fashion, the importance of style, the role of aesthetics in relation to politics. The "fable" can be identified as a harm-less fiction while calling attention to the parabolic uses of history in the interests of dramatizing conflicts over power and authority as in *La corona di ferro*. The film's play on matters of style and performance and double identity shifts attention from the real to the fictional and, therefore, iden-tifies the uses of history through the mediating role of art and imagina-tion. Like *La corona di ferro* and other 1940s films, this film is preoccu-pied with dramatizing the differences between the illegitimate and destructive uses of power and, like these films, the connection between aesthetics and politics confirms Walter Bejamin's insights about the increasing aestheticization of political life, a characteristic he identifies with fascism. In oblique fashion, *Salvator Rosa* offers yet another instance of the ways that the aesthetic uses of common sense as folklore at this time are dependent on theatricality as a means for creating consent and as a strategy that is far more complex than mere assent to the formal structures of power. The emphasis on painting, on impersonation, and on fictional-izing blurs boundaries between the "real" historical events and their rep-resentation that works in two directions: to reinforce a commonsense knowledge of the connection between theatricality and political represen-tation but, as an effect, to enhance a sense of helplessness about alterna-tives.

THE MUSICIAN AS NATIONAL SAVIOR

The films of the Risorgimento, by contrast, seem less inclined toward monumentalism, antiquarianism, or myth, and more inclined toward developing notions of popular struggle, toward a transformism that seeks to unify divergent political groups. It would be surprising if there were not films during this era that presented the biography of Giuseppe Verdi, since he was so much associated in the cultural imaginary with the Risorg-imento. His operas were drawn on abundantly by the cinema of the era. *Giuseppe Verdi* (1938) is a prime instance of the union of history, biogra-phy, melodrama, and the operatic,[46] though a review in *Bianco e Nero* in 1938 lamented that the film was not patriotic.[47] In the conventions of the biopic and of opera, the protagonist is shown to be a person whose eleva-tion to greatness is the result of his confronting and overcoming personal suffering most often in the service of the nation: "The way fame is linked to misfortune and in turn, happiness, is one of the most powerful instructive lessons the biopics display."[48] Verdi's sufferings are portrayed as the basis of his greatness, since he has overcome trials that might overwhelm ordinary human beings. It is thus not only his talent but his perseverance as well as his fortune in his relation to Giuseppina that enable Verdi to triumph. The prodigiousness of this talent is displayed in the segments that portray moments from his operas; his fortunate affair with Giuseppina and others enable him to persist and be successful.

The casting of Fosco Giachetti as Verdi enhances the patriotic image of the composer. Two years earlier, Giachetti had starred as patriotic Captain Santelia in *Squadrone bianco* (1936). His image as a man of determination, virile, dedicated, but also romantic is consonant with the image developed of Verdi. The film begins with Verdi as a young man, at the inception of his career as he goes off to study at the Conservatory in Milan. In Milan, he finds a lukewarm reception for his work, though the young Giuseppina Strepponi (Gaby Morlay) recognizes his genius. Verdi returns home, marries Margherita Barezzi (Germana Paolieri). Margherita becomes pregnant but expresses an anxiety about her impending death. Giuseppina comes to see him and tells him that he should return to Milan. He returns, has difficulty with the staging of his opera, and is struck by domestic and professional tragedy. One of his two children dies, then Margherita dies, operatically to the music of the as-yet-not-composed *Traviata*, and the audience is unreceptive to his first opera. Thus begins Verdi's dark night of the soul. He disappears, lives in a garret in squalid surroundings, though he continues to compose. He refuses any attempts to lure him back to the opera. His magnanimity is evident through his relation with a chestnut vendor who gives him a chestnut and Verdi, in turn, promises that someday he will give the woman a scarf. While in his garret, he reads a poem that becomes the scenario for *Nabucco*. At this point, Giuseppina finally discovers his whereabouts and convinces him to return. A sign for *Nabucco* signals the performance of Verdi's opera, which is greeted with enthusiasm and becomes associated with the spirit of the Risorgimento. After the performance, he goes to visit the chestnut vendor and gives her the promised scarf, indicating that fame has not altered him. Verdi's success is signaled by his association with the great men of his time. At a party to which Giuseppina brings him, he meets Balzac, who praises his music. Verdi's popular success and his identification with patriotic goals are highlighted in a scene where the masses are gathered outside with flags, banners, and a statue of Garibaldi. The people chant, "Viva Verdi," which has come to signify "Victor Emmanuele Re d'Italia" as he stands above on a balcony receiving their adulation. Verdi's personal life, however, is still problematic, since Giuseppina desires to marry Verdi but he feels that he is bound still to the memory of Margherita. Ultimately, he does marry her.

His creation of *Rigoletto* is portrayed through a gondola scene with Mirati, his tenor, played by the popular opera singer, Beniamino Gigli. The scene features the famous aria "La donna é mobile," sung by the gondolier, then by Beniamino Gigli, and then by a stage performance of the opera. *La traviata*, however, is blighted by the audience's laughter at the heavy Margherita, though later the work is successful. More difficulties arise with Giuseppina when Verdi begins to work with a young singer, Teresina Stoltz (Maria Cebotari), and Giuseppina becomes jealous of the young woman, staging angry and disruptive scenes. Verdi and Teresina continue their work, while he talks to her of the loss of youth and the debility of old age. He complains that everything around him is aged: "I am a living death." To her and to Giuseppina, he insists that "One must renew one self or die." The last operatic segment selected from *Aida* is lengthy and lavish, and Verdi's success with audiences is stressed as is his fame.

The biopic has followed the familiar trajectory from obscurity to fame, from suffering to a reward for perseverance. Verdi's exceptional talent becomes emblematic of national creativity, his creativity identified with the Italian national character and in the service of the nation, a thematic that is not unique to the cinema of the 1930s. By selecting an opera composer as its subject, linking the operatic and the melodramatic to the historical and the political, the text reveals connections between popular cinema and national identity. In particular, his popularity with people of all classes is emphasized through the shots of the aristocratic and middle-class audiences for the operas and the lower-class audiences on the streets. Consonant with the motifs of other films that make claims to historicizing, the elements of spectatorship and performance are highlighted. The film, like the musical generally, becomes a paean to entertainment in the form of opera, and entertainment becomes the force for creating a sense of community. Like the Hollywood biopic, the film draws on popular folklore surrounding the protagonist's life and links this mythology more generally to popular forms including the film itself as a means for creating community, a motif evident in such films as Camerini's *Figaro e la sua gran giornata*. *Verdi* corroborates the importance of style, of theatricality, and of performance, as preeminent factors in the recreation and circulation of commonsense meanings of history and representation.

THE OPERATIC IN FILM

Of all his historical films, Alessandro Blasetti's *1860* (1934) reaches deepest into the cultural and political life of Italy of the era. One of the most prolific and popular historical filmmakers of the era, Blasetti in *1860* focuses on the anticipation of Garibaldi's victory at Catalfimi and, according to Blasetti, the narration is consonant with Fascist ideology. The film draws on several art forms—painting, music, and literature—as well as on popular patriotic motifs. The Risorgimento is seen as a national melodrama through the eyes of its peasant protagonists, Carmeliddu (Giuseppe Gulino) and Gesuzza (Aida Bellia). The film, a combination of location and studio settings, of professional and nonprofessional actors, offers further verification of the compatibility between realism and melodrama. According to Angela Dalle Vacche, "In representing the Risorgimento, Blasetti confronted a dilemma previously tackled by the Macchiaioli painters, how to revitalize the historical classical scene with the insertion of elements drawn from daily life and regional genre paintings."[49]

Along with the insertion of images from paintings and the painterly creation of scenes, Blasetti created, through the action and the music, an operatic text that invokes the rhetorical tropes of nineteenth-century opera in contrast to the actual performance of an opera on film. I use the term "operatic" to stress the combined effect of character, image, and music to create the sense of scope of events and their melodramatic intensity in the service of heroic narratives of the nation and of power. The stylization of opera is further evoked through the emphasis on the southern Italian landscape, the choreographed character of the shots, and the highly stylized use of montage. In the cinematic representation of historical events, the bond between spectator and produced history is based on the effective marshaling of visual and auditory images derived from paintings. The film validates Pierre Sorlin's conception of cinematic history that "looks a bit like school history. . . . Classical history films were artefacts which attempted to reenact, recreate, dead events. The scenery had to be accurate and to conform to the models already offered by pictures or engravings. . . . Actors recited elaborate texts which were lectures on history and encapsulated what was considered the 'spirit' of an epoch."[50]

The strange conjunction of artifice with the emphasis on accuracy, the cohabitation of the fictional and the "authentic," is a major characteristic of opera and of historical/costume films, announcing themselves as both "possible and fallacious." The historical film demands to be read in complex fashion through the treatment of its various artifacts, its borrowings from the other arts, and the various ways in which it deploys music. From the opening moments of the film, the film enunciates its rhetorical concerns. The music functions there (and throughout the film) as a signifier for the intense emotions invested in a struggle for national unity. The music will also be identified with nature and with the innocence of the Sicilians. The orchestration serves as a bridge to the setting, connecting nature to revolution. Variations in tempo, volume, and intensity enhance contrasts in mood, character, and moral position. The images of the landscape assume a mystical significance, reinforced by music, that seems to transcend their specificity, becoming part of the film's dialectical structure, of the opposition between the foreigners and the Sicilian (soon to be Italian) population. The use of chiaroscuro lighting will distinguish the enemy from the clear images of the heroic villagers. The choreography also distinguishes between the unnaturalness of the Austrian mercenaries—their rigid mechanical movement in columns—in contrast to the more fluid and random movement of the Sicilians, movements that are identified with nature.

The visual and auditory distinctions paint a melodramatic canvas in which the lines are clearly drawn between friend and foe, patriot and interloper. The assignment of horizontal and vertical positions is metaphoric. The images of reclining and rising, like movement and stasis, become important as a way of measuring progress, but are also proleptic insofar as the notion of rising is associated with the notion of the Risorgimento. The enemy is also identified with jarring sounds, abrupt interruptions, entrances and exits, while softly played patriotic music identifies the Sicilians. To enhance the stages of the conflict a voice-over describes the course of events, losses and gains. The voice-over, like the voice of God narration in documentary, will be maintained throughout the film, commenting on the changes in the action and providing an oracular sense, explanation, and historical authority. The film does not depend on suspense; the outcome is known both by virtue of its historical subject matter as well as in its use of paintings and patriotic Italian theme music. The emphasis falls on the realization of the already-known, the rehearsal of events that are drawn from history but a history that requires repetition and heroic embellishment. A moving camera records the panorama, the sense of the forces arrayed, and the rhythm of events. The camera movements are accompanied by loud or soft orchestral music, depending on the rise and fall of action. The use of tableaux, characteristic of operatic performance and of historical films, militates against the very naturalness the film seeks to espouse. The immobile image of Carmeliddu and Gesuzza when they are first observed, lying affectionately next to each other until awakened at the priest's request to serve the cause, is a painting that comes to life. Their movement, too, seems choreographed rather than random. The various groups of villagers are also drawn from pastoral paintings as are the later scenes in the church. The rhythm of the peasants's lives is marked by tableaux of collectivity that are disrupted by the enemy. Time in the film is related to the future and to the anticipated arrival of Garibaldi announced at the outset.

The costumes by Nino Vittorio Novarese are instrumental in developing the dramatic class and national opposition that the film pursues in relation to the peasants, the Bourbons, and the middle-class intellectuals that Carmeliddu meets on his journey to Garibaldi. As befits her peasant status, Gesuzza is dressed simply, but she is filmed in a highly stylized manner. Despite her apparent similarity to the other women, she is frequently distinguished from them as an icon of familial and conjugal devotion through the use of low camera angles and through close-up. Carmeliddu, shot in similar fashion, is an icon of national purity and devotion in relation to the other men and to Gesuzza. The Bourbons are encased in their tightly fitting, ornate uniforms, while the Sicilian men are seen in their rough-hewn shirts and fleece pants, which, like the rocky landscape they inhabit, suggests primitiveness. One is again reminded of Antonio Gramsci's critique of Manzoni's treatment of the peasants in *I promessi sposi,* describing their portrayal as typical of ways in which subalterns are represented—childlike, inarticulate, and innocent.

The barbarism of the Bourbons is conveyed by their wanton killing of a young boy, a victim in this Manichean struggle between good and evil. The child is a significant figure in the films of the Fascist era as witnessed in such films as *Vecchia guardia* and *I bambini ci guardano,* a signifier of martyrdom, and often a vehicle for the legitimization of vengeance. The slow movement of the horse that brings the boy's body back to the village conveys a further reproach to the inhumanity of the enemy. The music swells as the animal approaches the waiting priest. The priest's (Gianfranco Giachetti) slow and methodical laying out of the boy's body under the impatient observation of the Bourbon officer heightens the sense in which the church is the aligned with the people, that the cause for which they fight is (to quote one Italian critic of the time) "sacred." The tableau of the people chanting their prayers in the church further enhances the motif of unity between church and emergent state. In the church scenes, the music serves especially to enhance ceremonial and ritualistic moment, fusing nation and church.

The scene of Carmeliddu's departure is accompanied by low lyrical music as he rides off saying, "Ritorno con Garibaldi." He is associated with water images that act as a metaphoric bridge between Sicily and Genoa, his destination. The passage of his journey is interrupted several times with scenes of battle between Bourbons and peasants, culminating in the brutal roundup of the peasants by their captors, thus underscoring the urgency of Carmeliddu's journey. Unconscious on his small boat, Carmeliddu is saved by a French ship, which brings him to port. Water shots will be reiterated on the return journey that brings Garibaldi and his men to Sicily. The journeys on the water function as a bridge, linking music to images of landscape, and individuals to a political destination.

The spoken language and dialect differentiate the various individuals and groups involved in the conflict. Linguistic differences highlight regional differences. The coexistence of spoken Italian, German, and French functions as a reminder of foreign domination and a means for distinguishing friend from foe. For example, Carmeliddu is unable to understand the French who saved him. Significantly, unlike neorealism, the Sicilians for the most part do not speak the Sicilian dialect but speak Italian, as if marking their assimilation into the future national landscape. The film also makes a distinction between the plain style of communication of the peasants and of Carmeliddu, in particular, and the style of communication of the middle- and upper-class intellectuals he meets on his arrival in Civitavecchia. His role as silent subaltern is underscored as Carmeliddu listens to men arguing about the number of French troops present and listing the atrocities committed against women and children and the destruction of churches. Later, he is also an audience to men of differing political persuasions arguing over the best course of events for the emerging nation—union between church and state, monarchy with Victor Emanuel, or a republic headed by Mazzini. These differences are to be resolved in the victory of Garibaldi, which will be identified with the triumph of the monarchy under the house of Savoy. Carmeliddu breaks his silence only to ask others on his journey penetrating questions about Garibaldi's identity. His demeanor and questions underscore his peasant origins and, hence, his lack of sophistication. His simplicity and directness distance him from the political machinations and from the sophistry of the various political groups struggling for control, and his difference from quarrelsome intellectuals. He is identified by his single-minded commitment to Garibaldi as a man of action.

The specifically contemporary perspective of the film can be seen in the valorization of action over thought, which is reminiscent of Gramsci's discussions of common sense as the "popular philosophy of the masses . . . an element of cohesive force exercised by the ruling classes and therefore an element of subordination to an external hegemony."[51] The commonsense rejection of thought and, hence, the rejection of difference, serves in this context to underline the impossibility of making difference disappear except by coercion. In its melodramatic treatment of the different groups, the film only exposes the depth of such differences. The uses of Risorgimento history come more clearly into focus as that earlier history is read as the authentic origin for the Fascist emphasis on national unity, and especially as the basis for the overcoming of differences between north and south. The figures of Carmeliddu and the peasants, the emphasis on their lack of complexity, their loyalty, and their single-minded devotion become the standard for action as opposed to effete contemplation.

The final scenes are reminiscent of the paintings of battle shown at the beginning of the film. The film choreographs the movement of the two groups, the Bourbons and the Garibaldians. Interspersed are scenes of Carmeliddu, seeking Gesuzza, whose father had kept her away from the battle through subterfuge. Also intercut are images of flowers and trees signifying rebirth juxtaposed to scenes of battle. Shots of the Italian flag are accompanied by the ever-swelling theme music. The Garibaldians sing as they go to fight, and music (especially the sound of trumpets) is skillfully edited to advance or retard the various lines of group movement. The sound is interspersed with moments of silence. An elegiac tableau is intercut with scenes of intense fighting as Gesuzza comes across a dying soldier—the boy shown earlier with his mother at the men's departure for Sicily. Gesuzza cradles his head and as he dies, Carmeliddu comes running to her, shouting, "Italy has been saved." The film ends with the waving of banners, a painting of the famous battle, and the playing of the national anthem, Mameli's Hymn. Thus, the film itself becomes an art work through fusion of the national anthem with this heroic painting, linking present to past and enshrining the actions of the men involved. Drawing on the heroic traditions associated with the Risorgimento and the mythic figure of Garibaldi, the film does not seek to analyze the dis-

FIGURE 11. Choreography of a battle scene in *1860*. Courtesy of New York Museum of Modern Art, Film Stills Archive.

course of nation but to enact it in terms of a public melodrama, pitting the forces of national and ethnic identity against the demonic forces of empire associated with a foreign culture.

THE MELODRAMA OF NATIONAL UNITY

The preoccupation with the Risorgimento functions as a way of identifying an originary moment in the creation of the Italian nation and as revolutionary movement. It serves, as Balibar describes, "in the history of every modern nation, wherever the argument can apply, there is never more than one single founding revolutionary event."[52] Furthermore, the impetus is to repeat these founding events, thus linking the past to the present. *Il Dottor Antonio* (1937), based on an historical novel by Giovanni Ruffini and directed by Enrico Guazzoni, reenacts the struggles of nation formation, linking them to romantic melodrama. Beginning with the shot of a prison fortress in Naples where the film's protagonist will later be imprisoned, the film traces the political and romantic activities of the doctor. Coincidence and chance are central to melodrama and it is through an accident that the doctor (Enrico Corlise) meets the Englishwoman, Miss Lucy Davenne (Maria Gamberelli), when her carriage rolls over. Through his concern for her, he is introduced to her family and he attends to her, despite her father's impatience to leave Naples for England. Lucy learns that Antonio, a Sicilian, has a "shady past." Blonde and childlike, Lucy is confused about Antonio's activities but when Antonio explains his patriotism to her, his struggles to free Italy from foreign domination, she is drawn to him. Her romanticism is conveyed through her novel reading, her "Englishness," and her sympathetic identification with the cause of freedom. Her sympathy for Italians is contrasted to her brother's view of Italians as uncivilized, akin to Africans. Now fully committed to Antonio, they exchange love vows, though he tells her he cannot make any deeper commitment until his country is free. The film climaxes with a street battle in which the civilians and soldiers clash. Antonio is arrested, and Lucy appeals to Ferdinand II to save him only to learn that, despite the monarch's promise to help her, Antonio is tried, found guilty, and imprisoned. However, with aid from others, he escapes from the fortress, and is reunited with Lucy and the promise of ultimate success.

The familiar union of romance and politics is reiterated. The romance between an Englishwoman and southern Italian takes on an allegorical character as she, a representative of "a free country," becomes identified with Antonio, the physician for his country's ills, and Italy's struggles for independence. His identification with southern Italy further connects the struggle for independence with the struggle to unify the north and south. Though upper class, Lucy is also identified with the union between workers and bourgeoisie. The melodrama functions in terms of stylistic oppositions between fair Lucy and dark Antonio, femininity and masculinity. In this respect, femininity provides the symbolic ballast, the necessary affective adhesive for nation formation, but masculinity is identified with commitment and action. Through the romance formula, the feminine figure becomes the nurture and support for national ideals. The film relies on the familiar ingredients of adventure to enhance the melodrama—the romantic meeting of Antonio and Lucy, his healing of her wounds and enabling her to walk again, the scenes in court, the balls, the trial scene, the street combats, and Antonio's dramatic rescue from prison.

The romance of nationalism, while tied to an English protagonist, is finally an Italian romance. As Gianfranco Mino Gori asserts, while the English play a role in the film, it is the Italians who are seen to create the Risorgimento.[53] While the film is committed through costume, setting, and allusion to historical personages, to its historical subject of the Risorgimento, its formulaic qualities derived from romance and adventure are, as in Hollywood's uses of history, amenable to a heterogeneous reading that undermines the specificity of the historical events. Critics of the time appreciated the film as "popular spectacle," the choreography of the crowd scenes, in particular.[54] In contrast to *1860* and its high rhetorical and operatic vein, the Risorgimento in this film can be acknowledged as an instance of the uses of national folklore that makes minimal polemic or critical demands on the spectator.

MELODRAMA AND HISTORY AS ELEGY

In a mode characteristic of calligraphism with its highly ornate, antiquarian attachment to history and to past forms of historical representation, *Piccolo mondo antico* (1941), directed by Mario Soldati, returns to the Risorgimento and to a literary novel from a prior time. Based on the novel by Antonio Fogazzaro, the melodrama focuses on a tension between the demands of family and of public duty. The domestic axis of the narrative involves the struggles of Luisa (Alida Valli) and Franco (Massimo Serato) with Franco's grandmother, the Marchesa Maironi (Ada Dandini), who seeks to prevent their marriage. They marry against her will, have a child, Ombretta, but their lives are continually disrupted by the marchesa's malevolence and by political machinations in behalf of the Austrians and against her grandson. The formal political dimension of the narrative involves Franco's immersion in the struggle to rid Piedmont of the Austrians. The marchesa refuses to aid the struggling couple, keeping from them a will made by her husband that left the estate to Franco. When they learn of the will, Luisa seeks to claim what is legally theirs against Franco's wishes. Their relationship deteriorates, and he takes a position in Turin, leaving his family. Luisa goes to see the marchesa but is intercepted by townspeople who inform her that her daughter has been drowned. Obsessed with Ombretta's death, Luisa visits the cemetery daily. Finally, the couple is reconciled and the marchesa, guilty over Ombretta's death, turns over the estate to Franco. The film ends with Franco departing with his regiment to fight against the Austrians as Luisa tearfully bids him farewell.

The style of the film was dubbed "calligraphic" by critics associated with the journal *Cinema*, because of its literariness, formalistic and highly stylized quality, and attachment to a hermetic form of expression. It was a style that brought down ridicule on Soldati along with Poggioli and Castellani. His choice of Fogazzaro rather than Verga as a source was a further sign of his identification with formalism rather than realism. The film does not lay claim to a literal rendition of the novel. Soldati claimed that he had not read the novel before signing the contract to direct the film. The number of characters is reduced in the film and Soldati claimed that rather than fidelity to the novel, he sought instead to create a sense of the ambiance of the period.[55] The film makes no pretense to fidelity via photographic realism. Instead, the acting and *mise-en-scène* are theatrical, painterly, and highly stylized, serving to produce a melancholy and elegiac ambience. From the opening with its heavily romantic music, its images of the mountains and water, and its view of the marchesa's substantial house, the film creates a sense of a dark and brooding atmosphere. The interior of the house is ornate, and the people gathered are carefully choreographed with the marchesa at center stage. Alone in his darkened room, the artistic and melancholy Franco plays the piano. The lighting is predominantly dark, light and dark functioning in the film to enhance not only the melodramatic contrasts but to underscore the narrative's overarching sentiment of misrecognition and loss. His piano playing punctuates segments of the film, functioning in opposition to the formal politics identified with both the grandmother and the men with whom Franco is politically aligned in opposition to the Austrians. Shots of him playing the piano are intercut with images of the lake and mountains, serving as a prolepsis of Ombretta's death.

The melodrama revolves around a number of oppositions: the marchesa against Luisa and Franco, the police against the "revolutionaries," and Ombretta against the adults. The world the characters inhabit is reliant on secrets, intrigues, familial machinations, and feminine hysteria, both the marchesa's and Luisa's. In the climactic scene of Ombretta's death, the images rely on the hyperbole of melodrama: scenes of the doomed child on the stairs with her dolls, the sounds of thunder, the ominous banging of shutters from the wind, and then of the child at the water's edge. These scenes are intercut with Luisa on the road, buffeted by the rain and the wind as she heads out to see the marchesa. The image of the child's boat floating on the water is reiterated, superimposed on Luisa's face. Luisa's grief is developed through her trancelike state, her refusal to talk to Franco, and her attempts to communicate with her dead child. An abrupt transition in time, introduced by a title, "1859," introduces the final moments of the narrative where Luisa and Franco are reconciled to each other after learning about the marchesa's restoration of the property to Franco. The intensity of the prior scenes is defused in Franco's departure as a tearful Luisa smiles and waves good-bye to him and his comrades.

The politics of the narrative are reinforced through the domestic melodrama. The film's dark and brooding style, its elegiac tenor, centers on the child's death and on the villainy of the marchesa. The *mise-en-scène* that isolates the characters from each other is paralleled, in Christine Gledhill's terms, by "the more global orchestration of the narrative structure. It is in this manner that the domestic melodrama thrives on the multiplication of silences, alibis, and misunderstandings generated in the characters' incomplete comprehension of the melodramatic situations in which they are implicated, or the degrees to which their actions (or lack of action) tend to further complicate those situations."[56] The film's ending is thus a closure and not a resolution, signaled by the mechanical shift in time. Instead of representing the Risorgimento in celebrational terms, the film presents the history in elegiac terms, focusing affectively on loss, on the sense of the reconciliation arriving too late to compensate for the suffering and death produced through incompatibility between familial

154

FIGURE 12. Mother and child tableau in *Piccolo mondo antico*. Courtesy of New York Museum of Modern Art, Film Stills Archive.

and national objectives. Thus, the film, unlike other Risorgimento films, eschews a celebrational mode, stressing rather the ravages of history. The theatricality of the film is perceptible in its uses of tableaux, in its operatic quality in which music plays a key role, in the stylized and excessive acting, and, above all, in the "orchestration of the narrative structure," which is reliant on a novelistic unfolding of the drama of personal loss against the historical panorama of the Risorgimento.

ITALIAN HISTORY AND THE WESTERN

Historical genres and their uses of the past are protean, creating a problem for the critic in assessing their readability to audiences. For example, *Passaporto rosso* (1935), directed by Guido Brignone, undertakes a recreation of the period from 1890 to 1922. The motif of the settlement of new lands, linked to the figure of the immigrant, relies on the folklore of the western, a protean genre that in Gramsci's sense combines the different strata of past and present history. This pastiche is productive of ambiguity. On the one hand, in the vein of common sense, *Passaporto rosso* is closely tied to questions of struggle and survival, a mistrust of existing institutions, and a valorization of past experience and inherited wisdom. On the other hand, the conflicts confronting the protagonists are a concession to the inevitability of change. The narrative of immigration provides affective resonance given its centrality to Italian life in the latter part of the nineteenth and early twentieth century.

The film focuses on a physician forced to leave Italy for political reasons and the trials and tribulations of emigration, particularly the relationship of the emigrants to their country of origin and their adopted country, Argentina. Beginning with a political gathering where men argue the pros and cons of the current government and of capitalism, the spectator is introduced to the film's protagonist, Lorenzo Casati (Filippo Scelzo). Casati is attacked for his political views, accused of fomenting trouble, and led away by friends who advise him of the necessity to leave the country. They tell him that they have arranged for him to go to Argentina. He will serve as the ship's doctor. Aboard ship he meets Maria Brunetti (Isa Miranda) and her father Andrea (Oreste Fares), Antonio Spinelli (Ugo Caseri) and Don Pancho Rivera (Giulio Donadio). Casati also discovers that the ship is overcrowded and that people will live in these dangerous cramped quarters for three months. Maria, sympathetic to the conditions of the emigrants, tries, with the assistance of Don Pancho, to get decent food for the children. The well-dressed, portly, cigar-smoking Don Pancho develops an amorous attachment to her, but she is romantically inclined toward Casati. She informs him that as soon as the railroad for which her father works is built, they will return to Italy.

The narrative shifts to Argentina and to the railroad company where an argument ensues about working conditions for the immigrants. Don Pablo Ramirez (Mario Ferrari) berates the company manager for taking land from tenant farmers and throwing them off the land without paying them. Don Pablo warns him that the men will rebel. Scenes of men working on the railroad and others huddling around a fire provide images of the rugged life. Upon the arrival of the immigrants, Don Pancho settles the women that he has brought over in his "hotel." In a further effort to seduce Maria, he offers her credit at his store. Catastrophes multiply. The hardships of life begin for the newcomers as they are made to do back-breaking work for the railroad, paid poorly, made to pay for their passage, and exploited at the company store. Casati has his hands full as he tries to save the immigrants, including Maria's father, who have fallen victim to yellow fever. Her father's death offers the opportunity that Don Pancho has been awaiting—to gain power over Maria. Though she has been working as a teacher, since she is in debt to him, she goes to work in his cafe as a singer but refuses to allow the men to fondle her.

She becomes the classic dance hall entertainer, a feminine figure at home in the Hollywood western. In fact, the film comes increasingly to follow the conventions of that genre in its emphasis on creating a community in the wilderness: its obvious distinctions between the exploitative railroad entrepreneurs who commercially exploit the helpless immigrant in the face of the hardships of frontier life, its clear melodramatic distinctions between victims and oppressors, its mistrust of excessive wealth, and its elevation of the concept of the "land." Earlier Antonio had given Casati a bag of soil from Italy and the thematic of turning this undeveloped land into an Italian enclave becomes a master motif of the film. Maria is saved from the clutches of Don Pancho by Casati. The farmers rebel against the railroad and in the tense battle, Don Pancho is killed. Maria and Lorenzo are married. The narrative moves forward to 1914, and their son, Gianni, has become an engineer and is married. He and his father differ about their politics. Gianni regards himself as an Argentinian, while his father is strongly identified with Italy and determined to go to Europe to fight in the war. With Maria's insistence, Gianni deters his father from enlisting and instead volunteers, ultimately affirming that "We have our country in our blood."

Like the western genre in its dependence on melodrama, the film relies on basic binary oppositions: nature and culture, civilization and wilderness, the individual and community, man of action and intellectual, tradition and change, Eastern and Western culture, unscrupulous moneyed interests and benign but oppressed agents of a reinvigorated social order. The affective dimensions of the melodrama rely heavily on the domestic drama where, as in *Scipione*, the community is threatened by violence directed against women, children, the elderly, and helpless inhabitants obstructed in their efforts to establish a secure and lawful community where the needs of all are enhanced and protected. The ever-present threat of the exploitation of women is underscored through the image of prostitution, a basic melodramatic trope that draws on the iconography of violence and exploitation. The women, and hence the positive values of the family, procreation, and continuity are under assault. The other melodramatic axis, reiterated in other films of the time (e.g., *Vecchia guardia* and *Cavalleria*), hinges on martyrdom, particularly on the martyrdom of youth. The son's death in Europe fighting for Italy serves to reconcile the parents to the son, the son to Italy, the community to its national past, and the past to the present. The narrative is melodramatic in its focus on social and economic hardship, in its focus on the conflicts over traditional regional and national ties, and in its emphasis on the invention of a new national identity. *Passaporto rosso* draws on the iconography of the western but weds it to contemporary exigencies that bear a relationship to Fascism. But its eclecticism, a primary feature of popular narrative, enables it to be read in multivalent fashion. The film inscribes the Fascist inclination to exalt ruralism, productivity, syndicalism, familialism, youthful ingenuity, and nationalism. However, given its folkloric vein, its melodramatic roots in the adventure saga, the theatrical and spectacular elements can, as with *Scipione*, overwhelm any specific political "message" that the film imparts.

THE NARRATIVE OF CONVERSION AND WAR

The war narrative often invokes history in its attempts to create a world where sacrifice and death cannot merely be entertained but where they can appear as desirable since they are sanctioned by past precedent. Of the melodramas that address heroism and war, Goffredo Alessandrini's 1936 film, *Cavalleria* (Cavalry, 1936), set in World War One, is most exemplary of the motif of conversion and a form of narrative that I examine in detail in the subsequent chapter. I include this film in the discussion of the historical film so as to provide a sense of the variety of forms and strategies adopted by the films' uses of the past. The conversion motif is central to the war narrative, involving the protagonist's conflict between pleasure and commitment to national aspirations. As Dana Polan argues, "If, as the war discourse will often argue, an individual gets out of place because he/she has internalized incorrect beliefs and values, then a potent narrative recovery from the violence of this bad internalization will be one in which an individual converts to a new and proper set of values and beliefs."[57]

The affective dimensions of conversion narratives arise largely from the tranformation of relationships from an erotic register of heterosexual desire to one of homosocial bonding, often leading to an apotheosis through martyrdom. The signposts of this transformation will be conveyed through the style, especially in the binary distinction between interior and exterior worlds through an operatic emphasis on music, dance, and social rituals in opposition to the images of nature and technology. The film idol, Amedeo Nazzari, plays the dashing Captain Solaro, a cavalry officer, later a flyer, who falls in love with a young noblewoman, Speranza (Elisa Cegani), during World War One. The spectacle exploits images of horse shows, cavalry exercises, and elegant people who inhabit this world. The world of the aristocracy is displayed as glamorous: sumptuous houses, salons, ballrooms, and exquisitely costumed bejeweled women. Speranza, the feminine protagonist, played by Elisa Cegani, is torn between her loyalty to her family and her love for Solaro. Solaro is split between duty and love, but with the help of his commanding officer, Ponza, he comes to accept duty. Ponza believes that his men, particularly brilliant officers like Solaro, must accept the seriousness of their military commitments. The striking aspect of Solaro's character is his lack of rebelliousness. His willingness to accept his superior officer's orders, his acceptance of the need to renounce Speranza, his discipline and self-control are offered as a model of heroism. His conversion to and immersion in duty and service are eroticized in terms of his filial-type of relationship to his superior officer, Captain Ponza. Solaro, not Speranza, is the film's specular object of desire. He is observed while dressing, on horseback, as leader of men, as lover, as dashing aviator, and as doomed hero.

FIGURE 13. Elisa Cegani as the obscure object of desire in *Cavalleria*. Courtesy of New York Museum of Modern Art, Film Stills Archive.

By contrast, Speranza is a figure of transgression who first becomes the agent of Solaro's death and then, ironically, of his transfiguration. Through Speranza, the film reverses the usual polarity between life and death, making death the entry into a higher form of existence. His identification with the fecundity of the land is equated to the nation that he has regenerated. The stages of the hero's conversion are formulaic and ritualized, marked specifically by stages of separation from the female. He must first suffer the pains of unrequited love, reconcile himself to the futility of his desire, which is identified with the taint of effeminacy. He must find a worthy object of emulation to replace heterosexual attachments. This substitution involves him in an Oedipal relationship with a significant paternal guide that signals his regeneration. His new life is associated with the isolated life of the flier, a glamorous image identified with the sky and with nature. Paradoxically, regeneration is identified with a symbolic or actual death. The protagonist is no longer passive, chained to the past and to his desire, but a liberated man of action. The airplane sets him apart from others, above the earth like a god. It also identifies him with the machinic and not the human.

The melodrama draws on fundamental romantic tropes, predominantly involving the tension between desire and inevitable loss. The initial obstacle to love is familial. Speranza must accede to a marriage of convenience to save her family from economic disaster, and her father's illness, the threat of his imminent death, forces her to conform. A masochistic aesthetic underpins the relationship of Solaro and Speranza connected to suffering that seems wilfully directed toward the obstruction of any type of heterosexual gratification. The film stresses spectatorship in the scenes of musical soirees and balls as well as in the cavalry shows, military maneuvers, and close-ups of the protagonists. The narrative relies on a bifurcation between familial and masculine worlds. In many ways, it is imitative of Tolstoy's *War and Peace* in its focus on the world of the aristocracy, tragic love, and on an opposition between nature and social conventions. The most ironic image in the film is of flowers. Solaro's relationship to Speranza is symbolized by an exchange of flowers culminating in the image of a field of flowers where Solaro is buried. The flowers signify passion, life, and hope, like Speranza's name, but they also signify indifference to life. Solaro's burial in the field of flowers fuses the images of love, war, and heroism. However, while the flowers are associated with life and creativity and with his insemination of the land, they also signify his mortality.

The ending rather than maintaining the divide between masculinity and femininity merges them. Solaro's death and union with the soil can be read in dual fashion. In polemic fashion, it can be seen as the fulfillment of a virile commitment to war and nationalism. Yet in Solaro's identification with the feminine imagery of a return to the earth and to fecundity, his character can be seen as subverting strict masculine identification. Ironically, he becomes what he sought to escape. Much as in Klaus Theweleit's description of the soldier-male and his relation to women, the figure of woman is presented as de-realized: "relationships with women are dissolved and transformed into new male attitudes, into political stances, revelations of the true path, etc. As the woman fades out of sight, the contours of the male sharpen. . . . It could almost be said that the raw material for the man's 'transformation" is the sexually untouched, dissolving body of the woman."[58] The theatricality of the film is most evident in its melodramatic, choreographed, and stylized acting, its costuming, its emphasis on an aristocratic *mise-en-scène* and entertainments, and, above all, its reliance on woman as spectacle that serves to unsettle and make undecidable the character of the male protagonist and his role in "history."

THE PRESENTNESS OF THE PAST

The uses of history are not restricted to those films that overtly portray a past historical period. History lives in the present in the ways that certain films invoke the past through their construction of character, their use of events to suggest historical parallels through choreography, gesture, and action, and their invocation of the folklore of war. Genina's *L'Assedio dell' Alcazar* (1940) dramatizes events from the Spanish Civil War from the perspective of the fascists, but everything about the film suggests its reliance on history, especially the feudal history associated with the Alcazar. The film focuses on the taking of the historic edifice of the Alcazar by the Italians, stressing the heroism and sacrifice of the men involved. In the same vein as those historical films that stress monumentalism, the narrative is created on a vast and epic scale in its battle reconstructions, intricate plots, and choreography of the masses.[59] The melodrama involves the heroism of the men in battle but also focuses on the necessary and romantic link between love and war. Beginning with militant music, the titles stress the threat of Bolshevism, the heroism of Francisco Franco in stemming the "red peril," and the taking of the Alcazar as a "freedom fight." Moreover, unlike Blasetti's acknowledgment of the fictional dimensions in *Un' avventura di Salvator Rosa*, this film purports to report the events "with historical accuracy."

The initial images are long shots of the Alcazar from different angles. Then in medium long shot, Captain Vela (Fosco Giachetti) reviews the Franchist troops. General Moscardó arrives (Raphael Calvo) to the accompaniment of martial music and a high-angle pan of the assembled men. In highly choreographed shots, he exhorts the men, invoking the "Spanish fatherland" and the importance of "honor." Following these conventional establishing scenes of military discipline and unity, the narrative introduces the two women, Carmen (Mireille Balin) and Conchita (Maria Denis), who will play a central role in the film's romantic scenario—one will be identified with Pedro (Andrea Checchi), the other with Francisco (Aldo Fiorelli). Like the typology of the men in the film, the women will come to represent the ideal of womanhood in wartime.

The film develops through a montage of contrasts: between the images of the orderly fascist troops and images of parliamentary disarray, between liberalism and the notion that the "fatherland is fate" and that Franco is the "savior of Spain, " and between the disorderly masses and the orderly soldiers. The hardships of war on the populace are portrayed in the images of the procession of the women and children who are leaving the city to seek shelter in the Alcazar. To underscore the hardships endured by the bombings, mothers are shown calling for their missing children, children crying for parents. The enemy appears to be gaining the upper hand, but Conchita is unflagging in her faith in the cause and in the positive outcome of the struggle. Carmen, who up to this point has been cynical and uncommitted, tells the captain that she wants to nurse the wounded. While conditions are deteriorating in the Alcazar, the enemy men are seen eating well and celebrating their victories. The melodrama is intensified when Colonel Moscardó learns that his son has been taken as a hostage. The Republicans negotiate with colonel for the life of the son, but neither Moscardó nor his son show weakness, and the son dies a hero. The emphasis on family and continuity is enhanced by the birth of a baby who is, not surprisingly, named "Francisco."

Romance flourishes as Carmen, rejecting Pedro's advances, confesses her love for Captain Vela. Pedro is shot in the thick of battle, but Vela and Carmen are united in their love for each other and now in their common commitment to the Franchist cause. The climactic scene of battle is shot with a large cast, highlighting contrasting shots from inside and outside the Alcazar, and stressing the tightly-choreographed and unified movement of the people until the Falangist flag is raised. The victory is marked by singing, men marching, and the emergence of the people (husbands, wives, and children) into the courtyard. The colonel greets the arrival of Franco as the camera pans the people greeting Franco with the fascist salute. The last images are of the damaged but still standing fortress.

The film follows the familiar conventions of the war film in its propagandistic emphasis on the defense of homeland threatened by a barbarous enemy. The frequent separation between home front and combat zone is brought together through the joining of the soldiers and the civilians in the Alcazar. The conflict serves to threaten the entire society, not merely the fighting men. The friendship of two men, Pedro and Francisco, is another staple of the war film, and the death of Pedro another instance of the inevitable and immemorial sacrifices demanded in war symbolized by the grand edifice of the Alcazar. The film invokes the typical triangulation of romantic wartime narratives, in this case of Carmen, Pedro, and Captain Vela, thus reinforcing Pedro's role as sacrificial victim, underlining the necessary acceptance of loss for a just cause. Life and death are marked by stoic acceptance. Unlike Hollywood and British World War Two films where the emphasis is on the coming together of different classes, this film assumes existing unity of class and purpose on the part of the various protagonists, focusing rather on sexual, familial, and psychological differences to be adjudicated. Captain Vela is invulnerable, honorable, and imperturbable. The colonel is the incarnation of stoic discipline. The sacrifice of his son is another instance of the Republicans' threat to paternal authority and the code of honor. Carmen is the only major character to undergo a change of heart from indifference to commitment, and the frightened civilians are reassured by the heroism of the troops. The assault on the Alcazar by the Republicans is portrayed as an act of aggression against civilization, family, and decency on the part of men lacking honor and decency. The Republicans are shown as barbaric, devoid of human compassion and of mercy.

The ritualistic and theatrical style of the film, its patterning of scenes of threat and confrontation of obstacles, its play on order and disorder, belongs to the forms of monumental history with its operatic penchant for inflating the magnitude and intensity of the struggle. The theatricality of the acting, the uses of incremental repetition of shots, the mingling of combat and romance narratives, the use of the Alcazar as symbol, and the thematic emphasis on sacrifice, duty, and honor intensify the melodramatic quality of the conflict and relegate the war to a drama of overarching proportions, affecting the twin poles of civil society and the state, suggesting that a loss of the struggle against the Republicans would result in the total demise of Spanish society and culture. The eroticism of the film seems, as in *Cavalleria*, to be directed toward the men, Pedro, Francisco, Vela and Moscardó as objects of desire, albeit unattainable desire. The distance between them and the others in the film is as vast as the distance between the everyday and the heroic, the leaders and the masses. The women fulfill the predictable function as maternal and nurturing figures. The film's pretension to realism is developed through its use of newspaper clippings, titles to provide a sense of the immediacy of events, but realism merges with theatricality and spectacle through the ritualistic shots of the troops, their review by the officers, the ceremonial quality of the military encounters, and the intensely melodramatic and stylized nature of the characters' interactions.

L'assedio dell' Alcazar belongs to the more overtly propagandistic Italian Films of the fascist era in its strictly binary and unrelenting representation of Republicans and fascists. However, by virtue of its adhering to the conventions of the war film—in its reliance on melodrama, on the commonsense of folklore with its melange of religion, national symbols, juridical discourse, on the valorization of romance as legitimation of gendered and familial relations as guarantor of continuity, and in its obsession with posturing—the film reveals itself as a throwback and almost a parody of past forms of representation in its blatantly contrived uses of literature, painting, and drama. Drawing in encyclopedic fashion on all the resources of the genre film, *Alcazar* reveals how the popular cinema in the service of fascism has abandoned its polyvalent relation to the audience that was the source of its appeal. In describing the breakdown of the movement-image, its devolution from the filmmaking of Griffith, Eisenstein, Vertov, the prewar French film, and the pre-Nazi German cinema, Gilles Deleuze writes that, "The revolutionary courtship of the movement-image and an art of the masses become subject was broken off, giving way to the masses subjected as psychological automaton, and to their leader as great spiritual automaton."[60] Deleuze's comments suggest the need to make an important distinction between the dynamic aspects of the popular cinema that opened up paths to new ways of seeing and thinking and of the cinema as propaganda where closure, constraint, and cliché are mechanically and inertly placed in the service of programmatic objectives.

An examination of the Italian films' uses of the past reveals that they are not all created from the same cloth: in their choice of generic form, involving epic and monumental forms of narration, reliance on genres such as the biopic, the western, or the drama of conversion, dependence on literary precursors, and preoccupation with the different types of national conflict as drawn from a selected historical moment. Whether set in the Roman period as in *Scipione l'Africano*, in the Renaissance as in *Lorenzino de' Medici*, or in the Risorgimento as in *1860*, these films reliance on theatricality and spectacle is not antiquarian; they do not conceal references to the present. They are mindful of their contemporary audiences in the ways that their use of theatricality overwhelms rhetoric through scenarios involving romance, adventure, fantasy, and, of course, the common sense of folklore that involves the address and redress of immediate conflicts. Their reflexive uses of theatricality—in their allusions to paintings, tableaux, architecture, landscape, opera, and music—places the audiences within the world of representation, not a real world. In this manner, the historical films offer an ambivalent sense of the past and an equally ambivalent sense of reality, requisites of how popular cinema functions to reach its various constituencies and of its willingness to share the knowledge of its artifactual character. In the case of *Alcazar*, in the film's striving to create a sense of verisimilitude, it is precisely this dimension of knowledge that reveals its fiction.

From the perspective of the films' discursive modes, the historical films reveal differences, varying from possible veiled critiques of the regime (e.g., Camerini's *Il cappello a tre punte*), to an encomium to nationalism (*1860* and *Passaporto rosso*), and to celebrations of Fascist heroics (*Condottieri*). Yet they are all invested in regarding the historical past, particularly the national past, as a necessary and viable fiction. Blasetti's *La corona di ferro* with its use of fairy tale and fantasy is perhaps a remarkable instance of the union of theatricality and history, where it becomes possible to see the ways in which popular culture through its use of folklore dramatizes the search for origins, the regaining of a repressed past, and the role of a savior in quelling disorder and violence. The highly stylized treatment serves to identify the historical past as a fiction that has designs on the present. What seems to animate the historical films and their treatments of the past in relation to the present—a trait that can be attributed to Fascism and fundamentally to mass spectacle—is their emphasis on visualization, performance, and melodrama as affective glue for cinematic representation. They are united in their awareness of themselves uppermost as cinema, and, as cinema, they speak to their audiences in a language that is determined by the demands of entertainment and by its capacity to simulate a sense of community. As products of popular culture, the films strive to reconcile the contradictions between desire and inevitable social constraints and necessities, between the public and the private, the individual and the group to overcome a sense of victimage through offering forms of compensation and rationalization for suffering. Their use of melodrama elevates the commonplace and endows it with a sense of intensity and meaning, making it appear operatic and significant. The individual passions and desires of ordinary people are equated with the actions of the great. This transformation is achieved by the folklore of common sense that valorizes survival and seeks forms of narration, a framework for neutralizing the sense of crisis and making it comprehensible. In relation to the presence of pathos in popular culture, Gramsci describes the importance of affect, a certain complex of overriding feelings and passions, inherent in common sense and in behaviors that appear conducive to collective action.[61]

The theatricality of the historical films can be be located in the ways that emotions are staged through the iconography of the characters, their actions, their reiteration of superstition, clichés, and a "morality closely tied to real religious beliefs. Imperatives exist that are much stronger, more tenacious and more effective than those of official 'morality.' In this sphere, too, one must distinguish various strata: the fossilized ones which reflect conditions of past life and are therefore conservative and reactionary, and those which consist of a series of innovations, often creative and progressive, determined spontaneously by forms and conditions of life which are in the process of developing and which are in contradiction to or simply different from the morality of the governing strata."[62] The theatricality of the films—their eclectic uses of the architecture, cultural artifacts, and costumes of the past—is not transparent and univalent but reveals the various strata of common sense as folklore, its official, fossilized, and innovative strands. As with the comedies, theatricality reveals the operations and mechanics of "putting on a show," dramatizing popular history for the fiction it is, "the privileged place where the gaze becomes unsettled, even if it is only that."[63] Moreover, particularly in the case of *Alcazar* in its construction of the present through the architecture of the past, the presence of theatricality also reveals how the Italian popular cinema of the era was indicative of a crisis in representation and how this crisis cannot be relegated to the past of the Fascist era but seen as an ongoing struggle in the cultural and political conflict over representation that stems from the hyperintensified character of popular culture and the increasing presence of mediated images. This crisis is particularly evident in the dislocation of boundaries between past and present and the real and the imaginary, even though this unsettling of parameters may do no more than manifest the existence of a crisis in knowledge that is integrally connected to the cinematic image and its relation to historicizing. This problem is not merely evident in the films of the Fascist era; it seems to be evident in the later peplum epics and spaghetti westerns, though these latter films are less identified with a particular ideology and more with interrogating history through the self-conscious uses of style.

CHAPTER FOUR

From Conversion to Calligraphism

In the previous two chapters, I focused on the various ways in which theatricality informs and complicates an understanding of the character of
two much-maligned genres of the Fascist era—comedies and historical
films. Through their focus on theatricality, the films share with their audiences a knowledge of their commodity status, a slippery relation to conformity and opposition, and a simultaneous sense of involvement and
detachment. Their treatment of spectacle is aligned to a reflexive use of
gesture, costume, and *mise-en-scène*, stressing artifice of setting and highlighting impersonation, disguises, doubling, carnival, and spectacle, the
ways in which they address and exploit "theatricality," a mode of expression where life is equated with performance—not authenticity. While the
narratives invoke familiar images of gender, sexuality, and work, conflicts
between the home and the world, the public and private spheres, tradition and modernity, personal desire and perceived social imperatives, their
reflexivity about performance produces an ambivalent and dialectical
interplay between realism and fiction, social conflict and fantasy, entertainment and seriousness, live entertainment and role playing, affective
involvement and distanciation.

In this chapter, I want to focus on two particular expressions of
melodrama—melodramas of "conversion" and melodramas of "calligraphism," designations that I adapt to identify the specific character of
theatricality that differs from the reflexive treatment characteristic of the
comedies and from the more monumental treatment of the historical

169

films. These forms of melodrama inform both the films that are set in the past and others that are set in a contemporary context. The aim of this chapter is to explore the nature and effects of their antirealism and use of narrative strategies that reach deep into the common sense of folklore. For the most part, these films dramatize embattled masculinity, marshalling familiar figures from folk tale and from religious narratives and myth but reworking these to suit contemporary dramas of nation formation, wartime sacrifice, and romantic and familial conflict.

What especially distinguishes these films from the historical dramas of the previous chapter is their treatment of character, both individual and collective, and of *mise-en-scène*. Character, action, and landscape are highly stylized, reliant on past folklore but transformed to suit the exigencies of contemporary life. In the dramas of conversion, for example, instead of the familiar and archaic hero of romance and earlier folklore, we find the new folklore clothed in the images of the aviator and the intrepid war hero and martyr. Instead of the Christian journey toward salvation, we have the national quest for purity and unity. Instead of the focus on the actions of the individual in behalf of the group, the individual stands in in exemplary fashion for the group. Instead of a union of romance and heroism, we are likely to have the subordination of heterosexual eroticism to homosocial bonding. The role of impersonation is still evident but impersonation is identified with the life that must be relinquished and purity and authenticity with the regenerated existence derived mainly through an encounter with death. However, in the films' melodramatic treatment, particularly in their highlighting the histrionic character of the masculine protagonist, and in his ambiguous transformation into a "new" existence, theatricality is still very much in evidence.

In the calligraphic melodramas, the environment that the films portray, whether in a rural or an urban context, is an unstable one, the lighting, the camera work, the acting, and the scripts themselves dramatize obsession, criminal activity, somnambulism, and violence. In so doing, the films rely on a highly ornate, baroque, and also theatrical style; this is not a world of realism but one of poses and artifacts where moral values and commitments are suspect. The protagonists in the films, largely masculine, appear to be the underside of the conversion dramas. If the former texts move to consolidate the protagonist's position through his identification with a spiritual goal, the latter move in an opposite direction by gradually revealing his decomposition, his loss of direction, and the corresponding dissolution of the community. I distinguish the films of conversion and calligraphism from the ones discussed in chapter 3 largely on the basis that they focus on the interiorization of antagonism, on the subjectification of conflict, and on a preoccupation with crumbling subjectivity. More than the comedies of the era that seem to be attuned to Hollywood style and values, those identified with the formalism of "calligraphism" and with such directors as Ferdinando Maria Poggioli, Mario Soldati, and Amleto Palermi, are narratives of dissimulation and disintegration, cast in the tradition of Italian literary and dramatic modes and characterized by a dark, claustrophobic, and obsessive world, images of paralysis but also of violence.

In the case of the films of both conversion and calligraphism, the films are a further validation of the need to understand the theatricality of popular culture, which both forms seem to address in their different ways. The terms in which spiritual dilemma are couched are those of melodrama, a highly theatricalized mode of expression relying on operatic excess. Melodramatic texts are heavily invested in theatricality. In their emphasis on the "mute gesture," their reliance on gesture, histrionic forms of expression, and music, the texts fuse past and present cultural forms, particularly an operatic style, to articulate and intensify the moral dilemmas confronting the protagonist.[1] On popular culture, Gramsci wrote: "popular theaters, with what are called arena performance (and today perhaps sound films, but also the subtitles of old silent films, all done in an operatic style) are of the utmost importance in the creation of this taste and its corresponding language."[2] Theatricality thus takes on a negative quality of being identified with a life and actions that are aimless and meaningless; by contrast, the life toward which the protagonist turns is identified with purpose and authenticity. In describing theatricality, Gilles Deleuze makes a crucial distinction between the theater of repetition and that of representation, which he derives in part from Marx:

> When Marx . . . criticizes the false movement or mediation of the Hegelians, he finds himself drawn to an idea, which he indicates rather than develops, an essentially "theatrical" idea: to the extent that history is theatre, then repetition, along with the tragic and the comic within repetition, forms a condition of movement under which the "actors" or the "heroes" produce something effectively new in history.[3]

The theater of representation seeks constantly to reduce differences to the principle of sameness, to tame multiplicity, while the theater of repetition offers gestures that develop before organised bodies, with masks before faces, spectres and phantasms before characters."[4] In the case of the melodramas under discussion in this chapter, they work by inversion, seeking to tame difference, subjecting affect and action to a false repetition in which the character seeks to undermine illusion and substitute instead another illusion as reality.

Melodramatic narratives of the era (whether from Hollywood or Italy) are preoccupied with portraits of transcendent or failed struggles on the part of the masculine protagonists to achieve attitudes and behavior appropriate to familial, romantic, or militant political and warlike expectations. The texts reproduce the moral polarities endemic to melodrama, and they rely on a folklore associated with the narrative of conversion as a conduit through which affect travels. An important component of these melodramatic scenarios is their ostensible focus on a quest for meaning and legitimacy in a world bereft of certainty, where values are in crisis, and where, consequently, the protagonists are engaged in a struggle to establish a meaningful identity and relation to society. While associated primarily with religion, the phenomenon of conversion is an essential component of many melodramatic narratives involving action, adventure, and forms of heterosexual and homosocial bonding. Basic to folklore, the melodrama of conversion is identified by its reliance on rituals of initiation, magical and rhetorical aides, and physical and spiritual trials. This form of melodrama also draws on a rhetorical, theatrical, operatic style and on juridical and religious discourses that have been assimilated into the folklore lexicon.

According to William James, religious literature from St. Augustine's *Confessions* to modernity has relied on two types of conversion.[5] One form of conversion is the starkly dramatic lightning-like type; the other form is more gradual. In each, the protagonist confronts a world that has lost its meaning, and he must struggle to find a meaningful alternative which he discovers in religious commitment. In each, the individual undergoes a dramatic reversal in his relations to his conception of himself and redefines his relations to others. Conversion dramatizes the hero's struggle to find an appropriate identity and his adoption of forms of action suitable to his "new" existence. The stages of the process involve a sense of dissatisfaction, even disgust, with his current life, an unsatisfactory attempt to accommodate to existing forms of behavior, an experience of emptiness, and a prolonged "dark night of the soul" in which he wrestles with himself and with others. A transformation in values and behavior is signalled by a headlong or gradual awareness of another form of life in spirituality and commitment to a higher cause even if this entails his own sacrifice and martyrdom.

Religious transformation seems especially congenial to those films that more obviously aligned to the Fascist regime and its dissemination of images identified with the "new" man and to wartime narratives. The most extreme expressions of the conversion narrative in the 1920s and 1930s are indebted to the literary and cinematic work of Gabriele D'Annunzio. The religious world inhabited by this masculine superhero is a world of homosocial bonding, where sacrifice and death are expected, epitomized by the quest for virility through the effacement of any trace of the stain of femininity. The portrait of this superhero is congenial to the language of cinematic melodrama, dependent as it is on hyperbole, monumentalism, and action. The situation in which the protagonist finds himself entails an all-or-nothing response. In the evolution of the nation-form, nationalism and patriotism are the religion of modern times, not merely of Italian Fascism. Conversion is not a matter of the religious, otherworldly salvation of individual souls, though theological discourse has provided models for their transubstantiation onto the idealization of the nation and the sacralization of the state, which make it possible for a bond of sacrifice to be created between men, and for the stamp of "truth" and "law" to be conferred upon the new order. As Etienne Balibar reminds us,

> Every national community must have been represented at some point or another as a "chosen people." . . . [N]ational ideology involves ideal signifiers (first and foremost the very *name* of the nation or "fatherland") on to which may be transferred the sense of the sacred and the affects of love, respect, sacrifice and fear which have cemented religious communities; but that transfer only takes place because *another type* of community is involved here.[6]

This other community is often the nation. Thus, the phenomenon of conversion takes on a secular, national, appearance but bears the traces of its religious source. The individual seeks regeneration and grace, but a grace conferred through his entry into the worldly, not religious, community. Before he can enter this community, he must contend with figures of authority and power, familial and sexual figures, representatives of social institutions and of the law. The narrative of conversion takes various forms derived from folklore, not all of them imbued with a radical nationalist ethos. The conversion paradigm is equally congenial to domestic drama, especially where these domestic dramas involve a radical choice between conformity to and rebellion against the existing social order. Most familiar is the pattern of the prodigal son who returns to the familial fold and makes peace with the father after having strayed. The narrative of the prodigal father who, too late, discovers his errors in disregarding the values of his son is also prominent. The Oedipal paradigm involves homosocial bonding. The bonding entails, first, antagonisms between two men, one, a surrogate paternal figure, who represents the path of duty, the other, a surrogate son, who seeks pleasure. Later, they are united, even fused into one identity. The conflict between commitment to a higher spiritualized cause and the pursuit of individual desire involves the centrality of the spectre of woman, split between the benevolent and sacrificial maternal image and that of the temptress, who offers the pleasures of the flesh inimical to the well-being and solidarity of the community.

Central to any view of melodrama is its emphasis on the personal and the affective. In relation to the individual, what is important is that his or her actions (or inaction) are not removed from the public sphere, though this relationship is masked by the centripetal drive of the narrative. It produces an illusion of individual agency and ostensible separateness from the arena of affairs of state, as Elsaesser states:

> The poverty of the intellectual resources in some of the characters is starkly contrasted with a corresponding abundance of emotional resources, and as one sees them helplessly struggling inside their emotional prisons with no hope of realising to what degree they are the victims of their society, one gets a clear picture of how a certain individualism reinforces social and emotional alienation, and of how the economics of the psyche are as vulnerable to manipulation and exploitation as is a person's labour.[7]

The narratives of conversion, in other words, oscillate between intellectual poverty and affective abundance of central characters. Through their affective ties to traditional folklore, common sense, and their roots in popular culture, they seek to mask the degree to which the protagonists are, in fact, emotional prisoners to a set of prescribed and choreographed imperatives. The films of calligraphism, while relying on similar narrative paradigms but in inverted form, take delight in exposing the vulnerability, emotional alienation, and histrionic quality of a world where the characters are victims. If religion is directly invoked, it serves less as legitimation and more as a further indication of the dissolution of the social fabric and the impotence of the individual and the community.

A PARADIGMATIC TEXT

Il fu Mattia Pascal (the Late Mattia Pascal), directed by Pierre Chenal was released in 1937.[8] The narrative had been produced earlier as a silent film in 1925 by the French director Marcel L'Herbier. Based on a novel of Luigi Pirandello, Chenal's film is a compendium of types, motifs, and images that derive from folklore and from its archetypal conversion strategies.[9] Nina da Vinci Nichols and Jana O'Keefe Bazzoni have described the vicissitudes of the novel as rendered on film, from modernist romance, to experimental and expressionist text invoking the grotesque, to a work that "may derive not from its cinematic merits but from its reminders of Pirandello's original work once again revived and transformed."[10] In particular, the motif of doubling is central to the work, once again reminding of the importance of theatricality and impersonation in so many films of the era. The Chenal film intermingles fantasy, folklore, and quotidian experience to produce a richly ironic portrait of the "new man." The film lays bare the mechanisms of representation that lie at the heart of the conversion narrative. Pirandello's work was involved with double consciousness, with "conflicts, opposites, the other side of the visible, the mask behind the mask," [11] and, as portrayed in the Chenal film, offers a version of theatricality that far exceeds the notion of theater transferred onto film to probe the power of representation as theatricality, as comprised of postures and semblances.

In commenting on Pirandello's work, Gramsci wrote "Luigi Pirandello is a 'stormtrooper' of the theatre. His comedies are so many hand grenades that explode in the brains of the spectators, bringing down banalities, wrecking feelings and ideas."[12] Mattia Pascal, the character, is for Gramsci, "the melancholic modern man, cross-eyed, a spectator of life who is at times cynical, bitter, melancholic, and sentimental."[13] In Chenal's hands the work vacillates between melodrama and irony as the text follows the vicissitudes and then the triumph of the protagonist over the forces that block his progress through the world. Nichols and Bazzoni have expressed the belief that the film had lost some of the Pirandellian grotesqueness and was less attentive to the original, adding peripheral scenes.[14] In particular, they feel that Chenal "departed . . . from the quixotic madness and tormented opportunism of Pirandello's deluded hero."[15] Though this position may correctly assess differences between original text and the film, it does not address the film's contributions to the relations between cinema and folklore of the Fascist era. The film is particularly important as a lexicon of the motifs and strategies of the conversion melodrama in its uses of character typification, its invocation of the symbolic landscape of the archetypal journey, and its reenactment of the stages of the drama of conversion.

Mattia Pascal begins deceptively as a pastoral idyll. Mattia (Pierre Blanchar) is romantically attached to Romilda Pescatore (Nella Maria Bonora), whom he is about to marry. An appearance of rural harmony is shattered by the harsh realities of money and family aggression. Signora Pescatore (Irma Gramatica), Romilda's mother, is the archetypal bad mother from a fairy tale, greedy, grasping, and tyrannical. Significantly, neither Romilda or Mattia have fathers, reinforcing that Mattia lives in a woman's world. Immediately after the wedding party, the mother-in-law, Pescatore, confronts Mattia with a bill for the festivities, completely disregarding that his mother has paid her 50,000 lire for the couple's housekeeping, all the money that she has in the world. By contrast, Mattia's mother is the good mother, completely devoted to her son and willing to go to any length to please him. The disrupted wedding feast is the prologue to a series of misfortunes that beset Mattia and his mother, following the motif of trials associated with the folklore of conversion. The characters in this world are highly stylized and divided between victims and aggressors. Very quickly, Mattia learns that Romilda is similar to her mother, and her first act on the wedding night is to refuse him the sexual pleasures of the wedding bed. His destitute mother, thanks to Signora Pescatore, Mattia goes to work as a librarian where he is further exploited, and the coup de grace comes when his mother dies. Signora Pescatore not only forbids Romilda to go to the dying woman but she arranges with the mayor for a pauper's funeral for Signora Pascal.

The element of contingency is central to the conversion narrative as the film dramatizes. Chance intervenes as Mattia after the funeral wanders off and in a haze finds himself on a train, and good fortune now follows as he heads for Marseilles and, on the advice of an old man, the proverbial wise man of folklore, ends up in Monte Carlo, where he wins at roulette. The contrasts between city and country, provincialism and cosmopolitanism become increasingly apparent, the countryside aligned to oppression, the urban world offering the possibility of freedom. With his winnings, Mattia returns to his home determined to reclaim Romilda and make Pescatore a "slave to him." However, he is unaware that he has been declared dead; the body of a drunk who drowned has been identified as Mattia Pascal, and he arrives home in time to view his own funeral. Thus, he becomes a spectator to his old world and his life of impersonation begins. Having shed one identity, he goes to Rome to the Luxor Hotel where he assumes another identity as Adriano Meis from Milan. It turns out that there is a Meis family at the hotel, and he is forced to manufacture evidence of his relationship to that family. Fortunately, he also makes the acquaintance in the park of a woman, Signorina Caporale (Olga Solbelli), a spiritualist who directs him to a boarding house where he meets Luisa (Isa Miranda), another resident. In the boarding house also live Luisa's tutor and a Count Papiano (Enrico Glori), who is engaged to Luisa. Again greed and exploitation rears its head, this time associated with the count. Caporale, Papiano's former mistress, decides to prevent his marriage to Luisa. Luisa and "Adriano" fall in love, but the count, having learned that Adriano has no identity papers, threatens him with exposure. Moreover, he steals Adriano's money, and, once again, Mattia is cast adrift. He tries to "kill" Adriano, and return home to his former life. Home once again, he learns that Romilda has remarried. Seeking to avoid embarrassment, the husband, a provincial official, gets Mattia identity papers, and he returns to Rome as Adriano Meis. Reunited with Luisa and having outsmarted Papiano, he tells Luisa, "Io sono . . . Io sono . . . Il fu Mattia Pascal." Thus, he finally has an identity that is validated. He has escaped from the tyranny of the past and entered into a "new life."

The stages of Mattia's "conversion" are consonant with the imagery of conversion: youthful naiveté and oppression, a journey to enlightenment, the "death" of the old life, the struggle to obliterate the past, and, finally, rebirth. The narrative is dependent on a strict binary structure. The figures whom he confronts are equally binary: good and evil mother figures, tyrannical male authority figures, cruel and benign women who alternately oppress or save him. The female characters associated with the village are domineering and exploitative. Identified with his self-sacrificing mother, he is passive and unable to combat the aggressiveness of his mother-in-law, his wife, and the mayor. The narrative is dependent on doubling: two mothers, two absent fathers, two women with whom he is involved romantically, two drownings and two false suicides, the countryside and Rome, and the protagonist's two identities. Other characters from folklore and fairy tale include the classic maternal shrew, the counterpart of the witch, the cruel decadent aristocrat who malevolently obstructs the protagonist's progress, and "orphans" (both Luisa and Mattia) who find an identity and romance.

The symbolism of the journey and of the water are also typical of the trajectory of conversion narratives. Spiritualism, as represented through Signorina Caporale, also reinforces the magical and folkloric aspects of the narrative. The fairy-tale quality of the film serves like a handbook, foregrounding the key elements in the drama of conversion. The protagonist's first "death" takes place in the country and his "rebirth" is associated with Monte Carlo and Rome. His second death in the city is only provisional since, after his return to the country to legitimize his new identity, he appropriates his former and only provisional role more fully. Money, equated with sexuality and power, is the instrument of his oppression, the means whereby Mattia is controlled but finally the means whereby he assumes power. In his new sense of self, he can subordinate the women from his past and, ironically, "march" on Rome. The "happy ending," like the rest of the film, is a fantasy. In the protagonist's journey toward the acquisition of a "proper" name and identity, in the forms of the trials he confronts, and through the imagery of light and darkness, the film provides a critical, even reflexive, blueprint of the conversion narrative. Ironically, the fiction of Mattia's death and rebirth are less the preconditions for a new and higher form of life, and more a satiric commentary on forms of social life as death. In its excessive reliance on stylization, coincidence, and magic, the film blatantly proclaims itself as artifice, perhaps invoking an audience that can entertain its ironies. In its emphasis on caricature, on blatantly stark oppositions between the characters, and in its repeated emphasis on forms of looking, such as Mattia contemplating his own image in death and in his repeated surveillance by others, the film complicates its familiar folklore and problematizes escapism and theatricality. The film takes the most familiar and popular of narratives, that of conversion, and, in making its strategies obvious through theatricalization, also makes them ambiguous, if not ludicrous.

THE PRODIGAL SON

In a much more serious and straightforward vein but consonant with the various narrative elements of *Il fu Mattia Pascal*, Blasetti's *Terra Madre*

(Earth Mother, 1931) is also a pastoral idyll and also dependent on a masculine protagonist who is converted to a new identity. The film is also
reliant on oppositions between country and the city, and, as in other
Blasetti films, the countryside is associated with the virtues of the "race,"
while the city is associated with decadence.[16] Much of the theatricality of
the film is associated with forms of entertainment identified with the
urban folk, on the one hand, and the peasants on the other. According to
Jean Gili, "in opposition to the indolent and unproductive rich, the peasants are the true riches of the country."[17] By contrast to the urban population, they are portrayed as honest and pious, with simple customs and
with a respect for work. Gianfranco Casadio describes the thematic of the
film as "the reconciliation between the peasants and the landed propri-
etors who have abandoned the earth (mother) for urban life."[18] Moreover,
the proprietor assumes, according to Casadio, "the figure of the *padre,
padrone, duce.*"[19] And it is through him that the drama of conversion is
realized

The film's protagonist, Duke Marco (Sandro Salvini), has returned
to his country estate to sell his land. Shots of land and workers are contrasted to images of shabby-looking peasants. The peasants look forward
to the return of the landowner, for productivity on the estate has been
sadly neglected. The initial images of the people highlight both young
and the elderly, men and women. A car appears in this rural scene as an
interloper. The master has arrived with his woman friend, Daisy (Isa
Pola), who is out of place in this environment and annoyed by its personal
inconveniences, its lack of modernity. The house is filled with paintings
and sculpture, books, and armor, signs of Marco's family lineage and of
the past. Outside, the camera travels over the landscape, the actual protagonist of the film. By contrast, the scene cuts inside to Daisy in bed,
being waited on by the serving woman and complaining of the sound of
water dripping in a basin brought in by the woman. The woman covers
the basin and looks with disgust at Daisy. Marco has already been out to
inspect the estate when he meets Emilia (Leda Gloria), daughter of his
superintendent. Unaware of the duke's identity, she complains to him of
the shameful way the duke has neglected his duty to the people. (She is
the link to the land, the other mother to whom the title refers.) The duke
is confronted by scenes of the death of his people in a peasant's funeral
reminiscent of the style of Dovzhenko's *Earth.* An outdoor scene of men
at work corralling a steer develops contrasts between the people and the
duke's friends and contrasts between Emilia and Daisy, who is playing

seductively with another man, as Marco, unaware, watches the men at work. Marco reveals his expertise when he steps into the corral and masters a steer. A country dance is performed with the peasants in regional dress, and Daisy laughs mockingly at the proceedings, looking fashionable and bored. Marco's city friends prefer dancing to American music. Entertainment becomes a major means of distinguishing between country and city life, between impersonation and authenticity.

Events worsen as a new agent arrives to take over management of the estate. His insolence is first expressed in his disrespect for Marco's serving woman. The peasants plan to plead with Marco to get him to change his mind about selling, but Marco informs the superintendent that it is too late to alter events. As the time draws nearer for Marco's departure, he becomes more involved with Emilia, but nonetheless he leaves. In the city, several tableaux of Marco and his friends are presented, showing them at their games, playing cards, dancing, listening to American-style music. When Marco is informed that a fire has broken out, he returns to the estate, learning that in his absence, the new superintendent has harassed the peasants. Chaos reigns as the fire rages and the peasants are hounded by Marco's agent. Emilia blames Marco for the disaster, for neglecting his people. He and the agent fight and Marco knocks him down, and announces his decision to stay. After saving peasants and animals from the fire, he announces that, "This land is mine and shall remain mine." He is united with Emilia and a title announces, "Progress. The earth again shall live. The happy past must be combined with a happy future." The film does not end here, but moves ahead in time to show images of the people working productively again and Marco on horseback overseeing the work. Emilia is also working as their children play in the hay. He tells her to go home—"Women don't work"—and she acquiesces. The final shots are of the landscape and of farm implements in the earth. This final scene, like the earlier scenes with the peasants' dancing, functions like a poster or advertisement for the happy and productive family. Emilia resembles the images of happy and fertile mothers circulated through posters and advertisements of the era and Marco the virile, active, and benign prototype of the new man, and both of them, along with their offspring, fused with the fertile land.

The drama of conversion is clear. As the "prodigal son," Marco has strayed from his proper responsibility, abandoning his family and his people. He has cast aside his playboy role and recognized his paternal responsibility to his peasants. But before Marco can be converted to a position of responsibility, he must undergo (literally) a trial by fire, must acknowledge his guilt and renounce his meaningless life in the city and his sterile relationship to Daisy, an unfit figure for maternal procreation. The agents of his conversion are Emilia and the disaster of the fire. While he is the source of the melodrama, the victims are the suffering people, and his conversion is, therefore, the consequence of his gradual acceptance of the paternal role and his renunciation of the deceptive attractiveness of modernity. Marco's role as paternal figure is complemented by the role of the peasants as childlike, defenseless, and in need of care and direction. Significantly, in his conversion, he assumes the burdens of leadership and its identification with paternalism after his old identity has been consumed by fire. He is responsible for regenerating the land as well as new life through Emilia and her children, fulfilling the role of fatherhood both in his own person and in his role as *padrone*.

Complementing Marco's role, Emilia is the eternal mother, identified with the land, with *strapaese*, with ruralism, with the people, and, of course, with reproduction. Her role is enhanced by its juxtaposition to that of Daisy, the urban dweller, uncreative, and lacking in compassion and nurture. Casadio describes her role as the disruptive element in the narrative, the woman who does not understand the patriarchal family and provincialism.[20] By contrast, Emilia is, "*la brava madre italiana,*" reminiscent of images of the mother in the demographic campaign conducted by the regime described by Victoria de Grazia and Lesley Caldwell.[21] She is presented as submissive and happy to assume the duties of wife and mother. The imagery makes it clear that she is identified, like the land, with fecundity. However, while the film lends itself to a reading that aligns it with Fascist ideology, it also reveals, in both Marco's drama of conversion and in the "earth mother" role of Emilia, how deeply Fascist ideology relies on pre-Fascist folklore and mythology. Blasetti's films in general seem consistently to be drawn to a mythology that overflows restrictive Fascist labels, subsuming them but also calling attention to the persistence and pervasiveness of folklore and common sense as the ballast for representation. Through melodrama's reliance on repetition and inversion, the "old" becomes the "new," and difference merges with sameness.

THE ORPHANS' RETURN

While the most recognized films of Mario Camerini are his comedies, especially those that he made with the young film idol, Vittorio De

Sica, he also directed melodramas. His lighter comedies as well as the more pathetic melodramas are reliant on the narrative of conversion, revealing errant young men who are brought to recognize their faults and repent their mistakes. The films are patterned on the motif of a journey, often featuring images of locomotion—cars and trains—to mark the stages of the protagonist's progress through the filmic world. The protagonists are either dissatisfied with their station in life, or as in the case of *Rotaie* (1929), are victims of familial misunderstanding and rejection, reducing them to the threat of being orphaned, without familial identity. A film that bears the marks of silent cinema, *Rotaie* is set in an urban context, where a couple, Giorgio (Maurizio D'Ancora) and Maria (Käthe von Nagy), estranged from family, registers in a hotel as husband and wife. Quickly their situation is revealed as hopeless. A letter from her mother indicates that the couple has cut themselves adrift from family. In this early sound film sparing of dialogue, the emphasis is mainly on the visual cues to their plight—the narrow and darkened room, the torn-up letter, and a glass with a dissolving poison pill. The couple is planning suicide, but vibrations from a passing train cause the glass to fall. The couple embraces and prepares themselves to leave. Penniless, they wander the streets until finally they find a wallet with money on the ground near the train station. For a second time, chance or fate has determined their behavior. They try unsuccessfully to find the owner, and Giorgio buys tickets with the found money. On the train (identified by the recurrent image of wheels), Maria asks where they are going, and he answers, "Where the others are going." The motif of wheels comes to signify multiple themes: the sense of movement though in ambiguous directions at the outset, of obsession later, and of release and purposive movement at the end of the film. The imagery from the perspective of the train is the countryside, buildings, and train tracks and wheels.

On the train, they meet a Frenchman, Marquis Mercier (Daniele Crispi) the prototypical "city slicker" and decadent aristocrat of traditional melodrama, a figure proleptic of the false and dissipating lures of wealth and cosmopolitanism. Through him, they find a hotel more elegant than the one where they had planned to commit suicide. That time has passed is evident from the situation of Maria and Giorgio. Maria is pursued by Mercier; Giorgio devotes his time to gambling, and is for a time successful. Entertainment is again highlighted and associated with the pitfalls of city life. Other than gambling, the characters' time is spent

FIGURE 14. The ersatz allures of city life, *Rotaie*. Courtesy of New York Museum of Modern Art, Film Stills Archive.

on dancing, drinking, and seduction, reminiscent of the urbanites in *Terra madre*. Escaping from Mercier, Maria hides in her room only to be reproached when Giorgio returns, his hands filled with his winnings. She begs to leave, but he indicates that they have nowhere to go and, moreover, he would have to give up his good fortune. This is their first disagreement, but they reconcile, only to find themselves in the throes of repetition. The wheels of the train have become roulette wheels as Giorgio's luck changes for the worse. He is forced to take money from Maria to pay for his now compulsive habit. Now become a shadow to him, Maria pawns items to survive and hovers in the background, observing Giorgio's fixation.

Mercier, however, enjoys Giorgio's obsession and encourages, even provides, him with money to continue. Furthermore, he sees Giorgio's distraction as a further opportunity to seduce Maria. After a desperate Maria has decided to succumb to Mercier's blandishments, Giorgio, alone in his room, observes through the window a domestic scene of a couple with their children sitting at table. He leaves his room and goes to Mercier's room in time to circumvent the impending seduction. Maria runs to him, and he and Maria leave the hotel and go to sit on a park bench where they reconcile. Again, Giorgio buys train tickets, again the image of wheels is evident, but the people on the train are working-class people. He sees a woman nursing a baby, a father with his young son, and the scene dissolves to Giorgio as a worker. This time, images of machinery are associated with the world of workers, and Maria appears, dressed in simple clothing, the wife of a worker, bringing him food.

Parallels with *Terra madre* are evident in the role of conversion as a precondition for the regeneration of social life, the focus being on the male protagonist and on his literal and figurative movement toward a new life associated with regenerating dimensions of labor. The emphasis on productivity is the key motif in both films and the contrast between the dissolute upper classes and the redemptive character of workers is also common to both. Both films stress the woman's role as the instrument of conversion, the type of woman who is identified with maternity, submission, and service to the man. Also as in the case of *Terra madre*, the familiar dichotomy between maternity and eroticism is evident. The major differences reside in the emphases on rural and urban life, *Terra madre* valorizing ruralism, *Rotaie*, urbanism, and the Blasetti film celebrating folklore and mythology, while the Camerini film draws on the classical folklore of melodrama, involving the threat to the woman's chastity as the device for the protagonist's change of heart. The upper-class Mercier, however, is not converted; he is not destroyed, but merely abandoned by the narrative, a sign that, though the protagonist is transformed, the world is not. Once again, the theatrical character of representation is evident, drawing its poses from the melodramatic potential of the orphan, of threatened female chastity, and of the fascinating but threatening lure of the metropolis and its vices.

MACHINES AND MODERNITY

An ambivalent attitude toward modernity is at the heart of so many of the melodramas of conversion in the ways that the films address not merely urban life but especially in the ways that they treat work and workers, relations between nature and technology, and seek to mediate traditional notions of masculinity, the family, and heterosexual romance with a sense of a transformed and transforming physical environment. In particular, the German filmmaker Walter Ruttmann produced a melodrama that alters traditional conceptions of conversion, casting them in modernist terms by subjugating individual conversion of the protagonist to a more collective notion of community transformation. *Acciaio* (1933), based on a Pirandello work, opens with a race of cyclists. The camera singles out the cyclists, the crowds, and the winner of the race, Mario (Piero Pastore). After his success, Mario returns to his hometown and to his childhood sweetheart, Gina (Isa Pola). The first images associated with Mario's return are of nature, highlighting a waterfall. The shots of the waterfall emphasize its power, a prolepsis of the melodrama to come. These images of nature and of agrarian scenes are contrasted with images of a factory as Mario rides his bicycle. The industrial photography and the style of editing of the factory shots are reminiscent of *Berlin, Symphony of a City*. The views of the machinery are, like the earlier views of the waterfall, seen from different angles, emphasizing design, intensity, and power. The sounds of the machinery cancel out other sounds. The workers' movements are stylized and mechanical. The images of the workers, while less prominent than those of the aesthetics of the machinery, foreground the dangerous relation between the men and the machines. Visually, the world is thus presented as a precarious one in which individuals are in danger of losing any sense of personal identity, overwhelmed by the machines.

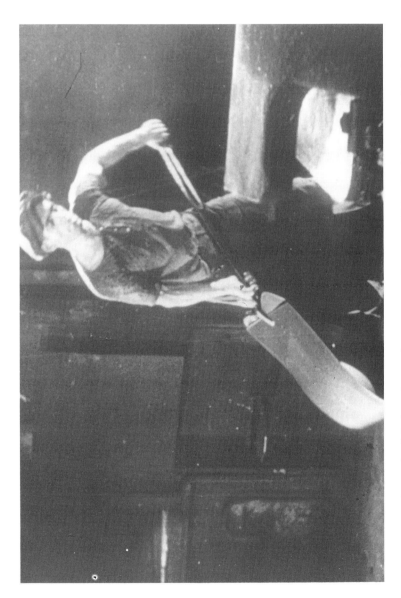

FIGURE 15. The work of feeding the machine, *Acciaio*. Courtesy of New York Museum of Modern Art, Film Stills Archive.

The relations among the characters threaten to erupt into violence. Thinking that Mario would never return, Gina has become engaged to another worker, Pietro (Vittorio Bellaccini). The narrative centers on the contrast between the men and their triangular relationship with the woman. Learning of the engagement, Mario becomes distraught and goes to a bar where he seeks to pick a fight with Pietro. Gina, who has come to the bar explains to Mario that since he has been away and did not write, she had no way of knowing that he was still interested. The three-some go together to an amusement park, which, with its merry-go-round, dancing, and games, is intercut with scenes of work where the men are moving their hands quickly and deftly with the machines. As the scenes alternate, the pace escalates, paralleling the intensity of the factory with the emotions of the men, their jealousy of each other, and the threat of violence. At the park, Mario dances with Gina, and Pietro becomes belligerent. Others intervene to forestall violence. At the factory, the antagonism of the two men is apparent as they work, their images intercut with dynamic shots of hot ingots, prefiguring disaster.

Pietro's father (Alfredo Polveroni) is told by the manager that he must let him go on account of the old man's illness and the risk of accident at the factory. However, he counsels him not to worry about his future, since his son is working. This scene introduces the tragedy of Pietro who is fatally struck by one of the falling ingots. Here, the contrast between machinic power and human frailty is stressed, but the scene also underscores the parallels between the power of nature and of machines that the film has repeatedly portrayed. The incremental, rhythmic, and escalating editing prior to Pietro's accident serves proleptically to suggest that someone is bound to be sacrificed. Before he dies, Pietro assures Mario that the accident was not Mario's fault. But the chance death of Pietro, a victim of the impersonal machine, is interpreted by the community as a premeditated act, not one of chance. Conflict intensifies as Mario is now ostracized despite the asseverations of the manager that he was not culpable. People ignore him; children turn away when he passes. He sees chalked messages on walls, insulting and indicting him. Women take their children's hands and cross the street when he appears. Gina tries to defend him but is vilified for her defense and told that she and Mario should leave town. Mario contemplates leaving and returning to his former life of racing. The turning point in the film comes when he learns about a local bicycle race and decides to participate. As Gina and the townspeople observe him, he rides to victory. The race provides an opportunity to rehearse images of the landscape: natural and manmade, rural and urban, fields and factory. In the final scenes, the conflict between work and racing is resolved as Mario joins the mass of workers on their way into the factory, finds a card waiting for him, and then is seen at his job. The camera pans the machinery; an image of smoke dissolves into a waterfall, reiterating the early images of the waterfall and the conjunction between nature and machinery. The struggles of the workers are inextricable from the overarching formal designs of the film that externalize individual and personal conflicts.

Concomitant with the melodramatic conflicts arising from the romantic triangle, the film offers another perspective on relations between nature, machinery, and human society, one that posits a transcendent image of the dynamism of industry and nature overarching the social life of individuals and of the community. A form of religiosity comes into play—identified with modernism, and the avant-garde, and the power of mechanized production and modernity voided of intentionality and human agency. In discussing the work of Marinetti, Walter L. Adamson comments that his political manifestos "'announced a new religion-morality of speed,' a machine aesthetic."[22] And James Hay describes Ruttmann's work as evoking "the kind of sacred and mystical aura traditionally associated with ritual caves or religious temples, as centers for the community's spiritual revitalization and unity of purpose."[23] The focus on individual power as a mainspring for the regenerated community merges with the fascination with speed, movement, and power identified in the film through an equation of factory machinery, waterfalls, and racing, also through its elevation of chance and contingency, and the incorporation of the human into the machinic. The narrative of conversion has not disappeared; it has shifted. The traditional conception of the protagonist's "dark night of the soul" and his struggle to affirm a new way of life is subsumed in the affirmation of a higher power that has been brought into being by the acknowledgement of the forces unleashed by technology but identified with the forces of nature. The film does not treat Pietro's death as a strategy for condemning the machine but as a way of recognizing and acknowledging the impersonality of power, and Mario's reintegration into the community is an acknowledgment of the existence of a higher power that also regenerates the community, traditional values, and behavior.

The film validates the persistence of folklore in its maintenance of a romance paradigm, its rural setting, its religious cast, and its movement from a focus on the protagonist's dilemma to that of the community.

Acciaio is particularly illustrative of the ways in which older forms of narrative are transformed to meet the exigencies of modernity in the sense that Gramsci has described the common sense of folklore, its absorptive and eclectic character, its functionality in producing a sense of community and consensus, and particularly its reliance on the residual forms of religion. In the context of theatricality, especially the film's focus on sports and on the events in the amusement park, the film reiterates the importance of spectatorship—through the involvement of the audiences within the film and, by extension, the external audience—as a ritual essential to the consolidation of community. If the traditional conversion narrative—its attempts to mediate between the human and the demonic—seems subordinated to the film's fascination with the organic nature of the factory machine, the film, nonetheless, maintains its ties to a religious sense of the world in terms of its spiritualizing technology, implicating, one presumes, the technology of cinema.

MARTYRDOM, MOURNING, AND COMMUNITY CONVERSION

Conversion is particularly identified with films of political propaganda and with the sacrifices deemed necessary in the commitment to the realization of political and social objectives. Blasetti's *Vecchia guardia* (1935) is identified as one of the few feature films that openly exalts Fascism and the *squadristi*.[24] The film was not unproblematically received, since the question of representing Fascist history carried the danger of "raking up unwanted memories" for those in authority.[25] Elaine Mancini sees parallels between Blasetti's film and *Hitlerjunge Quex* (1933), though Blasetti claimed not to have seen the film. Obvious similarities reside in the emphasis on and appeal to youth as a source of social and political transformation and also in the role of youthful martyrdom as the basis for solidifying the community. The film opens with a titled prologue that exalts the Fascists and situates the time of the narrative as preliminary to the "March on Rome." Like many of Blasetti's films, this one takes place in a small town and, as in a documentary, employs a voice-over that articulates the decadence of the present political situation, the impotence of the liberals and of other individuals to stem the tide of deteriorating social conditions.

The narrative begins with the arrival of a truck, filled with men and bearing an injured older man to Dr. Cardini (Gianfranco Giachetti), one of the major protagonists of the film. Roberto Cardini (Mino Doro), a Black shirt, goes home to rest after the trials of the prior night. At home, he finds his younger brother, Mario (Franco Brambilla), who is fascinated with working on machines, especially clocks. Clocks will play a central role in the film as they signify the sense of urgency of the Fascists, their struggling against the past and toward the future. The boy reveres his older brother, and the family is portrayed as a model of domestic unity. The mother is submissive and totally supportive of her sons, and the father will ultimately join his sons in their struggle to realize Fascism. The other important woman in the film is Maria (Barbara Monis), the next-door neighbor, a schoolteacher and Roberto's fiancée. Her role is conso-nant with prevailing portraits of women in the film. Victoria de Grazia describes how, according to the emphasis on the connections between fascistization and education, teachers were considered a fundamental pil-lar of the state, though increasingly women were excluded from this pro-fession.[26]

The film is not silent on its expectations of productive work and of orderly workers and on its repudiation of socialism as the demonic force responsible for the decay of community values. At Dr. Cardini's clinic, the physician is hampered by the inability of his employees to submit to the discipline of work, striking without regard for the necessary services per-formed by the hospital. The implication is that the leaders of their union and the socialists, not the workers, are to blame for the chaos. Concomi-tantly, representatives of the local government turn a deaf ear to Cardini's requests for help, spending their time at public events such as festivals, fishing, or plain idleness. The aggressive tactics of the *squadristi* in "ame-liorating" this hopeless situation are portrayed in a barber shop scene, where a Fascist, Aristide, gets revenge on a socialist and shaves off half his beard while others look on and laugh. Violence erupts as a band of unruly agitators throw rocks through the window of the barbershop and a young boy is injured, thus revealing the socialists' aggressiveness, indifference to young people, and the disruptiveness of their opposition to the Fascists. Maria scolds these "subversives," and takes the young boy out to care for him. The situation gets worse when Dr. Cardini learns that the strikers are creating further problems in organizing against the hospital. The leg-endary castor oil treatment is meted out to one of the socialists when he goes to the pharmacy to get medication for laryngitis, and later castor oil is given to the hospital workers, who are thus "urged" to return to work. In parallel fashion, the school is also under siege, since the town supervisor has canceled classes and locked the school. However, Roberto, Maria, and another man open the school, having gotten the keys from the custodian. The climax of the conflict between Fascists, socialists, and bureaucrats occurs in a street battle where Mario is shot, a martyr to the Fascist cause. His death becomes the rallying point for the Fascists. The boy's body is draped with the Fascist banner and an elegiac scene follows, focusing on the mother's and Maria's bereavement. Mario is given a hero's funeral that mobilizes the community. The Fascists march through the streets, singing, "Today no one stays at home, Mario is with us." The film ends in spectacle with lights, flags, and patriotic music, prefiguring the fascist march on Rome.

The narrative focuses on the conversion of the community—not just of individuals; its strategies are a form of pedagogy, directed at transforming the audience, inviting it to experience the trials and tribulations attendant on the quest for regeneration. The narrative draws on an assumed antipathy to violence against youth. In its contrasting typology of violent and unscrupulous socialists and benign Fascists, the film invites the audience to identify with the clean-shaven, virile, and well-meaning Fascists. In the film's orchestration of contrasting images of organization and disorganization, its portraying the threat of disruption to vital institutions such as the family, hospitals, and schools, it conjures a portrait of a world devoid of benevolence, trust, and predictability. But the mainspring of the narrative resides in the motif of martyrdom and the attendant mourning that follows it. In the death of Mario, the audience is invited to identify with the vision of an entire community grieving and to share in the sense of loss, in the collective ritual of mourning, and in the efforts at resolution through action.

Religious conversion is intimately tied to the necessity of reshaping identity in relation to the self and to the community. In order for one to experience conversion, one must first acknowledge the error of past ways and abandon past modes of thinking and behavior. Images of loss and recovery are central to the process. The death of an individual becomes the springboard to revaluation of erroneous and destructive relationships and forms of behavior, and mourning assumes a pivotal and dramatic function in the impetus toward change. Death and social transfiguration through the ritual of mourning serves as a means for cementing common bonds. In describing the ritualistic dimensions of mourning, Durkheim writes that "When someone dies, the family group to which he belongs feels itself lessened and, to react against this loss, it assembles. . . .

[C]ollective sentiments are renewed which then lead men to seek one another and to assemble together."[27] Blasetti's film invokes the spectacle of Mario's martyrdom and its galvanizing effects to consolidate a sense of community. Also, the film's use of typification, its distinction between profane and sacred figures, serves as a means of exhortation and pedagogy that is aligned to propaganda of the period with its emphasis on national renewal and its recasting of the notion of "the people" as a force transcending class distinctions, united in a common goal. The theatricality resides particularly in the film's emphasis on the ritual of mourning as the strategy for invigorating images of collective commitment and social solidarity.

THE PRODIGAL FATHER

Generational difference plays a role in the drama of conversion tied often to the family and particularly to the conflict between fathers and sons. The notion of youthful martyrdom is central to the narrative, the fulcrum on which the transformation of other characters turns, particularly that of the father or father-surrogate. The conflict between a father and his son is central to Mario Camerini's drama of conversion, *Il grande appello* (1936), a war film set in the context of the Italian war on Ethiopia. The melodrama of individual conversion is treated in familiar Manichean fashion, identified by sets of polarities that distinguish between a dissolute life and one of heroic commitment. The moral polarities are enhanced by the setting of the film, North Africa, underscoring a necessary distinction between Italy and the colonies. The film opens with a view of the city of Genoa from the vantage point of a ship bound for North Africa and parts east. A sailor goes to a hospital to receive a message from a dying woman whose husband is in Djibouti. She makes him swear that he will deliver the message and informs him that she has a son who is also in that part of the world. In Djibouti, the husband, Giovanni Bertani (Camillo Pilotto) is manager of a hotel, the Orient, where he lives with his mistress, surrounded by conniving individuals, the "dregs" of European society. His mistress, an indigenous woman, is perfidiously involved in anti-Italian activities, in smuggling arms to the Ethiopians. She is portrayed as untrustworthy, treacherous, opportunistic, aggressive, and as fascinating as the African landscape she is fused with. Her character suggests that her role as seductress, as exotic and threatening Otherness, is not uncommon in cinema and especially in the films of war and empire. Karen Pinkus comments that "it is a documentable, objective fact that white males in Africa were inevitably, almost fatally, drawn to black females. Once the gap had been breached, fascist disgust at this contact with the abject seems to break through the surface of the images in uncanny flashes."[28] Similarly, his mistress's treachery is tied closely to Bertani's betrayal and later conversion, a sign first of his lack of virility attributable to "his contact with the abject," and then to his identification with Italy and Italian culture.

When Bertani learns from the sailor of the death of his wife, he also learns of the presence of his son, Enrico (Roberto Villa), in Addis Ababa and goes to see him. The military camp contrasts to the hotel in Djibouti. The men are portrayed in terms of their bonding with each other and their zeal for winning the war. When Bertani invites his son to return to Djibouti with him, the young man tells him that his mission is here and that his patriotism comes before all other commitments. Bertani scoffs at Enrico's idealism and says that he does not want to die. When Enrico learns of his father's trading in arms smuggling, he is disgusted. Enrico is wounded in a battle, and when Bertani seeks to talk to him, his son rejects him. Now isolated, Bertani appears to experience conflict for the first time. He is filmed in close-up with the Italian flag displayed in the background, the emblem of his conversion. Returning to Djibouti, he rejects his mistress's call to profit from further smuggling. Alone in his room, he calls his son's name and when he emerges from his spiritual agony, he pretends to cooperate with the smugglers when, in fact, he turns on them and on the Ethiopians. Dressed as an Ethiopian, he uses the weapons he has transported to attack the Ethiopians and is fatally wounded. His actions ensure the victory of the Italians, and as he dies looking up at the sky filled with Italian planes he utters one word, "Italia."

His conversion is thus predicated on his reconciliation in spirit with his son. The father comes to see the error of his ways and redeems himself. Significantly, it is not the father who provides the prototype of committed behavior but the son who shows the way to the father, an instance of the younger generation guiding their elders. In his act of heroism, Bertani affirms his identity as a father, as a family man, as an Italian, and affirms Italy, symbolized through the son, as the bearer of the new world to come. Furthermore, in contrast to the Ethiopians and the other Europeans, he has affirmed the idealistic motives of Italian expansion in Africa—not for profit or for sexual adventure but for family, continuity, and the high-minded, even self-sacrificing goals of colonialism. His rejection of the Ethiopian woman and his reunion with his son, implies a reconciliation with his dead wife, whom he had denied and repudiated. He has, through his sacrifice, removed the stains of his fragmented, dissolute, and conflict-ridden life, their effects on his son and on the other soldiers. As is the case in other dramas of conversion, the melodramatic affect is dependent on a de-realization of both the dead and living woman, one overvalued as a martyr to her maternal role as the producer of heroes, the other undervalued as the emblem of feminine (and racialized) perfidiousness and as the subverter of masculine heroism.

Bertani turns away from the physical world identified as slippery, unstable, and illusory (another alignment with femininity), and his conversion entails a turning toward the symbol of nation identified with bonding between men, between the older and the younger generation emblematized in the relation between the father and son, to the exclusion of the mother and women generally. The figuration of woman in this film is reminiscent of Klaus Theweleit's description of how under fascism "relationships with women are dissolved and transformed into new male attitudes, into political stances, revelations of the true path, etc. As the woman fades out of sight, the contours of the male sharpen."[29] The language of conversion is evident in Theweleit's description of this metamorphosis; also evident is the fact that the illusion of mastery and clarity has found its appropriate theatrical language through the ritualized figures of conversion melodrama. Also important (and reiterated often by Theweleit) are the ways that figurations of masculinity and femininity, dependent as they are images from folklore, seem to overflow the categories of fascism and participate in a discourse of universalism.[30] This discourse provides the theatrical scenario for the portraits of masculinity.

SURROGATE FATHERS AND PRODIGAL SONS

The colonial narrative of conversion set in a wartime milieu and minus the embellishments of family melodrama, is best characterized by *Squadrone bianco* (1936), directed by Augusto Genina. The most outstanding feature of the film is the exemplary role played by Fosco Giachetti as the prototype of masculinity displayed in iconography and in gesture, suggesting that the "'true' body of the fascist is the phallic body, existing in a state of preparedness for war."[31] As played by Giachetti, Captain Santelia is filmed from various angles in a posterlike statuesque pose, identified with toughness and choreographed gestures. However, his heroic stance, his body mechanics, could appear ridiculous were it not for the reinforcement of his appearance through the *mise-en-scène*, in the alternating shots of him with his subservient troops and in the melodramatic character of the narrative dramatized in the conflicts between Santelia and one of his men. In particular, the drama of conversion is dependent on the antagonism developed between the captain and the playboy, Mario Ludovici (Antonio Centa).

The initial scenes of the film, a car hurtling forward in the darkness, are shot in chiaroscuro. The scene shifts abruptly to a group of upper-class pleasure seekers, among whom is Cristina (Fulvia Lanzi). In love with her, Mario finds himself subjected to her moods. He is enslaved to this woman, who plays with him and sends him away at her whim, already pointing to his weakness and his lack of decisiveness. By contrast, the narrative shifts to the Libyan desert. The portrait of Captain Donati (Olinto Cristina) is paternal; he is humane to the North Africans in this environment that is barren, hot, and dry. The motif of sacrifice is introduced through the figure of Captain Santelia, who has gathered the men to pay homage to a fallen comrade, Lieutenant Bettetini. "Death in combat is the most glorious end of a true soldier," he tells the men. He does not mingle with the men but stands apart from them, even though his presence is apparent. Even in a subsequent scene where Donati is playing cards with Lieutenant Fabrizi (Guido Celano), Santelia is in the shadows.

The arrival of Mario reiterates his identification with another, shady world, as he emerges from a car in the darkness. Greeted stiffly by Santelia, he is assigned an Arab, El Fennek (Cesare Polacco) as his guide and translator. Immediately and inevitably, antagonism is set up between Mario and the captain, who voices doubts about Mario's competence and commitment. El Fennek, an admirer of the captain, is also puzzled by Mario and his relationship to Cristina, whose photo he examines. Cristina continues to be recalcitrant, tearing up letters from Mario, who learns that the squadron is about to undertake a mission in the desert. The squadron takes off to the music of bagpipes and long shots from different angles provide a sense of the epic proportions of the task and of the heroic, ritualistic, and exotic quality of the squadron. The men's departure is intercut with the gaze of the North Africans, observing their movements. The squadron stops as Santelia pays homage to Bettetini at his grave in an elegiac moment, accompanied by music and again shot from several angles, again stressing Santelia's separateness. Frequently, the shots of the men are intercut with images of the sky and of the desert, endowing the procession of the squadron with a religious and operatic aura.

Mario becomes ill. Warned to be judicious with the water ration, he persists in drinking. The captain, learning from El Fennek about his illness, comes to see him and expresses concern about Mario's health. (The metaphor of health plays a central role in dramas of conversion.) In his weakness, Mario fantasizes images of Cristina and himself, but he finally takes a cigarette case she has given him and buries it in the sand. More men become ill. A sand storm rises, and the men are in danger of dying from thirst and exhaustion. Mario starts to hallucinate and tells Santelia, who is tending him like a parent, that he wants his respect. He is rewarded by the captain, who tells him that he has now earned it. Mario has come through his dark night of the soul and is a follower of and believer in the captain. Together, the men meet the rebels in a battle. At the base to which they will return, Cristina has arrived with other tourists, waiting to see Mario. As yet there is no news of survivors of the battle. When the squadron finally arrives at the base, one of the onlookers comments excitedly that these events are like a novel. Mario has now taken the dead Santelia's place and in appearance and action is a reincarnation of the captain. He rejects Cristina's advances, telling her he is no longer the same person: the Mario she knew is buried with Santelia.

In this drama of conversion, the paternal figure is not linked to stark generational but psychological differences (though Santelia is somewhat older than Mario), once again pertaining to the difference between feminine and masculine behavior and with the rejection of heterosexual pleasure. Homosocial relations triumph as the romance between the two men moves from hostility to fusion, founded on the exclusion of the feminine figure and of any signs of behavior identified with softness and femininity. And yet the progress of their relationship leading to the ultimate fusion evokes language similar to heterosexual romance. Femininity is not totally eradicated; it is transformed and rendered acceptable through its transposition into a wartime scenario, particularly in the transformation of Cristina from a seductress and object of desire into a mere spectator to Mario's transformation into a leader of men. The portrait of Cristina, her initial summary treatment of Mario, and later her banishment to the periphery would certainly seem to validate descriptions of the Italian Fascist body as armored against woman;

the problem is, however, that such treatments of women are not unusual in the other national cinemas of the era.

What may be unusual is the extraordinary emphasis on discipline and on its relation to the leadership principle to the exclusion of other relationships. The protagonists' relationship is intensified by its being set into this monumental, eroticized, and exotic landscape, into a world of "primitives," associated with a form of primal nature that is harsh and punitive but beautiful as evidenced by the aerial and long shots of the rippling dunes and the vastness of the terrain. The folkloric elements of the film reside in the religious stages of Mario's conversion: his initial immersion in an erotic and aimless existence, his trials and illness in the "desert," his awakening to a disciplined, self-abnegating, self-denying form of existence through contact with Santelia, and, finally, his assumption of Santelia's position and stance, becoming a copy of the ideal soldier as exemplified by Santelia. The tourist's comments that the events of Mario's return are like a novel seems apt from the perspective of both exposing the fiction of the events but also, and more significantly, of valorizing the necessary dimensions of theatricality, melodrama, and posturing inherent to masculine conversion. The excessive portrait of the men takes on the character of masquerade or impersonation that could be said to adhere to as well as evade the "controls of the regime."[32] Giachetti's and later Centa's posturing as the hero of the hour is drawn to the point of caricature. The film validates the notion that much of what has been termed consensus is dependent on an understanding of the fabrication, the imaginary strategies of consent that may, instead of producing adherence, result rather in the disorganizing effects of representation. In other words, like the comedies and historical films, and like Fascism itself, the films of conversion (and of calligraphism too) may produce a sense of disorientation rather than belief and even a sense of suspension between the illusory and the real.

THE NEW MAN, CONVERSION, AND COLONIALISM

Not all of the films set in the African context are war films. Certain films, such as *Sotto la croce del sud* (1938), link imperialism and colonialism to the drama of conversion. The film does not feature familial conflict, preferring instead to focus on a romance scenario. The role of the indigenous woman is given greater scope and a slightly fuller treatment than in *Il grande appello.* Starring Dori Duranti as Mailù, the film uses her as the unsettling center of the narrative. Along with the unscrupulous Simone (Enrico Glori), she is identified with this precarious, primitive, and dangerous world in need of containment and civilization and identified with popular and sentimental music and eroticism. When Mailù is first seen, she is smoking and listening to a song, "Nostalgia profonda" on the record player. The incarnation of everything that is contrary to wholesome conceptions of femininity as projected by the regime, she provides another instance of what Karen Pinkus has identified as inherent to Italian racism but often downplayed in discussions of Fascism—its focus on the African woman as an incarnation of the abject. Mailù is portrayed as a combination of a servile but also a potentially dangerous animal, a negative sign of the effects of fraternizing with the colonizers. Her masculine counterpart is Simone, the owner of the plantation, who is malevolent, greedy, and sadistic. With the arrival of Paolo (Antonio Centa) and Marco (Camillo Pilotto) conflict erupts. They have arrived to turn this exploited and unproductive area into a prosperous and useful colonial enclave. Prosperity, however, cannot be accomplished without conflict and this conflict will center in the need to eliminate Simone and his ilk, thereby turning this area into a pleasing extension of Italy.

Mario is seduced by the lure of the exotic, and Mailù responds to his compassionate treatment of her in contrast to Simone who goads her, treating her as no better than one of the African workers whom he kills in a subsequent scene. Consistently, contrasts are developed between the benevolent Italians and the "underdeveloped" and exploited Africans whom the Italians are trying to "save." Consonant with the "empire" film associated with Hollywood and British cinema, music and dancing becomes a central means of differentiating modern Westerner from the indigenous people.[33] Images of Africans working underscore the emphasis not only on the necessity of work to tame the land but also the importance of normalizing work, identifying it with Western values, eradicating the slavery of the indigenous people, and compensating them for their labor, a position articulated by Marco. By contrast, Simone gives the Africans whiskey in exchange for their work, encouraging their "backwardness." Under the guidance of Marco and Paolo, a "new order" is envisioned, one that contrasts with the tyrannical rule of Simone. Paolo's problem, his incomplete and ambiguous commitment to this work of building an Italian colony, is his attraction to Mailù, a situation that will finally erupt in violence, since it also involves her relationship to Simone.

The two declare their love during an indigenous ritual where the Africans dance and the camera focuses on the women's bare breasts.

Similar to many commercial (and ethnographic) films that involve Africa, dance here is associated with sexual desire and the exoticism of the African as Other. During the ceremony, Mailù and Paolo kiss, and they are observed by Simone, who plans to send her away. A fire on the plantation, set by the malevolent Simone, causes buildings to collapse, injuring a number of men. Simone attempts to escape in his truck, but the African workers turn against him. In an extended sequence, replete with the sound of drums and horns, the Africans track him into the jungle where he falls into quicksand and disappears. At the plantation, the smoking embers of the fire are the reminder of Simone's perfidy, but also symbolize the destruction of the old way of life identified with Simone. Mailù, realizing her difference and inappropriateness to the new order, plans to leave. She tells Paolo that her presence would create problems. She drives away with Paolo looking on, but Marco, always the paternal and reliable friend, gives Paolo the formula for life, "Let's go to work," and the final image is of clouds.

Aside from its obvious celebration of the Italian mission of colonization in Africa and its highlighting of the differences between the exploitation of the natives by greedy men like Simone and the helpless plight of the Africans (portrayed as in need of paternalistic guidance, supervision, and of enlightened treatment), the film builds the narrative on familiar strategies of melodramatic narration associated with the conventions of the empire film. The landscape relies on the familiar primitivism and exoticism associated with representations of Africa: sensuality, sexuality, and racial difference. The drama is constructed in line with the binary distinction between productive work and the disrupting effects of unbridled desire associated with otherness, especially the otherness of femininity and femininity aligned to racial difference. Woman in this film is, as Said describes woman in relation to Orientalism, identified with the racial Other, suggesting "not only fecundity but sexual promise (and threat), untiring sexuality, unlimited desire, deep generative energies."[34] Mailù represents Africa, its dangerousness and seductiveness that needs to be engineered into subjection. The aestheticization of place and character is reiterated especially through conjoining landscape to feminine transgressiveness.

Identified with the Africans, the African landscape (the sky, the clouds, the moon, the stars, and the jungle) underscores the necessity of controlling and refashioning nature, regarded as fascinating but threatening. The drama of conversion involves the elimination of the threat of disruptive sexuality, associated with violence in this film. Paolo has to be separated from Mailù and Simone to enable the progress of Marco's engineering project of transforming this land to conform to Italian objectives. In the background and through the portrayal of such figures as Marco and Paolo is the specter of Americanism and modernity as articulated by Gramsci. This new man is not merely a reiteration in new garb of the traditional hero but also introduces the image of Taylorized efficiency described in Gramsci's notes on Americanism and Fordism. By contrast to the undisciplined body, the new image of masculinity in this film also raises the question (relevant to American and European society, to "democratic" regimes as well as to Fascism), of how "one must make the body adapt while preserving its essential nobility."[35] The Italian emphasis on cleanliness and order in contrast to the filth and disorder associated with Africa in the film partakes of the problematic of social transformation that, like *Acciaio*, transcends the sense of individualism. The transformation of the individual relies on the fusion of the unruly individual body with the social body, putting aside desire and harnessing physical and psychic energy. Thus, we see in the iconography and character of Marco and Paolo ambivalent emblems and reminders of the material changes affecting Italian life and culture, predicated on the theatricalized imperative of the need for change identified with modernity and productivity.

THE FAMILY, HISTORY, AND THE NATION

The city plays a crucial role in many of the dramas of conversion. More than mere backdrop to the narrative, the city is a character in its own right, coming to be associated with history, culture, national aspirations, and tradition and modernity. In Amleto Palermi's *Napoli d'altri tempi* (1938), Naples is the locus for the conversion of a young man, Mario (Vittorio De Sica) into his proper role as artist, citizen, and family man. With a self-conscious emphasis on spectatorship, the film blends past and present. After opening shots of the city of Naples, the film's encomium to popular song is introduced by intertitles, identifying "music with nature, with history, with the city of Naples, and with the creation of the funicular railway." A group of people is assembled waiting to ride the funicular and anticipating a song, "Napoli mia," that will commemorate this occasion. Among the group of observers is Mario, destined to become an important composer of Neapolitan ballads. Images of Mario are intercut with images of the sea and of Mt. Vesuvius, identifying music with Naples. An intertitle introduces the departure of troops to Africa as Mario among the cheering crowd sings a song marking the occasion. Among the group of onlookers is Maddalena (Emma Gramatica), who will become his fairy godmother. Unknown to him, she is the sister of his deceased mother.

The question of his familial identity is a mainspring of the narrative that will transform him from an orphan to a man with a genealogy, from obscurity to fame, and from an uncertain class affiliation to a man of the people. Maddalena and the Cavaliere Baracchi (Giuseppe Porelli) live in the past, recollecting another time when Italian soldiers had gone to fight in Africa. At that time, her sister was engaged to a young man who died in the war. Maddalena undertakes to trace the child, Mario, but learns at the orphanage where the child had been placed that he now has another name. He has become a composer but in order to support himself works in a grocery store. Having traced him to this locale, Maddalena appears, asking for Mario Sposito. He informs her that his name is "Perla." Undaunted, she informs him that she has a piano that he can use, convincing him that this would be a favor to her. After initial reluctance, he accepts her offer. The delivery of the piano becomes a festive and musical occasion not only for Mario and Ninetta but for the entire neighborhood, thus highlighting the sense of community that prevails among the working classes.

Taking a position in an upper-class house through the aid of Baracchi, Maddalena furthers her plans for Mario, enlisting the daughter, Maria (Elisa Cegani), in advancing his career. Experiencing difficulty in selling his music to agents of publishers, he is urged to present his songs at a party given at Maria's house. Reticent about performing before this well-dressed upper-class gathering, he begins by playing familiar popular songs by other composers. The response is indifferent until he plays his own music, when the audience becomes attentive and enthusiastic. Excluded from this gathering, another audience, Ninetta and her family, also listen. The emphasis on spectatorship established at the outset of the film is maintained throughout, linking it to different social classes and to the importance of the reception of popular cultural artifacts.

Mario's rise to fame parallels his growing attraction to Maria, though her Aunt Bettina (Olga Vittoria Gentilli) disapproves of any relationship between the two, planning for Maria to marry a wealthy suitor. Maddalena, too, is unhappy about their relationship. Having discovered a note from Mario to Maria, she tries to convince him of the impossibility of marriage to Maria. Both she and Ninetta have recognized changes in his behavior toward his own class. Naively, he insists to Maddalena that Maria can live without her luxuries. However, after a final meeting with Maria again at the seaside, he acknowledges their class differences and tells her good-bye. Melancholy after Maria's departure from Naples, Mario works compulsively at his songwriting, determined to leave Naples. At this point, Maddalena, to deter him from leaving, tells him of their kinship and the identity of his mother. In place of Maria as his wife, he has now acquired a surrogate mother, one identified with him, Ninetta, and working-class culture. The final sequences of the film are festive. Once again there is a crowd scene as at the beginning. Once again Neapolitan music is heard and celebrated as "Napoli mia" is sung by the people. Having achieved his objective of being a composer, integrated into Neapolitan life and into a family, Mario, Maddalena, Ninetta, and the Cavaliere, along with the populace, walk together, arms linked, singing.

In contrast to the militant and warlike dramas of conversion, this drama of conversion is explicitly linked to conflicts arising particularly from class differences. The protagonist is torn between two identities, one linked to upper-class aspirations, the other identified with family, historical continuity, and regionalism. Once again elements from folklore are evident: the protagonist is an orphan who is adopted, given his rightful name, and must struggle against the temptations of wealth and privilege embodied in the figure of a beautiful but unattainable woman to attain proper understanding of his familial and class identity and his social role. Only after adversity through rejection by Maria and her family does he achieve a proper sense of his name and social position. In the Gramscian sense of folklore as striated, involving different layers of past and present, the film situates the protagonist (and the narrative) in an in-between space, repeating past forms in contemporary garb. In commenting on popular literature and its relation to popular knowledge in terms applicable to melodrama, Gramsci writes that "There is in the most primitive stratum of the 'people' this traditional esteem of birth which becomes 'affectionate' when misfortune strikes the hero and then becomes enthusiasm when the hero regains his social position in the face of his misfortune."[36]

Another aspect of the film that augments Gramsci's comments on misfortune, loss, and the regaining of social position involves the ways in which *Napoli d'altri tempi* conjoins images of the protagonist with those of community and community with entertainment. For example, the "resolution" of the film that relies on familial and conjugal union is fused with the idea of entertainment as being specifically a compensation for loss. The public space of the city is tied to performance, and performance is tied to individual and, hence, national identity. Naples, becomes central to the process of forging community, and the community is identified in terms of national aspirations. The city is the locus of trial and of discovery, the synecdoche for Italy and for an identification with nature through the emphasis on the sea and the mountains. But the role of the funicular functions to forge a connection between nature and mechanical and cultural production. Finally, the importance of the past, so often invoked in Palermi's films, is legitimated in the image of the rejuvenated Neapolitan community signified by Mario's reestablished connections to his deceased parents through the agency of Maddalena.

THE TENUOUSNESS OF CONVERSION

The melodrama of conversion becomes more problematic in the later years of the regime. A darker, more ambiguous, and potentially violent world emerges in the films especially of the 1940s. In some melodramas, the focus shifts to working-class protagonists whose lives are blighted by the threat of familial dissolution. The resolutions to narrative conflicts appear tenuous, marred by the looming antagonisms that erupt in relation to family and work. *Fari nella nebbia* (Headlights in the Fog, 1942) is different from the festive world of *Napoli d'altri tempi* in the ways it portrays squalor, urban dislocation, and disaffected domestic relations. Directed by Gianni Franciolini and based on a story by four writers—Rinaldo Dal Fabbro, Giuseppe Mangione, Alberto Pozzetti, and O. Gasperini—*Fari nella nebbia* also focuses on workers, featuring the conflicts of masculine protagonists over a space for themselves in a dark and conflict-ridden society. Similar to the noir films of Hollywood and France in the late 1930s and early 1940s, this film begins at night and with two men, Cesare and Gianni, driving in a truck (reminiscent of Raoul Walsh's *They Drive by Night* [1940]) to the accompaniment of intense music. Cesare (Fosco Giachetti) is disturbed about having quarreled with his wife, Anna. The motif of marital conflict and infidelity becomes the mainspring of the melodrama and the requisite hinge for the transformation of the protagonist. The men ride on to Savona where they learn that they have to deliver an emergency cargo. After bargaining for extra money, the men undertake the trip. However, Gianni, obsessed with returning home, urges that they take a route that will enable him to stop at his home. The men drive frenetically in the fog, and jumping a road signal they collide with a farmer's truck. The farmer complains of their driving and they argue, but, once again on the road, they drive to Acqui. Arriving at his home, a dark and drab lodging, Cesare does not find Anna, but a note that tells him she has left him.

At work, Anna (Mariella Loti) is told by a friend that she needs to be diverted, to meet new men, and Anna finally agrees. At a night club, Anna's friend is enjoying herself; however, Anna's date, Cavaliere Filippo (Antonio Centa), is not pleased with her. He tells her that he likes women who are young and happy, and he finds her morose. After they leave the club, he tries to kiss her and she angrily gets out of the car. On the road, Cesare and Gianni see a woman who has fallen from her bicycle. Gianni helps the woman up, while Cesare sits indifferently in the truck. He finally agrees to let her drive with them but insists that she can only ride with them until the next stop. When the men arrive at the trucker's headquarters, Cesare is berated by the dispatcher, who plans to dock him for damage to the truck and threatens dismissal. Cesare complains that he has been an employee for ten years and has made money for the firm. Their quarrel is interrupted by a call for the dispatcher, who learns that his child is ill. He rehires Cesare, though maintains that Cesare must pay the cost of damages.

At home, Anna prepares to go out on a date as her mother cautions her to remember that she is married. Anna's date with the Cavaliere is again unpleasant. He is adamant about having sex with her. He ignores her refusal and drives off with her into the night. At a bar, Cesare and Gianni again see the young woman, Piera (Luisa Ferida), that Gianni had helped on the road. She is trying to avoid the attentions of a man, Carlo. On the road again, the men stop over in Acqui, this time at Gianni's house where Cesare plays with Gianni's child. Gianni's wife, Maria, complains about the claustrophobia and dreariness of her domestic life. She informs Cesare that she has seen Anna and that she doesn't blame her for leaving. Reluctant to see Anna again and make amends, he finds Piera waiting for him, and invites her to eat with him. Maintaining her seduc-

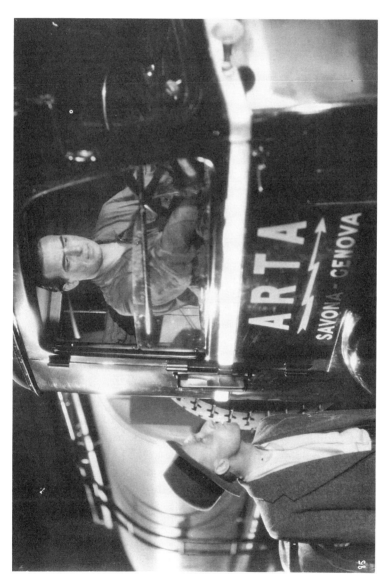

FIGURE 16. Theatricality and the world of the everyday, *Fari nella nebbia*. Courtesy of New York Museum of Modern Art, Film Stills Archive.

tive behavior toward him, she tells him he needs to have fun. They spend the night together and in the morning she behaves toward him in wifely fashion. Several flashbacks recall his life with Anna, their quarrels, involving her discontent about her lonely life, the squalor and dirt of a trucker's life, her dislike of having to visit Gianni and Maria, and her refusal to have a child. After a flashback of Cesare and Anna's quarrel, his ultimatum to her to be wife to him or leave, he invites Piera to live with him.

Anna is now tired of her life. She plans to leave work and to go home, enlisting the assistance of Maria and Gianni. Cesare's relationship with Piera has become complicated by Carlo, who is jealous of Cesare and ready to fight with him. Learning that Gianni and Maria's child is ill, Anna has gone to help the couple, while Piera learns to cook from her landlady as part of her plan to entrap Cesare. When he comes to see Piera, Cesare tells her that there is little hope for their future, prophesying that they will end up quarreling just as his friends have done. He returns home and, unaware that Anna is with Gianni and Maria, finds a neglected house and once again leaves. However, when he returns to Piera, his prediction is realized. She has begun to complain about being neglected. He leaves, and she turns to Carlo in her quest for pleasure. The climax of the film involves a confrontation between Carlo and Cesare. The men are given a job by the dispatcher. Cesare drives wildly, seeking to intimidate Carlo into admitting that he's been seeing Piera. When they arrive at Acqui, Cesare goes to his home and gets a gun, loads it, while observing himself in the mirror. Once in the truck with Carlo, he takes out the gun and unloads the bullets, the music rises, and the men drive off as rain falls on the windshield.

The melodrama ends with reconciliation between Anna and Cesare and Cesare and Carlo, but the tenor of the film seems to belie any notion of a "happy ending." While Cesare has recognized that life with Anna—after her return to domesticity—is preferable to the life he has been leading, the subdued and dismal aura of their lives has not been transformed. The characters have submitted to their marital responsibilities. Anna now will clean the house, visit Gianni and Maria, and, above all, wait for Cesare rather than seeking sexual pleasure elsewhere. The dark lighting, the somber *mise-en-scène*, the avoidance of idealized scenes of nature and marital relations, the less than idealized portraits of working-class figures, and the hardships of work and home mark the film as different from many of the films of the thirties, linking it more closely to such films as *Ossessione* and *Quattro passi fra le nuvole* and their critical view of working-class life and marital relations.[37]

The iconography of the characters, the ways they are filmed, and the use of mirrors and chiaroscuro lighting suggest a world of repetition and claustrophobia. The intensity and theatricality of the conversion motif—whether celebrating empire, colonialism, war, and homosocial bonding or familialism, artistic productivity, nation, and regionalism—is toned down, focusing on the reduced expectations of the characters, their guilt, psychological conflict, and accommodation to the constraints of their world. Cesare's reunion with Anna can better be described as a de-escalation and neutralization of the enthusiasm of the dramas that celebrate conversion with their quasi-religious and mythical character. A different form of theatricality is evident in *Fari nella nebbia*, evocative of film noir with its discontented characters, its dark world of violence, and its emphasis on entrapment, invoking difference in repetition.

"CALLIGRAPHISM"

Many films of late 1930s and early 1940s stress the darker and more formal characteristics of the historical film and melodramas. Their appearance, narrative structures, iconography, and uses of *mise-en-scène* has a certain coherence, despite differences in perspective, bespeaking a more critical, even antagonistic, and certainly contradictory relation to their subjects. In his discussion of the Italian cinema, Pierre Leprohon discusses a phenomenon known as "calligraphism" that was especially evident in the films of the last years of the Fascist period, a film style that came to be identified pejoratively with "brilliant arabesques in the void."[38] Unlike the conversion motif of many melodramas, these films do not focus on the drama of the creation of the new man or accommodations to the status quo. Instead, they portray a world of degeneration and masculine impotence conveyed through deliberate and highly crafted formal techniques. The films discussed below address a select group of these texts, identified with such directors as Mario Soldati, Renato Castellani, Ferdinando Maria Poggioli, and Luigi Chiarini. (While this chapter focuses on those films that feature masculine protagonists, the following chapter will examine "calligraphic" films that highlight problematic forms of femininity.)

The reception of the films of certain of these directors was at first positive, even enthusiastic; then, within the space of a few years, their works were discredited, dismissed for their crepuscular character, their infidelity to the past, their antirealistic style in relation to characterization and place, their rhetoricity, and their formalism. The turnabout was tied of course to the predilections of the critics of *Cinema* for realism. The association of these filmmakers with the cinema of the Fascist years was to condemn some of them, and their writers and technicians, for having been associated with such films as *Il grande appello, La corona di ferro,* and *Un' avventura di Salvator Rosa.*[39] The volte-face was thus not merely one of evaluating quality but rather tied to incipient ideological concerns. The volume, *La bella forma,* introduced by Micciché, is an effort to reexamine these filmmakers whose work has been consistently overshadowed by the years of neorealism, by critics, and by the preconceptions of historians of film about the Italian cinema of the sound era. According to Micciché, it is the duty of contemporary critics to reconsider these films, not for the purposes of absolution or condemnation but for an understanding of their directors' work and a rethinking of the role of these filmmakers within Italian cinema.[40]

To account for the work of the so-called calligraphers, those film-makers of "la bella forma," Andrea Martini argues that it is helpful to return to the film theory of the 1920s and 1930s, especially to the ways in which the new role of cinema was perceived.[41] The attempts to theorize connections between cinema and other arts, and with painting in particular, are central to an understanding of the sources and style of these films. Critics explored (much as Sergei Eisenstein did in his writings) the nature of the shot, the uses of the frame, the relation between horizontality and verticality, and between stasis and dynamic movement as a means of understanding the visual and the sensual potential of cinema. Moreover, critics were also concerned with color, the uses of decor, costuming, and photography, citing these as essential ingredients in cinematic representation. These critics' investigations are germane to the style of the calligraphers, who seem to be preoccupied with the pictorial quality of the shot.

The films of Castellani, Soldati, and Poggioli share this penchant for decor, design, choreographed movement, pictorial qualities. These qualities are intimately related to the uses of melodrama in the expressive treatment of character, place, and objects. The inspiration for these films came largely, though not exclusively, from nineteenth-century historical novels that provide portraits of an elaborate, baroque, and self-contained world. The world portrayed is inhabited by characters inflicted with nervous obsessional traits and preoccupied with psychological conflicts—auto-matic behavior, compulsion, jealousy, vengefulness, and aggression. The characters are, like characters in horror narratives, often somnambulistic, comparable to marionettes. The films' formal means to expressing these inward states are stylistic, depending on a predisposition to theatricality, the fusion of landscape and psychic states, and especially with an emphasis on mourning and melancholy. The pictorial quality of these films resides in the uses of mirrors, paintings, furniture, costume, and lighting. The sound track relies on the uses of natural sounds and music. The combined effect of the visual and auditory qualities is the creation of claustrophobia and dislocation. The tendency of the films is to denaturalize the natural and to defamiliarize the familiar. The acting style in the films is highly stylized. The characters appear caricatures rather than striving for naturalistic effects as can be seen in the acting of Roldano Lupi in *Gelosia* and the Gramatica sisters in *Sorelle Materassi*.

In certain ways, one might make general comparisons with these films and Hollywood melodramas of the 1950s, especially those of Vincente Minnelli and Douglas Sirk or the films of Max Ophuls, about which so much has been written regarding the connection between melodrama and visual style The films call attention to the signifying practices of the *mise-en-scène*, color, and music as opposed to realism and the rigid adherence to narrative structures. The same artifice governs these Italian films and also a similar sense of ambiguous critique of the dramatized social relations. Thomas Elsaesser's description of the role of style in these 1950s melodramas is applicable as a means of entry into these calligraphic melodramas. He writes that "the melodramas of Ray, Sirk, or Minnelli . . . deal with . . . what one might call an intensified symbolisation of everyday actions, the heightening of the ordinary gesture and a use of setting and decor so as to reflect the characters' fetishist fixations. Violent feelings are given vent on 'overdetermined objects'."[42] This tendency toward emphasizing decor has been uppermost in the identification of the calligraphic films as formalistic and self-contained and has led to problematic assessments of their discursivity. Jean A. Gili has written that it is often difficult to draw a line between those films that are involved in simple decorative exploration and those that on the contrary belong to an identifiable ideological discourse. "Is one witnessing a world grinding to a halt, a nostalgia for things that have ceased to exist, or an implicit critique of the present moment?"[43]

The examination of the films in the context of the melodramas of conversion would seem to suggest that these films are hesitant about adopting polemics or an affirmative or monumental style. While they cannot be read in terms of any express message or prescription, their subject matter and style suggest that they are portraying a set of events and types of characters that run counter to familiar discourses of Fascism. By offering up their models in such writers as Rosso di San Secondo they appear to retreat and evade the present and return to the past, but the subject matter that they choose to film from their selected literary sources in the portrayal of ego dissolution appears to address the milieu of the late 1930s.[44] Their fascination is with characters who are "abnormal," given to violating the law, manipulating others, driven to murder or suicide. The world of certainty has crumbled and the characters, though struggling to conform, find that they cannot. If there is nostalgia, it derives from "the construction of a totality that does not exist," a nostalgia that is itself fragile and threatened. The individual is powerless but his desires are boundless and unquenchable.[45] The films seem obliquely to represent an evasion of the present but this apparent regression is telling for the ways that the narration intersects with and parallels contemporary events through inversion and contrast, if not through analysis.

FRACTURED MASCULINITY

Most of the melodramas of conversion are preoccupied with conflicts that the masculine protagonist must face and overcome on his path to spiritual and social regeneration. In some of the films, most notably Blasetti's *Vecchia guardia,* the conversion entails the exemplary efforts of a select few whose actions are directed toward the regeneration of the community, the community within the film and the film community at whom the film is aimed. The films of calligraphism also feature masculine protagonists and also foreground conflicts between the protagonist and the social world. But instead of dramatizing a process whereby the masculine protagonist can move to defeat and overwhelm the obstacles in his path to transformation and commitment to the nation and to civil society, these films focus on his fragmentation, even defiance of and rebellion against, the social and legal order, leading to his demise. The society that is portrayed in the films is also tenuous, portrayed as venal and overly legalistic. The films are constructed on a primary disjunction between individual will and the community's efforts at control and restraint. The uses of religion and ritual in the film do not function as a critique so much as running counter to the overarching religious overtones of the conversion dramas, suggesting the frailty of institutional forces in the face of social forces, especially those of the law and social custom.

A film that has been cited as exemplary of the qualities of calligraphism is Ferdinando Maria Poggioli's *La morte civile* (1942). Based on a drama by Paolo Giacometti (1861), the original work has, according to Guglielmo Monetti, "a precise polemical objective: to demonstrate the injustice of a clerical law that desires the indissolubility of matrimonial bond, also condemning marriage to penal servitude, precisely to civil death."[46] Religion in this film takes a different form than in the melodramas of conversion. Spiritual values, especially those identified with institutional religion, offer little consolation, though religion is invoked if only to dramatize its impotence. The film does not dramatize the transcendent values of the state and its laws; nor does it portray the protagonist's struggles as serving those interests, though it does identify the other two major characters with piety and service to the common good, combatting the forces that produce "civil death." If the conversion dramas foreground the consolidation of identity, self-discipline, and altruism in the service of a common good, this film, in its portrait of fractured masculinity, reveals the antagonism between the spirituality of religion and the ways of the world.

Poggioli made changes from the Giacometti work, the foremost involving the transformation of the priest, the persecutor of the protagonist, to a lay councilor, thus moderating the antireligious elements from the play into the film. Also, the insertion of Dr. Palmieri, the benefactor of the protagonist's wife and child who is romantically inclined toward her, is an innovation, as is the ending that unites the couple. Highly theatrical, the film begins in the present with the wife of a convict, Rosalia (Dina Sassoli) and her child in a carriage with Dr. Palmieri, a physician (Renato Cialente) on the way to his house. He has undertaken to help this defenseless woman by offering her a position as a governess. Others in the carriage complain of the times, of the rampant injustice and the need for reform, particularly of the necessity of protecting oneself from criminals and outlaws, thus introducing the motif of social and political precariousness. A flashback identifies the history of Rosalia and her relationship to her husband, Corrado (Carlo Ninchi), an irascible and obsessed character driven by a sense of personal injury, a character common not only to this film but to others, as we shall see also to Poggioli's *Gelosia*. Obstacles in their marital life are intensified by economic difficulties (he is an artist who cannot support the family on his meager income). Also, her family disapproves of their marriage. Her brother comes to urge Rosalia to return home, but Corrado intervenes and the two men quarrel. In his rage against the aggressive treatment by the brother, Corrado strikes and kills the man, is sentenced, and sent to jail.

Returning to the present and to the carriage, the scene focuses on the bleak, rocky, and barren landscape, a landscape that will be central to the pilgrimage later in the film. Their arrival in town reinforces Palmieri's intentions to keep Rosalia's identity secret as the doctor introduces her as the woman he has hired to care for his daughter, his wife having died. While this explanation is accepted by some of the people, others are not so accepting, notably, Giacinto, a town councilor, himself a womanizer and troublemaker, who is suspicious of their relationship. The threatening texture of Rosalia's world is heightened through the machinations of Giacinto, who is both seductive with and intimidating toward her. While aggressive to Rosalia and Palmieri, he is portrayed ironically as under the rule of his wife. Dr. Palmieri's work is also threatened by challenges to his authority as a doctor. In treating a desperately ill child who has a high fever due to typhus, he insists that the child remain at home to be treated but others, especially Giacinto, are concerned about the possibility of contagion and thus eager to obstruct the doctor's authority and power to heal. The film's conception of "civil death" is enhanced by the imagery of disease, which becomes more than a narrative strategy to resolve conflicts in the community; it is a metaphor for the vulnerability of the society to narcissism, uncontrolled rage, and violence, the very crimes for which Corrado is incarcerated. The role of gossip in the film is linked to disease, serving, like the contagiousness of typhus, to destroy any sense of the community as a vital organism. The civil dis-ease spreads as Palmieri's personal situation also becomes public when, through gossip, the identity of Rosalia and her child becomes known, and he confesses that his own wife and child are dead. Giacinto seeks to make capital of this confession but is restrained by the mayor. The physically ill child improves, and the narrative intensifies its dramatization of the psychological and social illness known as civil death, specifically traced to the disease of sexual repression, the abuse of authority, and the defilement of language, underscored by the film's use of music (by Umberto Galassi) and the noir character of the lighting. While Palmieri experiences vindication in relation to his professional judgment, Rosalia experiences guilt about his situation and contemplates leaving with the child.

The climax of the film again focuses on the volatile state of the masculine protagonist as seen in his relations to women and children. Desperate and in a highly nervous state, having escaped from prison, Corrado has come to reclaim his wife and child. But he is not certain that the child he sees is his, and Rosalia appears and tries to divert him from his objective of discovering the child's identity. She seeks to keep guard over Emma-Ada so that Corrado cannot spirit her away, and tells Palmieri of Corrado's plans. Palmieri faces Corrado and tells him that he must not take the child, because it would be unfair to her, since a child cannot grow up well in itinerant and impoverished conditions. Again, as he was in the prison Corrado is identified with windows, the image of his internal and social imprisonment. Rosalia acknowledges his suffering, and he agrees that in prison, he was a dead man, canceled by society, living a civil death, but she acknowledges that she too has lived a civil death. She informs the daughter that Corrado is her father, but he, now more stable, relinquishes the child. In an operatic farewell scene, accompanied by funereal sounding music, Corrado tells her to inform her mother he is going alone, and the child gives him a flower. From a window, the child observes him as he leaves. When Rosalia learns of his departure, she runs after him, but he jumps to his death. He is found, clutching the flower tightly as Rosalia kneels over him and cries. The image of a cross can be seen in the background, and the final shots are again of pilgrims.

The uses of religion for which the film had been criticized by various critics of *Cinema* as sentimental and unrealistic[47] cannot be read simply and univalently. In particular, the portrait of Corrado, an ambiguous and devastating picture of fractured masculinity, has dimensions that are not reducible to a conventional religious reading. Portrayed as an unstable artist whose lot it is to suffer and agonize, he seems to bear resemblance to W. Somerset Maugham's anguished masculine figures, certainly to the portraits of fractured masculinity that are evident in Castellani's films as well. Neither Corrado nor Palmieri are prototypes of the committed individual, the virile "new man" confident in his assertive masculinity. Instead their presence attests to the failure of a religious ethos, the difficulty of containing and channeling the excessive sense of personal injustice. The image of the cross at the end—like the images of the madonna and child, and of the pilgrimage—is less related to the content of the narrative and the thematic of conformity than to a more functional role in terms of the film's formal visual patterning and organization.[48] The religious imagery—through the complex interplay between darkness and light, the choreography of the ritual of the pilgrimage, and the painting of the madonna and child, which are recapitulated in the scenes with Rosalia and her child, the scenes in the church, and the image of the cross at the end—seems almost detached from the other scenes that involve the more mundane and disruptive aspects of social life. These images are reflexive, calling attention to a hiatus between the limitations of existing representations of the individual and his milieu and the possibility of finding a language that can bring them into consonance.

The role of religion further seems to point to a number of extra-religious implications, centering on sexuality, associated less with eroticism and more with rage, violence, and irreparable loss. Rosalia's image as a maternal figure serves less to evoke religious associations with the madonna and more to dramatize threats to the civil status of women and children. Religion seems to function less in its own right than as a measure of the fragility of social institutions, highlighting the absence of moral and spiritual values. The film's melodramatic affect arises especially from the use of children to intensify the precarious state of social relations. The recurrent image of cut flowers (the flowers Rosalia cuts off her wedding dress and the flower that the child gives to Corrdao) are associated with violence and death, with the opposition, not union, between nature and civil society. The interplay of light and dark heightens the moral ambiguity of the portrayed relations, further heightening the distance between religion and the civil society. The melodrama portrays the debacle of civil society whether intentionally or not, focusing particularly on the threatened and threatening identity of the masculine figures. The formal elements seem to undermine a coherent reading of a "message,"serving to enhance the portrait of disequilibrium, the sense of an abnormal world, and of truncated lives and waste, a world that speaks to the horrors of a wartime situation, albeit indirectly. Not insignificant is the fact that Corrado is an artist, one who paints religious works. The allusion to artistic creativity situates the formal elements of the film within the broader context of an interrogation of the role of the artist and of art in the process of conceptualizing the crisis of representation that the film undertakes to dramatize and address.

THE FICTIONS OF HOMOSOCIAL CONFLICT

One of the major characteristics of the conversion dramas, seen especially in *Il grande appello* and *Lo squadrone bianco*, is its emphasis on relation-

ships between masculine figures instrumental in bringing one of the protagonists, usually the younger and more unsettled one, to a new sense of
himself, his relation to the past, and his commitment to a different future.
In a highly coded, ornate, and elaborate visual style, drawing on a
Pushkin story, *Un colpo di pistola* (1942), directed by Renato Castellani,
offers a more ambiguous instance of the relations between two masculine
figures and of the uses of the past as exemplified in the early 1940s cinema. Set in the nineteenth century, the film relies on the photography of
Gaston Medin and the costuming of Maria De Matteis, artists who were
identified with the growing stylistic and technical excellence of the Italian
cinema.[49] These artists were particularly attuned to the importance of creating a sense of place and historical moment. The film was excoriated by
De Santis in *Cinema* for its stylistic excess and its removal from contemporary conflicts.[50] On the surface and characteristic of most of the films
of calligraphism, *Un colpo* appears to be a hermetically sealed text, theatrical and operatic, seemingly inaccessible to any direct connection to
contemporary conflicts, especially to those confronting wartime Italian
society. However, in its preoccupation with the violence and competitive-
ness of masculine relationships, the fascination with and threat of
homosocial bonding, and with a vision of crumbling and tenuous social
relations, the film would seem to obliquely address the contemporary
context. Furthermore, the film also invokes the conversion paradigm in
the ways that it is preoccupied with masculine antagonism, particularly
conflict between the theatrical and externalized world of heroism and an
interior world involving obsession, jealousy, and injured self-esteem. But
if conversion is involved, it entails a de-escalation of the inflated and religious quest in the name of the nation, discipline, and martyrdom.

Like *La morte civile* and other films of this moment, the film also
is drawn to religious imagery. Also, like *La morte civile*, *Un colpo* uses the
imagery of nature in its various invocations of landscape as a metaphor
for psychic conflicts. The film begins in winter as two people observe a
man, Andrea Anschikoff (Fosco Giachetti), walking suicidally on an icy
lake until another man, Di Valmont (Renato Cialente), follows him and
forestalls the suicide. Later at a party, Andrea narrates to Di Valmont, a
novelist, the events preceding his suicide attempt. Through a flashback,
Andrea recounts his antagonistic relationship to Prince Sergio (Antonio
Centa). In a garrison in the south of Russia, Andrea is playing billiards
with fellow officers, including Sergio. Sergio's dislike of Andrea is manifest as is Andrea's discomfort with the prince. Leaving early, Andrea goes

to the general's house where the men play billiards and where the general's niece, Mascia (Maria Denis), sings at the piano. While Andrea gazes longingly at her, she appears not to be responsive to his attentions. When he tells her he will be leaving for a month on maneuvers, she is unconcerned, treating him with coyness and a mocking demeanor. In both the previous episode in his encounter with Sergio and here in relation to Mascia, Andrea is presented as awkward, naive, and inept in contrast to the highly theatrical role-playing of Sergio and Mascia. As the narrative develops, Andrea's character is tied intimately to Sergio and Mascia; he is neither an object of admiration to Sergio nor an object of desire to her. The order of events, the introduction first to Sergio and then to Mascia, suggests that the parallels not only reinforce his marginality but are linked to an ambivalent relation between homosocial bonding and heterosexual desire.

After a brief return to the present of the narration, the flashback resumes. The men are shown on maneuvers in the lush countryside, but their activities are interrupted by the arrival of a group of aristocratic visitors including Mascia. Throughout the film from the first icy scenes to this scene and to the duel in the woods, the countryside is presented with brilliant clarity as spacious and luxuriant. However, the shots of the countryside are contrasted to the interior settings with which they seem to compete. Like the character of Mascia, the images of nature seem to vie with artifice, its deceptive beauty disrupted by human conflict. The pastoral treatment of landscape is in tension with the portrait of choreographed and aggressive social relations. Confronting Andrea, Mascia tells him how she would love to live in the country. Misreading her enthusiasm, Andrea resigns his commission to marry her. Sergio, learning of the resignation, warns Andrea that his action may be premature. Oblivious, Andrea invites Sergio to meet Mascia, unaware that the two had met earlier at the maneuvers. In another outdoor scene, a picnic, the sadism and masochism of the relations among the three intensifies as Mascia flirts with Sergio and the two exchange looks, excluding Andrea, who observes them morosely. In a game of blind man's buff, Mascia, blindfolded, thinks she has caught Sergio only to discover that she has chosen Andrea. Her imperviousness to him reaches new heights as she orders him to serve sweets and to cut the cake, and teases him over his resignation. He realizes that the only way she could have learned about this is through Sergio. After the picnic and at the garrison, Andrea confronts Sergio angrily about the disclosure and challenges him to a duel.

FIGURE 17. Choreographing homosocial conflict, *Un colpo di pistola.* Courtesy of New York Museum of Modern Art, Film Stills Archive.

The duel scene was praised by the critics of the time. It takes place at dawn in the countryside covered by fog. The setting, like a pastoral painting, is idyllic and in as much contrast to the human drama as Sergio's ironic behavior is in contrast to Andrea's melodramatic stance. Alone and melancholy, Andrea waits for Sergio, who, arriving late, sees a cherry tree, nonchalantly plucks the cherries, eats them, and spits the pits onto the ground. He then approaches Andrea cockily and offers him some cherries from his hat that Andrea refuses. In fact, Sergio continues indifferently to eat the cherries as the ritual of the duel commences, and Andrea puts down his gun, saying that he will not shoot now but wait until a more opportune time when Sergio is happy and wants to live. The contrast between the two men is most evident here—Andrea, morose, brooding and intense, Sergio indifferent and mocking. Having brought Di Valmont into the present, Andrea's narrative ends his narrative with his comment that he hates Sergio more than ever and that, fed by this hate, he desires revenge.

A year later, Andrea and Di Valmont meet again now in Rome where Andrea has been living. The men meet by chance at a hunt and Andrea brings the novelist up to date on what has transpired since their last meeting. Through a flashback, he informs him that he has been visited by Mascia's sister, Antonietta, from whom he has learned that at the fateful picnic prior to his challenging Sergio to a duel, Mascia had entrusted her sister with a note of apology to Andrea for her flirtatiousness with Sergio. She had only acted in this way to make him jealous and she now awaits Andrea impatiently. Andrea sets out for Kiev, stopping only to change horses at an inn where he learns that Sergio is due to pass this way shortly. The rural scene with happy and friendly children, geese scurrying about, and warm hospitality mocks his unhappy state. Andrea waits at the inn, but Sergio never appears. Instead, he has gone on to Mascia's house in the city. The mother welcomes Sergio, informing him that Mascia has been in mourning for Andrea. She encourages Mascia to greet Sergio, and in a scene that highlights the role of women's clothing, Mascia goes to her room and pulls out dresses, finally choosing a white gown. She sits before the mirror and places a floral crown on her head as if preparing to go on stage. Looking radiant, she informs her mother that Sergio has twice proposed marriage to her and though she has refused him before, she is ready now to accept him. As she comes out to see him, the image of the house is foregrounded, its white pillars and shiny floors bespeaking opulence. She uncovers the piano and sits, telling Sergio that now she will be happy. Consistent with her role throughout the film, she is identified with entertainment and with posturing.

Later, Andrea appears at the house as a party is in progress. Finding Sergio, he takes him into another room, informing him that he is ready to finish the unfinished business of the duel. He hands Sergio a gun from a cabinet as Mascia enters and orders Andrea to leave the house, but as he leaves he tells Sergio that he will meet him at dawn. His angry departure and his desolate appearance contrast with the scene of a party where people dance the mazurka and the atmosphere is warm and lively. Mascia does not remain at home but leaves to find Andrea and stop the duel, wandering through the foggy city, seeking him vainly. Finally at dawn, she enters a church where she observes people praying. She crosses herself, lights a candle, and then she sees Andrea, who has decided not to duel. The shots of the couple are intercut with images of the church and of a priest reciting prayers. The couple exits with an image of light like a halo piercing the darkness. The two walk together in the fog as she tells him that she must leave him and keep her promise to Sergio. As Andrea walks away he calls her name; getting no answer he returns to learn that she has fainted. He carries her into a house and in a sentimental scene the two kiss good-bye. However, the film does not end here, but again in Rome and with Andrea united to Mascia. Di Valmont visits them and Andrea informs him that Sergio had not held Mascia to her promise. The image of Mascia singing at the piano ends the film.

While the film is more opulent looking than either Poggioli's and Chiarini's films, it shares with them a highly mannered style. The *mise-en-scène*, especially of the duel scene, is most exemplary of the film's penchant for formal patterning The landscape plays a major role seen in long and middle distance shots. The film also has a penchant for disorienting close-ups, especially of the three protagonists. The simulacrum of nineteenth-century Europe, and particularly Russia, is seen in the aristocratic splendor of the homes, the exoticism of the church, and rustic character of the way-side inn. The film is obsessed with the sense of place, costume, decor, and music, stressing spectatorship along with the theatricality of the acting and the stagelike character of the setting. Beginning with the couple's observing Andrea's attempted suicide, the narrative continuously highlights different forms of looking. Andrea and Sergio's relationship is developed through their mutual surveillance. Andrea's obsessive and masochistic obsession with Mascia takes the form of a macabre fascination in watching her with Sergio. She is the center of the other characters' gazes, both through her flirtatious behavior and through her entertaining others with her singing. The theatricality of the group scenes—the billiard playing among the men, the maneuvers, the picnic, the dual, and the parties—are carefully staged, stressing the role of the protagonists as performers. Mascia appears more like a doll or a plaything, the center of the drama and of the spectacle.

The carefully choreographed group movement resists any notion of randomness and spontaneity or naturalness. The underlying sense of disorder generated by the melodrama resides in the treatment of the characters, whose actions seem all the more dissonant in contrast to this well-constructed and aesthetically beautiful world. The violence is not virulent but constrained, like the games of cruelty that pass for playfulness on the part of Sergio and Mascia, later by Andrea. The duel scene in particular with its balletic quality and its stark contrasts between nature and society and between Andrea and Sergio, is a portrait of a world where form and content are at odds, touching a chord common to many films of the 1940s concerning tensions between the public and the private spheres, disjunctions between polite behavior and underlying conflict, between interiority and exteriority.

The world is exposed as capricious and irrational despite the religious imagery in the church scene. The presence of religion—due to the reliance on its nineteenth-century literary text and also perhaps to the contingent and unpredictable image of the world portrayed—is ambiguous. The consolatory vision of religion, like that of the reconciliation of the couple, is compromised by the unresolved nature of the antagonistic relations between the men. The role of Mascia complicates relations between Sergio and Andrea; she seems identified with the brittle, artificial, and aestheticized milieu, as much identified with the fictions of this upper-class milieu as is the novelist, Di Valmont. She is a necessary third party, serving to foreground and to mystify the basis of conflict between the men that is tied to incompatible notions of masculinity. Sergio's behavior is more closely identified with male aggressivity and power, Andrea's with a submissiveness more commonly identified as feminine. Unlike other conversion films, *Un colpo* does not celebrate homosocial bonding, though it does appear preoccupied with its failure. The film's theatricality, tied to the spectacle of the upper-class milieu, rather than providing the simulacrum of community as in the comedies, historical films, and the melodramas of conversion, serves rather to provide a sense of the fragility of male bonding, the imaginary character of harmonious social relations, and the underlying violence that subtends this world.

DECADENCE AND VIOLENCE UNREDEEMED

The films of conversion present a world that is amenable to control, where actions are portrayed as having affirmative consequences not only for the individual but for the society at large. They rely on a form of theatricality that is affirmative, couched in the language of familiar images of heroic and exceptional individual struggle. These heroic protagonists are part of the lexicon of popular literature and drama, modified to suit contemporary tastes, clearly fictional but appealing. In writing about these types of popular fictions, particularly about the prevalence of the "operatic conception of life," Gramsci describes this conception as "responsible for a whole range of 'artificial poses' in the life of the people, for ways of thinking, for a 'style.' 'Artificial' is perhaps not the right word because among the popular classes this artificiality assumes naive and moving forms. To many common people the baroque and the operatic appear as an extraordinarily fascinating way of feeling and acting, a means of escaping what they consider mean, low, and contemptible in their lives and passions to enter a more select sphere of great feelings and noble passions."[51] These comments validate the power of the theatrical on popular taste; they also suggest the persistence of such fictions and the fact that the audiences perceive them as *fictions*.

The calligraphic films are similarly preoccupied with theatricality, with the pervasiveness of acting and simulation but also with their destructive effects. The dark world portrayed in Poggioli's *Il cappello da prete* (The Priest's Hat, 1943) is centered on a demonic character, not on the spiritual hero of the conversion dramas. In his theatrical world, everything is exaggerated and everything is in a state of decomposition. This film dissects forms of obsessional behavior. In more excessive terms than in *La morte civile*, the characters are as acquisitive, dishonest, and aggressive as the world they inhabit. The tone of the film is grimly humorous, a satire that attacks individuals and institutions. A nobleman and a priest are the dominant characters in this film, which is based on a novel by Emilio di Marchi. The second Baron of Santafusca, played by Roldano Lupi, lives a dissolute life devoted to gambling. His addiction to the casino keeps him in debt and forces him into conflict with creditors and with an unscrupulous priest. Don Cirillo, the priest (Luigi Almirante), is portrayed as sinister and avaricious, eager to get every cent he can. He visits the baron's family home, which is bereft of furniture or ornament, everything having been sold to pay for the nobleman's habits. The priest's visit is for the purpose of appraising the house, which he has sold for the baron. While in the courtyard, the baron pushes the priest into a well and takes the money from the sale of the house. He embarks again on his pastimes, going to the theater, entertaining women, and gambling. The priest is discovered by the nephew of the old family retainer, who takes him to his quarters where Don Cirillo dies. The nephew also retrieves the priest's hat. News of the priest's death spreads, and the nephew is wrongly accused of killing the priest. The baron does not confess his crime, but is willing to let the innocent man be prosecuted. The priest's hat becomes the means of detecting the actual culprit, and the baron is arrested as he is about to take a trip with a woman.

The film's opening scenes, of a hand holding cards and then of the baron with the other men displaying his bravado in the face of losing, fore-shadows the film's preoccupation with money and with a society that is addicted to commercial transactions. The image of gambling applies not only to the nobleman but to the other figures in the film, including the priest. Poggioli even includes a public raffle where a poor man and his children suffer as the obsessed father waits for the announcement of the winning number. The low-key lighting and the presence of shadows convey a gloomy environment and a sinister sense of the individuals who inhabit it. In the earlier sequence in the baron's room, the shadow of the window blinds on the floor creates the effect of bars and is visually linked to the playing cards that lay scattered about. The arrival of Don Cirillo is announced by the ominous shadow of his head with his broad-brimmed priest's hat, and this image is repeated later in the film with another priest. The hat not only signifies the priest's office, but associates that office with the idea of stalking or hunting, and becomes the image too of retribution. An image of the duality that haunts the film, the hat is associated with the avaricious priest but also with the detection of the crime and the prosecution of justice. The dramas of conversion, as in *Lo squadrone bianco*, also present a precarious world but one that the protagonist rejects, affirming the possibility of overcoming its negative effects by his actions. In the case of *Il cappello*, the protagonist is of this world, his actions defining the character of the world and the world in turn reinforcing his character.

The image of concealing and withholding governs the actions of the characters. The priest withholds money from the nobleman. Don Cirillo's papers and money are concealed under his bed. The baron seeks to hide a portrait of his mother from the acquisitive priest. He also seeks to hide the body of his victim and to conceal the priest's hat by throwing it in the river. And, of course, he seeks to hide his complicity in the crime. Like

FIGURE 18. The "triumph" of the law, *Il cappello da prete*. Courtesy of New York Museum of Modern Art, Film Stills Archive.

film noir, *Il cappello* plays with chiaroscuro lighting, with tight framing of characters, with claustrophobic settings, with shadows, portraits, and reflections in order to visualize a world that is comprised of hunters and hunted in which all the people are hunters who prey on each other, a world where guilt and innocence is unclear and where it is only by accident, like the chance that governs gambling, that misdeeds are uncovered.

The source of corruption in the film is identified with the dissolute upper classes and an ineffectual, and malevolent, clergy. The baron has gambled away his patrimony and is bereft of any sense of tradition and continuity. His house is empty, and even the money for the sale of the house is squandered. The old retainer and his nephew are presented as the innocent victims of the baron's indifference and decadence. The nephew is almost destroyed by the nobleman's lack of moral fiber. Although justice is ultimately effected and the law enters to restrain the baron, the world is not rejuvenated. One crime may be detected but corruption seems unconfined. The film is preoccupied with concealment and with the difficulty of disclosure. The only hope for revelation resides in the workings of coincidence or chance ironically identified with the metaphor of gambling. The truth surfaces not because of the heroic efforts of any individual, but because, as in gambling, chance intervenes.

The motif of conversion, so dependent on the character and actions of exceptional individuals and on the idea of a world where social and political values can be assigned and validated, is alien to this film. The central figure is locked into an obsession, unwilling or unable to move except to express his destructive impulses toward others. Like so many other films of 1943, Il *cappello da prete* portrays a deformed world deprived of humanity, understanding, and feeling. While the film seems to take a strong moral stance, as do other Poggioli films, pointing a finger at contemporary abuses, it also seems to communicate its own form of nostalgia and entrapment in a hopeless and fantasmatic environment. Its theatricality is everywhere evident in the images of doubling through the highlighting of the shadows and through the interplay between withholding and concealment, making problematic the possibility of arriving at any clear vision of justice and truth.

DEATH IN LIFE

The dramas of conversion focus on martyrdom and sacrifice: death is seen not as closure but as entry to a higher and purer form of life purged of the dross of personal desire, difference, and contingency. As we have seen in *Lo squadrone bianco* and *Il grande appello*, the central dilemma in the dramas of conversion is the problematic position of femininity in relation to the male protagonist's struggle for identity and self-realization. While in the narrative the women appear peripheral to the protagonist's quest, the imagery and the *mise-en-scène* reveal otherwise. In fact, woman is the major obstacle to his self-realization, identified with the disorderly and destructive world that he seeks to escape. *La donna della montagna* (*The Woman of the Mountain* 1943), directed by Castellani, seems to recapitulate the paradigms of the conversion melodrama, focusing particularly on the role of two women in relation to its disturbed masculine protagonist. Through the familiar strategy of doubling, the problematic and seemingly marginalized role of femininity becomes visible.

The film was made under wartime exigency. Sections of the script were unfinished, and the work was edited by Mario Serandrei with approximately one-quarter of the film missing, accounting perhaps for the highly elliptical nature of the narrative. A contemporary review of the film compares it with Hitchcock's *Rebecca* (1940), though not in complimentary terms. The parallels involve the triangulation of a mysterious fascinating dead woman, her rather plain and commonplace successor, and a brooding husband whose attachment to his first wife remains to be deciphered. The style of *La donna della montagna* is less opulent than *Un colpo*, darker, and clearly melodramatic. According to Giovanna Grignaffini, the tension in Castellani's style derives from a union of diverse directorial styles and a blurring of comedy and melodrama.[52] In particular, she points to the director's use of "objects and figures that saturate the shots, literally exploding in a rebus of linear composition that creates so many obstacles and enigmas for seeing."[53] She also emphasizes Castellani's "abstract geometric style," and the ways that his films make the viewer aware of the "physiology of the visible."[54] *La donna* stars Amedeo Nazzari as Rodolfo and Marina Betti as Zosi as the protagonists in the melodrama.

The film opens with the funeral of Rodolfo's wife, Gabriella, filmed as a ritualistic spectacle, highlighting spectatorship as commented upon by Grignaffini. The event is observed by people on the street and from balconies as a procession of mourners moves through the street. Information is circulated that Gabriella died in an accident in the mountains, but the mystery of Rodolfo's relationship to this woman is withheld. The ensuing graveyard scene focuses on Rodolfo, a morose and surly charac-

FIGURE 19. Doubling and design in *La donna della montagna*. Courtesy of New York Museum of Modern Art, Film Stills Archive.

ter. Nature plays a dominant role as the title suggests, in particular in the images of snow-capped mountains associated with Gabriella's death and with the film's finale. A conflict between nature and art is reinforced by a consistent opposition between mountains and statuary. The symmetry characteristic of *Un colpo* is reiterated in this film, highlighting difference, particularly the differences between the animate and the inanimate, stasis and movement. In particular, life and death are inverted, the dead and spectral Gabriella more alive than the animate Zosi. The character of the protagonist is conveyed through static shots identified with his brooding and self-obsessed behavior. He is also identified with a crucifix and with his canine companions. Gradually it emerges as in *Rebecca* that Gabriella was not a saintly and submissive wife but was unfaithful to him. Zosi, totally devoted to Rodolfo despite his gloom and melancholy, persists in courting him, but nonetheless she is unable to communicate with him. In the face of his sadistic treatment of her, she remains with him, accepting the abject role he assigns to her. He ignores her, turns his back to her as she speaks, and is gruff when he does talk to her.

Rodolfo's ever-present dogs assume a dual signifying role. They are another facet of nature, animal and sentient nature, similar to his own snarling behavior. They are also identified with Zosi's animal-like devotion to him, the visual correlative of her submission to him. For example, when she is given a dress by a friend to replace her shabby garments, she wears it to feed Rodolfo's dogs and returns to the house with the dress torn and dirty. She justifies her decision to remain with Rodolfo despite his abusive treatment of her, by attributing his behavior to the impending anniversary of Gabriella's death. Obsessed by mourning for Gabriella, he locks himself in his room, gazes at a picture of her, and then burns a packet of her letters. On the following day, he goes to the mountains with a friend despite the fact that a storm is brewing. Zosi follows. The weather is wild, and the shots of Rodolfo and his friend fighting the wind are intercut with shots of Zosi braving the elements. When she finds Rodolfo, he angrily abuses her, but then his anger subsides. He takes off his jacket, covers her with it, and then, crying, takes her hand and begs her forgiveness. She holds his head to her breast, and the final shot is of her face looking toward the sky.

The narrative has all the earmarks of a conversion drama, beginning in loss, moving to express the sense of loss through the rage of mourning, and ending in the relinquishment of the rage and attachment to the past through Rodolfo's burning of Gabriella's letters and his reconciliation with Zosi. However, this type of linear reading does not take account of the nondiegetic elements and the melodramatic excess, which undermine a straightforward narrative analysis that would identify the film as a conversion drama. The enigmatic use of landscape, the equation between human and animal behavior, and the excessively abject character of Zosi function to call attention to the problematic role of woman in the narrative, suggesting an unresolved and mystified parallel between physical nature and the social constructions of femininity and masculinity. Absent from the film is the sense of movement on the part of the protagonist so central to dramas of conversion. Instead, the formal aspects of the film—the role of the absent Gabriella, the extreme self-abasement of Zosi, and the self-obsessed behavior of Rodolfo—call attention to the static role of the characters and to their pathology, which exceeds any attempts on the part of the narrative to situate them in new roles at the end. Much like Hitchcock's *Rebecca*, the power of the film resides in the entrapment and passivity of both the man and the woman and in the text's style that underscores the fantasmatic nature of their actions.

The film appears to have recourse to the pathetic fallacy in the anthropomorphizing of nature, mirroring human conflict. The sublime and tempestuous image of the mountains is linked to death and unrestrained feminine sexuality. (The storm settles after the couple's reconciliation.) It is too simplistic to leave the narrative at the level of the familiar opposition between the madonna and the whore, though the final imagery of the becalming of nature in the reconciliation between Rodolfo and Zosi seems to reinforce this dichotomy. Zosi's role, as much as Gabriella's, unsettles this equation. Her abjection invites questions about the boundaries of femininity. On the one side is the assumption that the parallel between physical nature and human nature can be homologized; on the other side are the excessive signs of the unrestrained, unrestrainable, and unresolvable character of difference, the "dialectical relations between identity and difference, the incessant dynamic between attraction and repulsion"[55] that cannot be set to rest through an act of conversion. The film corroborates what is at stake in the conversion drama, where masculinity is constantly threatened by a dissolution of boundaries. Yet what is interesting about the narrative is that Rodolfo does not succumb easily to Zosi's maternal solicitations. Her abjection is as disturbing as Gabriella's transgressions. He is attracted and repelled by both women, his character suspended, not resolved between these extremes, representing the poles between which he is suspended. The attempt to abstract woman, to subdue nature, is undermined by the excessive and disturbing figure of woman. If the actions of the masculine figure are based on the ability to subdue the indeterminacy of nature effectively as in the conversion dramas, the theatrical excess generated through the feminine characters in the film is a reminder of how the process of control and mastery is intimately tied to woman and to her representation as a threatening and unsettling force. The ending of the film thus appears to provide a conventional form of closure in the union of the heterosexual couple, but not the sense of transcendence characteristic of conversion.

A PORTRAIT OF ABJECTION

The dramas of conversion and of calligraphism have a common basis in their concerns with power, but in the case of the calligraphic films the dissection, not consolidation, of power is central to the texts. Power is coded in relation to conflicts involving sexual transgression, dissonances between public and private spheres, and particularly violations of law. Furthermore, while both conversion and calligraphic films are united in their theatrical styles, the calligraphic films seem to be seeking a different cinematic and philosophic position from which to dramatize their conflicts. In its encyclopedic treatment of power and heterosexual and homosocial relations, Poggioli's *Gelosia* (1943) exemplifies most of the tensions inherent to calligraphic films. The film does not deviate much from the novel by Capuana on which it is based, *Il Marchese di Roccaverdina*. The marchese's world as developed by Poggioli is not Blasetti's celebration in *Terra madre* of the rural world of *strapaese* but one "in which the agrarian aristocracy considers itself above the law and inviolable."[56] The protagonist, Antonio (Roldano Lupi), is not brought to a realization of his responsibilities to the people. At the center of this world, as its sole determinant, the marchese controls the fate of the people, their lives and deaths. However, his power operates in an inverse direction in his wanton murder of one of his peasants and in the ways that the murder sets in motion his defiance of all existing social institutions. The title of Visconti's *Ossessione* is equally applicable to this film as well as to the films of Castellani, Soldati, and Chiarini, revealing the films' predilection for an affective register in portraying social relations, the turning from the external world to probe the subjective dimensions of power. The spectacle of masculinity as developed through Antonio's character is rendered through a range of figurative elements, animals, a crucifix, clothing, and lighting. The lighting and the use of symmetry and asymmetry invite reflection on the illegibility of this world, the ways in which the familiar is estranged.

The film begins with two riders on horseback. The scene is dark to the point of obscurity, though it becomes evident that one rider is the hunter, the other his prey. One man, the one who has been singing, falls to the ground, but the identity of the other is not clear. In the following scene, the police enter a house. A man can be heard proclaiming his innocence. He is dragged out and arrested. Antonio, the Marchese di Roccaverdina, is approached by a lawyer who seeks to enlist his help to save Neli, the man accused of the murder of Rocco Curcione and one of Antonio's peasants. The lawyer informs Antonio that there appears to be no apparent motive for the murder, since Rocco, once a womanizer, became a changed man after his marriage to Agrippina (Luisa Ferida). Agrippina confronts Antonio with her plight, but he treats her dismissively. The Baronessa di Lagomorto (Wanda Capodoglio), who runs the affairs of the estate, confronts Agrippina, concerned that the peasant woman will resume her relationship with Antonio, if not become his wife. Agrippina informs her that she knows her station and does not aspire to become his wife. However, the baroness decides to find Antonio a proper wife as quickly as possible and settles on Zosima Munoz (Elena Zareschi), an upper-class and socially responsible woman. Parallel to the baroness's efforts to marry Antonio off are the lawyer's efforts to involve him in the freeing of Neli. Antonio agrees to help, but he is silent at the trial.

The trial scene is highly choreographed, filmed from Antonio's perspective. Witnesses attest to Neli's innocence. A sign, "The law is equal for all," is posted in the courtroom and serves as an ironic reminder of the travesty of justice to be enacted. At a dinner party, Antonio's friends accuse the court of injustice, but Antonio, enraged, asserts his belief that Neli was the assassin. He is confronted by Agrippina, who reproaches him for arranging the marriage between her and Rocco, and he treats her roughly. As she turns to leave, he embraces her passionately. In a night scene that borders on Gothic horror, Antonio, wearing a cape with which he partially covers his face, passes through a corridor containing a statue of Christ, on his way to seek absolution from the priest. He confesses his long-standing affair with Agrippina, that he arranged the marriage between her and Rocco, and that he had ordered Rocco not to consummate the marriage. Tortured by jealousy, he finally murdered Rocco. The priest counsels him to make reparation and to confess his crime, for an

FIGURE 20. "The law is equal for all," *Gelosia*. Courtesy of New York Museum of Modern Art, Film Stills Archive.

innocent man will die because of him. Scornfully, Antonio responds that he is a Roccaverdina and above the law. He reminds the priest that he is constrained by his priestly office from revealing Antonio's confession. In the following scene, the reproachful Christ figure is removed at his orders by a group of acolytes to be taken elsewhere.

Antonio, beginning to experience the pangs of guilt, writes a note of confession to be given to the public prosecutor and contemplates shooting himself, but he is interrupted by the arrival of Zossima, who has come, at the instigation of the baroness, to collect money from him for charity. Antonio is filmed standing in the doorway as she leaves, as if on the threshold between life and death, then he takes the suicide note and burns it. Shortly thereafter, he proposes to her, expressing the hope that she will help to banish the ghosts in his life. No sooner married then Antonio begins again to seek out Agrippina. Zossima complains to her mother that Antonio has become melancholy. When Antonio learns that Zossima has agreed to care for one of Neli's children, he becomes enraged, shouting at her that he does not want a reminder of an unpleasant situation. Not submissive, she tells him that she has had enough of his behavior, alluding to his silences and to his relations with Agrippina.

Antonio's growing discomfiture is portrayed in yet another night scene. In bed in a candlelit room, he begins to hallucinate, hearing the sound of horses' hooves. He gets up and goes to Zosima's room, but her door is locked. When she opens it, telling him that she locked it because of her fear of him, repentantly he proposes that they take a trip together to the country. The trip is marred by their meeting a peasant who asks Antonio permission for his son to marry Agrippina, and he angrily refuses, as Zosima looks on. At home, Antonio is disturbed by the absence of the religious statue from the corridor. Immediately thereafter, Zosima informs him that Neli has died in prison. Agata, the wife of Neli, comes to the house with her children and exhorts them to remember that their father was innocent, and she curses the murderer of Rocco. Antonio goes to his room. The scene is darkly lit. A shadow of a cross and his own shadow are visible on the wall, and these are superimposed onto images of the murder and of the priest in judgment. The music is harsh and dissonant. Antonio becomes delirious, and, as Zosima tends him, he raves about the sound of the horses' hooves and the priest's voice. He fears that he will have no peace. Following this night, Zosima leaves for good, but Agrippina returns. The doctor tells her that Antonio's condition is serious, and she goes to see the dying man. In his room, he sits paralyzed in a chair, oblivious to everything. She is led out as the sound of choir boys chanting the Miserere can be heard. The boys pass her in procession, and she falls to the floor. When she gets up, the corridor is empty. Her shadow can be seen as she exits, and the last shot is of the empty corridor, the one where the Christ figure was seen earlier.

The film's lighting is highly expressive from the opening shots where the obscurity of the events functions proleptically, foreshadowing the obscurity of Antonio's actions, the complexity of his jealousy, and his succumbing to obsession. The night scenes, as he descends into guilt, hallucination, and madness, reinforce his ambiguous and shadowy interior world, magnifying, not simplifying, the nature of his fixation. The film's reliance on parallelism, repetition, and symmetry does not convey any sense of balance and harmony but rather of disorientation and imbalance. The image of a corridor seen first with a religious icon, later with the image of Antonio slinking like a vampire on his way to confess to the priest, and, finally, with the empty corridor highlights the desolate and discordant character of this world, the disparity between inner and outer worlds. The religious images, rituals, and landscape stand in opposition to Antonio's decomposing inner world. He is also filmed from the rear as if to signify further the difficulty in reading his state of mind and actions. His incipient madness is identified with suggestions of diabolism in his uneasy relation to the crucifix, his satanic suffering that admits of no mitigation, and his paralysis, his inability to escape his monomaniac fixation.

The contrasting portraits of Zosima and Agrippina highlight the familiar conflict between the idealized upper-class maternal figure, associated with religion and the family, and the sexualized lower-class peasant figure, associated with transgression. Both women, in relation to Rocco, serve to highlight his inability to accept the privileges and responsibilities of his social class. His aristocratic position is more than a designation of social class. It is also the mark of his unchecked power. In his identification with criminality and his flouting of the law as well as in his manipulation of the peasants as exemplified in his arrangement of Agrippina's marriage to Rocco, this film too probes the abuse of power, its illegitimacy. Religion functions in the text as an ironic correlative to his arbitrary and excessive behavior. In one sense, the role of the priest, rather than enhancing the positive character of religion, only underscores its impotence. The melodrama has turned the world upside down, revealing through the protagonist's madness and disintegration an insight into the loss of fixed boundaries, the eruption of difference, and the rampant character of unrestrained desire.

The calligraphism of *Gelosia* thus exemplifies a style and subject that diverges from many conversion films of the era with their upbeat treatments of history, their attempts to present a world amenable to control, their presentation of feminine figures as sources of or threats to redemption, and their attempts to hold at bay the unsettling effects of difference, reflection, contemplation, and social and especially social class disunity. Films such as *Il cappello del prete* seem to turn such narratives on their head by opening up a vision of a world that is demonic and disruptive. If the conversion dramas seek to portray a world of resemblances, the calligraphic dramas struggle with difference, difference that centers on questions of power and identity, particularly masculine identity. In their melodramatic excess, their veiled and ambiguous treatment of character and context, their emphasis on form, the calligraphic films implicate the spectator in a world that transgresses narrative limits, secure boundaries, and conventional moral positions, substituting in their place darkness and doubt. The conversion films regard theatricality in terms of life as performance, a form of performance that is dependent on the common sense of folklore derived from religion, the law, habit and custom, from reiterated and familiar structures that reinforce a sense of the known world. The calligraphic films plunge the spectator into another form of theatricality that turns spectacle into horror. In *Gelosia* as in *Il cappello da prete*, the underside of spectacle is exposed, its demonic and anticollective character. Theatricality no longer serves as a means of bonding between text and spectator in a shared sense of the necessity of performance to community as in the comedies and many of the historical films. Instead, what is emphasized is the destructive and violent consequences of power.

The films of conversion are, however, not simply the binary opposites to these films. The world that they portray is not hermetic. The melodramas expose the sense of threat attendant on a loss of self, of ego boundaries, and of relations to the social world, but they adopt familiar affective strategies to dissipate the danger of thinking differently. They address conversion from a vantage point that Klaus Theweleit in *Male Fantasies* describes in the following terms:

> These men experience their affinity with power as "natural." To them, powerlessness means the threat of permanent exclusion, both from justice and from pleasure. Their every action becomes an *assertion of themselves*; they are always in *opposition*. Yet their transgressions are organized within systems of absolute obedience. Their sta-

tus as components within totality machines gives them the feeling of being-in-power, but the machines themselves function according to strictly hierarchical positions; each component is allotted a single position. . . . While every component experiences a sense of power, the power is neither individual nor can it be gained in isolation. The machine partakes of, and represents, a larger social power which it functions to maintain and celebrate.[57]

In this sense, the paradigm of conversion underpins the folklore of consensus, revealing its dual character, both the tenaciousness of its hold and its constitutive character as entertainment. The melodramas with calligraphism are the underside of the conversion dramas, bringing forward more explicitly and graphically that which is submerged but not invisible in the conversion narratives. The conversion melodramas work to contain disorder and destruction, while the images and structures of calligraphism release a vision of dissolute and decomposing masculine personas in a disintegrative system of social relations, a cinematic vision of the world that allows for the possibility of challenging, if only obliquely, the form and substance of received ideas. In many ways, the calligraphic films in their form, style, and subject matter open a window onto an unfamiliar world that, while antirealistic, touches on contemporary realities. They, like the "neorealist" films that follow them, are, in the terms of Gilles Deleuze, responsible for the breakdown of the "collapse of traditional sensorimotor situations"[58] in their intense focus on character and in their challenge to clichéd and formulaic images.

The calligraphic films that cluster in the late 1930s and early 1940s cannot be accounted for in univalent terms. A number of factors can be adduced for their appearance: the horrendous conditions of a country at war, dislocations of populations, disillusionment and fatigue with the Fascist regime, the ongoing inflow of Americanism as derived from literature and from Hollywood, and the innovation of the film industry from 1935 not merely technically but in terms of different narrative forms, characters, and situations.[59] Their theatricality must also be accounted for in terms beyond the persistence of melodramatic modes. One of the characteristics of modernity, and its relation to what we term the "postmodern"—connected to the proliferation of newspapers, magazines, advertising, radio, popular records, and cinema—is an increased sensitivity to and awareness of media, not as a reflection of reality but, in Godard's famous dictum, as the "reality of a reflection." The "politics of style" served to

produce audiences who were increasingly drawn into the various spectacles of modern life whether in the formal political arena or in the cinema.
On the one hand, this offers a challenge to commonsense formulations of
the self and the world; on the other, a desperate need to fill the void. By
breaking down the rigid lines between reality and illusion, the theatricality of these conversion and calligraphic texts produced a situation that
may be more terrifying than the notion of "fascinating fascism," eroding
a secure sense of the world but not necessarily replacing it with a more
complex understanding of performance. While the uses of theatricality
encompass and dramatize both an adherence to and aberration from history, time, social value, and possible change, they remain elusive, ambivalent, and affectively invested in performance, and their character and
reception also remain elusive as befits popular and mass culture's eclectic
uses of common sense as folklore.

CHAPTER FIVE

The Affective Value of
Femininity and Maternity

Femininity is central to the early and late melodramas of the Italian silent and sound eras, always present and always problematic even when the figure of woman appears marginal to the narrative resolution. In the case of the films that feature masculine conversion, femininity is something other than the biological female and something more than a material entity. Femininity is, like money, a medium of exchange and circulation, serving as an abstraction, a semblance, that has no intrinsic value but is assigned value through its differential relations to commodities. The dual character of money—as representation and as differential, as commodity and as value, as general and specific form—appears to take on a fixed, measurable, and univalent character. In the realm of social relations, femininity, inherently abstract and valueless in itself, becomes the source of specific kinship, sexual, and reproductive values, assuming a univalent character. However, we have seen through an examination of forms of the various expressions of theatricality in the cinema of the era that the constitutive character of representation emerges through the various expressions of transgression and abjection that are associated with the threatening figure of woman as mother, wife, sexual object, and worker. The transgressive nature of femininity opens into the abyss of the social production of meaning, overturning stable categories of social life involving sexual difference, the family, and regional and national communities. Femininity is synonymous with uncertainty, with that which is disruptive to the world of the masculine protagonist and to the social order. Its threat and its power lies in its protean character. The figure of woman becomes the impediment to masculine self-realization and power, to forms of desire that are identified with the loss of commitment to a higher cause, particularly the cause of service to the community and the nation, serving to isolate the protagonist from the community of men.

The recent criticism of sexual relations as exemplified in Fascist culture and society, has tended to accord greater importance to the position of women. The writings of Victoria de Grazia, Lesley Caldwell, and Jacqueline Reich stress the contradictory position of women under Fascism, exploring the question of how Fascism ruled women, the ways in which the media disseminated various portraits of femininity, and the reception and impact of these portraits.[1] If there was a fantasy circulating at the time of the coming into being of a "new man," there was also the corresponding emphasis on the creation of the "new woman" as his "counterpart." Magazines, newspapers, and documentaries by LUCE were increasingly devoted to this project, aligning it particularly with government campaigns to enhance the birth rate as well as with the battle to restore the primacy of the family presumed to be under siege. The emphasis on the valorization of motherhood corresponded to the devalorization of feminist aspirations.[2] With the aim of making motherhood attractive and profitable, the regime offered honorific and monetary incentives. Writing of the character and effects of maternity practices under the regime, de Grazia says:

> This pattern of relegating women to domestic duties, while diminishing their authority in the family, will come as no surprise to anybody familiar with how modern welfare states operate. What distinguished fascist Italy is perhaps only that the state's claim to promote a modern maternity was so vigorous, while government services were so unevenly administered. The fascist family welfare services offered the allure of the modern without its underpinnings. They set new standards, interfered with old customs, and stigmatized traditional practices. Yet they failed to provide the wherewithal for women to feel empowered by a modernized maternal craft— either as the providers or as the beneficiaries of new services, Italian mothers of all classes were thus made to feel inadequate, anxious, and dependent.[3]

In its efforts to prescribe maternity, the regime was zealous in seeking to reinvent the family, aligning it with the nation: "The state claimed that the family was sacrosanct and indivisible, yet, in the name of nation, the dictatorship justified every kind of intrusion."[4] While propaganda insisted on the sexual puritanism, economic frugality, and austere leisure habits associated with early industrialism, the tendencies toward the creation of a modern consumer society were bound to create contradictions between past and present practices, between political injunctions and personal need.

The work of de Grazia is valuable for highlighting the programs and practices of the regime as they affected women. However, as Lucia Re indicates, a focus on Fascist institutions does not adequately reveal the character of "fascist theories of 'Woman.'" Lucia Re writes that "if we want to gain a less limited understanding of all the levels and complexities of the cultural construction of gender in the Fascist era, we need to consider the ways in which the hegemonic discourse of the regime finds philosophical as well as political and ideological grounding in its *theories* of gender."[5] Examining the writings of such philosophers as Giovanni Gentile, Re probes the ways in which the theorization of sexual difference must be accounted for, its modernity, and yet its insistence on motherhood as "something innate, original, and essential to woman."[6] Specifically in relation to modernism and avant-guardism, Re explores writings on femininity that denaturalize the biological and maternal, using techniques of estrangement, irony, and satire (as well as theatricality), thus indicating that while there were tendencies toward totalization, there were also fissures in the cultural fabric, fissures also evident in the popular commercial cinema. These fissures exposed the various attempts at totalizing and the impossibility of producing a seamless narrative.

The composite and contradictory tension between tradition and modernity as it inflects gender and sexuality is addressed in Karen Pinkus's *Bodily Regimes*, which makes that tension central to Fascist struggles for hegemony.[7] In her examination of advertising under Fascism, she documents the collusion between capitalism, modernism, and the production of desexed bodies, but she underscores the fact that sexuality in Fascist terms must be understood in terms established by Deleuze and Guattari and by Theweleit as actually moving through and beyond gender in its de-realization of the body, both affirming and denying it simultaneously. Pinkus asserts that "At times, the body seems to erase any traces of its own gender—to masquerade or cross dress—as a security measure, almost as if to escape the controls of the regime."[8] The ways in which gender and sexuality function are not transparent. While forms of impersonation as masquerade are central to an understanding of the constitution of femininity, gender is not erased but staged. In the process of staging, the dual character of femininity—as symbol and as measure of value, as amorphous and as coded—is not invisible.

The common sense of folklore enables a rudimentary recognition of this duality in ways that reductive notions of propaganda cannot. The media of the period, and especially the newsreels and commercial cinema, are a striking instance of the necessity of drawing on a number of discourses to reach audiences in terms that are sufficiently eclectic, flexible, and even playful, always attentive to the necessary anastomosis between the formulaic and the innovative. The notion of propaganda has to be qualified through examining the dual role of forms—as an opportune strategy for staging consensus and as a shared recognition of the artifice entailed in the process of creating meaning. Once the conception of folklore as purely residual is abandoned and its protean and emergent character acknowledged, the possibility of tracking "the contradictory, disjointed quality both of the mass cultural product and of the commodity with its fluctuating status of 'meaning' becomes possible in relation to capital and to the State."[9] This recognition, however, is not synonymous with subversion or resistance; it ironically complicates and enhances the nature of the folklore of consensus. Thus, by broadening the range of documents, by challenging reductive conceptions of cultural hegemony, by stressing the innovative aspects of Fascism in relation to modernity, and especially by rethinking the politics of style that is derived from conceptions of femininity, it is possible to see the character and uses of femininity as exposing the folklore of consensus, revealing its role in constructions of social value.

This chapter addresses how femininity is expressed in melodramas of the 1930s and early 1940s. It explores the ways the films' uses of narrative, spectacle, and theatricality offer insights into the management of femininity and into the ways that femininity exposes representational constraints. Melodramatic excess, in particular, stages these constraints, revealing femininity as the mainspring of representation that produces conflict between the real and the imaginary. The concept of consensus as constituting "real" conditions of totalization inhibits the possibility of identifying and understanding the "compromises, or forms of adaptation, to various institutions and ideologies of the regime."[10] The concept of consensus thus becomes a more flexible and dynamic means for assessing the slippery and subtle relations between the production and consumption of cinematic images of femininity under Fascism.

In addressing these issues, this chapter will examine melodramas that dramatize conflicts over representation involving maternity, the family, the school, entertainment, and heterosexual and homosocial relations. Consonant with recent scholarship in cinema and cultural studies, my critical treatment of these films produced under Fascism will show them to be a resource for understanding the overdetermined and tenuous nature of cultural and political representation, shedding light on the complex nature of consensus, which "should never be mistaken for a finished product. It is always contested, always trying to secure itself, always 'in process.'"[11] The theatricality of the conversion melodramas discussed in the previous chapter is an important index to the contested, not secure, character of representation. While the films appear to thrive on a familiar and static discourse of sameness, their emphasis on sexual and gendered fictions must perforce engage with and reveal the processes of difference and indeterminacy that their attempts at mediation attempt to quell. Since the popular cinema thrives on the sexual politics of femininity for the creation of spectacle, for narrative complication, and for affective value, an examination of the protean forms of femininity will yield insights about the always contested nature of production, reception, and, hence, the folklore of consensus.

Throughout the era, from such films as *La segretaria privata* to *Zazà*, the films feature a range of feminine figures: working-class women, department store clerks, telephone operators, secretaries struggling to make their way in the world; single women, often entertainers, bereft of lovers, languishing for companionship but fated to isolation; women of color as in the case of such films of *Il grande appello* and *Sotto la croce del sud*. These feminine figures are central to the transformation of the male protagonist and then peripheralized or finally eliminated from the narrative. Often, the female characters are barred from the realization of desire by their social class or by their "irresponsible" and personal and socially destructive quest for pleasure and self-realization. In those narratives featuring an unwed mother, she is doomed for a time to wandering with her child, subject to social ostracism and often driven to crime and prostitution until redeemed. The maternal figure or maternal surrogate, whether as a paragon of self-abnegation or as errant and destructive, is inescapable. Usually, a figure of self-sacrifice, the mother renounces her own desires in behalf of her offspring. Even when the mother is not directly invoked, the scenario of maternity guides the narrative, images, and relations among characters. But the treatments of femininity are not uniform but vary according to genre, style, and directorial perspective. For example, the comedies of Camerini and Neufeld, the historical films of Blasetti, and the various dramas of conversion are more likely to celebrate theatricality through their romantic fictions, relying on the feminine figure as the foundation of the social fictions enacted—the fictional and often reflexively portrayed source of discord and the fictional source of reconciliation between the individual and the community. While femininity remains problematic throughout the films of the era, there is a subtle transformation visible in the final films produced under the regime. The calligraphic films of Soldati, Castellani, and especially of Poggioli produced during the war, while still adhering to the identification of femininity with illusion, use theatricality to cast a jaundiced and critical eye on a society where conceptions of masculinity and femininity are identified, but not celebrated. They function as masquerade, puppetlike creations, dramatizing the sexual politics of power and the power of sexual politics.

THE MATERNAL MACHINE

I begin my discussion with *Il carnevale di Venezia* (1940) an exemplary film for examining a commonsense view of sexual and familial relations as they are theatricalized through the portrait of the feminine maternal. The film is a maternal melodrama, focusing on the ways in which the position of the mother is essential to the consolidation of the family, expressly tied to conceptions of theatricality. The dual valences of impersonation are evident. "Putting on a show" comes to represent more than entertainment and escapism; it is a strategy for "producing" social performance that dramatizes the conflation of the domestic and public spheres.

Directed by Giuseppe Adami and Giacomo Gentilomo, the film contains a melange of opera arias (orchestral work by the Royal Opera of Rome), folk songs, and ballet (performed by the Corps de Ballet of La Scala). The central figure in the film is the opera singer Toti Dal Monte, a lyric soprano, who plays the role of Ninetta. The city of Venice also figures largely in the film as more than backdrop, central to the spectacle and theatricality of the text. The film opens with images of Venice, of the Grand Canal, a view of palaces, bridges, and people scurrying about. A title, "The Bridge of Sighs," gives way to the pages of a musical score and then to a view of musicians under the direction of a conductor, Montini. The conjunction of the city with musical culture provides a prolegomena to the ways the film seeks to establish the relationship between urban life and the characters' domestic conflicts.

Ninetta, Montini's daughter, an opera singer, is not a successful stage performer but works as a foreman in a tobacco factory. Ninetta warns one of the women that she will have to perform better or be reported. In response, the woman taunts her about Tonina (Junie Astor), Ninetta's daughter, revealing that she is carrying on with Paolo, Count Sagredo (Guido Lazzarini). Tonina is studying music at the Conservatory. A fight, reminiscent of opening scenes in Bizet's *Carmen*, ensues between the two women and others join the fray. The film poses a number of oppositions between success and failure, working-class life and upper-class aspiration, Venice's visual splendor set against domestic conflict, and problematic mother-and-daughter relations. Misrecognition and confusion multiply as Ninetta assumes that her daughter is having an affair with the baker, Marchetto (Stefano Sibaldi), who is in possession of a scarf of Tonina's that he found on the street. Confronting her daughter with her suspicion, Tonina does nothing to dispel it, concealing that she is actually involved with Paolo, but Marchetto is delighted and begins to entertain the thought of being engaged to her.

In a scene at San Marco, Tonina, disaffected with her family and with the neighbors, meets Paolo and tells him that she is going to leave home, but he urges her to think of her mother. Meanwhile, Marchetto makes preparations to celebrate his engagement to Tonina at the Feast of the Redeemer to be held that evening. After the family is dressed for the feast, Ninetta discovers that her daughter has run way. Stoically, she goes with her father to the festival. Asked to sing by her father, she at first refuses but relents after he commands her not to expose publicly how she feels. As she sings, the editing intercuts between her and the assembled company in the boats and on the shore (among whom is Tonina with Paolo). When she performs a traditional lullaby that Tonina recognizes from her childhood, the daughter decides to return to her mother. She finds her praying before an image of the Madonna and the two embrace. Determined now to succeed as a performer, Tonina makes an attempt to practice her singing. She asks her mother to perform arias for her, and Ninetta sings arias from *Lucia da Lammermoor* and from *La Sonnambula*. The mother's exemplary performance discourages the daughter, though it provides Montini the opportunity to lament that Ninetta's voice is wasted in her working at the factory. Paolo, zealous for Tonina, plans for her to perform publicly. Posters and signs broadcast the appearance of the "nightingale of San Marco." Confusion escalates as Marchetto seeks restitution for the money he has spent for the engagement party, threatening to appropriate Montini's piano as compensation.

Much has been written in recent years about carnival, derived largely from the work of Mikhail Bakhtin, in which the concept of carnival relates to folk culture in certain ways parallel to Gramsci's conception of folklore as polyphonic, heteroglossic, hybrid, parodic, and indicative of a dual vision of the world, seen largely through the festive or saturnalian occasion where the world is temporarily turned upside down.[12] In relating carnivalization to the cinema, Ella Shohat and Robert Stam write, in terms reminiscent of Jane Feuer's discussion of "live entertainment" that "Carnival, then, is not only a living social practice but also a general, perennial fund of popular forms and festive rituals; it promotes participatory spectacle, a 'pageant without footlights' erasing the boundaries between spectator and performer."[13] The film draws on a popular form of entertainment in its dramatization of the festive and ritualistic dimensions of carnival, highlighting participation, and focusing on relations between performer and spectator but in its reflexive treatment of entertainment subdues and qualifies the heterogeneous and festive character identified with the notion of carnival. The carnival, the climax of the film, begins with an elaborate ballet sequence, mingling it with the dancing of crowds. Tonina's performance is threatened when she loses her voice, but Ninetta, concealed, sings in her stead as Tonina mimes the words. The audience is wildly enthusiastic. Tonina seeks to confess but is stopped by Paolo who drags her away to his friends. The final shots of the film are indoors with Ninetta alone at the piano until joined by Montini, who tells Ninetta that he alone knows that she was the singer. She comments, "But he'll marry her" as she leans against Montini. On the surface the film provides a narrative of reconciliation. Marchetto has relented in his claims, Tonina will marry well, and the secret of the fraudulent performance is safe.

Il carnevale di Venezia offers an affectively intense and ambiguous version of the benign and selfless face of motherhood, reenacting the melodramatic motif of a mother's total devotion to her daughter to the point of self-abnegation, subordinating her own career to further her daughter's ambitions. However, the daughter's "career" does not turn out

to be a musical one but marriage to a nobleman. The film does not reconcile talent, success, and domesticity. Rather, creativity is subordinated
in both the cases of the mother and the daughter to work and to the
domestic sphere. Though the film has certain classic elements of the opera
and the musical film—romance, spectacle, the struggle to succeed in the
world of entertainment, and self-reflexivity about performance and spectatorship—its treatment of spectacle does not resolve the conflicts generated by the mother and daughter relationship or the conflict between art
and social life.[14] Moreover, the festive aspects of carnival that usually function as vehicles for undermining conventional behavior and restraints are
complicated and diluted by the knowledge of Ninetta's fraudulent act of
ventriloquism and by the image of Ninetta's isolation at the end, which
tends to distinguish the film from many of the comedies discussed in
chapter 2.

   Unlike Victor Savile's British melodrama *Evergreen* (1934) where
the heroine impersonates her mother, is forced to confess so as to be
absolved for her crime of fraudulence, and hence is enabled to continue
as a performer in her own right, *Il carnevale* suppresses the confession and,
hence, the requisite absolution.[15] Ninetta uses her vocal talent to conceal
her daughter's inadequacies. In the final analysis, she not only "gives up
the child to the social order," but in so doing she negates her own identity.[16] The film can be seen to reiterate the pathos of a film such as *Stella
Dallas* (1937), which dramatizes the familiar maternal dilemma through
"Stella's displacement of her desires onto her daughter."[17] The film's
silences—like Ninetta's—argue for the text's working on commonsense
assumptions shared with the audience, playing with the commonsense
subordination of the public to the private sphere, of collective submission
to individual action, and of self-expression to self-suppression. The viability of the private sphere is maintained by suppressing truth, by keeping
the secret of impersonation intact. Melodrama as the language of muteness serves commonsense in *Carnevale* at the same time that it enacts the
paradigm of maternal service, it also—intentionality aside—exposes how
common sense is based on maintaining silence and, therefore, how this
silence is the instrument of consensus.

   In the context of challenging escapism, this emphasis on silence can
be read in ambiguous terms as either prescription or as cynical revelation.
The daughter's incorporation of the mother's voice and the silence that
attends this action is uncomfortably conspiratorial. This silence, not
obscured for the external audience, undermines the conventional utopian

characteristics of musical. The musical's reflexivity depends on performance to create a sense of shared community between internal and external audience. In this film, the exposure of secrecy works on several levels to fracture the semblance of unity. The narrative is exposed as relying on fraudulence. Most especially, the film denaturalizes femininity by inadvertently revealing how the maternal figure does not exist in her own right. The silence surrounding the mother's actions further reveals itself as another instance of the instrumental and enigmatic nature of femininity. As surely as a radical text might seek to provide a critique of commodification, the maternal discourse in this film serves to expose its commodification. If in advertising, as Pinkus suggests, "the product itself gains power and prestige over the means of production [and] . . . the human subject is gradually elided, mechanized, or annihilated by a violent representational act,"[18] in this film, the removal of the usual affective props reinforcing maternal sacrifice calls attention to form over content, style over substance. Femininity thereby is potentially exposed as a theatrical strategy, an artifact. The melodramatic ending does not, however, negate affect. In the image of Ninetta at the end of the film, supported by Montini, another affective valence can be discerned, one that portrays the cost of suppression and compliance. Most especially, the film inadvertently reveals how the maternal figure serves as a determinant of social value, though receiving by way of compensation only an image of her sacrifice, an analogue to the film itself. Thus, escapism in the form of theatricality is not devoid of a knowledge of its contradictions, which it is even willing to share with the audience. Yet there is still another twist. As the recognized star of opera and of the film, Toti Dal Monte's role serves both to reinforce the image of maternal sacrifice in the narrative while at the same time intertextually undermining it through the audience's knowledge of her own success as performer, yet another indication of the common sense and theatricality that underpins consensus.

WORKING-CLASS DIVAS

Theatricality is not confined to those films that highlight forms of entertainment; it flourishes through another route, namely through melodramatic excess and its exposure of the affective investment in the family through the staging of social transgression. The major protagonist in this drama is the solitary female who, through willfulness or impulse or due to the threatening and oppressive character of working-class life, violates expectations of female purity. Feminine transgression opens up to the threat of (and the fascination with) social dissolution; it is also the necessary hinge for entertaining forms of restabilizing order. Camerini's *T'amerò sempre* (I'll Always Love You, 1933) is a melodrama that focuses on the plight of the unwed mother and her attempts to resist repeating her mother's fate. The imagery evokes prevailing representations of femininity as exemplified by the propaganda and advertisements of the time. In its opening scenes, the film bears a resemblance to documentaries produced by LUCE for the edification of women in their requisite roles as producers for the nation.[19] In a maternity ward, scores of babies are photographed as nurses tend newborn infants. The camera pans a line of babies in their cribs, providing a curious vision of regimentation, clinical hygiene, and modern care. No sound is heard of crying infants. The babies are then delivered to their mothers. In the midst of this scene of maternal care, a well-dressed woman appears and approaches bed number "seven." The woman in the bed is Adriana (Elsa De Giorgi), and it is quickly apparent that Adriana is unlike the other mothers. Her baby is born out of wedlock, and the woman visiting her, sister to the aristocratic father of the child, has come to inform Adriana that her relationship to her brother, the count, is a nuisance to the entire family. This encounter is intercut by shots of others in the ward, looking on at this drama. The woman informs Adriana that she is young and will in time forget her brother.

On the woman's departure, Adriana, clutching her baby, begins to cry, and the baby begins to cry as well. A nurse comes and takes the infant. The woman in the next bed asks Adriana if there is anyone who can help, and Adriana confesses that she is alone and has always been alone. This statement is the prologue to a flashback of Adriana as a child, alone until her mother exits from the building with a man who pats the child on the head as she cringes. "You are very bad," he tells her. She is scolded by her mother for this behavior, and in an ensuing scene, yet another man visits as Adriana is left alone as her mother and the man go into another room and close the door on her. After sounds of violence, the man emerges and Adriana discovers the lifeless body of her mother. The scene shifts in time to an orphanage where Adriana is brought by one of the mother's male acquaintances. He informs the director that her mother is dead and that there is no one to care for her, and he leaves her with the injunction to be "good." Once again, the motif of the orphan is central to the working out of the melodramatic and affective preoccupation with identity and its relation to the family and social community.

Within a flashback and with another shift in time, Adriana is seen with other young women in the orphanage as they observe through the window a man walking with a young woman and kissing her. The girls refer to the woman as a "sinner." The flashback ends with Adriana as a young woman herself walking with a man, and then the scene dissolves to her in her bed, crying. Now the count is introduced, interrogating his sister about the visit to the hospital. She informs him that she has told Adriana to stay away from them and not to trouble the family. Adriana is dismissed from the hospital with her baby as a nurse tells her to be brave, and a slow fade moves the narrative ahead in time to when the child, a girl, is playing and Adriana fondles the child before leaving her with a sitter. The beauty parlor, Oscar's, where Adriana works, is reminiscent of the scenes of regimentation that were introduced at the beginning of the film. The women under the hair-dryers are portrayed in terms of regimentation, as if part of an assembly line for the production of femininity. In the midst of this vision of sameness, a woman enters imperiously with her docile husband in train, demanding to see Oscar as the other women laugh at her and at her submissive husband. A new character is introduced, Mario (Nino Besozzi), an accountant, who is attracted to Adriana. He remains after closing hours, and follows Adriana out to the street where he also meets his sister and introduces the women to each other. Rejecting their invitation to join them, Adriana leaves as the sister makes complimentary comments about her.

The count phones Oscar's to make an appointment for a woman friend. Adriana answers the phone as the count, unaware of her identity, makes seductive comments to her about how nice she sounds and asks whether she is a blonde or a brunette. She hangs up. The count appears, complaining of the rude manner in which he has been treated. The images of the beauty parlor highlight the artificiality of the upper-class women who come to transform themselves into fashion plates and narcissistically admire themselves before the mirrors. Oscar berates Adriana for rudeness on the phone, but, on seeing the count, she hides in the accountant's office without explaining to him her reason for hiding. When the count and his friends leave, Mario invites Adriana to his house for a family party, and she accepts. While offering a homely contrast to the regimentation, pretentiousness, and sterility of the beauty parlor, the Fabbri home, characterized by food, family photos (including one of

Mario as a child), and dancing, is not idealized. According to James Hay, the scene "both valorizes and satirizes the Italian petit-bourgeois sensibility and family ideals."[20] The disruptive elements are Mario and Adriana, both offering eccentric and flawed portraits of gendered and familial ideals. A contrast to his sister's more virile fiancé, he violates conventional notions of masculinity, his behavior suggests the "taint" of effeminacy. In this milieu, Adriana is awkward too, presenting, because of her past, a flawed image of conventional femininity. Escorting Adriana home, Mario proposes to her, and, silent about her situation, she tells him that marriage in not possible.

Returning to her apartment, she finds the count waiting for her. He tells her how beautiful she is and how remorseful he is for neglecting her and the child. Despite his offers to set her up in more suitable lodgings, to offer her a life of leisure, and to support her financially so that she need not work, she tells him to leave. Clear contrasts are set up between the two dominant male characters. The count is lithe, imperious, sophisticated, and also menacing, while bespectacled Mario is reticent, awkward, humble, and gentle. Mario has become distracted. Deciding that he doesn't feel well, he leaves only to realize that he has forgotten his work. When he emerges on the street, he encounters Adriana with her child. She informs him that the child is hers, and walks off. At home, he is told by his mother how much she liked Adriana, a further indication of family pressure on him to marry. Once again at work, he encounters Adriana, who is reluctant to talk to him. The count appears and again importunes Adriana. Mario eavesdrops on the charged conversation of the pair as she pleads with the count to leave her alone, that she is interested in someone else. He approaches her, threatening violence, as Mario breaks in and the two men fight. Oscar fires Adriana, and Mario leads her out of the beauty parlor. On the street he apologizes for his behavior but tells her he could not bear to stand by and see her treated in such rough fashion. Once again, he invites her with her child to his home. The last shot of the film is of the couple walking off together,

The melodrama draws on familiar conventions: the vicissitudes of the orphan in the impersonal world of the city without any familial identity and social support, the lower-class woman at the mercy of parasitic, immoral, and violent aristocrats, the unwed and unprotected mother seeking to fend for herself and her child in a threatening environment, the dangers of prostitution that confront dependent women, and the appearance of a savior of motherhood and hence of the sanctity of family. Consonant with Camerini's other films, the visual codes are an index to the sexual and social class dimensions of the narrative. Especially crucial are the visual contrasts between the upper-class women and Adriana conveyed through the opposition between the marcelled and overdressed women who visit Oscar's shop and Adriana's simpler dress, hairdo, and makeup. The film's preoccupation between "natural" behavior and artifice is conveyed through the regimented images of the beauty parlor with the heads of dummies and the bizarre bust of Oscar, the effeminate owner of the establishment. The images of the orphanage as well as of the aristocratic milieu are contrasted to the centerpiece of the film, the family gathering with its emphasis on domesticity and community.

The plight of the unwed mother is intimately tied to this image of the home as less than perfect haven from the depredations of the world of work and upper-class leisure. In certain ways the film seems to parallel the propaganda of the regime in its insistence on the return of women to the family, on the importance not only of reproduction but on the proper responsibility of mothers to guard and care for their children. The vision of Adriana's mother's tragic end and her aggressive treatment at the hands of the count and his sister underscores the necessity of proper familial support and nurture from childhood to maturity. "Promiscuous" feminine sexuality appears to be the danger, the outcome of the absence of the proper guidance and care of female children. The lack of these social constraints reinforces the imagery of the dangers of unconfined feminine sexuality, subject particularly to social exploitation in the form of prostitution that threatens to undermine the role of woman as "a moral human being."[21] In the Fascist education of women as mothers, their role as reproductive agents of the nation means a denial of desire, a dematerialization of their bodies, and their transformation into an abstract entity known as the mother. The projection of femininity, however, is slippery, for while the appeal to motherhood is usually couched in terms of the inherent naturalness of reproduction, it is feminine "nature" that is threatening and, therefore in need of cultural intervention in the form of surveillance, discipline, and masculine support. Mario's "rescue" of Adriana is tied to his assertion of virility, and thus partially purged of the threat of femininity.

The maternal melodrama in *T'amerò sempre* thus addresses the contradictions inherent to femininity and evokes Fascist discourse of women, but the film is not hermetically sealed. As James Hay maintains:

While the ending promises a union between these two refugees from the decadence of Oscar's factory of fashionable facades, their future family would not necessarily seem to be a "natural" one—only one that is marginally acceptable in terms of the film's ideal couple (Mario's sister and her fiancé). Nor does the film clearly resolve Adriana's ambiguous role in the family/social structure. Marriage may redeem her past and her social stigma as an unwed mother, but Camerini has already satirized the rituals of petit-bourgeois family life in the earlier scene at Mario's home. And herein are the contradictions of the movie's ideology. The audience is encouraged to enjoy and accept lovers who are misfits but who, in their rejection of the fads of upper-crust society, appear quite stable.[22]

Hay's observations illuminate the contradictions in the film that emerge through the narrative's refusal to valorize clear-cut alternatives. However, his comments need to be further explored in the context of the film's preoccupation with artifice that pertains to both the portraits of domesticity as well as the beauty salon. The world in which the protagonists find themselves is highly choreographed, calling attention to the socially constructed nature of gendered relations. Both protagonists are exemplary of a deviation from conventional conceptions of gender and familialism, but their portraits do not suggest stability. Rather, their roles are a further reminder of the unstable and slippery nature of femininity and masculinity. The iconography of the two "misfits," their contrast to the film's reiterative images of regimentation and sameness, their problematizing conceptions of "naturalness," are exemplary of folklore as common sense at work in the film. Rather than presenting a unified and reiterative image of prevailing ideology and of consensus, the film touches more profoundly on the eclecticism of consensus that, through its misfitting of irreconcilable differences, reveals, not mystifies, its contradictions.

THE FAMILY MELODRAMA
AND BECOMING MOTHER

In the family melodrama, the focus is on the problematic and unresolved character of a paternal figure in need of rehabilitation. In this context, the figure of woman serves as the major obstacle to his recuperation or as its instrument. *Come le foglie* (Like the Leaves, 1934), a Camerini melo-

drama, recapitulates this scenario. Like many Hollywood films of the
1930s, the film is preoccupied with the world of the wealthy and with
their foibles. The feminine protagonist is not the source of conflict but of
reconciliation, and the focal point of the conflict is the mother and son in
an elaborate dissection of and satire on upper-class life, this time characterized by a sexually "promiscuous," extravagant, and social-climbing
mother, a dissolute and narcissistic playboy son, and a father who is
unable to control his domestic affairs. The film, derived from a play by
Giuseppe Giacosa, stars Isa Miranda. Beginning in the home of a businessman, Rosani (Ernesto Sabbatini), whose economic and familial affairs
are in a state of disarray, the initial scenes dramatize the decadent character of upper-class family life. The house is filled with guests, each with his
own eccentric and self-centered demands on others. The servants are
made frantic by these demands, and, finally, one of the maids rebels,
refusing to serve a guest who is laying in wait to seduce her. Much to the
consternation of the guest, a manservant appears instead. The maid who
serves the daughter of the house, Nennele (Isa Miranda), informs her that
Tommy, Nennele's brother (Cesare Bettetini), has been out all night
cavorting. The mother, Giulia (Mimi Aylmer), is identified with the fast-
moving and morally lax upper classes. Dressed in a peignoir, flurrying
nervously about, she is obsessed with her lack of funds to entertain her
guests. The settings are luxurious, similar to the films identified as "white
telephone" films. The images of the assembled guests single out their preoccupation with eating, seduction, and sports. Camillo, Nennele's fiancé,
is preoccupied with staging his mother's, the duchess, arrival, and the
hope that the two women will get to know and accept each other.

Outside the chauffeur complains that he has not been paid, but
Tommy arrives in his sports car and, overhearing the complaint, nonchalantly offers the man money as if the lack of payment was a mere over-
sight. Similarly, he pays two other servants. When he greets his mother,
she confronts him with the sad saga of her debts. Knowing that he was
gambling, she asks him for money to pay for the duchess's visit, and he
complies. Cynically, he tells her that the aristocrat she is going to great
trouble to impress has no money. Through these theatrical vignettes of
family life, the film establishes the dissolute and destructive tenor of
upper-class relationships. The father, conspicuously absent from this portrait, is now introduced in a scene with business associates that sets up a
contrast between his character and that of his wife and son. Deeply in
debt as a consequence of his family's extravagance, he is determined to sell

off everything in order to settle his accounts despite the fact that his colleagues tell him that he is much too scrupulous about his obligations.

Some time later, at a construction site, Massimo (Nino Besozzi), having learned about his uncle's bankruptcy, decides that he will visit the family, whom he has not seen for many years. He recollects fond memories of Nennele. She, equally concerned for her father's situation, seeks to solicit her brother's cooperation in aiding their father, but Tommy is indifferent to her pleas, preferring to concentrate on his wardrobe. As for Giulia, the thought of bankruptcy drives her to hysteria, her predominant concern being the threat to her lifestyle. Massimo arrives in time for the party for the duchess and is totally ignored. Tommy exits for another night of gambling. When the father arrives home, he is assaulted by some of the guests who advise him not to sell, that he is ruining his family. No less distraught, but for self-centered reasons, Giulia complains of having to part with the villa.

Unable to hold the job and resentful of Massimo for interfering in their family affairs, Tommy blames his situation on his difference from Massimo. Tommy has become involved with Madame Orlo, who encourages his visits to her house and lends him money to gamble. Deeply in debt to her, Tommy informs Nennele, to her consternation, that he will marry Orlo in a scene that is climaxed by images of leaves blowing in the wind. Giulia's affair with the Englishman escalates into a romantic liaison as she makes plans for a nighttime rendezvous, and Nennele complains to Massimo that their family is disintegrating. He offers marriage but she rejects his proposal, saying that she cannot accept charity. He tells her that he is leaving for Berlin on business, and exits. After his departure, she writes a suicide note. When Rosani, looking for Nennele, finds the note, he runs out of the house and stops her from plunging to her death in the water. Massimo returns and finds the two together. He and Nennele are united as the father observes them embrace.

Nennele's attempted suicide can be read as a melodramatic act of desperation and of rebellion, but even more as a theatrical strategy to force a reconciliation between her and her father as well as with Massimo. Earlier in the film, she and Massimo had seen a laborer fall to his death as the two walk by a waterfall. The death of the workman and Nennele's contemplated suicide serve to reinforce an underlying sense of the power of nature and also of the need to guard oneself against its threats. Massimo becomes the family redeemer, supporting not only the father but the daughter, becoming the founder of a new and more industrious and responsible family. Giulia and Tommy are excluded from this vision as are the parasitic guests who inhabited their home earlier. The redemption of Rosani and Nennele thus bridges generations. The father's role is not unsympathetic. Not an authoritarian figure, he is portrayed as in need of cooperation and support. Massimo replaces the biological son as the renewed source of family continuity and stability. Nennele replaces her undisciplined and irresponsible mother, dramatizing through her suicide attempt and its narrative parallel to the death of the worker earlier, the dangers of physical vulnerability and isolation from others.

Nennele is not a femme fatale, racked by desires that cause her to go astray and undermine the sanctity of the family. She is not directly threatened with abuse or exploitation at the hands of unscrupulous men. She is not a recapitulation of her mother but her inverted mirror image. Only briefly and to save the family finances, does she seek independence. First and foremost, she exists as a creation of the family, instrumental in its reconsolidation and in the recuperation of the conjugal and maternal role, more acted upon than acting. Nonetheless, her role is central insofar as she is both the victim of the violence that threatens to destroy the family and the necessary symbol of its revitalization. While the upwardly mobile characters, Massimo excepted, are satirized as parasites and as sexually irresponsible, the characters that have reduced desires are those that prevail. The film seems consonant with the regime's emphasis on the strengthening of the family as well as on requisite feminine and masculine models. However, the representation of family at the end falls short of a celebration, acting more as a critique of familialism than its mainstay. There has been no action to control the more destructive forces that have undermined familial relations. Giulia and Tommy disappear but are not constrained. With their elimination, the family appears, as in *T'amerò sempre*, more as an escape (like the film itself) from the antagonisms that threaten its survival, rather than an image of utopia. The dark lighting employed at the reconciliation scenes seems to reinforce the sense of the ambiguous, fragile vision of a family in a harsh world.

The role that nature plays reinforces the compromises of the film's seemingly affirmative resolution. Like the title that is identified with decay and contingency, and like the images of blowing leaves punctuating the text, the film associates nature with isolation and death. Nennele's salvation by her father and by Massimo seems to be a salvation from the instability and unsettling nature of femininity characterized by her mother. Tommy's gambling is another metaphor for contingency and instability, also identified with the threat of nature, like the falling leaves. However, the film does not pose urbane culture and society as the alternative to the vicissitudes of nature. Urban life is identified with violence and sexual excess, and sexual excess with an undermining of the protective boundaries of family life. Thus, family comes to signify something in excess of the conventional nuclear family, becoming identified more broadly with the threat of social and economic predation and the need for protection against its incursions in relation to generational, sexual, and gendered differences. Audiences might well have responded to this combined vision of upper-class licentiousness and petit-bourgeois constraint as antidote. The film, with its echoes of Hollywood melodrama, simultaneously provides a window into the spectacle of upper-class leisure and luxury, while at the same time disavowing its appeal.

"PHALLIC" FEMININITY

Melodramas of beleaguered femininity are also set in the public sphere, and, as Mollie Haskell has described in relation to Hollywood films of the era, are structured by the conflict between career, especially a career on the stage, and marriage, signalling the interconnectedness of theatricality and femininity. The Italian cinema of the 1930s dramatizes this conflict, as exemplified by *Ballerine* (1936). Based on Giuseppe Adami's, *Fanny ballerina della Scala*, and directed by Gustav Machaty, a Czech director (*Ecstasy* [1933] is his most notable film with Hedy Lamarr), the film was plagued by production problems mostly due to Machaty. The director could not communicate with his actors and technicians because of language and personality problems. According to Silvana Joachino and Antonio Centa, the stars, the film was disappointing, necessitating a re-editing for its premiere in Venice.[23] The film opens with an iris shot of a woman being photographed amid Greek ruins. The camera lingers on the woman's body as spectacle, thus introducing the film's focus on spectatorship, on connections between femininity and spectatorship, and, further, on the threatening nature of feminine desire. These outdoor shots give way to a stage. Technicians are working, and the corps de ballet is rehearsing with their ballet master, who is angry about the absence of the prima ballerina about whom the other women gossip. The manager Rochetti appears and complains about having to wait for her. There are other dancers who can take her place. He reiterates his demand for discipline. The film is a backstage narrative in which the importance of performance is established with its conventional exploration of the relation between theatricality and "life."

The prima ballerina continues with her tantrums, and Fanny is designated to perform in her place. Before going on stage, she feeds a cat, picks up one of its kittens, and strokes it, identifying her with maternal qualities, unlike the imperious prima ballerina. However, she does not perform. An argument between the manager and the ballet master ensues. Rochetti falls to the floor and the ballerinas surround him. He exhorts Fanny to continue with her dancing as he is carried out on a stretcher. The view of the stage gives way to images of printing presses and to a group of men in a newspaper office. Mario Verandrei (Antonio Centa), a newspaperman, has announced that he will go to America, when he learns of Rochetti's sudden death. Though he is not sympathetic toward Fanny's career, he goes to see her, offering his sympathy and telling her that he realizes that Rochetti was like a father to her. Together, they examine mementos from her past—a scrapbook and a stuffed animal—as he commiserates with her loss and tells her to have courage.

In the following scene, a friend of Fanny's, also having difficulties establishing herself as an entertainer, performs a melancholy song to a group of people in a night club, but the manager tells her after the performance that while the song was well executed, it is not appropriate for his establishment. However, she meets a wealthy businessman who expresses an interest in her, and she leaves the club with him. On the way home, she tells him of her distaste for discipline, for the alarm clock that forces her to awaken when she would like to remain in bed. She brings him, half-asleep to her quarters, where he spends the night. Upon awakening, her businessman, alone in the room, confronts a cleaning woman who informs him that she too was once young and beautiful like his young woman. For a while, she was well taken care of, but now she is reduced to domestic work. The man asserts his intentions to gratify his young woman's wishes, though he will not marry her. In contrast to her friend, Fanny is single-minded in her desire for a career. The two quarrel when she informs him that her only passion in the world is dancing. While Mario continues to woo Fanny unsuccessfully, Fanny's friend allows herself to be set up in a hotel room by the businessman. As she reclines in bed, she is visited by the members of the corps de ballet. Fanny arrives and the young women remind her of Rochetti's prophecy of Fanny's success. Fanny's friend, however, extols the life of leisure. Her businessman arrives, and is delighted that he does not have to remain with her, pleading work. When the women leave, the young woman is alone, a foreshadowing of her future and a highlighting of the estranging and isolated world of the feminine entertainer.

Fanny finally gets her chance for a leading role in a ballet when she auditions with Madame Alexa. She and Mario attend the opera where *La Traviata* is being performed, and the two hold hands. He confesses his love for her, and she in turn is responsive to his advances. When he goes to get her coat, she stands before a mirror, scrutinizing her face, a prefiguration of the conflict to come between her desire for self-realization and Mario's insistence on her relinquishing her career. Her relationship with Mario is again threatened, when, at a rehearsal, he introduces himself as her fiancé, telling Madame Alexa that Fanny intends to give up her career, to be his wife, and to travel to America with him. The woman and the ballet master protest that Fanny would be making a great mistake, since she is an artist and has a great career ahead of her. Again, Mario and Fanny quarrel. He tells her how different they are from each other, accusing her of driving ambition and of narcissism. She, in turn, accuses him of being a vulgar bourgeois, and they part. Fanny's friend also receives a farewell letter from her businessman, saying that he had to leave suddenly and that he will not be returning. He has removed all of his belongings.

Fanny's big night begins frenetically, with her removing her costume and announcing that she will not perform but will leave for America with Mario. Having seen Mario in the theater and thinking that he has returned for her, she runs from her dressing room to greet him only to learn that he is there to do an interview with her for the newspaper. Once again, she dresses for the performance, and in an elaborately choreographed scene, she dances her number. When the curtain falls, the audience applauds enthusiastically. In Mario's interview with her, he is ironic and rude, and she responds tartly to his questions. They quarrel, and he slaps her, then exits. The last image of him is at the train station. A montage of her dancing and of applauding audiences signifies the passage of time and her rise to success. Later, at a café, she sees a newspaper with an article by Mario and adjacent to it an announcement of her coming successful repeat performance at San Carlo. Her dancing at San Carlo climaxes the film. After an interlude with the corps de ballet, she is framed performing alone as the film ends.

The film suffers from abrupt transitions from episode to episode. Furthermore, images that suggest a meaningful role within the narrative are either treated in cursory fashion (like the shots of the cat) or mechanically (like the photos that introduce the film and are later repeated). Nonetheless, the film's ellipses and ambiguities are illuminating for what they suggest about femininity. The dual structure of the film rests on parallels between Fanny and her friend. Success or failure in career both lead to the same end—isolation. The major difference in Fanny's case lies in the success she receives for her disciplined attitude toward her work. In both cases, the alternative of marriage is precluded for these two women. In the case of Fanny's friend, her lack of commitment to career leads her to repeat the fate of the cleaning woman. Fanny's portrait is far more complex. It is enmeshed in conceptions that exceed the opposition between marriage and career. Her portrait is exemplary of the enigmatic and multivalent character of femininity. She is torn between self-love (as exemplified in the brief scene of her examining her face in the mirror) and the claims of love and the desires of others for her. She is the object of scrutiny for Mario, her peers, and audiences to her performance. She is dissociated visually and in the narrative structure from others in the film, and her isolation serves not only to call attention to her as an artifact but also to elevate the image of the film's star, Silvana Joachino, from others in the film. Fanny is the creation of her surrogate father, Rochetti, and of Madame Alexa, subject to those who, like the film's director, shape, determine, and assign meaning to femininity, captured and isolated through the discipline of performance. The portrait of Madame Alexa, cast in the mold of the successful entrepreneur and of the masculine woman, is parallel to Fanny's, since the implication is that Madame Alexa prefigures the future ahead for Fanny, just as the cleaning woman signals her friend's fate.

The film's exploration of entertainment flouts a familiar convention identified with Hollywood cinema of the 1930s and 1940s—the utopian union of romance and theatrical success. In the case of *Ballerine*, the celebratory union of life and art is erased, isolating art from life. The film provides a portrait of the successful woman bereft of a male mate. The film's emphasis on discipline seems opposed to heterosexual desire. Identified with bodily discipline and control, the dance becomes the antithesis of eroticism, akin to the disciplining of the soldier. The film also poses the possibility that successful creativity is identified with the defying of bourgeois values (as Fanny complains to Mario in his refusal to acknowledge her attachment to ballet). Fanny's friend, by being a kept woman and by not taking her career seriously, also scorns bourgeois expectations both in relation to work and in relation to marriage. But the film also suggests that there is no pleasure in these rebellions, since the price for anti-bourgeois behavior is economic or social punishment through isolation.

In its eccentric modifications of its literary source, whether due to the director's lack of clarity, an inability to communicate his objectives to his actors, or his desire to cram as much as possible into the narrative, the film's treatment of femininity sheds light on its ambiguities and contradictions, on the sources of its affective value, expressing its necessary function as a means for representing the social order and, at the same time, revealing its excessive character.[24] The female figures are disruptive to the narrative, presenting them in opposition to heterosexual coupling. The film offers not one but several portraits of transgression—Fanny, her friend, Madame Alexa—as a strategy in fracturing any consolidated portrait of the feminine position. Furthermore, by highlighting performance, the film focuses on the spectacular nature of femininity. The emphasis on the theater and of the role of the entertainer may not dramatize what femininity is, but it does dramatize its fictive nature. By calling attention to artifice and reproduction, the film subsumes the conflict between career and marriage to entertain the painful and contradictory faces of imaginary femininity.

VISUAL PLEASURE AS UNPLEASURE

Film melodramas foregrounding women escalate in the latter part of the Ventennio. They offer problematic images of femininity, suggesting a crisis of representation inextricably tied to the figure of woman. Woman appears as malcontent, disrupter of the family, and corrupter of socially sanctioned behavior, not merely as its victim. Renato Castellani's *Zazà* (1942) features Isa Miranda as a chanteuse who is, like Fanny in *Ballerine*, suspended between career and romance. However, this opposition is too schematic, since the film is, like the films of Josef von Sternberg to which *Zazà* has been compared, a complex portrait of what Gaylyn Studlar has described as the "visual pleasure of unpleasure."[25] The pleasure derives from the portrait of the female protagonist as the conduit for the conflict between the sadistic power of the text to dominate her and the ways in which her character struggles, finally vainly, to elude that control.

According to Castellani, he had initially wanted to star Luisa Ferida in the role of the entertainer. His conception of the character of Zazà was "earthy," even comic, and he saw Ferida's persona as sensual, human, and popular. Bound to Isa Miranda by prior contractual arrangements, he had to rethink the role, since Miranda's persona, despite the actress's actual lower-class origins, was aristocratic, genteel, and sophisticated.[26] Transforming the comedy into a melodrama, he strove to create the ambiance of the epoch and to model Zazà's role in terms more consonant with the character of his female star. And characteristic of his other films (e.g., *Un colpo di pistola*), *Zazà* became more "calligraphic" and melodramatic, relying on a finely developed and symbolic *mise-en-scène*, a nuanced and highly charged use of detail, a fascination with masochistic desire, and a scrupulous attention to spectatorship as it centers on the body of femininity.

Zazà is thus not simply another portrait of violated womanhood but an exemplary text for perceiving the ways that "cinema seduces its viewers by mimetically exacerbating tension in an orgy of unproductive expenditure."[27] Also, instead of a mere exercise in reinforcing mechanisms of control in relation to femininity, it opens the window onto "abjection, fragmentation, and subversion of self-identity."[28] Instead of a closed ideological document or an anti-ideological celebration of subversion and counterhegemony, cinema constantly oscillates between control and dissolution. The foregrounding of entertainment and conventional familial conflict in *Zazà* calls attention to the tension between desire and its blockage, fixing reflexively on entertainment as the instrument for mobilizing these contradictory positions. The film, characteristic of the woman's film with its focus on beleaguered femininity, offers the familiar narrative of a woman who falls in love with a married man and relinquishes him for the sake of his family. But through the images, the fascination is shifted onto the terrain of spectacle associated with the figure of femininity. Consonant with Steven Shaviro's observations on Fassbinder's treatment of Lysiane in *Querelle, Zazà* "obsessively narrates the process by which she is frozen out of the action, culminating literally in a freeze-frame on her anguished, isolated figure."[29]

The film is preoccupied with time, conveying the sense of the too-lateness of actions and perceptions characteristic of the operatic dimensions of melodrama.[30] The film begins with an image of a Frenchman, Dufresne (Antonio Centa), asleep on a train, suggesting a connection between film and dream experience. The man awakens, goes into a restaurant, and when he returns, discovers that he has missed his train. The film ends with this same image. As a result of his mistiming, he meets a journalist who tells him about the entertainment offered at the local theater.

FIGURE 21. Isa Miranda performing as Zazà in *Zazà*. Courtesy of New York Museum of Modern Art, Film Stills Archive.

There he becomes fascinated with Zazà, a descendant of the lady of the camellias. She is the object of men's admiring glances when he first sees her, but she is attracted to him. Dropping her glove like a gauntlet, he picks it up, hands it to a woman, who, in exchange, gives him a message. He follows her backstage. Ambivalent, he returns to the station only to return again to the theater. After Zazà's performance, he spends the night with her. He awakens, picks up his wedding ring from the floor, unseen by her. He informs her that he must return to Paris, but she is determined to see him again. She walks to a window, another image like that of mirrors that will punctuate the film's complex play on vision. From her perspective, she looks into an apartment across the street where a family is gathered, underscoring the contrast between her role as a seeker of love and romance and that of family life. She, who is the theatrical object for others, has become an audience to the scenario of domestic life.

At the train station with Dufresne, she gives him the key to her apartment. On the train, he once again falls asleep, and when he awakens throws the key out of the window. Returning to Paris, he finds that his wife and daughter have left for several days. He lies down on his bed, holding a handkerchief laden with Zazà's perfume, and the scene cuts to her spraying herself with perfume as she stands before a mirror. She hears the doorbell and, opening the door, sees Dufresne. The two take a holiday together where they register as man and wife. The problematic character of domesticity for Zazà is reiterated as again the image of the woman at the window is reintroduced. Dufresne disappears, and she is alone in the room. Looking out, she sees a wedding party, people drinking toasts and making speeches to the young couple. She descends to congratulate the couple, and, as in the earlier scene of her gazing on a scene of domesticity, her separateness is stressed. Dufresne returns home briefly to discover his wife and daughter. His holiday plans thwarted, he returns to Zazà and informs her that unfortunately they must cut short their holiday, still concealing the fact of his married state. When she returns to her apartment, she finally learns that Dufresne is married. Dressed in black, like a widow, she comes to his apartment, determined to get revenge.

When the maid opens the door, Zazà pretends that she is a foreigner and asks to see the wife, who is out. She insists on waiting, and the maid brings her into the parlor. A few moments later, a child enters and introduces herself to Zazà. In contrast to the lively popular songs sung by Zazà in the theater, Nino Rota's music in these scenes is somber and heavily emotive. The child asks Zazà if she is married, and she responds that she

FIGURE 22. Barred from maternity, *Zazà*. Courtesy of New York Museum of Modern Art, Film Stills Archive.

is a widow. Showing Zazà a religious book that her father has given her, the child also entertains her at the piano. As the two sit at the piano, Zazà cries, thus highlighting once again her exclusion from maternity. The mother arrives, and Zazà does not confront her but manufactures an excuse for her visit. She praises the child to the mother, and exits. At home, she is beset by demands from others for money, alone with only her manager as her confidante. Her alienation from others is again identified with images of time as she is shown alone, glancing at a calendar. But time is identified with recurrence, though with a difference: Dufresne returns to the same station and again meets the journalist, though he tells him that he has left home for good. The role of the journalist parallels that of the novelist in *Un colpo*, serving as more than a device for bringing the characters together at the outset, for marking the passage of time, for highlighting repetition and difference, but also as a means for focusing on Antonio's conflicts and anxieties. In her room, Zazà contemplates her image in the mirror, evoking too the sense of time and change as well as isolating and imprisoning her in her reflected image. When he arrives, Dufresne informs her that he has left his family and wants to be with her. She informs him of her visit to his apartment, of her encounter with his child, and tells him to return home. As she urges him to leave, her face is bathed in shadow, and when he leaves, she goes to the window, and observes him on the street as his image diminishes in size until the street is empty. The last shot is of Zazà alone as she turns away from the window.

The film reproduces the classic elements of the woman's film, the tension between desire and self-sacrifice, the incommensurability between the world of entertainment and that of domesticity. The film's complex interplay of pleasure and desire is the legacy of romanticism, provoking contemplation on the inevitable, necessary, spectacular, and pleasurable aspects of suffering and renunciation. The aestheticized suffering provides pleasure in its acknowledgment of the impossibility of gratification. The focus on the female protagonist's role as an image captured for the consumption of others has a dual valence. By appropriating her image for common consumption, the threat of her disruptiveness can be framed and contained, but the strategies of containment through the discipline of looking make specific the conditions of that containment. The ways in which she is filmed repeatedly isolate her as an object of inspection, of others' and of her own. The two striking images in the film, the mirror and the window, as well as the scenes where Zazà performs—separate her from others through visualization particularly by highlighting an image of femininity dissociated from the familiar world of family life. The film's identification of femininity with the maternal role and the maternal role with the family could be read as yet another form of disciplining wayward femininity. However, the opposition between the world of entertainment and domestic life is not a simple reiteration of the injunction for women to be fruitful and multiply but instead undermines this expectation.

In the ways that Zazà is filmed, in constantly differentiating and isolating her through the emphasis on specularity, the film places her in an ambiguous position that frustrates narrative recuperation of the feminine position as wife and mother. In this film, as in Castellani's *La donna della montagna* and *Un colpo di pistola*, the estranging character of femininity reveals a world where power, including the filmmaker's power over his feminine subject, cannot be disarticulated from sexuality and where female sexuality is isolated from conventional images of family and religion. In the film, masculinity also deviates from conventional expectations. Dufresne's character, identified with reiterated images of him asleep, is associated with an oneiric world (like the film itself), a world of mistiming and paralysis, disjunctive to conventional conceptions of masculinity. The film, like many of the calligraphic films, through its form, style, and imagery and especially in its preoccupation with performance, engages with questions of power and sexuality reminiscent of Visconti's work, which is identified with the cinema of antifascism. Significantly, femininity is central to these dissections of power. In the case of *Zazà*, the the role of femininity becomes ambiguous: it can be regarded as yet another instance of the disciplining of a wayward and recalcitrant female; it can also be seen highlighting the impossible and spectral position of femininity outside the conventional boundaries of heterosexual union and maternity by highlighting her role as an entertainer and by isolating her from the other characters.

RETURN TO THE MOTHER

The woman's film is distinguished by its female protagonist, its female point of view, and its ostensible focus on female experience: "the familial, the domestic, the romantic—those arenas where love, emotion and relationships take precedence over action and events."[31] And the maternal melodrama, in particular, is associated with "scenarios of separation . . . —

dramas which play out all the permutations of the mother/child relation."[32] While these scenarios appear to be disjoined from the public arena, they are in fact intimately related to a division of labor involving masculinity and femininity that inflects on connections between the home and the social world. Amleto Palermi's *La peccatrice* (The Sinner, 1940) recapitulates the maternal scenario but with a difference. The pursuit of upward mobility and success is systematically precluded in the text as is the possibility of heterosexual union. Initial scenes at a bar establish the setting as a house of prostitution and focus on an employee, Maria (Paola Barbara), who is in a darkened room, tending a sick fellow worker, Anna. The accompanying music is somber, heavy, and unsettling, the room claustrophobic. Anna bewails her sinful life, calls for her mother, and begs Maria to stay with her, but Maria is angrily summoned to meet her clients. Though she pleads that she must help Anna, she is told that someone else will take care of the sick woman. The scene dissolves to images of Maria with a young man, Alberto (Gino Cervi), as they enter a church and Maria kneels before an altar to pray as the man observes her.

In a restaurant scene (which is reiterated with a difference toward the end of the film), she tries to move him with the seriousness of her situation, the fact that she is pregnant and unemployed, but he is indifferent to her plight. In a subsequent scene with her mother, Maria conceals that she is pregnant. She informs a friend of the family that she is leaving to find work, while her mother sits in another room, praying. In a darkly lit scene, she descends the stairs and goes to Alberto's lodgings only to discover that she has been abandoned. Still part of the flashback, but after a lapse of time, the scene shifts to a hospital where Maria, who has lost her own child, now works, isolated from family and friends. Appreciative of the care she has given his child, Andreas, a farmer, invites her to come live with his family and care for the child, and she agrees. At the farm, she meets Erminio (Fosco Giachetti), who tries to force his attentions on her, berating her for being promiscuous; she decides to leave.

Once again, she finds herself in the city, where she encounters Pietro (Vittorio De Sica) and his friend Paolo. The men compete for her attention, but she is drawn to Pietro. She moves in with him, but their affair is short-lived as Pietro's underworld past comes between them. The narrative returns to the present with her on her bed. She rises, splashes water on her face, and discovers that she has been locked in the room. Banging loudly on the door, she summons a woman, who releases her and informs her that Anna has been taken to the hospital. On the street, she buys flowers from a vendor and goes to the hospital to see Anna, where she learns of her death. Her troubles continue to mount. She is assaulted by Ottavi, an underworld kingpin, who roughhandles her. She accuses him of having ruined Anna, and he threatens her, saying that she owes him money. Though she again finds Pietro who gets her a job at a laundry, this employment is terminated when she learns from Pietro that, at Ottavi's instigation, the police are after her. Again she packs to leave. The image of her packing punctuates segments of the film, underscoring her homelessness.

Andreas too reappears, and after learning of her situation, invites her to return to the farm. This time, her stay is less fraught with conflict. The photography of the outdoor scenes is idyllic, bright in contrast to the somber urban setting. The industriousness of the peasants is highlighted as they are shown working and singing at their labor. Erminio is now friendly, apologizing for his previous behavior, and commiserating with her about her sad plight; however, she decides to return to her mother. After she leaves, Pietro comes looking for her, but is told by Andreas that Maria is seeking peace at home. Before her reunion with her mother, she stops at the restaurant that was the initiating point of her odyssey, where she again sees Alberto. She sits apart at another table and observes him self-absorbed in his meal. On his way out, he sees her and the two have a perfunctory conversation as her hand moves gently to a knife on the table but remains there. After he exits, she emerges onto the street. The lighting is again low key as she walks across a bridge. The scene cuts to the mother, but, through a series of intercuts between the mother and daughter shot from different angles, the moment of reunion is deferred. Finally, the two meet and embrace as the music rises to a crescendo and the film ends.

Commentators on the film praised it for its convincing melodrama.[33] The episode from the film most often commented upon is Maria's final encounter in the restaurant with Alberto. This scene, one of great economy, is characterized by a controlled use of dialogue, dependent mainly on visual detail and gesture to communicate affect. The melodramatic intensity arises not from excessively emotive and stylized acting but from the suppression of intense melodramatic affect. The banality of Alberto's eating without registering the presence of others, his tidy folding of his napkin upon finishing is registered from the perspective of Maria's steady gaze, bringing into focus the man and woman's distance from each other. All that has preceded is encapsulated in this wordless interaction: his indifference to her, her rage at his callousness, and, in her rejection of revenge, her abandonment of her life as "sinner."

The film invokes the familiar landscape of the woman's film, its emphasis on the plight of the unwed mother, the long-suffering or abandoned mistress, the anguished mother. In all these instances, the maternal figure "throws into question ideas concerning the self, boundaries between self and other, identity."[34] She is as a portrait of abjection, not a figure of reconciliation but a reminder of loss. In *La peccatrice* the "concept of motherhood" is unsettling, portrayed in terms of suffering and deprivation. Maria's mother is presented only twice in the film, and associated with isolation and inarticulateness. The daughter, separated from the mother, is buffeted from one man to another—Alberto, Pietro, Erminio, and Ottavi. The narrative rejects romantic love as an alternative to the threatening aspects of desolation and dependency. Urban life is associated with the world of masculine predatoriness, prostitution, and crime, the agrarian world identified with the land, work, nurture, and forgiveness. And Maria belongs in neither place. If in Camerini's *T'amerò sempre* and *Come le foglie*, the nuclear family with its paternal figures and paternal surrogates provides the haven from social depredation, in *La peccatrice*, it is finally the maternal home—minus the father—that is identified as a source of safety. In this respect, the film seems to offer another ambiguous instance of femininity common to all the Italian films of the era. While the film offers a sympathetic portrait of Maria, in ways similar to *Zazà*, it situates femininity in a fantasmatic, in-between space, again isolated and reduced to a spectral figure.

Religion plays a role in the film, both directly and indirectly, and is associated with femininity and, in particular, maternity. The flashback introduces Maria through her praying in church to the Madonna. Her name, the images of her with the babies in the hospital that frame her as a madonna figure, and the film's emphasis on sin and redemption suggest the collusion between femininity and religion, not surprisingly given the aura of the sacred that attaches to the maternal figure, a form of neutralizing its threat of abjection through the dissolution of sexually-sanctioned boundaries. However, similar to Poggioli's *La morte civile*, the crux of the film does not lie in affirming religion. The film's investment in the maternal feminine conjoined to the religious imagery serves as a yardstick to measure the distance between social dissolution identified with aggressive masculinity and social responsibility identified with quiescent and buffeted femininity. The masculine figures, with the exception of Andreas, a paternal figure, are associated with violence, criminality, arbitrariness, narcissism, and the uses and abuses of women. The style of the film, with its noir lighting, its emphasis on night scenes and mirrors, its angular composition and tight framing, dramatizes the threatening and disorientating character of this world. There are no feminized male figures such as Mario in *T'amerò sempre* to provide a complementary mate for Maria. However, the fact that after her separation from the mother she returns home again seems to suggest the impossibility of locating any bridge between masculinity and femininity, the private and the public spheres. If many of the melodramas of the 1940s dramatize the problematic character of femininity, they do so in the context of flawed and insufficient masculine figures, a reproach perhaps to the elevation in the previous decade of disciplined, controlled, and insulated masculine characters invested in the project of national recuperation. Palermi's woman's melodrama offers an oblique dramatization of the irreconcilability of gender differences. The maternal figure, identified with nurture and religion, is presented as an impossible ideal. The idea of returning to the mother can be read as an escape from prevailing values or as a utopian desire for renewal, of beginning again, and in any case as a representation of a sexual economy where femininity serves as a measure of social order or its failure. The film's recourse to the iconography of religion, the identification of the sinner with the Madonna, and perhaps also with Mary Magdalen, is especially theatrical, highlighting as it does the film's recourse to one of the enduring masks of femininity, reinforcing the circularity and repetitiveness of femininity as representation.

CALLIGRAPHISM AND FEMININITY

The tenuousness of social relations as emerging from the problematic character of femininity is most dramatically exemplified by the countless melodramas that focus on the female character's descent into madness, a major trope for feminine abjection. The fall into abjection is the sign of the loss of boundaries, order, and identity. No stranger to melodrama, the abject comes to signify for both feminine and masculine characters the impossibility of the social positions prescribed for them, but it would seem that femininity occupies the central position in the creation or dissolution of social boundaries. Such films as *La canzone dell'amore* (1930) and *La signora di tutti* (Ophuls, 1934) testify to the ubiquity of this motif from the early 1930s into the 1940s. In the Ophuls film, the identification of the feminine protagonist as entertainer reinforces the identification of femininity with theatricality and illusion and problematizes the borders between the real and the imaginary, the cinematic and the "real."

Particularly in the works of the "calligraphers," who derive their material from nineteenth-century novels, the presence of tormented femininity (in the case of both male and female characters) is central to their works. Mario Soldati's *Malombra* (1942) provides an instance of a Gothic melodrama, focusing on a female protagonist whose madness is identified with mysticism, occultism, and history. The Fogazzaro novel on which the film is based has been described as an example of "the nervousness of decadent romanticism."[35] The common strategy of polarization is evident in the delineation of feminine characters: Marina is the incarnation of the *femme fatale*, whereas Edith signifies a pure and more spiritualized femininity. Moreover, the novel's penchant for psychologizing is linked to an aestheticization of experience.[36] The Gothic melodrama is the instrument for ruminating on the past, occultism, sexuality, and power. In Soldati's cinematic rendition of the novel, the conflict is generated from the dissolution of social and psychic boundaries, and from the obsession with time, death, difference, and repetition. The specifically Gothic elements involve the ancient villa, an orphaned young woman, an imperious uncle, the Count D'Ormengo, the presence of ghosts, an overwhelming fascination with the threat of nature, and the fragility of the protagonist's mental state.

As in *Piccolo mondo antico*, the lake and mountains provide the correlative for unstable femininity. Marina (Isa Miranda) arrives by boat with another young woman, and is brought to the villa. Her uncle shows her to her room but she is dissatisfied, wanting one that overlooks the sea. The room she selects had been formerly inhabited by Cecilia, a young woman who had been imprisoned in the room when her husband learned that she was in love with a young officer. In her mad state, she entertained herself by playing wildly on the spinet. One of the servants tells Marina that she resembles Cecilia. At first, Marina dismisses this talk as superstitious, but increasingly, she becomes curious about Cecilia in ways that resemble the novel and also Hitchcock's *Rebecca*. Once again, a young woman is haunted by a dead female figure from the past, and, once again, the image of a window is identified with the female protagonist as Marina observes the world through her window. As in melodrama, music becomes the protagonist's medium of communication. She begins to play

FIGURE 23. The woman in the window, Isa Miranda in *Malombra*. Courtesy of New York Museum of Modern Art, Film Stills Archive.

the piano, but when she hears a bad note, she opens its lid and finds a packet containing a lock of hair, gloves, a silver brooch, and a note. The note enjoins the reader to wear the brooch and to carry out revenge on the descendant of the Count of D'Ormengo.

Marina, enlisting the aid of the physician, wants to leave for "reasons of health," but the count refuses to let her go. When her uncle finally decides to let her go, realizing that she is ill and feverish, she has already moved into the past and decides to remain in her uncle's house. She reads a book, *Phantasms of the Past,* and hears Cecilia's voice. Marina decides to write a letter to the author in which she seeks information about returning from the grave, the possibility of living twice. The author writes back, calling her deluded. At the villa, a young man, Corrado Silla (Andrea Checchi), arrives to assist the count with research. From a Hungarian named Steinegge (Jacinto Molteni), Corrado learns that Marina has become obsessed and is in the habit of wandering. He shows Corrado to his room. The room is lit by candlelight and the camera moves closer to Corrado as he examines a picture on the wall of his mother. Corrado asks Steinegge to see the count immediately to unravel the mystery of how this picture came to be here, but Steinegge tells him that he will have to wait. Later, when he meets the count, he presses him for information but is told that they will not talk until later. The mountains loom menacingly in the background.

Marina in her room, playing the piano wildly, refuses to come down to meet Corrado, preferring to be alone. She is seen by Corrado as she stands at the window, looking out. When she finally meets him, she treats him imperiously. Increasingly he becomes obsessed with her. He sees Marina about to take a boat out during an impending storm. The two struggle as he seeks to restrain her and finally he returns her to the pier. After this incident, Corrado leaves for Milan, and Marina is ordered by her uncle to marry Count Nepo Salvador. He and his mother (Ada Dondini) are fortune hunters, only concerned with Marina's inheritance and, like Marina's uncle, preoccupied with wealth and power. By contrast, the relationship between Steinegge and his daughter, Edith (Irasema Dilian), who has arrived on the same boat as Nepo and his mother, is exemplary of familial respect and reciprocity. In Milan at Steinegge's home where he and Edith have returned, Corrado and Edith have become acquainted, but a pleasant familial scene is marred by the news of Marina's wedding, which is to take place on the following day. After a title announcing Marina's vigil as she waits for Corrado, she is shown sitting before her mirror, impatient for his return. Cecilia's voice is heard, saying that the moment for revenge has come. Still in Milan, Corrado asks Edith to marry him, but she hesitates out of fear and the knowledge of his relationship with Marina. The lighting is dark, the street scene filled with shadows. Corrado receives a telegram, informing him that the count is ill, and he decides to return to the villa. After he leaves, Edith expresses misgivings about her dismissive treatment of Corrado and decides to follow him to the villa. At the villa, the count is suffering from a mysterious illness. Delirious, he calls "Cecilia." The priest informs an assembled company of the disfigured expression on the suffering count's face and that Cecilia's brooch was found in the count's hand.

Marina, totally demented, has a reunion with Corrado in the garden, where she obsessively asks him "Do you remember?" He confesses his love for her and tries to kiss her, but she evades his embraces. In her room, she plays the piano for him and asks if he remembers the brooch he gave her. He tells her he knows nothing of the brooch (given to Cecilia by Renato), and she tells him the time has come for her vendetta. Informed that the count is dying, Marina goes to the count's room where she hysterically shouts that she "is here with her lover to see him die," and she laughs wildly and has to be escorted from the room. Though the count is not yet dead, the Salvador family is rifling through his papers to find his will. When the will is read, it is learned that the count has not left his money to Marina. Marina continues to act strangely toward Corrado, informing him that she will never leave the villa. She has planned a dinner for the remaining guests, but he does not attend. In an extremely ornate scene on a verandah, candle-lit with the wind blowing, Marina entertains a group of men at a lavishly set table, asking them to share a toast with her to a long journey that she is about to undertake. Nervously she gets up, though the men try to calm her, announcing that she is going to the library. She confronts Corrado and, taking out a gun, shoots him. The final shots of her are in her boat, alone as she heads toward the grotto, her figure becoming smaller until she disappears. The film ends with an image of a calm sea and of mountains. Edith, with a priest at Corrado's grave, hears him express the hope that Corrado will now rest peacefully.

The priest's words sit ironically with all that has preceded, since the narrative has dramatized the problem of laying the past to rest. *Malombra* is obsessed with history, a history that is intimately tied to writing in the film, as exemplified in the references to books, letters, and wills. Writing reinforces Malombra's question, "Can a person live twice?" but, at the same time, explodes reductive connections between time and memory, language and death. The film's self-conscious focus on writing troubles a univalent reading of the narrative and reinforces its theatrical character, frustrating any sense of secure knowledge, confounding boundaries between fantasy and reality, truth and untruth. In its obsession with repetition, the text seems preoccupied with challenging the boundaries and limits of conventional historicizing and, by extension, of representation. In Derrida's terms, "Representation is death. Which may be immediately transformed into the following proposition: death is (only) representation. But it is bound to life and to the living present which it repeats originarily."[37] Through the character of Malombra, the narrative enacts the violence associated with representation, its insistence on resemblance and on identity. Threatricality thus has a greater valence than the notion of "putting on a show" as a mode of escapism: it is the indication of the impossibility of regarding representation as a sure guide to knowledge. And through Malombra's excessive and unsettling character, which raises the spectre of madness, femininity becomes manifest as the troubling and uncertain element identified with death and difference. While Edith serves as a representation of the recuperation of order and the forgetting of the past, Marina is a reminder of the impossibility of erasing that past, of its continuity in the present.

The Oedipal conflict identified with a domineering masculine paternal surrogate is enacted first through Cecilia, then recreated through Marina, a conflict that generates murder and suicide. It is not conveyed through dialogue but through gesture and image—the wild images of the sea, the ravings of Marina, her piano playing, the candle-lit scenes, the world of shadows, heightening and making more ambiguous any effort to interpret the events in a literal and moralistic fashion. Instead ambiguities proliferate, ambiguities concerning the legibility of past events and, even more, of femininity and its discontents. In discussing differences between Soldati's film and an earlier silent version by Gallone, Antonio Costa comments on the absence of flashback in the later film, preferring to focus on the *mise-en-scène* and character to signal "the origins of Marina's disquieting behavior."[38] Thus, Soldati restores and reinforces the ambiguous and mysterious character of the Gothic elements in a vein closer to the novel. Costa also underscores the importance of writing in the film— *Phantasms of the Past*, Baudelaire's *Fleurs du mal* that Corrado peruses, the note from Cecilia and Marina's letter, tying it to the film's obsession with the past and to the enigma of Marina's actions.[39]

Marina's behavior is identified with hallucination and dream, with the visual elements of the film, and with costume and *mise-en-scène*. In certain ways, this film can be compared to the "escapist" and sumptuous costume dramas produced by Gainsborough during the 1940s: their preoccupation with aristocratic protagonists, conventional social boundaries, and conflicts involving sexuality and power.[40] *Malombra*—enclosed as it may seem within the parameters of the past, within the conventions of Gothicism with its brooding castles, malignant patriarchal figures, characters driven to insanity, and communion with ghosts—speaks indirectly to the present. Marina's descent into madness is an obliteration of boundaries, conventional and predictable rules of behavior, in ways similar to Antonio's fall into madness in *Gelosia*. However, because the film keeps "out-of-field" her motivation or questions of legal guilt and punishment, the emphasis falls on the more complex problem of femininity as the destroyer of political and social boundaries. In invoking a world of tyranny and violence as characterized by the count and by Nepo and his mother, the film does not judge Marina. In identifying her with writing and writing with "phantasms of the past," the film appears to pass judgment on the repetitiousness and violence of history, seeking vainly to lay its phantasms to rest.

BLURRING "BOUNDARIES"

Increasingly in the 1940s, rigid distinctions between femininity and masculinity become blurred. In its obsession with affect vainly in search of an object of attachment, its theatricality, and its mistrust of spoken language, melodrama is uniquely suited to dramatize the slippery nature of gendered and sexual representation, its striving for consensus, and also the impossibility of fixity and closure. Raffaello Matarazzo's *Il birichino di papà* (1943) has been identified as a film that undermines fascist ideology and its practice,[41] but the film does not undermine Fascist ideology so much as it exposes the fragmentary character of consensus that relies on both concealment and disclosure. In its conjoining of the school to the family, it draws on melodrama and on a form of melodrama that is identified with the woman's film and specifically on conflicting conceptions of femininity. The film centers on the socially disruptive actions of a young girl, Nicoletta (Chiaretta Gelli), in relation to the family and to other social institutions. What has been remarked in regard to the film is its stress on the liberatory dimensions of the narrative as engineered through its young female protagonist. While commentary focuses on the film's critique of Fascist educational policies in relation to young girls, thus challenging prevailing gender discourses, the film situates the school in relation to the family. An examination of the "subgenre" of the schoolgirl films from the 1930s to the 1940s reveals changing relations to forms of consent and coercion. The Italian school films provide a window on educational practices as promulgated first by Minister of Education Giovanni Gentile and later by his successor Giuseppe Bottai. Since education was a high priority for Fascism in the regime's attempts to fascistize youth and especially to domesticate young women, it is not surprising that films should focus on the school as source of dramatic conflict. However, an examination of such school films as *Mädchen in Uniform* (1931), *Zéro de conduite* (1933), and *Tom Brown's School Days* (1940) among others reveals that the school film has been a form that requires melodrama. However, the affective investment in the socialization of the young is not restricted to Fascism but inheres in all forms of nationalism. Locating tensions in their narratives is not a matter of excavating hidden discourses, but of tracking how melodrama and its "structures of feeling" are part of a "constant reworking of values . . . elements of a wider and more general signifying system" that inheres in the social text.[42] This signifying system is not purely formal and abstract but produced out of a social symbology that draws on familiar and contradictory, folkloric elements that circulate in the culture at large.

Il birichino is a pastiche of traditional and contemporary images, drawing on the school, the family, and youth as they converge on questions of femininity. In orchestrating these various elements, the film is mindful of Hollywood cinema, its predilection for youth, its emphasis on familial values, its uses of spectacle, its populism, and its "celebration, in *modern* images, of spiritual community and conservative values."[43] But the incorporation of Americanism was reworked to accommodate Italian and even Fascist values or, conversely, their critique. In *Il birichino*, the protagonist, Nicoletta is a counterpart to Deanna Durbin, a young Hollywood star popular with Italian audiences of the time.[44] Associated with the musical, Durbin's persona was a source of misrule and reconciliation within the narrative. Her character functions to unsettle the rigidified structures of family and of education and to inject the illusion of spontaneity and freedom into the reigning order of social institutions by invoking the world of entertainment. Music, particularly song, links entertainment to the utopian desire for the management of crisis, but in the process the terms of the crisis are made manifest as well. Thus, Matarazzo's film, through the role of its musical protagonist, addresses and redresses the repressive functions of the educational system.[45] How the film is directed at Fascist politics as a whole is more ambiguous.

The film opens with light and frenetic music conjoined to images of carriage wheels, horses' hooves, and of a young girl singing, stressing movement and energy. These images will reoccur at the film's ending. By contrast, the scene changes to a large house seen first from outside and then from within. (Opposition between images of inside and outside is central to the film.) Nicoletta's father and aunt are arguing about her lack of femininity, her unwillingness to conform to prescribed feminine behavior. The father, Leopoldo, calls her "Nicola" and defends her right to act like a boy, though he acknowledges that his other daughter, Livia (Anna Vivaldi), assumes a more acceptable heterosexual and passive form of feminine behavior and appearance. Thus, femininity is at stake in the unraveling of the dramatic conflict and tied to the film's exploration of both family and school life. The family is in a state of disorder, awaiting the arrival of the aristocratic Della Bellas, whose son Roberto (Franco Sanderia) is betrothed to Livia. The first view of the Della Bellas— mother, son, and daughter—in their car on the road presents them as upper-class snobs. The daughter, Irene, complains about having to visit the country and predicts that Roberto will be bored with Livia. Nicoletta, again in the carriage, passes them, singing, and sends their car off the road, a foreshadowing of her later conflicts with and victory over them. Upon their arrival at the house, the Della Bellas are given the once-over by the servants. Livia is uneasy about Roberto's philandering past and wonders if he can settle down, and Nicoletta is scolded for her wild driving.

The Marchesa Della Bella, highly critical of Nicoletta's behavior, recommends that the girl be placed in a school where Nicoletta can be disciplined and where, since she is connected with the school, she can survey the girl's progress. One of the incidents that motivates the marchesa's suggestion is Nicoletta's talk about the horse giving birth. Shocked, she insists that the girl be socialized, and her school is just the place for such a preparation. Nicoletta gets momentary revenge when she sends a rug she has rolled up down the stairs and it reaches its destination, the marchesa. In her room, Nicoletta complains to her father about Livia's going to live at the marchesa's, but he tells her "to be a man." Their conversation is interrupted by fireworks that Nicoletta has arranged in Livia's honor, another proleptic sign of the trouble to be engineered by Nicoletta. Nicoletta goes off to the school, despite her father's misgivings and her nightmares about the school. In images reminiscent of scenes from Sagan's *Mädchen in Uniform*, critical of the Prussian quality of German upper-class schools, *Il birichino* focuses on regimentation of the girls through a montage of feet and bodies. According to Jacqueline Reich, the images of the school "reek with militaristic connotations," which she finds in the use of shadows, the choreography of the girls in orderly, regimented movement, and the sounds of their clicking heels.[46] In class, Nicoletta fails to answer teachers' questions and is repeatedly given a "zero." By contrast to the classroom scenes, the girls are shown less formally, singing and lounging about until the moment of spontaneity and leisure is disrupted by a teacher. Nicoletta is called to the office, where she sees her sister, who, in turn, complains of the boredom of her life. Nicoletta tells Livia that she purposefully does not answer teachers' questions about such issues as the dates of Napoleon, because she does not want to give them any satisfaction.

Domestic conflict is paralleled at school, where an audience is assembled to watch the girls perform, but Nicoletta is perched on a window ledge singing about the oppressiveness of school life. Her father, one of the guests, is unperturbed by her youthful prank, but the principal is not pleased, and Nicoletta is confined to the infirmary, where she takes the opportunity to phone her sister. After several fruitless phone calls, she reaches the number of a lawyer, Giulio Marchi, who knows the Della Bellas, and he agrees to assist her. Escaping from the school, Nicoletta goes home to her sister and finds Roberto in a compromising clinch with his former fiancée. She gives Roberto and Irene a tongue blistering and goes to pack Livia's clothes. At first, Livia is reluctant to leave, but when she learns of Roberto's behavior with Marianella, she joins her sister in packing. Leopoldo comes to school to discover that Nicoletta has absconded. Then he learns that his daughter Livia has also disappeared. The sisters have sought refuge with Marchi. They spend the night with him, and he informs the family of their whereabouts. Livia informs Nicoletta that she is pregnant, and Nicoletta, delighted, begins making preparations and expresses her hopes for a boy, singing of her pleasure. At the film's denouement the lawyer informs the gathered family of Livia's plans for divorce and of Nicoletta's demands that she be allowed to withdraw from school. Livia and Roberto are reconciled, he promising to reform, and Nicoletta is permitted to return home as the families settle down to a festive meal. The film closes with Nicoletta, her father, aunt, and Marchi in the carriage, suggesting Marchi's future incorporation into the family through union with the aunt.

The narrative conventions associated with young women in the school film are predictable, deriving from the repressiveness of school discipline and its containment and repression of femininity. As in the films by Camerini, *Il birichino* relies on images of upper-class decadence, irresponsibility, and cruelty, especially the flouting of the integrity of the family. The marchesa is the bridge between the school and the family, linking them in their oppressiveness. By contrast, Leopoldo is, like the paternal figure in *Come le foglie*, representative of a more enlightened attitude toward familial relations and, in particular, toward feminine behavior. Within his family, Nicoletta is permitted her rebelliousness, her challenging of rigid gender typing of girls. The paternal family is juxtaposed to the maternal one, identified with the marchesa and her daughter, portrayed by contrast as rigid as they are sadistic. While the school is, as Reich indicates, a locus of control and power, power in this film is not exclusively identified with masculine figures: it is identified with its female personnel.

The crucial element for reading the film resides in the film's homologizing of school and family, dramatizing both as complicit in the deformation of femininity. The paternal family can be read as less repressive than the one headed by the maternal figure, offering an illusion of freedom. Significant in this juxtaposition is how the film can be seen to represent, on the one hand, a critique of authoritarianism, the repression of youth, the constraints on feminine behavior, while, on the other hand, patriarchy is reaffirmed as less repressive and more enlightened. This reading conjoins the sense in which the film offers a critique of the status quo represented by the institutions of both the family and the school. In the film, the school signifies the public dimensions of the state's attempts at control over social life, a form of control integrally related to producing and reinforcing conceptions of gendered and sexual behavior.[47] However, the film's conjoining of school and family is central to the social production of youthful subjects. While critical of the institutional setting of the school in its caricature of education, the film remains within the parameters of the family, offering both an apparent critique of Fascist practices while adhering, in ways reminiscent of Camerini, to the notion of the patriarchal family as haven. It is in this context that the role of melodrama in relation to comedy becomes important. The melodrama in the film arises from two directions, both identified with femininity—Nicoletta's persecution at the hands of the marchesa and of the school authorities and Livia's persecution at the hands of the Della Bella family. In both instances, the affect arises from the excesses identified with femininity that threaten to undermine social, especially gendered, boundaries.

Nicoletta's ambiguous and protean character, identified with the excessive character of melodrama, is itself legitimized through comedy. Points of convergence between the comedic and the melodramatic, the feminine and the masculine, are to be found in their reliance on forms of typification, a mistrust of verbalization, the splintering and dissolution of consolidated identities, a troubled relation to physicality and aggression, the blurring of boundaries between interiority and exteriority, and the incommensurability between achievement and desire. Comedy sets up situations that contain the potential for melodrama in the dramatization of abuses of power, of sexual, generational, and gendered antagonisms, and the potentially disastrous effects of misrecognition and miscommunication. But, after entertaining the possibility of melodrama, the comedy veers away from melodramatic expression though the adoption of strategies for the management and reduction of affect: through irony, parody, understatement, and the audacious role of the music, strategies that serve to contain emotional surcharge relating to gender and familial transgression. Moreover, as in Camerini's films, the focus on the paternal family privileges the private sphere over the public, thus introducing the notion of the family as a place of safety against the incursions of the depersonalized and depersonalizing forces identified with the school (as in *Amarcord's* schoolroom). By indirection, the film touches on subjects dear to the heart of the folklore of the time, involving the family, forms of leisure and entertainment, the law, especially the care and upbringing of youth. The film is not unique in its focus on youth but is one of a number of films of the era that takes place in the school and focuses on the disruptive antics of the young in a vein similar to Hollywood film comedies. Most particularly, as discussed by Reich, these films are not clear-cut in their portraits of youth and its relation to tradition and modernity, or in their uses of genre: their "lack of ideological coherence reflects the very nature of Italian Fascism and its policies toward women, which were themselves riddled with conflicts and contradictions."[48] In this respect, *Il birichino* captures the ambiguities and contradictions inherent to many of the melodramas and comedies of the era, but particularly evident in the films of the early 1940s that highlight femininity—such films as *Sissignora, Sorelle Materassi,* and *Malombra*—in their portraits of threats to the family, their images of endangered femininity and masculinity, and their portraits of the arbitrary and destructive uses of power.

WOMEN BEWARE WOMEN

In melodramatic representations of femininity, less attention has been devoted to the intricacies of female bonding. For example, in *La peccatrice,* the bonding between Maria and Anna as well as between Maria and her mother stands in opposition to the largely divisive portraits of masculinity. Similarly, the portrait of Nicoletta's affection and defense of her sister in *Il birichino* is set against that of the marchesa and the teachers at school, representing not merely a generational but a class and sexual difference. In the case of Ferdinando Maria Poggioli's *Sissignora* (1941), the presentation of femininity relies on binary distinctions not only between upper- and lower-class women but between those who are bonded in adversity and those who are oppressors. The film is not a maternal melodrama of sacrifice. If anything, it is preoccupied by the absence of nurture, renunciation, altruism, or self-sacrifice in relation to the maternal figures. Based on a literary work of the same name, Poggioli's film features the familiar melodramatic scenario of orphans and orphanages, illness and hospitals, cold and heartless maternal figures, and familial relations that are sterile and repressive. The two sisters are played by Emma and Irma Gramatica. Emma, a prominent theater actress, was associated with the first successes of the sound film in Italy and both sisters enjoyed long and acclaimed careers in theater and cinema.

Set in the city, the film begins by introducing the viewer to the vision of a bereft and dependent young woman, Cristina (Maria Denis), who upon visiting her aunt in the hospital learns of her death through the sight of an empty bed. Alone, Cristina turns to a Catholic convent to seek employment. At the convent, life is presented in as depersonalized fashion as the hospital. Through Sister Valeria (Rina Morelli) she gets a job with the Robbiano sisters whose home is as regimented as the public institutions. They train her to say, "Si, Signora" (Yes, madam) to them, rehearse her chores, caution her not put her suitcase on the bed, and outfit her with a uniform. They set her to work cooking, washing dishes, cleaning windows, doing laundry, and barrage her with constant complaints about her lack of precision. Parsimonious, they complain about her use of a light in bed to read. They are affectionate, if controlling, with their nephew Vittorio (Leonardo Cortese), a sailor who meets Cristina when the sisters are out as she, with the sea as backdrop, is hanging laundry, and he is attracted to her. The sisters return and invite Vittorio to lunch but look disapprovingly at Cristina.

On the street as a group of soldiers march past a cheering crowd, Cristina goes to the market to shop for her employers, but is shortchanged by a vendor. Observing the transaction, Emilio (Elio Marcuzzo) comes to her defense. The two discover that they are from the same village and make plans to visit there some time. At the Rabbiano home where Cristina is serving dinner, the sisters are annoyed with Vittorio for his familiar attentions to Cristina. On Sunday, however, she meets Emilio and they are joined by two of her friends, Enrichetta and Maria. The foursome goes to a dance hall where Enrichetta flirts with Emilio. Vittorio enters the hall when he sees Cristina and asks her to dance, telling her he will teach her the steps. Jealous and annoyed, Emilio watches the couple dance. Cristina and Vittorio exit for a walk on the strand, and he tries to embrace her but she is fearful. In the dance hall, Enrichetta comments on the fate of many innocent young women who often end up with a child that they must place in a foundling home.

Cristina returns to her work and is berated by the sisters for her lateness. Still at the dance hall, Vittorio is instructed by Emilio on women, how their simple faces conceal dramas of deceit, seduction, and betrayal. At the Robbianos, Cristina is fired for refusing to relinquish a photo of Vittorio and her taken at their outing, enraging the women because she says, "No, Signora." Having found another position with the Valdatas, she goes with Maria to a foundling home where Maria's child is being kept. By chance, Vittorio is visiting the child of a friend. When he sees her holding Maria's child, he assumes it to be hers until he sees her return it to Maria. Her good fortune at having found employment is transitory, for her employers inform her that they are bankrupt and cannot afford even to pay her back wages. Instead, the woman gives her a dress and a fur-trimmed coat in payment. Again, she is thrown into dependency. Her affair with Vittorio fares no better, since his aunts are furious that he contemplates marrying a servant. Hysterically, they remind him of all they have done for him, and, angry, he leaves them.

Cristina's new job, assigned to her by Sister Valeria, introduces yet another portrait of upper-class femininity in the character of Mrs. Valdata. The woman has little interest in her child, Giorgio; she is more interested in Cristina's hairdo. Giorgio is at first reluctant to come to her, but she wins him over. The child becomes ill, but Mrs. Valdata minimizes the illness, more upset about the fact that her lover admires Cristina's braids. She goes to Cristina's room and orders her to have her hair cut. Cristina is summoned to Sister Valeria at the instigation of the Robbianos. The sisters confront Cristina, accusing her of stealing Vittorio from them. Sister Valeria tells Cristina that she has brought discord to the Robbiano family and that as a servant she must not think of marrying Vittorio, lecturing her on the spiritual virtues of sacrifice and renunciation. Cristina promises to choose the path of spirituality. At her place of employment, the situation has become dire. Giorgio is ill with scarlet fever, and the doctor cautions Mrs. Valdata not to let Cristina sleep in the same room with him. Mrs. Valdata, unconcerned about the child and Cristina, merely tells her not to inform her lover of the illness, and Cristina continues to remain by the side of the child.

At a final meeting with Vittorio, whose orders to sail have arrived, Cristina urges him to forget the idea of marriage. The two walk in the rain as he insists that he will return to her. On the day of Vittorio's departure, she goes to the port, observing him saying farewell to his aunts. There she sees Emilio again. Delirious with fever, she watches the ship leave port. The Robbiano sisters pass her haughtily, and with Emilio she returns to the Valdata house to learn that Giorgio is out of danger. Emilio informs the physician of Cristina's fever, and the physician berates Mrs. Valdata for her irresponsibility. An ambulance arrives and Cristina is carried out on a stretcher as Giorgio cries, and his mother does nothing to comfort him. When Sister Valeria learns of Cristina's hospitalization, she informs the Robbiano sisters of the illness but they refuse to see Cristina. The film closes with Maria and Enrichetta sitting on a bench, crying and lamenting Cristina's subsequent death.

Aside from the emotional sustenance she receives from her friends, Cristina is a portrait of precarious and abject femininity. The situation of women like Cristina and her friends, Enrichetta and Maria, is portrayed as one of unmitigated suffering. Like the other women of her class, Cristina is barred from union with her lover. Her employers exploit and abuse her. The institutions are aligned with the upper classes, even the church as exemplified by the character of Sister Valeria. Unlike the situation in *Il birichino*, family is not proffered as a haven from institutional abuse, in her case from the threat of poverty and isolation, but, in fact, seems to be the aggravating source of her unhappiness and finally of her death. Similarly, the church offers small consolation and mitigation of her condition. Like the marchesa and Irene in *Il birichino*, the upper-class women in *Sissignora* are portrayed as indifferent, dishonest, and cruel. They characterize a world where power is conferred through wealth, institutional support, and by the drive for control and self-interest. This is a world where masculine figures are either absent or peripheral, and where the feminine characters are divided between maternal/predatory figures and young women who are their prey, pointing once again to the disintegration of the patriarchal family and to the assumption of power by women like the Robbianos or Mrs. Valdata. The only source of pleasure is the dance hall, identified with youth, companionship, and momentary release from hardship, but it is also a place where young women are subject to the dangers of seduction and abandonment.

The setting of the film—the sea, the street life, the dance hall, the convent, and the interior of the upper-class homes—reinforces the sense of estrangement, the separation between the different worlds. As opposed to the clearly lit outdoor scenes, the interiors are darkly lit, emphasizing shadows, creating a sense of claustrophobia. Death, illness, and loss, are ubiquitous, beginning with the death of Cristina's aunt and ending with her own illness and death. Everything is infected by the malignancy of power. Images that signify control are evident, as exemplified by Cristina's first meeting with the Robbiano sisters, where one of them stands above her on the stairs looking down at her, and in other scenes where she is the object of their surveillance. The urban setting, however, is not the sociological culprit. The film does not posit a conflict between nature/nurture and tradition in opposition to modernity. Rather, the narrative focuses on the internalized relations of power, especially those identified with the family, reinforced by other social, economic, and religious institutions.

In contrast to films such as *Ballerine* or *Zazà*, *Sissignora* does not offer the compensation of an independent, if constraining, life of work. Cristina's isolation in the hospital excludes her from the sight of others, rendering her invisible to the internal as well as the external audience. Her illness and death are metaphoric, signifiers of a society where power is visible and where its victims are finally rendered invisible. The naked rule of power goes unchecked, and Cristina's illness is the outward manifestation of social corruption. Christina is not a femme fatale, nor is she a willing victim to her demise. She can say, "No, signora." She is not an heroic amazonian spirit who is greater than her world. Instead, like her illness, she is the recipient of social ills, ills that do not admit of narrative cure. To the end, she remains an unrelieved figure beyond rescue, a counterpart to the last years of fascist rule where crisis was evident and where the possibilities for amelioration were in question. The film is a powerful dramatization of the operations of power and control stretched to the limits of the spectator's credibility: excessiveness of affect and image function almost as a camouflage, confounding the real and the illusory, complicating the possibility of restitution. As in all of Poggioli's films, femininity is at the center of his melodramatic anatomies of power, signaling that more is at stake than a simplistic correction of specific social abuses.

SEXUAL POLITICS, POWER, AND FEMININITY

In an even more striking, theatrical, and unsettling vein, Poggioli's *Sorelle Materassi* (1943) is a dissection of the sexual politics of power and the power of sexual politics. Once again, Poggioli utilizes the Gramatica sisters in roles that are satiric and melodramatic. The film is a portrait of a world gone berserk, where accumulation, venality, hypocrisy, and exploitation are commonplace. More than *Sissignora*, the film portrays a woman's world comprised of three sisters, an assistant to the sisters, a cook, a princess, and a South American woman from Argentina. This haremlike world is invaded by a man, Remo (Massimo Serato), the nephew of the Materassi sisters, whose presence transforms the home into bedlam. Based on a novel by Aldo Palazzeschi, the film begins on a street where a car turns into a gate bearing the sign, "Materassi Sisters." Women are gaping out of the window excitedly as the car arrives. The visitor, a priest, goes to a workroom where two of the sisters, Teresa (Irma Gramatica) and Carolina (Emma Gramatica), are fitting a customer with lingerie. When the priest enters, one of the sisters discreetly covers the customer. At Teresa's request, Carolina gives the priest vestments they have made for the church, and he commends them for their excellent work, telling them that they have been honored for their work by a visit to the Pope. Niobe (Dina Romano), the cook, rushes out, shouting the good news for all to hear.

In a highly stylized scene of the sisters at the Vatican, the sisters walk down a long hall decorated with murals and paintings until they reach an ornate door and are stopped. When the Pope is announced, the sisters kneel as he blesses them and others. Starkly in contrast to this scene of

FIGURE 24. Honored at the Vatican, *Sorelle Materassi*. Courtesy of New York Museum of Modern Art, Film Stills Archive.

hard work rewarded, Remo is seen on a train, traveling in a first-class compartment with a third-class ticket. When confronted with this discrepancy by the conductor, he is saved by a young woman who offers to pay the difference between the tickets as an older man observes the transaction shaking his head. When the sisters return home, they are again observed by others from the window and on the street. The element of voyeurism is central to the film. The film's recurrent use of mirrors and windows highlight spectatorship. The opposition between inside and outside, looking and being looked at, will be reiterated throughout the film. Inside their home, the sisters babble about their visit to the Vatican, but their narrative is interrupted by the sounds of crying. The two sisters walk upstairs to enter the room of their third sister, Giselda (Olga Solbelli), who from her bed complains that they have fun while she languishes. However, she accuses them of being ignorant of life, and when Teresa and Carolina leave, she picks up a photo of a man, her husband who deserted her, kisses it, and cries. This photo is her weapon against the unmarried sisters. The preoccupation with inanimate objects (photos, bikes, cars, clothing, and money) will gain in intensity through the narrative.

When Giselda ventures downstairs, she finds Teresa, Carolina, Laurina (Anna Mari), their assistant, and Niobe hovering around Remo, who has arrived on the scene. He tells the women a sad story of maltreatment at the hands of an uncle, while leering seductively at Laurina. He complains of being forced by his uncle to take work that was unworthy of him. Teresa and Carolina invite him to stay with them, while Giselda adamantly refuses to have a man in the house. Against her wishes, he stays, and Teresa and Carolina offer him a bike for transportation. Six months later, Remo is still with them, and the two sisters rave about their nephew to the priest, calling him a "perfect saint." The "perfect saint" is at that moment putting on his jacket, and a woman on the bed takes out money from a wallet to pay him for his services. The sisters continue to wait servilely on Remo and refuse to believe anything negative about his behavior. When a mother comes to the house to complain of Remo's taking advantage of her daughter, Teresa and Carolina angrily send her away. After meeting a sculptress who has asked Remo to model for her, he sees a motorcycle that he covets. When he asks the sisters for money to buy it, they refuse. He leaves the room, and the sisters are disconsolate that he has not kissed them. They decide to purchase the motorcycle, but Remo has already charmed Niobe, who, fearful that he might leave, gets him the money.

Remo's conquests with women now include the sisters, the sculptress, Niobe, and also Laurina. In the hope of placating Remo, the sisters now buy him a car. Remo's rise in this world is marked by his graduation from a bike to a motorcycle to a car. The two sisters' situation is characterized by increasing fear and desperation over the possibility of losing Remo. The more they suffer, the more Giselda gloats. When the princess who has also been supporting Remo comes to the house to pick up lingerie, Teresa and Carolina tell her they no longer want her business. Giselda shows the sisters a card she has found in Remo's jacket from the sculptor, another indication of her constant spying and of her desire to torture them. Remo, appearing to be grateful for the gift of the car, invites the sisters to dinner at a restaurant. He sets down one sister before a mirror and fashions her a new hairdo as the other looks on jealously. At the restaurant, Remo's regular haunt, a place where he meets his cronies and engages in shady transactions, he cavorts with the men, while the sisters sit alone at a table looking at him admiringly and giggling. They are left paying for the meal but are unperturbed. At home, they wax enthusiastic about him, seeing him as a prince, a soldier, or a bishop. When they learn that Laurina is pregnant and that the father is Remo, their shining image of him remains untarnished. He brings his cronies to the house, and the aunts are displaced. They sit on the stairs, observing the men carouse and giggling at Remo's antics. Only Giselda complains of the noise. Remo makes fun of them as he parades around for his friends in lingerie he has taken from the work room but still the aunts are not offended. When the friends leave, Teresa and Carolina confront him with Laurina's situation. He offers to marry her, but they, along with Niobe, do not want him to waste himself on her, and they plan to find her a more suitable husband.

The two sisters' relationship with Remo reaches new heights when he, pressed to pay back a loan, asks the sisters for the money. Despite the fact that the sisters' property is totally mortgaged, he insists that they sign a promissory note. They refuse, and he locks them in a closet, pocketing the key. Smoking indifferently in the doorway, he meets Niobe, who also seems unperturbed by the aunt's incarceration. She informs him that she has found a man who will marry Laurina. He opens the closet, and the sisters file out with the signed note. Giselda is pleased, thinking that they have seen the end of Remo. However, the sisters behave as if nothing unusual has happened. At the automobile showroom where he works, Remo waits on a client, a rich South American woman, Peggy (Clara Calamai), and makes a sale. She insists on going for a drive in the car, and

FIGURE 25. The deserted "brides," *Sorelle Materassi*. Courtesy of New York Museum of Modern Art, Film Stills Archive.

he takes the wheel, she urging him to drive faster. When they stop the car, he smokes a cigarette, and then they resume their ride, she driving this time at a furious pace. The car runs out of gas, because unbeknownst to Remo, she put sugar in the gas tank. He insists on going home, but they are forced to spend the night at an inn. He has met his match.

At the Materassi house, the sisters, huddled in a blanket, wait for news of Remo. A telegram arrives, announcing Remo's marriage to Peggy. The sisters accuse Peggy of being old and a witch. A dissolve to the street by the Materassi establishment reveals a group gathered to see the arrival of Peggy and Remo. Their arrival is also observed from the window by the sisters, and Peggy turns out to be young and beautiful, not at all as the Materassi have imagined her. Teresa and Carolina greet her stiffly. At the church, where again a crowd is assembled, Peggy appears radiant as a bride. Teresa and Carolina arrive next—also dressed as brides to the amusement of the crowd. After the wedding, the two sisters still in their bridal finery learn from Remo that he is leaving. In a scene that borders on the surrealistic, the women like deserted brides part with Remo. He says his farewell as the camera pans to the window where the aunts look out at a show of fireworks. The film ends with the sisters again at work.

The film's satire develops through the excessively stylized character-ization. Each character—especially Teresa, Carolina, Giselda, and Remo—is drawn in caricature to the straining point of credibility. Their speech, gestures, and movement convey their self-imprisonment, obses-sion, and inability to hear or see. Remo is the focus of their obsession, the source of their impossible desires. The consummate exploiter of women, he is portrayed as entrapped in a fetishized relation to the world, a cari-cature of the commodification of social connections. To say that he is cruel and sadistic would make him a melodramatic villain. What negates such an identification is the film's portrait of the sisters as equally fetishis-tic, and Remo is their fetish. They are complicit in their treatment of Remo, in their blindness to his manipulations.

The film valorizes looking in ways that also serve to undermine the melodrama or at least make it appear self-consciously theatrical. Theresa and Carolina observe the world through their window. They observe Remo's every movement even when what they see is designed to make them look ridiculous. Giselda observes her sisters and Remo through peepholes. The crowds watch the comings and goings at the Materassi house, amused at the events they see. The sisters are voyeurs, gratifying their desire through viewing photographs and especially through constant scrutiny of their nephew. The number of spectators on the street who increase as the film progresses serves as an ambiguous and ironic surrogate for the external audience, a distancing device that permits sardonic laughter. By extension, the external audience is implicated in the voyeurism. The emphasis on looking serves as a means of distanciation, undermining identification with the characters and its habituating affect. Looking also functions as a way of underscoring the disjunction between desire and attainment, heightening the sense of their incommensurability. Seeing is not aligned to acting. The shifting perspectives inhibit the stabilization of one spectatorial position. Where an unchanging perspective might insure an affective involvement with the character, the shifting of positions draws identification away from any one character, dispersing attention among the various characters and directing it toward the situation. The treatment of spectatorship in the film is triangulated, shifting from the characters to the internal audience and to the external audience.

The characters' mechanical gestures and responses are like dream condensations, contributing to a sense of the de-realization and the abstract character of their world. The objects in the film—the clothing, the bicycle, the motor cycle, and the car—are more substantial than the people. The metamorphosis of the characters into puppetlike creations and their interchangeability with objects serve to dramatize the film's preoccupation with power exemplified by the characters' manipulation of each other and the role of money as the medium of domination indifferent to any human interaction. Teresa and Caroline seek to control Giselda and Laurina. Giselda in turn seeks to undermine that control through her own machinations. Remo seeks to control his aunts. His mastery over them is predicated on his ability to play on their desire to possess him and on the threat of his withdrawal of affection. The essential force that animates their interactions with each other and with others is their fear of isolation. Locked into their sexual fantasies, vainly waiting for someone to free them, their desire for affection and recognition plunges them into degradation, violence, and exploitation. The sisters' entrapment is made literal by Remo's locking the sisters in a closet until they accede to his financial demands.

Through Remo's protean and disingenuous character, the film probes the excessive and destructive side of bourgeois attitudes toward family and respectability. Economics and sexuality (money, cars, and sex) are the terrain on which the game of dominance and subordination is played out between Remo and the sisters. The job Remo finally acquires is as automobile salesman, and motor vehicles become signifiers of his sexuality. If he is the women's object of desire, their fetish, locomotory objects are his fetishes. They are corollaries of his inability or unwillingness to confront human needs, and his exploitation of people for the acquisition of material goods. In this film, basic thematic elements of many of the films that address familial virtues are overturned—the sanctity and security of family relations, the elevation of industriousness, and the imperative of loyalty and service.

The melodramatic conflicts are orchestrated in several ways: in the sisters' aggressive and competitive relationship with each other, in their "adoption" of and conflict with Remo, and in their competition with Peggy, who wins Remo. The petty bourgeois world they inhabit can be read in the sisters' conspiracy with Remo to maintain the ideal of being "useful" even to the point of tolerating verbal and physical debasement. The emphasis on looking also underscores the film's obsession with vicarious experience. The mannered theatrical style of acting and the claustrophobic *mise-en-scène* create an alienating effect, producing an uncomfortable relationship to the events viewed. The ending of the film is an ironic commentary on the fantasy of the happy ending. Remo is successful in finding a rich woman to gratify his economic and sexual aspirations, and the sisters are freed of his tyranny. However, the sisters are once again alone, illusions intact, as they were at the beginning before Remo's arrival. Nothing appears to have changed, but the internal as well as the external audience has witnessed their consummate degradation.

In the sisters' situation, the film obliquely invokes a reminder of the war and of the scarcity of men away fighting in Greece, Russia, Africa, and even in sections of Italy. In the interactions between Remo and the sisters, the film also provides an unsettling portrait of masculinity as violent and exploitative that runs counter to official legitimations of virility, sexuality, and power. But the binarism of melodrama is undermined by the excessiveness of representation in the women's desperate attachment to a dominant masculine figure, their endowing that person with great power, and their willingness to endure any humiliation to maintain that relationship. The stylized acting of the female protagonists and the claustrophobic *mise en scène*, unsettles a univalent reading of the sisters' role. Desperate and fragile, they are victims of desire culpable in their willingness to endow Remo with power over them. All the characters dramatize the desire to possess, to manipulate, and to dominate through the obsession with money, respectability, and the terrifying fear of isolation. The lingerie and linen, the house, the objects of locomotion, the photograph, and the clock that signifies Remo's absence and the sisters' longing for him testify to the film's exploration of the commodification of desire.

In its negative and interrogative view of this topsy-turvy world, a parody of the utopian portraits of the carnivalesque, the film orchestrates problematic connections between familialism, sexuality, and power. The inclusion of the American, Peggy, is not an exception. She merely turns the tables, augmenting the chain of exploitation, inviting reflection on marriage as another dimension of the exchange of commodities and of human beings as indistinguishable from inanimate objects. However, though everyone is corrupt, none is beyond empathy. Similar to *Il birichino di papà*, the film has all the appurtenances of melodrama in its focus on obsession, consuming, endless, and ungratified desire, though the pathos is tempered by the characters' opaqueness and invulnerability. Nothing enters in to disturb this enclosed and histrionic world except the possibility of recognition, and the only locus for such perception remains with the external audience. The film offers the remote possibility, through its focus on spectatorship, that seeing, not merely looking, might offer an avenue of escape, if only for the audience. More than many other films of the early 1940s, including *Ossessione*, *Sorelle Materassi*, in encyclopedic fashion, lays bare the grotesque and theatricalized character of dearly held values—the self-sacrificing nature of feminine maternal behavior, the sanctified haven of the family, the phantasm of masculinity and femininity, and the vain and destructive desire to master and to be mastered associated with sexual politics and with the politics of melodrama. Nothing has changed, neither improved nor worsened. The film appears to complicate escapism, suggesting that, through its portraits of obsessional behavior and the self-deceptions that it generates, it is possible to gain an insight into the complex character of theatricality that does not stand in binary opposition to authenticity but rather puts the belief in genuineness into question. The idea of "putting on a show" and of "keeping the show going" is central to the film, to all the films discussed above, to the "folklore of consensus," and to the production and reception of cinematic texts, but theatricality expresses more than blind adherence to spectacle; theatricality involves a recognition of performance but not necessarily a belief in its truth value. The more frightening truth is that we are still in the dark when it comes to understanding how theatricality invites its audiences through common sense as folklore to share knowledge of its artifices but also inhibits the possibility of thinking differently about and acting on that knowledge.

CHAPTER SIX

Conclusion

The critical focus on "fascinating fascism" calls attention to the ritualistic and spectacular public face of fascism. Such a perspective tends to impede an understanding of the immediate, everyday, and eclectic dimensions of cinematic representation that the films inflect and that subtend questions of their reception. Critics have highlighted the practices of the regime in its public manifestations of power, involving the restrictive laws that governed woman's reproductive life, the repression of alternative sexualities, the erosion of civil life, the increasing intervention of the state into all areas of social life, the preparation and execution of an imperialist war, and the racist practices that are the inevitable accompaniment of nationalistic and imperialistic aspirations. These realities cannot be ignored. But what are the connections to be made between these displays of power and the role of popular culture as an instrument of consent?

Throughout this book, I have attempted to find strategies for analysis that can elicit forms of congruence between the public and private spheres, between these coercive repressive practices of power and their relation to the modes of expression and reception in the popular culture of the time. I have argued that an examination of the commercial sound films produced during the era offers important clues to the intricate, multilayered, indirect, and often oblique relationship between public and private spheres. I have further argued that to regard the films either as a retreat to the private sphere, a mode of escapism from the harsh realities of life under a totalitarian regime, or, conversely, as an accession to the "dominant ideology" of Fascism does a disservice to the necessary enterprise of identifying the more intricate ways in which the public and the private are mutually imbricated.

An examination of fascist practices is often confined to Italy and Germany, while their connections to and their impact on other Western countries has been ignored or understated to the detriment of an analysis of fascism. In Detlev J. K. Peukert's terms, a comparative as well as everyday analysis of fascism tends to blur the boundaries between "stereotypes of the utterly evil fascist and the wholly good anti-fascist,"[1] allowing for a more complex portrait of social consensus and its relation more broadly to the culture of modernity. The problem with a binary analysis of popular culture and particularly with binary analysis of cinematic representation (but also of sports, music, dance, and other forms of leisure life) under fascism in terms of escapism and realism, conformity and opposition, is that the notion of consensus that emerges is based on a monolithic sense of adherence or resistance. Binary views of escapism or conformity presume collective guilt and uniform involvement in the construction and maintenance of fascism. Even more, such views disregard precisely the specificity of those areas of life where difference is evident. The character, quality, and degree of differences needs to be understood not for the purposes of judgment but for the purposes of gaining a more adequate conception of the various ways in which people were indifferent to and confused and disorganized by the economic, political, and cultural conditions that were brought into existence under fascism, involving the challenges of modernization, the tensions between modernity and tradition, and the role of media in the reorientation of Italian life.

The cinema in the interwar years was an important social function. From 1936 on, the size of audiences grew spectacularly. As Pierre Sorlin comments, "We must bear in mind that the cinemas were highly popular places of sociability."[2] In relation to the question of the film's subject matter and points of view, he adds, "We are tempted to ascribe to Fascism such features as the reverence for leaders, the importance of family life, the dependence of women and the overvaluation of nationalism. In fact, the same characteristics can be found in pictures and in Hollywood or in democratic European countries."[3] Without completely dismissing the power of these features cited by Sorlin, I have sought to indicate where there is more commonality between the Italian films and those of Hollywood and Europe, a commonality that can be accounted for by the character of media, but, even more, by the specific and differentiating strategies of popular culture in its struggle for the hearts and purses of their audiences.

The labor of cinema, both in its production of texts and in its reception is affective. It demands the time and the attention of the spectator as well as her money, but in so doing cinema must be able to identify the different constituencies that it addresses. It must be both traditional and innovative; it must be engaging; it must be knowledgeable of the power of folklore; and it must compensate the different audience members for voluntarily offering their time and money. In order to pay this price, the audience must feel that they have been adequately compensated. Too often, however, the critics of popular culture have underestimated the state of the audience's knowledge. Popular culture has been a contentious subject, giving rise to all kinds of uncritical generalizations about its influence and impact, relegating popular culture to the sphere of the fantasmatic. In returning to and elaborating on Gramsci's conception of common sense as folklore, I have sought to identify the ways the films, like common sense itself, operate within the realm of formula, habituation, and convention, wily in the ways they fuse realms of knowledge from all areas of cultural and social life—from high and low culture, opera and detective literature, juridical practices, music, and past history. This folklore constantly renews itself to adapt to contemporary life. Common sense is central to everyday life and expression, to modes of survival, and only at their peril do films ignore this.

While acknowledging the specificity of different media and other forms of cultural expression, it is possible to see the cinema as exemplary of the emergent state of popular culture in the interwar and war years. What differentiates the folklore of consent from prevailing notions of consent is its reflexivity and theatricality; it is a politics of style as much as it is a style of politics. Theatricality occupies a major position in the culture of Fascism, a legacy the silent cinema, theater, avant-garde painting, and music, steadily refined upon in the 1930s and 1940s. In the context of many descriptions of Fascism as disorganizing rather than organizing cultural and political life, theatricality functioned in the cinema as a feature of modernity, with its shocks, dislocations, and disorientations. Through its emphasis on theatricality, impersonation, doubling, disguises, and carnival, the cinema of the Ventennio played a role in undermining traditional belief systems with far-reaching implications for the politics of culture not only for the Ventennio but for the post–World War Two era. In the previous chapters, I have suggested that the problem of theatricality of the films of the 1930s and early 1940s was less a crisis of ideological manipulation than one of a crisis of representation.

Throughout this book, in my examination of the comedies, the historical films, the films of "conversion" and "calligraphism," and the films that dramatize femininity, I have sought to challenge the notion of the cinema of the era as "escapist." I regard this appellation as yet another permutation of the view of mass culture as void of meaning and of the audiences as dupes of the media, drawn unthinkingly to a fascination with the world of commodities. Instead of offering audiences "the experience of being able to migrate temporarily to the world of their own dreams, and of returning to their own lives and private spaces enriched and enlivened,"[4] the cinema more fundamentally confused relations between interiority and exteriority, reinventing the world as cinema. In challenging the notion of escapism through the conception of theatricality, I have sought to describe how the cinema as a major form of popular culture played a major role in reeducating and reorienting audiences to the world of visualization. My argument against the thesis of escapism relies on the more profound and possibly insidious hypothesis that what the Italian cinema of the era, like that of Hollywood, inaugurated was an uneasy relationship to representation, one that undermined traditional conceptions of a binary opposition between illusion and reality and rather sought to conflate the two in the interests of illusionism.

The films of the Ventennio are self-conscious about their need to be entertaining and about sharing their strategies for entertainment with audiences. Even where they seem to adopt a polemic stance, they present themselves in terms of theatricality, stressing spectatorship, artifice, doubling, disguises, and impersonation, which complicates the role of the narrativity and perspectivalism. As exemplified by the comedies, the texts do not univalently conform to a model of the "dream factory" identified with Hollywood and, more generally, with mass culture. In certain instances, such films as Camerini's *Figaro e la sua gran giornata, Il Signor Max, Gli uomini che mascalzoni, Darò un milione,* and *Batticuore* blur the lines between life and film in ways that cannot be merely assigned to their escape from reality. Perhaps they are realistic precisely in the ways they foreground theatricality and spectacle. The films are blatant about the fact that they are sharing a "secret" with their audiences, the secret being the necessity for "putting on a show," for maintaining the appearance of common sense of performance. In this sense, they wink at their audiences, indicating that they share a knowledge of the necessity and normality of posturing and artifice rather than functioning as a mode of merely foisting their fictions on their unaware and unsuspecting victims.

The comedies were not the only films that reveled in theatricality. In the historical films, history becomes a stage too, a masquerade for the great and powerful, and the forms of drama enacted are reminiscent of earlier silent epics. Such films as *Scipione l'Africano, Condottieri, Cavalleria,* and *1860* obey the dictates of popular culture by reinventing folklore, and by taking figures, images, and narratives from the past and clothing them in the melodramatic affect of theatricality. In these films, too, the theatricality enhances the national imaginary, underscoring the fictions of nation, colonialism, and war, less in the interests of persuading their audiences of the truth, vitality, and viability of their rhetoric but more in the direction, in a Pirandellian sense, of foregrounding their illusion and the inescapability of performance. The cinema could thus become a necessary agent of the "folklore of consensus," as well as an archive for later critics to gain a complex insight into this.

The narratives of conversion and calligraphism offer another permutation of theatricality, couched in the familiar folklore and iconography of religious narrative paradigms, focusing on impersonation but in a melodramatic rather than comic mode. The religious dimension of the conversion melodramas focuses on the turning away from a dissolute life toward one of commitment and sacrifice even unto death, presenting the protagonist with a new identity. The traditional spiritual paradigm of the psychomachia has been restaged in the newer agon and images of the divine nature of the nation, which thrives on the masks of masculinity. The fictional dimension of the narrative resides, as one might suspect, in the role of the woman as the generator of illusion and fiction, the necessary illusion for the metamorphosis of the masculine protagonist. In these narratives (e.g., *Il grande appello, Sotto la croce del sud,* and *Terra madre*), femininity is both the source of illusion, generating confusion for the protagonist and providing him with a rationale for rejecting and banishing woman, or turning her into a spectator. Theatricality is most evident in the melodramatic excesses generated in her name, in the strategies whereby femininity serves to mask the threat of disorder and fragmented masculinity.

The calligraphic films are similarly preoccupied with masculinity. Where feminine figures play a role, they too are identified with doubling (e.g., *Lo squadrone bianco*), with the threat of difference, and with the ambiguous, ritualistic, often impotent, and even ironic role of religion. Profoundly preoccupied, too, with dissimulation, the calligraphic melodramas move in a different direction from the conversion dramas. Sub-

traction is fundamental to the conversion dramas as the masculine protagonist strips away difference, multiplicity, and any attribute that could
be identified with femininity. In the case of the calligraphic melodramas,
addition, augmentation, and elaboration predominate as excess piles on
excess. Their theatricality relies on the magnitude of the protagonist's
malevolence and on the dark and intimating portrait of a world in a state
of decomposition. In the case of both forms of melodrama—conversion
and calligraphism—the preoccupation with illusion is evident. In the
conversion dramas, the theatrical elements are presumably contained by
the disciplining of femininity. In the calligraphic melodramas, theatricality and fiction are not tempered and mitigated (e.g., *Gelosia*); they are
acknowledged as akin to madness and obsession.

The discussion of femininity, therefore, that ends this book explores
how femininity is identified with theatricality and theatricality with the
inadequacies, limits, and snares of representation. The figure of woman
becomes the precursor of illusion and, at the same time, its victim. The
films discussed in Chapter 5 exemplify the ways femininity serves to
reestablish familiar and commonsensical gendered and sexual borders in
social relations; through melodrama and comedy, through the emphasis
on entertainment, fiction, and performance, the films also reveal the violence with which these boundaries are formed and the slippery and tenuous modes of their construction. Centering on two female protagonists,
Poggioli's *Sorelle Materassi* is a complex and ambiguous treatment of theatricality, a dissection of the dominance and power of illusion. The sisters
are embroiled in a world where reality is dissimulation. More succinctly
and starkly than the other films discussed throughout the book, the characters are irretrievably lost in their fictional world, including the audiences within the film who are entertained by the sister's abject performances. In its self-referentiality, uses of melodramatic affect for satiric
effect, and its highly stylized and caricatural treatment of character, *Sorelle
Materassi* makes evident that the strategies of theatricality are inseparable
from cinematic spectatorship. The audience within the film regards the
sister's performance through laughter, and the laughter thus inhibits the
external audience from regarding the sister's obsessions within the heightened affect of melodrama.

If *Sorelle Materassi* reiterates the strategies of the other films discussed in my book, presupposing a bond with audience through a shared
recognition of the fictional nature of what is being enacted, this film also
highlights the cinematic experience as one of entrapment and cruelty. The

narrative seems to equate theatricality with looking, looking with obsession, and obsession with the eroded boundaries between the imaginary
and the real in its emphasis on the mundane aspects of everyday life as
"putting on a show," the consequences of adhering to prescribed social
scenarios, a situation evident in all the films discussed above but in varying intensities. The film compounds questions concerning the real. Is the
real actually fiction? Is the reality of this reflection an opening to a different way of critically assessing representation, or is it a form of nostalgia
for a time when roles and disguises are cast aside and when the true
essence of things will become manifest? In either case, the compounding
of the actual and the virtual is a legacy of Italian Fascism and of the mediated world it inaugurated that is with us still.

The preoccupation with theatricality does not come to an end with
the appearance of the phenomenon named as "neorealism"; actually it
continues, taking new stylistic forms in the battle between the real and
the imaginary, the actual and the virtual. Neorealism has not abandoned
the problematic of the character of spectatorship in its ambiguous treatment of reality and representation. In fact, what Deleuze describes as the
"time-image" identified with neorealism is similarly characterized by "a
principle of indeterminability, of indiscernability: we no longer know
what is imaginary or real, physical or mental, in the situation. . . . It is as
if the real and imaginary were running after each other, as if each was
being reflected in the other around a point of indiscernability."[5] Looking
backward to the films discussed in this book as well as forward to the films
of the late 1940s and early 1950s, while the styles, the images, the characters, the *mise-en-scène*, and the rhetoric shifted in the films of neorealism, what remained continuous was the preoccupation with the role of
cinema as a major force in the deconstruction and reconstruction of the
folklore of popular culture as a feature of consensus, and as a profound
indication of the crisis of representation that characterizes modernity and
postmodernity and, further, the potential for fascism.

NOTES

PREFACE

1. See Gian Piero Brunetta's monumental studies of the mass media of the era as well as those by Philip V. Cannistraro, Adriano Aprà and Patrizia Pistagnesi, Francesco Savio, Jean Gili, and Lino Micciché. The work of British Gramscian scholars Geoffrey Nowell-Smith and David Forgacs also appeared in the 1980s along with the works of Elaine Mancini, Marcia Landy, and James Hay. For a recent study, see also Pierre Sorlin, *Italian National Cinema, 1896–1996* (London: Routledge, 1996).

2. Lino Micciché, "Il cadavere nell' armadio," *Cinema italiano sotto il fascism*, ed. Riccardo Redi (Venice: Marsilio, 1979), 9–19.

3. See Karen Pinkus, *Bodily Regimes: Italian Advertising under Fascism* (Minneapolis: University of Minnesota Press, 1995); Robin Pickering-Iazzi, ed., *Mothers of Invention: Women, Italian Fascism, and Culture* (Minneapolis: University of Minnesota Press, 1995); Mino Argentieri, ed., *Risate di regime: La commedia Italiana, 1930–1944* (Venice: Marsilio, 1991); Gianfranco Casadio, Ernesto G. Laura, and Filippo Cristiano, eds., *Telefoni bianchi: Realtà e finzione nella società nel cinema italiano degli anni quaranta* (Ravenna: Longo, 1991); Victoria de Grazia, *How Fascism Ruled Women: Italy, 1922–1945* (Cambridge: Cambridge University Press, 1992).

4. Gilles Deleuze, *Cinema 1: The Movement-Image* (Minneapolis: University of Minnesota Press), 101.

5. See Peter Brooks, *The Melodramatic Imagination: Balzac, Henry James, Melodrama and the Mode of Excess* (New York: Columbia University Press, 1989); Christine Gledhill, ed., *Home Is Where the Heart Is: Studies in Melodrama and the Woman's Film* (London: British Film Institute, 1987); Marcia Landy, *Imitations*

304 NOTES TO CHAPTER 1

of Life: A Reader on Film and Television Melodrama (Detroit: Wayne State University, 1991); Jackie Byars, *All that Hollywood Allows: Re-reading Gender in 1950s Melodrama* (Chapel Hill: University of North Carolina Press, 1991).

CHAPTER ONE. FILM, FOLKLORE, AND AFFECT

1. Giambattista Vico, *On the Study Methods of Our Time*, trans. Elio Gianturco, ed. Donald Phillip Verene (Ithaca, N.Y.: Cornell University Press, 1990), 13–14.

2. Antonio Gramsci, *Selections from the Prison Notebooks*, eds. and trans. Quintin Hoare and Geoffrey Nowell-Smith (New York: International Publishers, 1978), 91. Hereafter referred to as *SPN*.

3. *SPN*, 21.

4. Antonio Gramsci, *Selections from the Cultural Writings*, ed. David Forgacs (Cambridge, Mass.: Harvard University Press, 1985), 273. Hereafter designated as *SCW*.

5. *SCW*, 202.

6. "Americanism and Fordism," *SPN*, 277–316.

7. Pierre Sorlin, *Italian National Cinema, 1896–1996* (London: Routledge, 1996), 76–83.

8. *SCW*, 380.

9. *SPN*, 324.

10. *SPN*, 325–29. For an extended discussion of Gramsci's notion of common sense and its implications for understanding consensus, see Marcia Landy, *Film, Politics, and Gramsci* (Minneapolis: University of Minnesota Press, 1994), 128–32.

11. Friedrich Nietzsche, "On the Uses and Disadvantages of History for Life," *Untimely Meditations*, trans. R. J. Hollingdale (Cambridge: Cambridge University Press, 1991), 57–125.

12. *SPN*, 304–5.

13. Maria-Antonietta Macchiocchi, "Female Sexuality in Fascist Ideology," *Feminist Review* 1 (1979): 67–82.

14. Karl Marx, *Capital*, vol. 1, trans. Eden and Cedar Paul (New York: Dutton, 1977), 47.

15. Gilles Deleuze and Félix Guattari, *A Thousand Plateaus: Capitalism and Schizophrenia*, trans. Brian Massumi (Minneapolis: University of Minnesota Press, 1988), 7.

16. Gilles Deleuze, *Cinema I: The Movement-Image* (Minneapolis: University of Minnesota Press, 1986), 11.

17. Ibid., 97.

18. Ibid., 99.

19. Michael Hardt, *Gilles Deleuze: An Apprenticeship in Philosophy* (Minneapolis: University of Minnesota Press, 1993), 92.

20. Ibid., 92–93.

21. Karl Marx, *Capital*, vol. 1, trans. Ben Fowkes (New York: Vintage Books, 1976), 163–65.

22. Gayatri Chakravorty Spivak, "Scattered Speculations on the Question of Value," *In Other Worlds: Essays in Cultural Politics* (New York: Routledge, 1988), 164.

23. Ibid., 166.

24. *SCW*, 189.

25. *SCW*, 195.

26. Gianni Vattimo, *The Transparent Society*, trans. David Webb (Baltimore: Johns Hopkins University Press, 1992), 29.

27. Ibid., 29.

28. Ibid., 37.

29. Ibid., 40.

30. *SCW*, 9.

31. *SCW*, 189.

32. Vattimo, *The Transparent Society*, 42.

33. *SPN*, 318.

34. *SCW*, 123.

35. Philip V. Cannistraro, *La fabbrica del consenso* (Rome: Laterza, 1975); Victoria de Grazia, *The Culture of Consent: Mass Organization of Leisure in Fascist*

Italy (Cambridge: Cambridge University Press, 1981) and *How Fascism Ruled Women, 1922–1945* (Berkeley: University of California Press, 1992).

36. Detlev J. K. Peukert, *Inside Nazi Germany: Conformity, Opposition and Racism in Everyday Life*, trans. Richard Daveson (London: Penguin, 1987), 244.

37. Pierre Sorlin, "Italian Cinema's Rebirth," *Historical Journal of Film, Radio, and Television* 14.1 (1994): 11.

38. Ibid., 11.

39. Ibid., 10.

40. James Hay, *Popular Film Culture in Fascist Italy: The Passing of the Rex* (Bloomington: Indiana University Press, 1987), 29.

41. Sorlin, "Italian Cinema's Rebirth," 11.

42. Joanne Hollows and Mark Jancovich, eds., *Approaches to Popular Film* (Manchester, U.K.: Manchester University Press, 1995).

43. Renzo De Felice, *D'Annunzio Politico* (Rome: Laterza, 1978).

44. Gian Piero Brunetta, "The Long March of American Cinema in Italy," *Hollywood in Europe: Experience of a Cultural Hegemony*, ed. David Ellwood and Rob Kroes (Amsterdam: Vrije Universiteit University Press, 1994), 143.

45. Sue Harper, "Historical Pleasures: Gainsborough Costume Melodramas," *Home Is Where the Heart Is*, ed. Christine Gledhill (London: British Film Institute, 1987), 167.

46. Ibid., 188.

47. Ibid., 191.

48. See de Grazia, *Culture of Consent*, 16–17.

49. See de Grazia, *How Fascism Ruled Women*, 1.

50. Ibid., 2.

51. Ibid., 132.

52. Ibid., 132–33.

53. Ibid., 135.

54. Hay, *Popular Film Culture in Fascist Italy*, 35.

55. Karen Pinkus, *Bodily Regimes: Italian Advertising under Fascism* (Minneapolis: University of Minnesota Press, 1995), 16.

56. Gledhill, "The Melodramatic Field: An Investigation," *Home Is Where the Heart Is*, 50.

57. Peter Brooks, "The Text of Muteness," *The Melodramatic Imagination: Balzac, Henry James, and the Mode of Excess* (New York: Columbia University Press, 1985), 56–81.

58. Thomas Elsaesser, "Tales of Sound and Fury: Observations on the Family Melodrama," *Imitations of Life: A Reader on Film and Melodrama*, ed. Marcia Landy (Detroit: Wayne State University Press, 1991), 88.

59. Kristin Thompson, *Eisenstein's Ivan the Terrible: A Neoformalist Analysis* (Princeton, N.J.: Princeton University Press, 1981), 290, 293.

60. Christine Gledhill, *Stardom: Industry of Desire* (London: Routledge, 1991), 218.

61. Gian Piero Brunetta, *Storia del cinema italiano* (Rome: Riuniti, 1979), 78.

62. Brunetta, *Storia del cinema italiano*, 73.

63. Brunetta, "The Long March of American Cinema in Italy," 139.

64. Bruno Wanrooji, "Dollars and Decency: Italian Catholics and Hollywood," *Hollywood in Europe: Experience of a Cultural Hegemony*, ed. David Ellwood and Rob Kroes (Amsterdam: Vrije Universiteit University Press, 1994), 248, 249.

65. Brunetta, "The Long March of American Cinema in Italy," 142–43.

66. Ibid., 143.

67. Elaine Mancini, *Struggles of the Italian Film Industry under Fascism* (Ann Arbor, Mich.: UMI Research Press, 1985), 33.

68. Ibid., 33.

69. Sorlin, "Italian Cinema's Rebirth," 3–4.

70. Ibid., 9.

71. Peukert, *Inside Nazi Germany*, 23.

72. Ibid., 21.

73. Philip Morgan, *Italian Fascism, 1919–1945* (New York: St. Martin's Press, 1995), 3.

74. Ibid., 4.

75. Jared Becker, *Nationalism and Culture: Gabriele D'Annunzio and Italy after the Risorgimento* (New York: Peter Lang, 1994), 1.

76. ibid., 211.

77. Renzo De Felice, *D'Annunzio Politico, 1918–1938* (Rome: Laterza, 1978), xv.

78. Becker, *Nationalism and Culture*, 3.

79. David Forgacs, "The Left and Fascism: Problems of Definition and Strategy," *Rethinking Italian Fascism: Capitalism, Populism, and Culture*, ed. David Forgacs (London: Lawrence and Wishart, 1986), 42.

80. Ibid., 43.

81. Ibid., 44.

82. Morgan, *Italian Fascism*, 48.

83. De Grazia, *How Fascism Ruled Women*, 72.

84. Ibid., 81.

85. Morgan, *Italian Fascism*, 131.

86. De Grazia, *How Fascism Ruled Women*, 170.

87. Ibid., 279.

88. Ibid., 282.

89. Doug Thompson, *State Control in Fascist Italy, 1925–1943: Culture and Conformity* (Manchester, U.K.: Manchester University Press, 1991), 32.

90. Mancini, *Struggles of the Italian Film Industry*, 29.

91. Sorlin, "Italian Cinema's Rebirth," 8.

92. Ibid., 10.

93. Susan Sontag, "Fascinating Fascism" in *Movies and Methods*, vol. 1, ed. Bill Nichols (Berkeley: University of California Press, 1976), 31–44.

CHAPTER TWO. COMEDY, MELODRAMA, AND THEATRICALITY

1. Francesco Savio, *Cinecittà anni trenta: parlano 116 protagonisti del secondo cinema italiano (1930–1943)*, vol. 3 (Rome: Bulzoni Press, 1979), 1139.

2. Gerald Mast, *A Short History of the Movies* (New York: Macmillan, 1986), 316.

3. Andrew Horton, "Introduction," *Comedy/Cinema/Theory*, ed. Andrew Horton (Berkeley: University of California Press, 1991), 2.

4. See also Stanley Cavell, *The Pursuit of Happiness: The Hollywood Comedy of Remarriage* (Cambridge, Mass.: Harvard University Press, 1981); Kristine Brunovska Karnick and Henry Jenkins, eds., *Classical Hollywood Comedy* (New York: Routledge, 1995).

5. Hay, *Popular Film Culture*, 28.

6. Ibid., 27.

7. Kathleen Rowe, "Comedy, Melodrama, and Gender: Theorizing the Genres of Laughter," in Karnick and Jenkins, *Classical Hollywood Comedy*, 40.

8. Gian Piero Brunetta, *Cinema italiano tra le due guerre: fascismo e politica cinematografica: problemi di storia dello spettacolo tra due guerre* (Milan: Mursia Press, 1975), 92.

9. Jane Feuer, *The Hollywood Musical* (London: BFI, 1982), 82.

10. Ibid., 3.

11. Ibid., 23.

12. Savio, *Cinecittà anni trenta*, 3:1068.

13. Ibid., 3:989.

14. Ibid., 3:1021.

15. Brunetta, "The Long March of American Cinema in Italy," 143.

16. Ibid.

17. *SCW*, 317.

18. Steve Neale and Frank Krutnik, *Popular Film and Television Comedy* (London: Routledge, 1990), 155–56.

19. Ibid., 149.

20. Ted Sennett, *Laughing in the Dark: Movie Comedy from Groucho to Woody Allen* (New York: St. Martin's Press, 1992), 63.

21. Siegfried Kracauer, *The Mass Ornament: Weimar Essays* (Cambridge, Mass.: Harvard University Press, 1995), 291.

22. Tina Olsin Lent, "Romantic Love and Friendship: The Redefinition of Gender Relations in Screwball Comedy," in Karnick and Jenkins, *Classical Hollywood Comedy*, 315.

23. Savio, *Cinecittà anni trenta*, 3:885–986.

24. Immanuel Wallerstein and Etienne Balibar, *Race, Nation, Class: Ambiguous Identities* (London: Verso, 1991), 101.

25. Sennett, *Laughing in the Dark*, 86.

26. Ernesto G. Laura, *Comedy Italian Style* (Rome: National Association of Motion Pictures and Affiliated Industries, n.d.), 7.

27. Ibid.

28. Hay, *Popular Film Culture*, 115.

29. Savio, *Cinecittà anni trenta*, 3:844.

30. Dyer, Richard, *Stars* (London: BFI, 1986), 49–50.

31. Laura, *Comedy Italian Style*, 8–9.

32. Ibid., 9.

CHAPTER THREE. THE USES OF FOLKLORE

1. Gerald Mast, *A Short History of the Movies* (New York: Macmillan, 1986), 316; see also David A. Cook, *A History of Narrative Film* (New York: W. W. Norton, 1996), 353–54.

2. Walter Adamson, "The Language of Opposition in Early Twentieth-Century Italy: Rhetorical Continuities between Pre-war Florentine Avantgardism and Mussolini's Fascism," *Journal of Modern History* 64 (March 1992): 22–23.

3. Robert Rosenstone, ed., *Revisioning History: Film and the Construction of a New Past* (Princeton, N.J.: Princeton University Press, 1995), 7.

4. Ibid., 6.

5. Gianfranco Mino Gori, *Patria Diva: La storia d'Italia nel film del ventennio* (Florence: Usher, 1988), 9–16.

6. *SPN*, 377–78.

7. Gian-Paolo Biasin, *Italian Literary Icons* (Princeton, N.J.: Princeton University Press, 1985), 76–77.

8. Caroline Springer, *The Marble Wilderness: Ruins and Representation in Italian Romanticism* (Cambridge: Cambridge University Press, 1987), 1–13.

9. Brooks, "The Text of Muteness," *The Melodramatic Imagination: Balzac, Henry James, and the Language of Excess* (New York: Columbia University Press), 56–62.

10. *SCW*, 296.

11. *SCW*, 116.

12. Thomas Elsaesser, "Tales of Sound and Fury," in *Imitations of Life: A Reader on Film and Television Melodrama*, ed. Marcia Landy (Detroit: Wayne University Press, 1991), 69.

13. Millicent Marcus, *Italian Cinema in the Light of Neorealism* (Princeton, N.J.: Princeton University Press, 1986), 12.

14. Morena Paglai, *Mito e precarietà: Studi su Pascoli, D'Annunzio, Rosso di San Secondo, Malaparte, Diddi* (Florence: Franco Casati Press, 1989), 65–102.

15. Becker, *Nationalism and Culture*, 137, 150.

16. A. Nicholas Vardac, *Stage to Screen* (Cambridge, Mass.: Harvard University Press, 1968), 20.

17. Vardac, *Stage to Screen*, 214.

18. Pierre Leprohon, *The Italian Cinema* (New York: Praeger, 1972), 34.

19. George Custen, *Bio/Pics: How Hollywood Constructed Public History* (New Brunswick, N.J.: Rutgers University Press, 1992), 9.

20. Nietszche, "The Uses and Disadvantages of History," 72.

21. Gilles Deleuze, *Cinema I*, 70.

22. Hay, *Popular Film Culture*, 158.

23. Harper, "Historical Pleasures," 191.

24. Deleuze, *Cinema 1*, 96.

25. Claver Salizatto and Vito Zagarrio, *La corona di ferro: Un modo di produzione italiano* (Rome: Di Giacomo, 1985), 16.

26. Luca Verdone, *I film di Alessandro Blasetti* (Rome: Gremese, 1989), 101.

27. Brian Taves, *The Romance of Adventure: The Genre of Historical Adventure Movies* (Jackson: University of Mississippi Press, 1993), 94.

28. Christopher Frayling, *Spaghetti Westerns: Cowboys and Europeans from Karl May to Sergio Leone* (London: Routledge & Kegan Paul, 1981), 11–12.

29. Ibid., 20.

30. Hay, *Popular Film Culture*, 164.

31. Julian Petley, *Capital and Culture: German Cinema 1933–1945* (London: BFI, 1979), 120.

32. Brunetta, *Storia del cinema*, 398.

33. Petley, *Capital and Culture*, 122.

34. Hay, *Popular Film Culture*, 155.

35. Ibid., 177–79.

36. Walter Benjamin, "Theories of German Fascism," trans. Jerolf Wikoff, *New German Critique* 17 (Spring 1979): 125.

37. Ibid., 128.

38. Ibid., 123.

39. Nietzsche, "The Uses and Disadvantages of History," 72.

40. Biasin, *Italian Literary Icons*, 72.

41. Gianfranco Mino Gori, *Patria diva: La storia d'Italia nel film del ventennio* (Florence: Usher, 1988), 90–91.

42. Taves, *The Romance of Adventure*, 156.

43. Gori, *Patria Diva*, 37–39. See also Savio, *Ma l'amore no*, 162.

44. Wallerstein and Balibar, *Race, Nation, Class*, 93.

45. Gilles Deleuze, *Difference and Repetition*, trans. Paul Patton (New York: Columbia University Press, 1994), 69.

46. Gori, *Patria Diva*, 78–91.

47. Ibid., 54.

48. Custen, *Bio/Pics*, 75.

49. Angela Dalle Vacche, *The Body in the Mirror: Shapes of History in Italian Cinema* (Princeton, N.J.: Princeton University Press, 1992), 106.

50. Pierre Sorlin, *European Cinemas/European Societies* (London: Routledge, 1991), 174.

51. *SPN*, 419–20.

52. Wallerstein and Balibar, *Race, Nation, Class*, 87.

53. Gori, *Patria Diva*, 51.

54. Savio, *Ma l'amore no: realismo, formalismo, e telefoni bianchi nel cinema italiano di regime 1940–1943* (Milan: Sonzogno, 1975), 114.

55. Antonio Costa, "'Risotti con i tartufi': Soldati, Fogazzaro e il calligrafismo," *La bella forma: Poggioli, i calligrafici, e dintorni*, ed. Andrea Martini (Venice, Marsilio, 1992), 99.

56. David N. Rodowick," Madness, Authority and Ideology: The Domestic Melodrama of the 1950s," in Gledhill, *Home Is Where the Heart Is*, 275.

57. Dana Polan, *Power and Paranoia: History, Narrative, and the American Cinema, 1940–1950* (New York: Columbia University Press, 1986), 75.

58. Klaus Theweleit, *Male Fantasies* (Minneapolis: University of Minnesota Press, 1987), 1:35.

59. Savio, *Cinecittà anni trenta*, 2:524.

60. Deleuze, *Cinema II: The Time Image* (Minneapolis: University of Minnesota Press, 1989), 264.

61. *SCW*, 413.

62. *SCW*, 190.

63. Michel De Certeau, "The Beauty of the Dead: Nisard," *Heterologies: Discourse on the Other* (Minneapolis: University of Minnesota Press, 1995), 136.

CHAPTER FOUR. FROM CONVERSION
TO CALLIGRAPHISM

1. Brooks, *The Melodramatic Imagination*, 56–80.

2. *SCW*, 380.

3. Deleuze, *Difference and Repetition*, 10.

4. Ibid.

5. William James, *The Varieties of Religious Experience* (Cambridge, Mass.: Harvard University Press, 1985).

6. Balibar and Wallerstein, *Race, Nation, Class*, 95.

7. Elsaesser, "Tales of Sound and Fury," 66.

8. Marco Pannunzio, "Chenal di fronte a Pirandello," *Cinema* (November 10, 1936): 391.

9. Tvzetan Todorov, *The Poetics of Prose* (Ithaca, N.Y.: Cornell University Press, 1977).

10. Nina da Vinci Nichols and Jana O'Keefe Bazzoni, *Pirandello and Cinema* (Lincoln: University of Nebraska Press, 1995), 114.

11. Ibid., 5.

12. *SCW*, 83.

13. *SCW*, 80.

14. Nichols and Bazzoni, *Pirandello and Cinema*, 113.

15. Ibid., 114.

16. Jean Gili, *L'Italie de Mussolini et son cinema* (Paris: Henri Veyrier, 1985), 79.

17. Ibid., 79.

18. Gianfranco Casadio, *Il grigio e il nero: Spettacolo e propaganda nel cinema italiano degli anni trenta (1931–1943)* (Ravenna: Longo Press, 1989), 63.

19. Ibid.

20. Ibid.

21. De Grazia, *How Fascism Ruled Women.*

22. Walter Adamson, "Modernism and Fascism: The Politics of Culture in Italy, 1903–1922," *American Historical Review* (1990), 95: 378.

23. Hay, *Popular Film Culture*, 102.

24. Mancini, *Struggles of the Italian Film Industry*, 113–18.

25. Ibid., 116.

26. De Grazia, *How Fascism Ruled Women.*

27. Durkheim, *Elementary Forms of the Religious Life*, trans. Joseph Ward Swain (New York: Collier, 1961), 445.

28. Pinkus, *Bodily Regimes*, 73.

29. Theweleit, *Male Fantasies*, 1:35.

30. Ibid., 1:31.

31. Pinkus, *Bodily Regimes*, 86.

32. Ibid., 154.

33. Landy, *British Genres* (Princeton, N.J.: Princeton University Press, 1991), 97–101.

34. Edward Said, *Orientalism* (New York: Vintage Books, 1979), 188.

35. Pinkus, *Bodily Regimes*, 124.

36. *SCW*, 351.

37. Brunetta, *Storia del cinema*, 466, 467.

38. Leprohon, *Italian Cinema*, 77.

39. Lino Micciché, "Introduction," *La bella forma: Poggioli, i calligrafici, e dintorni*, ed. Andrea Martini (Venice, Marsilio, 1992), 21.

40. Ibid., 25–26.

41. Andrea Martini, "Soldati—Poggioli—Chiarini: Una questione di spazio, di simmetri e di artificio," in *La bella forma: Poggioli, i calligrafici, e dintorni*, ed. Andrea Martini (Venice, Marsilio, 1992), 29–43.

42. Elsaesser, "Tales of Sound and Fury," 56.

43. Gili, *L' Italie de Mussolini et son cinema*, 145.

44. Morena Paglai, *Mito e precarietà: Studi su Pascoli, D' Annunzio, Rosso di San Secondo, Malaparte, Diddi* (Florence: Franco Casati Press, 1989), 136.

45. Ibid., 141.

46. Guglielmo Monetti, "A proposito de *La morte civile* e di *Gelosia*: dall'istanza realista all'entropia cinematografica," in Martini, *La bella forma*, 59.

47. Micciché, "Introduction," in Martini, *La bella forma*, 62.

48. Monetti, "A proposito de *La morte civile* e di *Gelosia*," 62.

49. Stefano Masi, "La bellissima immagine," in Martini, *La bella forma*, 179.

50. Mino Argentieri, *Risate di Regime: La commedia italiana, 1930–1944* (Venice: Marsilio, 1991), 208.

51. *SCW*, 377–78.

52. Giovanna Grignaffini, "Una certa maniera: Il cinema di Renato Castellani," in Martini, *La bella forma*, 109.

53. Ibid.

54. Ibid., 110.

55. Ibid., 107.

56. Mino Argentieri, ed., *Risate di Regime: La commedia italiana, 1930–1944* (Venice: Marsilio, 1991), 191.

57. Theweleit, *Male Fantasies*, 2:368–69.

58. Deleuze, *Cinema II*, 12.

59. Sorlin, *Italian National Cinema*, 84.

CHAPTER FIVE. THE AFFECTIVE VALUE OF FEMININITY AND MATERNITY

1. De Grazia, *How Fascism Ruled Women*, 75–115; Lesley Caldwell, "Madri d'Italia: Film and the Fascist Concern with Motherhood," *Women and Italy: Essays in Gender, Culture, and History*, ed. Zygmunt G. Baranski and Shirley W. Vinall (New York: St. Martin's Press, 1991), 43–64; Jacqueline Reich, "Reading, Writing, and Rebellion: Collectivity, Specularity, and Sexuality in Italian Schoolgirl Comedies," *Mothers of Invention: Women, Italian Fascism, and Culture*, ed. Robin Pickering-Iazzi (Minneapolis: University of Minnesota Press, 1995), 220–51.

2. De Grazia, *How Fascism Ruled Women*, 78.

3. Ibid., 60.

4. Ibid., 81.

5. Lucia Re, "Fascist Theories of 'Woman' and the Construction of Gender," in *Mothers of Invention: Women, Italian Fascism, and Culture*, ed. Robin Pickering-Iazzi (Minneapolis: University of Minnesota Press, 1995), 80.

6. Ibid., 85.

7. Pinkus, *Bodily Regimes*, 15.

8. Ibid., 154.

9. Ibid., 86.

10. Ibid., 8.

11. Stuart Hall, *The Hard Road to Renewal* (London: Verso, 1988), 7.

12. M. M. Bakhtin, *The Dialogic Imagination*, ed. Michael Holquist, trans. Caryl Emerson and Michael Holquist (Austin: University of Texas Press, 1981); John Docker, *Postmodernism and Popular Culture: A Cultural History* (Cambridge: Cambridge University Press, 1994), 168–233.

13. Ella Shohat and Robert Stam, *Unthinking Eurocentrism and the Media* (London: Routledge, 1994), 306.

14. Christian Viviani, "Who Is without Sin: The Maternal Melodrama in American Film, 1930–1939," *Wide Angle* 4 (1980): 4–17.

15. Marcia Landy, *British Genres: Cinema and Society, 1930–1960* (Princeton, N.J.: Princeton University Press, 1991), 200–203.

16. Mary Ann Doane, *The Desire to Desire: The Woman's Film of the 1940s* (Bloomington: Indiana University Press, 1987), 74.

17. Ibid., 75.

18. Pinkus, *Bodily Regimes*, 15.

19. Lesley Caldwell, "Reproducers of the Nation: Women and the Family in Fascist Policy," *Rethinking Italian Fascism*, ed. Davis Forgacs (London: Lawrence and Wishart, 1986), 110–41.

20. Hay, *Popular Film Culture*, 126.

21. Mariella Graziosi, "Gender Struggle and the Social Manipulation and Ideological Use of Gender Identity in the Interwar Years," *Mothers of Invention, Women, Italian Fascism, and Culture*, ed. Robin Pickering-Iazzi (Minneapolis: University of Minnesota Press, 1995), 26–52.

22. Hay, *Popular Film Culture*, 126.

23. Savio, *Cinecittà anni trenta*, 1:307; 2:653.

24. Spivak, "Scattered Speculations on the Question of Value," *In Other Worlds*, 154–75.

25. Gaylyn Studlar, *In the Realm of Pleasure: Von Sternberg, Dietrich and the Masochistic Aesthetic* (Urbana: University of Illinois Press, 1988), 192.

26. Savio, *Cinecittà anni trenta*, 1:277.

27. Steven Shaviro, *The Cinematic Body* (Minneapolis: University of Minnesota Press, 1993), 56.

28. Ibid.

29. Ibid., 188.

30. Deleuze, *Cinema II*, 97.

31. Maria Laplace, "Producing and Consuming the Woman's Film: Discursive Struggle in *Now, Voyager*," *Home Is Where the Heart Is: Studies in Melodrama and the Woman's Film*, ed. Christine Gledhill (London: BFI, 1987), 139.

32. Doane, *The Desire to Desire*, 73.

33. Francesco Savio, *Ma l'amore no*; Adriano Aprà and Patrizia Pistagnesi, *I favolosi anni trenta: cinema italiano 1929–1944* (Rome: Electa, 1979), 102.

34. Doane, *The Desire to Desire*, 83.

35. Sergio Pacifici, *The Modern Italian Novel from Manzoni to Svevo* (Carbondale: Southern Illinois University Press, 1967), 138–49.

36. Alfredo Sisca, *Cultura e letteratura: rapporti tra cultura regionale e nazionale: Manzoni, Verga, Fogazzaro* (Ravenna: Longo Press, 1970), 205; Lanfranco Caretti, Giorgi Luti, *La letteratura Italiana: per saggi storicamente disposti: L'ottocento* (Milan: Mursia, 1985), 738–45.

37. Jacques Derrida, *Writing and Difference* (Chicago: University of Chicago Press, 1978), 227.

38. Antonio Costa, "Risotto con i tartufi," in Martini, *La bella forma*, 100.

39. Ibid., 101.

40. Sue Harper, *Picturing the Past: The Rise and Fall of the British Costume Film* (London: BFI, 1994).

41. Landy, *Fascism in Film*, 55–57; Brunetta, *Storia*, 484; Reich, "Reading, Writing, and Rebellion," 220–39.

42. Hay, *Popular Film Culture*, 10.

43. Ibid., 98.

44. Landy, *Fascism in Film*, 20.

45. Reich, "Reading, Writing, and Rebellion," 227.

46. Ibid., 239.

47. Ibid., 223.

48. Ibid., 222.

CHAPTER SIX. CONCLUSION

1. Peukert, *Inside Nazi German*, 14–15.

2. Sorlin, *Italian National Cinema*, 76.

3. Ibid.

4. Brunetta, "The Long March," 143.

5. Deleuze, *Cinema II*, 7.

BIBLIOGRAPHY

Adamson, Walter. "The Language of Opposition in Early Twentieth-Century Italy: Rhetorical Continuities between Prewar Florentine Fascism and Mussolini's Fascism." *Journal of Modern History* 64 (March 1992): 22–51.

———. "Modernism and Fascism: The Politics of Culture in Italy, 1903–1922." *American Historical Review* 95 (1990): 359–90.

Alexander, Foscarina. *The Aspiration towards a Lost Natural Harmony in the Work of Three Italian Writers: Leopardi, Verga, and Moravia. Studies in Italian Literature*, vol. 1. Lewiston, N.Y.: Edwin Mellen Press, 1990.

Aprà, Adriano and Patrizia Pistagnesi. *I favolosi anni trenta: cinema italiano 1929–1944.* Rome: Electa, 1979.

Argentieri, Mino, ed. *Risate di Regime: La commedia italiana, 1930–1944.* Venice: Marsilio, 1991.

Bakhtin, M. M. *The Dialogic Imagination.* Michael Holquist, ed. Caryl Emerson and Michael Holquist, trans. Austin: University of Texas Press, 1981.

Baranski, Zygmunt G. and Shirley W. Vinall. *Women and Italy: Essays on Gender, Culture and History.* New York: St. Martin'sPress, 1991.

Barthes, Roland. *Mythologies.* Annette Lavers, trans. New York: Hill and Wang, 1972.

Becker, Jared. *Nationalism and Culture: Gabriele D'Annunzio and Italy after the Risorgimento.* New York: Peter Lang, 1994.

Benjamin, Walter. *Illuminations.* New York: Schocken, 1976.

———. "Theories of German Fascism." Jerolf Wikoff, trans. *New German Critique* 17 (Spring 1979).

Berezin, Mabel. "Cultural Form and Political Meaning: State-Subsidized Theater, Ideology, and the Language of Style in Fascist Italy." *American Journal of Sociology* 99.5 (March 1994): 1237–86.

Berman, Russell A. "The Aestheticization of Politics: Walter Benjamin on Fascism and the Avant-Garde." *Stanford Italian Review* 8 (1990): 35–52.

Biasin, Gian-Paolo. *Italian Literary Icons*. Princeton, N.J.: Princeton University Press, 1985.

Bobbio, Norberto. *The Future of Democracy*. Roger Griffin, trans. Minneapolis: University of Minnesota Press, 1987.

Bondanella, Peter. *Italian Cinema: From Neorealism to the Present*. Bloomington: Indiana University Press, 1993.

Braun, Emily. "Illustrations of Propaganda: The Political Drawings of Mario Sironi." *Journal of the Decorative and Propaganda Arts, 1875–1945* (Winter 1987): 84–108.

Brooks, Peter. *The Melodramatic Imagination: Balzac, Henry James, and the Language of Excess*. New York: Columbia University Press, 1984.

Brunetta, Gian Piero. *Cinema italiano tra le due guerre: Fascismo e politica cinematografica: Problemi di storia dello spettacolo tra le due guerre*. Milan: Mursia Press, 1975.

———. "The Long March of American Cinema in Italy." In *Hollywood in Europe: Experiences of a Cultural Hegemony*, ed. David E. Ellwood and Rob Kroes. Amsterdam: Vrije Universiteit University Press, 1994, 139–55.

———. "Mille lire e più di mille (lire al mese)." In *Risate di Regime: La commedia italiana, 1930–1944*. Venice: Marsilio, 1991, 97–109.

———. "Il sogno a stelle e strisce di Mussolini." In *L'estetica della politica: Europa e America degli anni trenta*, ed. Maurizio Vaudagna. Bari: Laterza, 1989, 173–87.

———. *Storia del cinema italiano, 1895–1945*. Rome: Riuniti Press, 1979.

Bruno, Giuliana. *Streetwalking on a Ruined Map: Cultural Theory and the City Films of Elvira Notari*. Princeton, N.J.: Princeton University Press, 1993.

Byars, Jackie. *All that Hollywood Allows: Reading Gender in 1950s Melodrama*. Chapel Hill: University of North Carolina Press, 1991.

Caldwell, Lesley. "Madri d'Italia: Film and the Fascist Concern with Motherhood." *Women and Italy: Essays in Gender, Culture, and History*, ed. Zygmunt G. Baranski and Shirley W. Vinall. New York: St. Martin's Press, 1991, 43–64.

———. "Reproducers of the Nation: Women and the Family in Fascist Policy." In *Rethinking Italian Fascism*, ed. Davis Forgacs. London: Lawrence and Wishart, 1986, 110–38.

Cannistraro, Philip V. *La fabbrica del consenso: Fascismo e mass media.* Rome-Bari: Laterza, 1975.

Caretti, Lanfranco and Giorgi Luti. *La letteratura Italiana: per saggi storicamente disposti: L'ottocento.* Milan: Mursia, 1985.

Casadio, Gianfranco. *Il grigio e il nero: Spettacolo e propaganda nel cinema italiano degli anni trenta (1931–1943).* Ravenna: Longo Press, 1989.

Casadio, Gianfranco, Ernesto G. Laura, and Filippo Cristiano, eds. *Telefoni bianchi: Realtà e finzione nella società e nel cinema italiano degli anni Quaranta.* Ravenna: Longo, 1991.

Castagno, Paul. *The Early Commedia Dell'Arte 1530–1621: The Mannerist Context.* New York: Peter Lang, 1994.

Cavell, Stanley. *Pursuits of Happiness: The Hollywood Comedy of Remarriage.* Cambridge, Mass.: Harvard University Press, 1981.

Cook, David A. *A History of Narrative Film.* New York: W. W. Norton, 1996.

Costa, Antonio. "'Risotti con i tartufi': Soldati, Fogazzaro e il calligrafismo." In *La bella forma: Poggioli, i calligrafici, e dintorni*, ed. Andrea Martini. Venice, Marsilio, 1992.

Custen, George. *Bio/Pics: How Hollywood Constructed Public History.* New Brunswick, N.J.: Rutgers University Press, 1992.

Dalle Vacche, Angela. *The Body in the Mirror: Shapes of History in Italian Cinema.* Princeton, N.J.: Princeton University Press, 1992.

———. "Nouvelle Histoire, Italian Style." *Annali d'Italianistica* 6 (1988): 98–123.

Debord, Guy. *Society of the Spectacle.* Detroit: Black and Red, 1983.

De Felice, Renzo. *D'Annunzio Politico, 1918–1938.* Rome: Laterza, 1978.

De Grazia, Victoria. *The Culture of Consent: Mass Organization of Leisure in Fascist Italy.* Cambridge: Cambridge University Press, 1981.

———. *How Fascism Ruled Women: Italy, 1922–1945.* Berkeley: University of California Press, 1992.

Deleuze, Gilles, *Cinema I: The Movement-Image.* Hugh Tomlinson and Barbara Habberjam, trans. Minneapolis: University of Minnesota Press, 1986.

————. *Cinema II: The Time Image.* Hugh Tomlinson and Robert Galeta, trans. Minneapolis: University of Minnesota Press, 1989.

————. *Difference and Repetition.* Paul Patton, trans. New York: Columbia University Press, 1994.

Deleuze, Gilles and Félix Guattari. *A Thousand Plateaus: Capitalism and Schizophrenia.* Brian Massumi, trans. Minneapolis: University of Minnesota Press, 1988.

Derrida, Jacques. *Writing and Difference.* Chicago: University of Chicago Press, 1978.

Di Giammateo, Fernaldo. "*Sorelle Materassi* sepolte vive con sussiego." In *La bella forma: Poggioli, i calligrafici, e dintorni,* ed. Andrea Martini. Venice, Marsilio, 1992.

Doane, Mary Anne. *The Desire to Desire: The Woman's Film of the 1940s.* Bloomington: Indiana University Press, 1987.

Docker, John. *Postmodernism and Popular Culture: A Cultural History.* Cambridge: Cambridge University Press, 1994.

Durkheim, Emile. *The Elementary Forms of the Religious Life.* Joseph Ward Swain, trans. New York: Collier Books, 1961.

Dyer, Richard. *Stars.* London: BFI, 1986.

Ellwood, David W. and Rob Kroes, eds., *Hollywood in Europe: Experiences of a Cultural Hegemony.* Amsterdam: Vrije Universiteit University Press, 1994.

Elsaesser, Thomas. "Tales of Sound and Fury: Observations on the Family Melodrama." In Marcia Landy, ed., *Imitations of Life: A Reader on Film and Television Melodrama.* Detroit: Wayne State University Press, 1991, 68–93.

Ferrarotti, Franco. "Sogni di potenza e amnesia sociale indotta." In *Risate di regime: La commedia italiana, 1930–1944,* ed. Mino Argentieri. Venice: Marsilio, 1991, 3–19.

Feuer, Jane. *The Hollywood Musical.* London: BFI, 1982.

Forgacs, David, ed. *Rethinking Italian Fascism: Capitalism, Populism and Culture.* London: Lawrence and Wishart, 1986.

Forgacs, David and Robert Lumley, eds. *Italian Cultural Studies: An Introduction.* Oxford: Oxford University Press, 1996.

Frayling, Christopher. *Spaghetti Westerns: Cowboys and Europeans from Karl May to Sergio Leone.* London: Routledge & Kegan Paul, 1981.

Galli, Giorgio. "Nazionalismo e esoterismo." *L'estetica della politica: Europa e America degli anni trenta,* ed. Maurizio Vaudagna. Bari, Italy: Laterza, 1989, 203–21.

Gili, Jean A. *L'Italie de Mussolini et son cinema.* Paris: Henri Veyrier, 1985.

Gledhill, Christine, ed. *Home Is Where the Heart Is: Studies in Melodrama and the Woman's Film.* Lodon: BFI, 1987.

———. *Stardom: Industry of Desire.* London: Routledge, 1991.

Golsan, Richard J. *Fascism, Aesthetics, and Culture.* Hanover, N.H.: University Press of New England, 1992.

Gori, Gianfranco Mino. *Patria diva: La storia d'Italia nel film del ventennio.* Florence: Usher, 1988.

Governi, Giancarlo. *Vittorio De Sica: Parlami d'amore Mariù.* Rome: Gremese, 1993.

Gramsci, Antonio. *Selections from the Cultural Writings.* David Forgacs, ed. Cambridge, Mass.: Harvard University Press, 1985.

———. *Selections from the Prison Notebooks,* Quintin Hoare and Geoffrey Nowell-Smith, eds. and trans. New York: International Publishers, 1978.

Graziosi, Mariella. "Gender Struggle and the Social Manipulation and Ideological Use of Gender Identity in the Interwar Years." In *Mothers of Invention: Women, Italian Fascism, and Culture,* ed. Robin Pickering-Iazzi. Minneapolis: University of Minnesota Press, 1995, 26–52.

Grignaffini, Giovanna. "Una certa maniera: Il cinema di Renato Castellani." In *La bella forma: Poggioli, i calligrafici, e dintorni,* ed. Andrea Martini. Venice: Marsilio, 1992.

Hall, Stuart. *The Hard Road to Renewal.* London: Verso, 1988.

Hardt, Michael. *Gilles Deleuze: An Apprenticeship in Philosophy.* Minneapolis: University of Minnesota Press, 1993.

Harper, Sue. "Historical Pleasures: Gainsborough Costume Melodramas." *Home Is Where the Heart Is.* London: BFI, 1987, 167–297.

————. *Picturing the Past: The Rise and Fall of the British Costume Film*. London: BFI, 1994.

Harvey, James. *Romantic Comedy in Hollywood: From Lubitsch to Sturges*. New York: Knopf, 1987.

Hay, James. *Popular Film Culture in Fascist Italy: The Passing of the Rex*. Bloomington: Indiana University Press, 1987.

Hollows, Joanne and Mark Jancovich. *Approaches to Popular Film*. Manchester, U.K.: Manchester University Press, 1995.

Horton, Andrew S., ed. *Comedy/Cinema/Theory*. Berkeley: University of California Press, 1991.

James, William. *Varieties of Religious Experience*. Cambridge, Mass.: Harvard University Press, 1985.

Jarratt, Vernon. *The Italian Cinema*. New York: Macmillan, 1951.

Kaplan, Wendy. *Designing Modernity: The Arts of Reform and Persuasion, 1885–1945. Selections from the Wolfsonian*. New York: Thames and Hudson, 1995.

Karnick, Kristine Brunovska and Henry Jenkins, eds. *Classical Hollywood Comedy*. New York: Routledge, 1995.

Kracauer, Siegfried. *The Mass Ornament: Weimar Essays*. Cambridge, Mass.: Harvard University Press, 1995.

Krause, Elizabeth. "Forward vs. Reverse Gear: Politics of Proliferation and Resistance in the Italian Fascist State." *Journal of Historical Sociology* 7.3 (September 1994): 261–88.

Landy, Marcia. *British Genres: Cinema and Society, 1930–1960*. Princeton, N.J.: Princeton University Press, 1991.

————. *Fascism in Film, The Italian Commercial Cinema, 1931–1943*. Princeton, N.J.: Princeton University Press, 1986.

————. *Film, Politics, and Gramsci*. Minneapolis: University of Minnesota Press, 1994.

————. *Imitations of Life: A Reader on Film and Television Melodrama*. Detroit: Wayne State University Press, 1991.

La Place, Maria. "Producing and Consuming the Woman's Film." In *Home Is Where the Heart Is: Studies in Melodrama and the Woman's Film*, ed. Christine Gledhill. London: BFI, 1987, 138–76.

Laura, Ernesto G. *Comedy Italian Style*. Rome: National Association of Motion Pictures and Affiliated Industries, n.d.

————. "Il mito di Budapest e i modelli ungheresi nel cinema italiano dal 1930 al 1945." In *Telefoni bianchi: Realtà e finzione nella società e nel cinema italiano degli anni Quaranta*, ed. Gianfranco Casadio, Ernesto G. Laura, and Filippo Cristiano. Ravenna: Longo, 1991, 31–49.

Lent, Tina Olsin. "Romantic Love and Friendship: The Redefinition of Gender Relations in Screwball Comedy," in *Classical Hollywood Comedy*, ed. Kristine Brunovska and Henry Jenkins. New York: Routledge, 1995, 314–32.

Leprohon, Pierre. *The Italian Cinema*. New York: Praeger, 1972.

Lizzani, Carlo. *Il cinema italiano, 1895–1979*. Rome: Riuniti Press, 1979.

Lowenthal, Leo. *Literature, Popular Culture and Society*. Palo Alto, Calif.: Pacific Books, 1961.

Lutti, Giorgio. *La letteratura nel ventennio fascista: Cronache letterarie tra le due guerre, 1920–1940*. Florence: La Nuova Italian Press, 1973.

Macciochi, Maria-Antonietta. *La donna "nera": Consenso femminile e fascismo*. Milan: Feltrinelli, 1976.

Mancini, Elaine. *Struggles of the Italian Film Industry during Fascism*. Ann Arbor, Mich.: UMI Research Press, 1985.

Marcus, Millicent. *Italian Cinema in the Light of Neorealism*. Princeton, N.J.: Princeton University Press, 1986.

Martini, Andrea. "Soldati—Poggioli—Chiarini: Una questione di spazio, di simmetria e di artificio." In *La bella forma: Poggioli, i calligrafici, e dintorni*, ed. Andrea Martini. Venice: Marsilio, 1992, 29–43.

Masi, Stefano. "La bellissima immagine." In *La bella forma: Poggioli, i calligrafici, e dintorni*, ed. Andrea Martini. Venice, Marsilio, 1992, 175–81.

Mast, Gerald. *A Short History of the Movies*. New York: Macmillan, 1986.

Marx, Karl. *Capital*, vol. 1. Ben Fowkes, trans. New York: Vintage Books, 1977.

————. *The 18th Brumaire of Louis Bonaparte*. New York: International Publishers, 1990.

Micciché, Lino, ed. *De Sica: Autore, regista, attore*. Venice: Marsilio, 1992.

————. "Introduction." In *La bella forma: Poggioli, i calligrafici, e dintorni*, ed. Andrea Martini. Venice: Marsilio, 1992.

Micheli, Paola. *Il cinema di Blasetti, parlo così: Un'analisi linguistica (1929–1942)*. Rome: Bulzoni Press, 1990.

Mida, Massimo and Lorenzo Quaglietti. *Dai telefoni bianchi al neorealismo*. Rome-Bari: Laterza, 1980.

Modleski, Tanya. *The Women Who Knew Too Much: Hitchcock and Feminist Theory*. New York: Methuen, 1988.

Monetti, Guglielmo. "A proposito de *La morte civile* e di *Gelosia*: dall' istanza realista all' 'entropia cinematografica.'" In *La bella forma: Poggioli, i calligrafici, e dintorni*, ed. Andrea Martini. Venice: Marsilio, 1992.

Morgan, Philip. *Italian Fascism, 1919–1945*. New York: St. Martin's Press, 1995.

Mosse, George. "L'autorappresentazione nazionale negli anni trenta negli Stati Uniti e in Europa." *L'estetica della politica: Europa e America degli anni trenta*, ed. Maurizio Vaudagna. Bari, Italy: Laterza, 1989, 3–25.

Neale, Steve and Frank Krutnik. *Popular Film and Television Comedy*. London: Routledge, 1990.

Nello, Paola. *L'avanguardismo giovanile alle origini di Fascismo*. Bari, Italy: Laterza, 1978.

Nichols, Nina Davinci and Jana O'Keefe Bazzoni. *Pirandello and Cinema*. Lincoln: University of Nebraska Press, 1995.

Nietzsche, Friedrich. "The Uses and Disadvantages of History for Life." *Untimely Meditations*. R. J. Hollingdale, trans. Cambridge: Cambridge University Press, 1991, 57–125.

Nowell-Smith, Geoffrey. "The Italian Cinema under Fascism." *Rethinking Italian Fascism*, ed. David Forgacs. London: Lawrence and Wishart, 1986, 142–61.

Ostenc, Michel. *L'éducation en Italie pendant le fascisme*. Paris: Sorbonne, 1980.

Pacifici, Sergio. *The Modern Italian Novel from Manzoni to Svevo*. Carbondale: Southern Illinois University Press, 1967.

———. *From Verismo to Experimentalism: Essays on the Modern Italian Novel*. Bloomington: Indiana University Press, 1969.

Paglai, Morena. *Mito e precarietà: Studi su Pascoli, D'Annunzio, Rosso di San Secondo, Malaparte, Diddi*. Florence: Franco Casati Press, 1989.

Pannunzio, Marco. "Chenal di fronte a Pirandello." *Cinema I* (November 10, 1936): 391.

———. *L'estremista moderato: La letteratura, il cinema, la politica.* Cesare De Michelis, ed. Venice: Marsilio, 1993.

Perry, Ted. "The Road to Neorealism." *Film Comment* 14.6 (Nov.–Dec. 1978): 8–13.

Petley, Julian. *Capital and Culture: German Cinema 1933–1945.* London: BFI, 1979.

Peukert, Detlev J. K. *Inside Nazi Germany: Conformity, Opposition and Racism in Everyday Life.* London: Penguin, 1989.

Pickering-Iazzi, Robin, ed. *Mothers of Invention: Women, Italian Fascism, and Culture.* Minneapolis: University of Minnesota Press, 1995.

Pinkus, Karen. *Bodily Regimes: Italian Advertising under Fascism.* Minneapolis: University of Minnesota Press, 1995.

Polan, Dana. *Power and Paranoia: History, Narrative, and the American Cinema, 1940–1950.* New York: Columbia University Press, 1986.

Re, Lucia. "Fascist Theories of 'Woman' and the Construction of Gender." *Mothers of Invention: Women, Italian Fascism, and Culture,* ed. Robin Pickering-Iazzi. Minneapolis: University of Minnesota Press, 1995, 76–100.

———. "Gabriele D'Annunzio's Theater of Memory: Il Vittoriale degli Italiani." *Journal of Decorative and Propaganda Arts, 1875–1945* 3 (Winter 1987): 6–52.

Reich, Jacqueline. "Reading, Writing, and Rebellion: Collectivity, Specularity, and Sexuality in Italian Schoolgirl Comedies." In *Mothers of Invention: Women, Italian Fascism, and Culture,* ed. Robin Pickering-Iazzi. Minneapolis: University of Minnesota Press, 1995, 220–51.

Rentschler, Eric. *The Ministry of Illusion: Nazi Cinema and Its Afterlife.* Cambridge: Harvard University Press, 1996.

Roda, Vittorio. "Appunti sulla costruzione del personaggio dannunziano." *Annali d'Italianistica* 5 (1987): 87–111.

Rodowick, David N. "Madness, Authority and Ideology: The Domestic Melodramas of the 1950s," in *Home Is Where the Heart Is: Studies in Melodrama and the Woman's Film,* ed. Christine Gledhill. London: BFI, 1987, 268–83.

Rosenstone, Robert, ed. *Revisioning History: Film and the Construction of a New Past*. Princeton, N.J.: Princeton University Press, 1995.

Rowe, Kathleen. *The Unruly Woman: Gender and the Genres of Laughter*. Austin: University of Texas Press, 1995.

Ryan, Michael and Avery Gordon. *Body Politics: Disease, Desire, and the Family*. Boulder, Colo.: Westview Press, 1994.

Said, Edward W. *Culture and Imperialism*. New York: Knopf, 1993.

——— . *Orientalism*. New York: Vintage Books, 1979.

Salizatton, Claver and Vito Zagarrio. *La corona di ferro: Un modo di produzione italiano*. Rome: Di Giacomo, 1985.

Savio, Francesco. *Cinecittà anni trenta: Parlano 116 protagonisti del secondo cinema italiano (1930–1943)*. 3 vols. Rome: Bulzoni Press, 1979.

——— . *Ma l'amore no: Realismo, formalismo, propaganda e telefoni bianchi nel cinema italiano di regime 1930–1943*. Milan: Sonzogno, 1975.

Schulte-Sasse, Linda. *Entertaining the Third Reich: Illusions of Wholeness in Nazi Cinema*. Durham: Duke University Press, 1996.

Sennett, Ted. *Laughing in the Dark: Movie Comedy from Groucho to Woody Allen*. New York: St. Martin's Press, 1992.

Shaviro, Steven. *The Cinematic Body*. Minneapolis: University of Minnesota Press, 1993.

Shohat, Ella and Robert Stam. *Unthinking Eurocentrism: Multiculturalism and the Media*. London: Routledge, 1994.

Sisca, Alfredo. *Cultura e letteratura: rapporti tra cultura regionale e nazionale: Manzoni, Verga, Fogazarro*. Ravenna: Longo Press, 1970.

Smith, Denis Mack. *Mussolini*. New York: Random House, 1983.

Sorlin, Pierre. *European Cinemas/European Societies*. London: Routledge, 1991.

——— . "Italian Cinema's Rebirth, 1937–1943: A Paradox of Fascism." *Historical Journal of Film and Video* 14.1 (1994): 3–13.

——— . *Italian National Cinema, 1896–1996*. London: Routledge, 1996.

Spivak, Gayatri Chakravorty. *In Other Worlds: Essays in Cultural Politics*. New York: Routledge, 1988.

Springer, Caroline. *The Marble Wilderness: Ruins and Representation in Italian Romanticism*. Cambridge: Cambridge University Press, 1987.

Stone, Marla. "Staging Fascism: The Exhibition of the Fascist Revolution." *Journal of Contemporary History* 28 (1993): 215–43.

Studlar, Gaylyn. *In the Realm of Pleasure: Von Sternberg, Dietrich and the Masochistic Aesthetic.* Urbana: University of Illinois Press, 1988.

Taves, Brian. *The Romance of Adventure: The Genre of Historical Adventure Movies.* Jackson: University of Mississippi Press, 1993.

Theweleit, Klaus. *Male Fantasies,* 2 vols. Steven Conway, trans. Minneapolis: University of Minnesota Press, 1987.

Thompson, Doug. *State Control in Fascist Italy, 1925–1943.* Manchester, U.K.: Manchester University Press, 1991.

Thompson, Kristin. *Eisenstein's Ivan the Terrible: A Neoformalist Analysis.* Princeton, N.J.: Princeton University Press, 1981.

Todorov, Tzvetan. *The Poetics of Prose.* Ithaca, N.Y.: Cornell University Press, 1977.

Vardac, A. Nicholas. *From Stage to Screen: Theatrical Method from Garrick to Griffith.* New York: Benjamin Blom, 1968.

Vattimo, Gianni. *The Transparent Society.* David Webb, trans. Baltimore: Johns Hopkins University Press, 1992.

Vaudagna, Maurizio, ed. *L'estetica della politica: Europa e America degli anni trenta.* Rome: Laterza, 1989.

Verdone, Luca. *I film di Alessandro Blasetti.* Rome: Gremese, 1989.

Vico, Giambattista. *On the Study Methods of Our Time.* Elio Gianturco, trans. Donald Phillip Verene, ed. Ithaca, N.Y.: Cornell University Press, 1990.

Vitti, Antonio. *Giuseppe De Sanctis and Postwar Italian Cinema.* Toronto: University of Toronto Press, 1996.

Viviani, Christian. "Who Is Without Sin? The Maternal Melodrama in American Film, 1930–1939." *Wide Angle* 4 (1980): 4–17.

Wallerstein, Immanuel and Etienne Balibar. *Race, Nation, Class: Ambiguous Identities.* London: Verso, 1991.

Wanrooji, Bruno. "Dollars and Decency: Italian Catholics and Hollywood." *Hollywood in Europe,* ed. David E. Ellwood and Rob Kroes. Amsterdam: Vrije Universiteit University Press, 1994, 247–66.

Zagarrio, Vito. "*Malombra* ovvero della dissimulazione onesta." *La bella forma: Poggioli, i calligrafici, e dintorni,* ed. Andrea Martini. Venice: Marsilio, 1992.

INDEX

THE FOLKLORE
OF CONSENSUS

THE SUNY SERIES
CULTURAL STUDIES IN CINEMA/VIDEO

Wheeler Winston Dixon, editor